Homicide in the Biblical World

Homicide in the Biblical World analyzes the treatment of homicide in the Hebrew Bible and demonstrates that it is directly linked to the unique social structure and religion of ancient Israel. Close parallels between biblical law and ancient Near Eastern law are evident in the laws of the ox that gored and the pregnant woman who was assaulted, but when the total picture of the process by which homicide was adjudicated comes into view, what is most noticeable is how little of it is similar to ancient Near Eastern law. This book reconstructs biblical law from both legal and narrative texts and analyzes both law collections and documents from actual legal cases from the ancient Near East.

Pamela Barmash is Assistant Professor of Hebrew Bible and Biblical Hebrew at Washington University in St. Louis. She received her Ph.D. from Harvard University and her rabbinic ordination from the Jewish Theological Seminary. She has published in various journals, including *Vetus Testamentum, Journal of Near Eastern Studies, Jewish Quarterly Review, Journal of Biblical Literature,* and *Hebrew Studies*.

Homicide in the Biblical World

Pamela Barmash
Washington University in St. Louis

CAMBRIDGE
UNIVERSITY PRESS

PUBLISHED BY THE PRESS SYNDICATE OF THE UNIVERSITY OF CAMBRIDGE
The Pitt Building, Trumpington Street, Cambridge, United Kingdom

CAMBRIDGE UNIVERSITY PRESS
The Edinburgh Building, Cambridge CB2 2RU, UK
40 West 20th Street, New York, NY 10011-4211, USA
477 Williamstown Road, Port Melbourne, VIC 3207, Australia
Ruiz de Alarcón 13, 28014 Madrid, Spain
Dock House, The Waterfront, Cape Town 8001, South Africa

http://www.cambridge.org

First published 2005

Printed in the United States of America

Typefaces Sabon 10/12 pt. *and* Albertus *System* LaTeX 2_ε [TB]

A catalog record for this book is available from the British Library.

Library of Congress Cataloging in Publication Data
Barmash, Pamela, 1966–
Homicide in the biblical world / Pamela Barmash.
p. cm.
Includes bibliographical references and index.
ISBN 0-521-83468-6 – 0-521-54773-3 (pb.)

2004
2004045668

ISBN 0 521 83468 6 hardback
ISBN 0 521 54773 3 paperback

To my mother and father,
Sarah J. and Isadore Barmash

...וְתִפְאֶרֶת בָּנִים אֲבוֹתָם.

"...and the glory of children is their parents."
(Proverbs 17:6)

Contents

Abbreviations

AASOR	Annual of the American Schools of Oriental Research
AB	The Anchor Bible
ABD	*Anchor Bible Dictionary*
ABL	Robert Francis Harper, *Assyrian and Babylonian Letters Belonging to the Kouyunyik Collection of the British Museum* (Chicago: University of Chicago Press, 1892–1914)
ADD	C. H. W. Johns, *Assyrian Deeds and Documents* (Cambridge: Deighton, Bell, and Co., 1901, 1924)
AfO	*Archiv für Orientforschung*
AHw	Wolfram von Soden, *Assyrisches Handwörterbuch* (Wiesbaden: Otto Harrassowitz, 1959–1981)
$ANET^3$	*Ancient Near Eastern Texts Relating to the Old Testament* (ed. J. B. Pritchard; 3d edition; Princeton: Princeton University Press, 1969)
AnOr	Analecta Orientalia
AnSt	*Anatolian Studies*

AOAT	Alter Orient und Altes Testament
AOS	American Oriental Series
ARM	Archives royales de Mari
ARMT	Archives royales de Mari, transcrite et traduite
ArOr	*Archiv Orientálni*
AuOr	*Aula orientis*
b.	Babylonian Talmud
BA	*Biblical Archaeologist*
BASOR	*Bulletin of the American Schools of Oriental Research*
b.e.	bottom edge of tablet
BBSt	L. W. King, *Babylonian Boundary Stones and Memorial Tablets in the British Museum* (London: British Museum, 1912)
BDB	F. Brown, S. R. Driver, and C. A. Briggs, *A Hebrew and English Lexicon of the Old Testament* (Oxford: Oxford University Press, 1907)
Bib	*Biblica*
BM	Symbol for tablets in the British Museum
BWAT	Beiträge zur Wissenschaft vom Alten Testament
BZAW	Beiheft zur Zeitschrift für die alttestamentliche Wissenschaft
CAD	*The Assyrian Dictionary of the University of Chicago* (Chicago: Oriental Institute, 1956–)
CahRB	Cahiers de la Revue biblique
CANE	*Civilizations of the Ancient Near East* (ed. Jack M. Sasson; New York: Scribners, 1995)
CBQ	*Catholic Biblical Quarterly*
CC	Continental Commentaries
CCT	Cuneiform Texts from Cappadocian Tablets in the British Museum
CIJ	Corpus inscriptionum judaicarum
CT	Cuneiform Texts
CTH	Emmanuel Laroche, *Catalogue des textes hittites* (Paris: Klincksieck, 1971)
CTN	Cuneiform Texts from Nimrud

DMOA	Documenta et Monumenta Orientis Antiqui
DO	Symbol for tablets in Musée National de Damas
EA	El-Amarna
EI	*Eretz Israel*
GKC	Wilhelm Gesenius, E. Kautzsch, E. Cowley, *Gesenius' Hebrew Grammar* (Oxford: Oxford University Press, 1910)
HL	Hittite Laws
HSM	Harvard Semitic Monographs
HSS	Harvard Semitic Series
ICC	International Critical Commentary
IDB	*The Interpreter's Dictionary of the Bible* (ed. G. A. Buttrick; Nashville: Abingdon, 1962)
IEJ	*Israel Exploration Journal*
Int	*Interpretation*
ITT	Inventaire des Tablettes de Tello
JAOS	*Journal of the American Oriental Society*
JBL	*Journal of Biblical Literature*
JCS	*Journal of Cuneiform Studies*
JJS	*Journal of Jewish Studies*
JNES	*Journal of Near Eastern Studies*
JSOT	*Journal for the Study of the Old Testament*
JSOTSup	Journal for the Study of the Old Testament Supplement Series
KAI	H. Donner and W. Röllig, *Kanaanäische und aramäische Inschriften* (Wiesbaden: Otto Harrassowitz, 1964)
KBo	Keilschrifttexte aus Boghazköi
KUB	Keilschrifturkunden aus Boghazköi
l.e.	left edge of tablet
LE	Laws of Eshnunna
LH	Laws of Hammurapi
LL	Laws of Lipit-Ishtar
LOx	Laws about Rented Oxen
LU	Laws of Ur-Nammu

LXX	Septuagint
m.	Mishnah
MAL	Middle Assyrian Laws
MANE	Monographs on the Ancient Near East
MRS	Mission de Ras Shamra
NABU	*Nouvelles assyriologiques brèves et utilitaires*
ND	Symbol for tablets excavated at Nimrud
NEB	New English Bible
NICOT	New International Commentary on the Old Testament
NSG	Adam Falkenstein, *Die Neusumerische Gerichtsurkunden* (Munich: Bayerische Akademie der Wissenschaften, 1956)
NJV	New Jewish Version = *TANAKH, The Holy Scriptures: The New JPS Translation According to the Traditional Hebrew Text* (Philadelphia: The Jewish Publication Society, 1988)
obv.	obverse of tablet
OEANE	*Oxford Encyclopedia of the Archaeology of the Ancient Near East* (ed. Eric M. Meyers; New York: Oxford University Press, 1997)
OIP	Oriental Institute Publications
Or	*Orientalia*, n.s.
OTL	Old Testament Library
PBS	Publications of the Babylonian Section
PPA	J. N. Postgate, *The Governor's Palace Archive* (Hertford, U.K.: British School of Archaeology in Iraq, 1973)
PRU	*Le palais royal d'Ugarit* (ed. Jean Nougayrol; Paris: Imprimerie nationale, 1955–)
RA	*Revue d'assyriologie et d' archéologie orientale*
RB	*Revue biblique*
rev.	reverse of tablet
RIDA	*Revue internationale des droits de l'antiquité*
RIMA	The Royal Inscriptions of Mesopotamia, Assyria Periods
RLA	*Reallexikon der Assyriologie und vorderasiatische Archäologie* (Berlin: Walter de Gruyter, 1932–)
RS	Ras es-Shamra

RSV	Revised Standard Version
SAA	State Archives of Assyria
SAAS	State Archives of Assyria Studies
SBL	Society of Biblical Literature
SBLDS	Society of Biblical Literature Dissertation Series
ScrHier	Scripta Hierosolymitana
Si.	Symbol for tablets excavated from Sippar
SLEx	Sumerian Laws Exercise tablet
SLHF	Sumerian Laws Handbook of Forms
SVT	Supplements of Vetus Testamentum
TCL	Textes cunéiformes, Musée du Louvre
TEO	Henri de Genouillac, *Textes économiques d'Oumma de l'époque d'Our* (TCL 5; Paris: Librairie Orientaliste/Paul Geuthner, 1922)
TUAT	Texte aus der Umwelt des Alten Testaments
Ukg.	Symbol for UruKAgina texts
VAT	Symbol for tablets in the Vorderasiatische Teil der Staatlichen Museen, Berlin
VT	*Vetus Testamentum*
WMANT	Wissenschaftliche Monographien zum Alten und Neuen Testament
YBC	Symbol for tablets in the Yale Babylonian Collection
ZA	*Zeitschrift für Assyriologie*
ZAW	*Zeitschrift für die alttestamentliche Wissenschaft*
ZSS	*Zeitschrift der Savigny-Stiftung, Romanischen Abteilung*

Symbols in Cuneiform Transliterations

[ ]	gaps or reconstructed text
< >	scribal omissions
<< >>	scribal superfluity
x	cuneiform sign that cannot be read

Acknowledgments

THIS STUDY has its origins in a doctoral dissertation I completed at Harvard University. I would like to express my gratitude to my dissertation advisor, Professor Peter B. Machinist, for his constant encouragement and kindness. His meticulous reading and his generous and consistently good advice have been indispensable to my work. He is a shining example of the best in scholarship and teaching.

Washington University in St. Louis granted a research leave in which I was able to completely restructure this study and advance the argument magnitudes further. Professor Shalom M. Paul, with his brilliant mastery of biblical studies and Assyriology, provided inspiration and good counsel during the difficult process of revision.

I would like to thank Harvard University and the National Foundation for Jewish Culture for their support during my Ph.D. studies. I am grateful for the support of Yad Hanadiv/Beracha Foundation and the Lady Davis Fellowship Trust for funding a research leave at Hebrew University.

I would like to thank Rabbi Edward S. Romm for his technical assistance during the preparation of the manuscript. I would also like to thank my students Corey M. Helfand and Evan I. Weiner for checking the index for accuracy.

Chapters of this manuscript were presented as lectures at Hebrew University, Bar-Ilan University, and the Schechter Institute of Jewish Studies, as well as at a number of community forums. I am grateful for the questions and comments of the listeners.

This study has been greatly improved by suggestions from Gary A. Anderson and Charles Donahue, Jr. Avi Hurvitz and David Weisberg provided invaluable help.

Professor Gary Beckman generously provided assistance with the Hittite texts.

Most of all, I would like to thank my parents, Sarah J. and Isadore Barmash, for providing a home filled with boundless love and encouragement.

Introduction

I BEGAN this project interested in the question of how much of biblical law was transplanted from the law of the rest of the ancient Near East. It swiftly became obvious to me that I had to expand the scope of the project to examine the broader spectrum of procedures, institutions, and literary forms connected with the adjudication of homicide in the Hebrew Bible and its relationship to aspects of Israelite society and religion. It is among the laws on homicide that the closest parallels between biblical law and ancient Near Eastern law are evident, in the statutes on the ox that gored and fatal assault on a pregnant woman, but a different picture comes into focus in the complete process by which homicide was adjudicated. Indeed, what is most noticeable is how little of the adjudication of homicide in the Hebrew Bible is similar to that of ancient Near Eastern law.

It is essential to understand that the treatment of homicide in the Bible is dependent on the institutions and conceptual underpinnings of biblical society. Biblical law did not come into existence in a vacuum, and law in general is part and parcel of a cultural system. Without such a holistic point of view, law could very easily be taken out of its context and misunderstood.[1]

[1]Shemaryahu Talmon, "The 'Comparative Method' in Biblical Interpretation – Principles and Problems," *Congress Volume: Göttingen* (SVT 29; Leiden: Brill, 1978), 320–356 (reprinted in his *Literary Studies in the Hebrew Bible: Form and Content* [Jerusalem: Magnes Press, 1993],

The treatment of homicide in the Bible is directly linked to aspects of biblical culture outside the legal sphere. Indeed, the contours of Israelite society and religion generated specific institutions and principles. This study will highlight the relationship of biblical law to Israelite society and religion, allowing us to see how the adjudication of homicide fit into the cultural pattern of Israelite society.

Law in the Bible must be investigated in its own environment before any meaningful or valid comparison can be made. Nonetheless, interpreting biblical law in its ancient Near Eastern context is also essential. The Bible did not come into existence in a vacuum. Biblical culture and society stemmed from the cultures of the ancient Near East, especially that of Mesopotamia, whose influence is felt in almost every chapter of the Hebrew Bible.

The striking convergences and divergences in form and content between biblical law and ancient Near Eastern law with regard to homicide in particular have profound implications. (The law from the ancient Near East appears to be part of a common tradition, and since it is all written in cuneiform script, whether in Sumerian, Akkadian, or Hittite, it is called "cuneiform law.")[2] Some scholars have focused on the question of how biblical writers knew of cuneiform law. Raymond Westbrook suggests that biblical writers actually possessed copies of ancient Near Eastern laws: Cuneiform law collections were literary works used as school texts in Canaanite scribal workshops and, by implication, were used the same way during the Israelite period.[3] Reuven Yaron thinks that there was a common law throughout the ancient Near East, including ancient Israel, law that was sporadically put into writing, and that the similarities between biblical and cuneiform law reflect this common law.[4] Shalom M. Paul and J. J. Finkelstein argue that biblical law and ancient Near Eastern law had a direct connection but that the exact method of transmission cannot be ascertained.[5] Other scholars have focused on elucidating the guidelines by which cuneiform law was reworked. Moshe Greenberg argues that a general legal/theological principle of biblical law that contradicted a general principle of cuneiform law generated divergent law on the same subject despite biblical law's basis in

11–49); David P. Wright, *The Disposal of Impurity* (SBLDS 101; Atlanta: Scholars Press, 1987), 5–7.

[2]The term "cuneiform law" was coined by Paul Koschaker, "Keilschriftrecht," *Zeitschrift der Deutschen Morgenländischen Gesellschaft* 89 (1935), 26, and "Forschungen und Ergebnisse in den keilschriftlichen Rechtsquellen," *ZSS* 49 (1929), 188–189.

[3]Raymond Westbrook, *Studies in Biblical and Cuneiform Law* (CahRB 26; Paris: J. Gabalda, 1988), 2–3.

[4]Reuven Yaron, *The Laws of Eshnunna* (revised edition: Jerusalem: Magnes Press, 1988), 294–295.

[5]Shalom M. Paul, *Studies in the Book of the Covenant in the Light of Cuneiform and Biblical Law* (SVT 18; Leiden: E. J. Brill, 1970), 104–105; J. J. Finkelstein, *The Ox That Gored* (prepared for publication by Maria deJ. Ellis; Transactions of the American Philosophical Society 71/2; Philadelphia: The American Philosophical Society, 1981), 20.

cuneiform law.[6] Finkelstein contends that theological differences account for the disparate laws in the Bible regarding a case that was borrowed from cuneiform law.[7] A few have dissented from seeing a connection between biblical law and cuneiform law: A. Van Selms claims that the differences were too great, even in a case like the goring ox, and that the dependency of biblical law on cuneiform law seems unlikely.[8] Albrecht Alt holds that the geographic distance between ancient Israel and Mesopotamia was simply too great and that biblical law was based on Canaanite law, which is no longer extant.[9]

This study therefore operates on two levels: analyzing biblical law in its own context and comparing biblical law to cuneiform law. This two-front approach prevents the distortion of cultures, when the features and significance of a parallel phenomenon are transferred from one to the other, and allows for a more accurate assessment of cultural phenomena.[10]

A few words on the comparative method are in order. The comparative method in general has benefits and perils. It always walks the fine line between a comparison of contrasts and a comparison of similarities. Indeed, the pendulum of biblical studies has swung regularly from emphasizing the continuity of the Hebrew Bible with the rest of the ancient Near East to emphasizing the discontinuity of the Hebrew Bible with the rest of the ancient Near East and back again.[11] This is partially because the comparative method suffers from the danger of generalization in which uniqueness is lost. First, arranging one set of data against another set may organize the comparison so that there is a matching of components in a Procrustean bed, whether or not there is a correspondence. A culture in its complete phenomenology can easily be obscured. Second, combining what is in each set makes that set appear monolithic. The comparative method, as it is used in biblical studies, locates the Hebrew Bible on one side and everything from the rest of the

[6] Moshe Greenberg, "Some Postulates of Biblical Criminal Law," in *Jubilee Volume for Yehezkel Kaufman* (ed. Menahem Haran; Jerusalem: Magnes Press, 1960), 20, 14–15 (reprinted in *The Jewish Expression* [ed. Judah Goldin; New York: Bantam, 1968], 18–37). Bernard S. Jackson attacks Greenberg's views in *Essays in Jewish and Comparative Legal History* (Studies in Judaism in Late Antiquity 10; Leiden: Brill, 1975), 25–63. Greenberg replies to Jackson's attack in "More Reflections on Biblical Criminal Law," *Studies in Bible* (ed. Sara Japhet; ScrHier 31; Jerusalem: Magnes Press, 1986), 1–18.

[7] Finkelstein, *The Ox That Gored*, 5.

[8] A. Van Selms, "The Goring Ox in Babylonian and Biblical Law," *ArOr* 18 (1950), 321–330.

[9] Albrecht Alt, "The Origins of Israelite Law," in *Essays on Old Testament History and Religion* (trans. R. A. Wilson; Garden City, New York: Anchor Books, 1968 [1966]), 124–126.

[10] Richard G. Fox, *Urban Anthropology: Cities in Their Cultural Settings* (Englewood Cliffs, New Jersey: Prentice-Hall, 1977), 4; William W. Hallo, "Biblical History in Its Near Eastern Setting: The Contextual Approach," in *Scripture in Context: Essays on the Comparative Method* (Pittsburgh: The Pickwick Press, 1980), 1–26.

[11] Cf. Meir Malul, *The Comparative Method in Ancient Near Eastern and Biblical Legal Studies* (AOAT 227; Neukirchen-Vluyn: Neukirchener Verlag, 1990), 13–78.

ancient Near East on the other. The Hebrew Bible becomes uniform, as does all the rest of the ancient Near East. One might well imagine a different focus: The Neo-Assyrian or Hittite texts could occupy center stage, with every other source from the rest of the ancient Near East (including the Hebrew Bible) assembled in comparison and analyzed in a comparative light.

Furthermore, the time span from which the cuneiform texts originate is broad, from the Neo-Sumerian period (twenty-first century B.C.E.) to the end of the Neo-Assyrian period (seventh century B.C.E). They stem from a wide geographical sphere encompassing the entire ancient Near East, including Egypt, Ugarit, the Hittite empire, Assyria, Babylonia, and Sumer.[12] They are written in Sumerian, Akkadian, and Hittite. Despite this diversity, there is much uniformity across these cultures in the realm of law, but any analysis of such greatly diverse material must avoid blurring differences and be sensitive to the variations between cultures. It is also essential to be wary of importing alien categories on ancient Near Eastern cultures, a warning to be heeded ever since Benno Landsberger defended the "conceptual autonomy of the Babylonian world."[13]

This study has attempted to bypass these pitfalls in two ways: 1) by utilizing all the textual sources that these cultures offer in order to present the treatment of homicide in each culture in its fullness; and 2) by being conscious of the variety within each set of data as a corrective to the polarization inherent in the comparative method. This study will treat the cuneiform material as a whole only when it is warranted and will emphasize where the cuneiform material does not cohere. As we will see, Assyrian law differs at times from the rest of Mesopotamian law, and the adjudication of homicide as reflected in legal records occasionally diverges from law collections.

Generally, studies of biblical law and cuneiform law have been confined to formal collections of statutes, but in this study, I will make use of a broader repertoire. First, in addition to the formal collections of law in the Bible, I will treat narrative texts touching on homicide because these texts can shed light on legal matters by providing evidence for elements essential to legal practice omitted in legal texts.[14] They can provide insight into the social setting in which law was used. Narratives can be used as a means of accessing key aspects in law not necessarily included in legal texts. They can identify what are felt to be the inadequacies of a legal system. They can provide insight into how the law appears to operate in actuality, whether well or poorly, and how law relates to general concepts of law and government. They can reveal

[12]There is only a single document from Egypt on homicide, and it is in fact Babylonian in origin. This text, EA 8, addresses the murder of the Babylonian king's merchants by Egyptian vassals and does not treat homicide internal to Egyptian society.

[13]Benno Landsberger, *The Conceptual Autonomy of the Babylonian World* (1924; reprint, MANE 1/4; Malibu: Undena, 1976).

[14]For a fuller discussion of this methodology, see my article "The Narrative Quandary: Cases of Law in Literature," *VT* 54 (2004), 1–16.

the inherent flaws of a legal system, unanticipated in statutes. Narrative texts are, therefore, critical to the study of biblical law, and their absence from previous studies is a lacuna this study hopes to remedy.

Second, in contrast to many other studies, attention will also be paid to the legal records from the ancient Near East as well as to the formal legal collections. The former include records in a variety of forms from actual legal cases and treaties covering cases that might arise in the future. The records of actual cases reflect how the legal process was carried out and what was deemed essential to a transcript of a case. The treaties and other international documents encapsulate the shared features of the legal procedure and principles between countries and may shed light on the common denominator of the treatment of homicide in the ancient Near East, if one should exist. With few exceptions, scholars have concentrated on the formal legal collections.[15] Thorkild Jacobsen's 1959 article on a Sumerian homicide trial[16] and Martha T. Roth's reconstruction of Neo-Assyrian homicide procedure[17] represent rare examples of analysis of legal records. Horst Klengel identifies common legal practices of West Semites in the Late Bronze Age by studying the treaties and other interterritorial documents of the period.[18] The cuneiform texts treated here appear in a variety of forms, such as legal records of a wide variety, letters referring to actual cases of homicide, and treaties and formal collections of law containing provisions on unlawful death, but there are lacunae that call for comment. Cuneiform narrative texts deal with killing during war or with generations of younger gods superseding the previous generation by killing the older gods, not with the type of slaying treated in this study. Oddly enough, although the Neo-Babylonian period is the second-best documented period in Mesopotamian history, there are no Neo-Babylonian texts treating homicide (except for an attempted homicide, TCL 12 117). This may not be as surprising as it seems initially, since the Neo-Babylonian texts originate almost exclusively from the archives of temples, religious institutions that did not have jurisdiction over cases of homicide.

[15]Even a study as recent as Ulrich Sick's *Die Tötung eines Menschen und ihre Ahndung in den keilschriftlichen Rechtssammlungen unter Berücksichtigung rechtsvergleichender Aspekte* (Ph.D. diss., Eberhard-Karls-Universität, 1984), did not make reference to any legal records, though the records were available in edited form by then, some in a number of editions.

[16]Thorkild Jacobsen, "An Ancient Mesopotamian Trial for Homicide," *Studia Biblica et Orientalia* (Analecta Biblica et Orientalia 12; Rome: Istituto Biblica Pontificio, 1959), 3.130–150, reprinted in Thorkild Jacobsen, *Toward the Image of Tammuz and Other Essays on Mesopotamian History and Culture* (ed. William L. Moran; HSS 21; Cambridge, Massachusetts: Harvard University Press, 1970), 193–214.

[17]Martha T. Roth, "Homicide in the Neo-Assyrian Period," in *Language, Literature, and History: Philological and Historical Studies Presented to Erica Reiner* (ed. Francesca Rochberg-Halton; AOS 67; New Haven, Connecticut: American Oriental Society, 1987), 351–365.

[18]Horst Klengel, "Mord und Bussleistung in spätbronzezeitlichen Syrien," in *Death in Mesopotamia* (ed. Bendt Alster; Copenhagen Studies in Assyriology 8; Copenhagen: Akademisk Verlag, 1980), 189–197.

Undoubtedly, homicides occurred during the Neo-Babylonian period. Unfortunately, we have no records of them.

We must be aware of our limited access to sources. It must be acknowledged that there is no way of determining the extent to which the Hebrew Bible reflects a representative cross section of ancient Israelite culture. The Bible may incorporate only selected aspects of Israelite society, offering us a skewed picture of ancient Israel. Nor is there any certainty whether the statutes in the Bible were used in a court system. There is only one inscription from ancient Israel that deals with a legal matter, the Meṣad Ḥashavyahu or Yavneh-Yam letter, in which a complaint is lodged with an official regarding an object left in pledge that was not returned.[19] We must ask, therefore, whether the differences that are found between the Hebrew Bible and the documents from the rest of the ancient Near East are real differences, or whether they simply reflect a limited, and therefore distorted, database, due to the accidental nature of tradition, for the Hebrew Bible, and of archaeological discovery, for inscriptions from the ancient Near East as a whole. A critical distinction needs to be drawn between the Hebrew Bible and ancient Israel. The Hebrew Bible is not a representative cross section of ancient Israel. It comprises products of particular individuals and ideological circles. The idiosyncracies of these writers and theological factions may distort the law.

These strictures, however, could be applied to any collection of texts: Could any finite collection of works, like the Hebrew Bible or even the fifty-odd documents amassed from cuneiform cultures, ever suffice? How many documents from a particular era in a particular territory would ever be a sufficient number? We can only base a historical reconstruction on what we have, keeping in mind how our sources skew our perception. We are always at the mercy of the next archaeological discovery. In the absence of court records or other documents shedding light on actual legal procedures in ancient Israel, a reconstruction of the law based on the material in the Bible must be qualified by the acknowledgment that a distinction needs to be drawn between the legal system as described in the Bible and the actual legal system of ancient Israel.

A hotly debated issue in the study of cuneiform law is whether the statutes in formal collections of law were precedent setting and comprehensive. In other words, were the formal collections of law ever used in court? This issue has been subsumed in scholarship under the question of whether the Laws of Ur-Nammu, the Laws of Lipit-Ishtar, the Laws of Eshnunna, the Laws of Hammurapi, and the Middle Assyrian Laws should be called "law codes." Objections have been made to calling the Mesopotamian laws and the Hittite Laws law codes because they were neither binding nor comprehensive nor

[19] J. Naveh, "A Hebrew Letter from the Seventh Century B.C.," *IEJ* 10 (1960), 129–139; KAI 200.

apparently ever cited; rather, they should be called "law collections."[20] However, James Lindgren argues that the word "code" is rarely used to refer to a country's comprehensive body of law and that restatements of laws already in force are generally considered to be codifications of law even if the restatements themselves have no binding force.[21] In this study, I shall call them law collections for convenience.

Lastly, I must emphasize that the comparative method is not a method of evaluating the superiority or inferiority of any culture in contrast to another. Especially in regard to a topic such as homicide that is the subject of such heated debate in contemporary society, we must be aware of the ways we belong to biblical tradition, as well as the distance we are from it in light of modern legal and political ideals.

OUTLINE OF THE BOOK

The first chapter focuses on the story of Cain and Abel. This tale adumbrates many of the critical issues involved in the treatment of homicide in the Bible. It is the most famous case of homicide in the Bible, and as a tale intentionally set in hoary antiquity, it both concurs with and diverges from the treatment of homicide as described in the rest of the Bible. It sets the stage for the analysis that follows.

The second chapter, "Blood Feud and State Control," deals with social history and comparative law. I analyze the institution that ensured that a homicide would be punished in biblical law. In biblical Israel, the victim's family assumed the primary responsibility for ensuring that the slayer was punished: One member of the victim's family, "the blood avenger," possessed the right to kill the slayer on sight with impunity. I argue that this process should be understood as blood feud, a legal institution with particular characteristics, basing my interpretation on an anthropological model. Blood feud was a legal mechanism, not an aberration outside of the law, and was directly linked to the role of the clan or lineage, the association of extended families, in other legal matters. The identification of the process as blood

[20] Cf. Finkelstein, *The Ox That Gored*, 15–16; Jean Bottero, *Mesopotamia: Writing, Reasoning, and the Gods* (trans. Zainab Bahrani and Marc van de Mieroop; Chicago: University of Chicago Press, 1992), 156–184; F. R. Kraus, "Ein zentrales Problem des altmesopotamischen Rechts: Was ist der Codex Hammurabi?" *Genava* n.s. 8 (1960), 292. What is ironic about this stricture is that it appears that whatever law is studied is compared unfavorably to any other law, which appears to be binding and comprehensive in comparison. Cf. the lament about the Icelandic laws *Grágás* by Andrew Dennis, Peter Foote, and Richard Perkins, *Laws of Early Iceland: Grágás* (University of Manitoba Icelandic Studies III; Winnipeg: University of Manitoba Press, 1980), 9.

[21] James Lindgren, "Measuring the Value of Slaves and Free Persons in Ancient Law," *Chicago-Kent Law Review* 71/1 (1995), 150–151, n. 3.

feud is critical because it allows us to understand it as an intrinsic element of the legal process and how blood feud is by its nature rule-bound. The potential for violence actually limits violence and promotes the acquiescence of the killer to a trial. In a society without specialized judicial personnel, such as police or prosecutors, a lineage acting as a mutual aid society ensures that the crime would be punished. This understanding of the process is in direct contrast with the prevailing idea that the actions of the family are outside the law and that the excesses of the family's activities must be curbed by the law.

At the institutional level, therefore, biblical Israel differed radically from its neighbors. Blood feud did not operate elsewhere in cuneiform law, where a central government exerted control over the legal process. The difference is due to disparate conceptions of society. I argue that a social system based on kinship ties persisted in ancient Israel. This is contrary to the dominant models of the social development of ancient Israel, which claim that kinship ties broke down during the monarchy. My argument is based on both textual evidence and archaeological data. The organization of society based on kinship ties in ancient Israel is in sharp contrast to the pervasive urbanism of Mesopotamian society, in which kinship ties dissipated. This chapter concludes with three excurses on matters essential to my analysis. In the first, I evaluate and reject the argument that the blood avenger was *not* a member of the victim's family. In the second, I present the evidence that the Akkadian term *bēl damê,* "owner of the blood," refers both to the slayer and to the claimant from the victim's family. This terminology reflects the difference between biblical and Mesopotamian law. Biblical law is focused on the representative of the victim's family, whereas the participation of both parties is the assumption of Mesopotamian law. In the third excursus, I reconstruct the Neo-Assyrian process of the adjudication of homicide from a series of documents. This set of texts is the only one available that allows us to reconstruct a Mesopotamian example of the adjudication of homicide from start to finish.

The third chapter, "The Development of Places of Refuge in the Bible," sketches the history of the development of asylum and analyzes the cities of refuge as described in the Pentateuchal sources. I argue as faulty the claim that altar asylum for killers developed into the cities of refuge as a result of the consolidation of control by the early monarchy or for the monarchy by the Deuteronomic reform. The narrative evidence depicting asylum during the period of the early monarchy actually shows political offenders, not killers, seeking asylum from their political opponents, and the texts from Deuteronomy do not present the cities of refuge as an innovation, contrary to how other Deuteronomic reforms are depicted. The statute in the Covenant Code, Exod 21:12–14, is ambiguous: It is equally plausible that it refers to asylum at an altar or to a city of refuge. The second part of the chapter shows that the differences between the Pentateuchal sources designated P/H and D on a number of the basic features of these sanctuaries is as a direct result of their ideological and theological programs and is not based on a historical development from altar asylum to cities of refuge. The number of refuges in the Priestly tradition is linked to its program of schematicizing Israelite history, and its linkage of Levitic cities to the cities of refuge reflects its evaluation of the Levites. The Priestly law is concerned with the purity of space, whereas the Deuteronomic law is focused on the Israelite people. The Deuteronomic crystallization of the cities of refuge is informed by a Deuteronomic interest in social aspects of the law. Finally, I demonstrate how the different traditions of P/H and D are brought together in the description of the cities of refuge in the book of Joshua.

The relationship of the treatment of homicide to Israelite religion is the subject of the next chapter, "Pollution and Homicide." Homicide had a cultic valence. I demonstrate that blood was considered to be both a polluting and cleansing substance. The spilling of blood was a serious offense not only because a person was slain but because the spilled blood itself was a polluting substance. A slaying not only contaminated the slayer but affected the purity of the nation as a whole because biblical religion extended the concept of impurity to include certain nonritual offenses, such as homicide. The only viable remedy was to remove the contamination by spilling the blood of the killer, a cleansing act because of the decontaminating power of blood. This concept is reflected in the title given to the avenger from the victim's family, גאל הדם, "the redeemer of the blood."

Even an accidental killing polluted. According to the Priestly traditions, this meant that the accidental killer was forced to remain in a city of refuge until the death of the high priest: His death acted as expiation for the contamination incurred by the accidental death. A city of refuge was therefore both a sanctuary and a prison. In Deuteronomy, the concept that any unlawful killing pollutes was manifested in the concern that an accidental slayer might be killed by the avenger before reaching the city of refuge and in mandating a public ceremony removing the ill effects of spilled blood when a corpse whose killer cannot be identified is discovered.

By contrast, the pollution caused by homicide is generally ignored in sources from the rest of the ancient Near East. In the event of a corpse being found in an open field, the concern is with determining who is responsible for compensating the victim's family, not with any possible contamination. I argue that, at least in the case of Mesopotamia, this difference is due to fundamental differences between Israelite religion and Mesopotamian religion. In the latter, blood was considered only to be a polluting substance, not a cleansing substance, and the blood spilled in an unlawful death did not contaminate anyone besides the killer. Impurity was thought to be caused by demons, and committing a sin subjugated a person under the control of demons. The solution then was to send the demons back to their home. Biblical religion manifests the anxiety that pollution had an effect on national institutions and concerns and that the misdeeds of a single individual could pose a danger to the larger group – these are concepts not extant in Mesopotamian religion.

In Chapter Five, "Typologies of Homicide," I deal with the typologies of homicide reflected in the biblical laws and narratives and compare them to the typologies found in ancient Near Eastern law. I argue that both biblical law and narrative share a common denominator in that only homicide caused by direct physical assault is subject to legal action. Biblical narratives show characters utilizing this loophole in the law to evade punishment and differentiating between legal culpability and ethical responsibility, phenomena we would not be aware of except for narrative texts. The laws manifest a struggle to distinguish between intentional and accidental homicide.

The biblical texts lay out different criteria for determining responsibility, a presentation that appears to reflect the dilemmas of an actual court, whereas the ancient Near Eastern texts reflect scribal conventions divorced from court procedure. For the Bible, justice is grounded in actual cases, in the gray areas that make the determination of justice difficult. For cuneiform law, justice is abstract: It is articulated in conventional cases that shy away from complexity. The ancient Near Eastern law collections share more than this: I demonstrate that they are part of a common literary tradition in which a certain number of conventional cases make up the repertoire from which an author then composes his own variations. What is striking about the difference between biblical and ancient Near Eastern law is that the ancient Israelites actually used the conventional cases common to ancient Near Eastern law while reworking them in an Israelite idiom. I argue that the presence of certain highly unusual and specific cases of homicide in biblical law and ancient Near Eastern law collections show that biblical law was related to a common literary tradition of law because the differences between the two are at times of the same magnitude as the differences between the ancient Near Eastern law collections themselves. Other scholars have claimed that the similarities are due to the biblical jurist actually having a copy of ancient Near Eastern law collections in front of him or that there was a common legal practice used extensively but rarely put into writing throughout the ancient Near East. I attempt to demonstrate that particular statutes on homicide in biblical law are part of the ancient Near Eastern literary tradition of writing formal law.

The chapter concludes with two appendixes. The first examines and dismisses the claim that the principle that only intentional homicide merits the death penalty is a later development in biblical law. The second analyzes whether the biblical principle that only an individual who kills another human being by direct means is subject to legal action is applied in cuneiform law.

Chapter Six addresses *lex talionis*, "an eye for an eye," perhaps the most controversial citation from the Bible. Capital punishment was the rule for killers because the Bible holds that the punishment must be similar to the offense in the aspects in which the original offense was wrong. The agent of harm becomes the recipient of the same action of the type that constituted the offense. It was a reversal of roles: The slayer became the slain. This concept applied to other offenses. Just as a thief, for example, has taken a particular type of animal away from its owner, so was that particular type of animal demanded from the thief. The offender suffers a loss in the same coinage. This is what lex talionis, "an eye for an eye," signified. It was a principle of equivalence, not of harsh justice. Capital punishment as the punishment for homicide in cuneiform law is not a consequence of lex talionis; rather, it is an example of the harsh punishment meted out for severe crimes. Lex talionis is utilized in cuneiform law in some cases of nonfatal bodily injuries. The chapter ends with an excursus examining the claim that the Laws of Eshnunna contains alternate penalties and concludes that this claim is unfounded.

Chapter Seven addresses the question of whether there were general assumptions about the treatment of homicide in the ancient Near East, including ancient Israel. A way of answering this question is to examine the interterritorial documents from the ancient Near East to see whether there were basic ground rules that were followed or whether every aspect had to be negotiated from scratch. There are a number of documents internal to the Hittite empire as well as documents sent between states. At the basis of all the documents is the general assumption that homicide is wrong, but there is very little more than that. In the area under Hittite hegemony, the Hittite viceroy could force the parties to come to terms because of his political power, but rulers of independent states would have only the power of rhetoric to convince another ruler to remedy the wrong.

In the interests of space, only the translations of the texts from law collections are provided since the original Sumerian, Akkadian, and Hittite texts can easily be found in a number of recent publications. (See the book appendix for this information.) However, I will provide transliterated texts for the other cuneiform documents because they are far more difficult to locate and their publications are marred by errors.

CHAPTER ONE

A First Case: The Story of Cain and Abel

ONE OF the first stories in the Bible is about a homicide:

> 1 Now, the man had known his wife Eve, and she conceived
> and gave birth to Cain, saying, "I have acquired a male child with
> [the help of] the LORD." 2 Once again, she gave birth, [this time]
> to his brother Abel. Abel became a keeper of sheep, and Cain be-
> came a tiller of the soil. 3 In time, Cain brought an offering to the
> LORD from the fruit of the soil, 4 and Abel, for his part, brought
> the choicest of the firstlings of his flock. The LORD looked with
> favor upon Abel and his offerings 5 but did not look with favor
> upon Cain and his offerings. Cain was depressed[1] and saddened.
> 6 The LORD said to Cain, "Why are you depressed, and why are
> you saddened? 7 Is it not true that whether[2] you are good at being

[1] A distinction is to be drawn between חרה ל־, "to be depressed, be despondent," and חרה אף, "to be angry." Cf. Mayer Gruber, "The Tragedy of Cain and Abel: A Case of Depression," in *The Motherhood of God and Other Studies* (South Florida Studies in the History of Judaism 57; Atlanta: Scholars Press, 1992), 121–131.

[2] In this clause, אם functions as a coordinating conjunction introducing two alternatives in a protasis, הלוא אם תיטיב שאת ואם לא תיטיב, contra the translations and commentaries. Another example of this may be found in Ezek 2:5 ("And they – whether they listen or not, for they are a house of rebellion – they will know that there was a prophet among them"). The word תיטיב

> patient[3] or not, sin is a demon at the door; toward you is its de-
> sire, but you control it." [8]Cain said to his brother Abel, and when
> they were in the field, Cain arose against his brother and killed him.
> [9]The LORD said to Cain, "Where is your brother Abel?" He said, "I
> do not know. Am I my brother's keeper?" [10]The LORD said, "What
> have you done? Listen, your brother's blood is crying out to me from
> the soil. [11]Now, you are cursed from the soil, which has opened its
> mouth to take your brother's blood from your hands. [12]When you
> till the soil, it will no longer yield its strength to you. You will be
> a fugitive and a wanderer on the earth." [13]Cain said to the LORD,
> "My punishment is greater than I can bear. [14]Today you have driven
> me from the soil, and I shall be hidden from your face. I will be a
> fugitive and wanderer on the earth, and anyone who meets me may
> kill me." [15]The LORD said to him, "Therefore, whoever kills Cain
> will suffer sevenfold vengeance." The LORD put a mark on Cain so
> that no one who came upon him would kill him. [16]Cain went away
> from the presence of the LORD and settled in the land of Nod, east of
> Eden. (Gen 4:1–16)

The forcefulness of this narrative is that it is about social relations and violence; it is not just an internal linguistic affair of signs and signifiers.[4] Cain is portrayed not simply as a cold mechanical killer, but as one drawn in subtle emotional nuances. The story of Cain and Abel is fraught with dramatic, psychological, and social possibility, and each turn of the story escalates the tension and complexity. God confronts Cain with a warning about the unpredictability and tenacity of the impulse to sin and then returns to confront him about his role in his brother's slaying. God does not mention Abel's death explicitly at first but asks Cain about his brother's whereabouts. Cain evades the question, knowing exactly what befell his brother, but unwilling to admit his part in it. When God rebukes Cain and announces his punishment, Cain is filled with feelings of shame and acute despair, and his

acts adverbially in describing שאת. The adverbial usage of the root יטב in Hiphil is discussed in Bruce K. Waltke and Michael O'Connor, *An Introduction to Biblical Hebrew Syntax* (Winona Lake, Indiana: Eisenbrauns, 1990), 592.

[3] The verb נשא rarely appears intransitively in Qal, and since it is used so infrequently, translators have failed to understand it. NJV translates, "If you do well, there is uplift . . ." reflecting the pun on "Why is your face fallen?" from the previous verse, but it is unclear what "uplift" signifies. E. A. Speiser, *Genesis* (AB; Garden City, New York: Doubleday, 1962), 33, suggests, "If you do well, there is exaltation . . . ," but the root in Niphal, not Qal, means "exaltation." RSV's translation, "If you do well, will you not be accepted?" also transforms the root into its Niphal meaning. However, in our passage, Gen 4:7, the root appears in Qal. The meaning of נשא in Qal depends on whether it has an object. When this root is used intransitively in Qal, it means "patient," as can be extrapolated from Ps 99:8.

[4] Cf. William Ian Miller, *Bloodtaking and Peacemaking: Feud, Law, and Society in Saga Iceland* (Chicago: University of Chicago Press, 1990), 3.

pleading inspires God to mitigate the punishment. In addition to the dramatic and psychological, the story reflects or raises questions about typical social and legal matters. What motives serve as causes for murder? Can a killer ever justify his actions? Who remedies the crime? What is the appropriate sanction for a slaying? What rules, customs, and norms govern the prosecution and punishment of a killer? And if a killer is not punished by execution, what kind of life can he be expected to lead?

Genesis 4 is a good entryway into many of the issues of central concern in the adjudication of homicide in the Hebrew Bible. It adumbrates the considerations that inform the treatment of homicide in other biblical texts. The focus on Cain's psychology and the impulse to sin reflects a desire to determine the killer's responsibility, an essential element in the biblical adjudication of homicide. The selection of a slaying as the first offense committed by one human being upon another indicates the seriousness with which slaying is taken. The killing is set in the field, a place often the site of crime where the infrequency of bystanders complicates the determination of guilt (cf. Deut 22:25; 2 Sam 14:6). Divine protection of Cain reflects the anxiety over the appropriate form of punishment for a killer. And the דמים, "blood," of Abel is not simply a powerful image invented by a creative author for the tale of Cain and Abel. It is something real that has an existence of its own, and when blood is spilled, serious consequences result. The story of Cain and Abel thus opens up some of the critical issues in homicide for the Bible.

There is a preoccupation, even a morbid fascination, with the inner life of the killer in Genesis 4. The narrative is concerned with the circumstances leading up to the killing, the motive and *mens rea,* the state of mind, of the slayer.[5] Cain's enmity and jealousy toward his brother are aroused by the

[5]The other main line of interpretation of the story of Cain and Abel shifts the focus from murder. Rather, this episode illustrates the inevitable conflict between nomads and farmers, between the desert and the sown. The murder arose naturally and invariably out of this inevitable conflict and, therefore, the implication is that the killer himself does not really bear responsibility. (Cf. D. Bernhard Stade, who worked out the interpretation in detail, "Das Kainszeichen," in *Ausgewahlte Akademische Reden und Abhandlungen* [Giessen: J. Ricker'sche Verlagsbuchhandlung, 1899], 229–273; G. S. Kirk, *Myth: Its Meaning and Functions in Ancient and Other Cultures* [Cambridge: Cambridge University Press, 1970], 146; Speiser, *Genesis,* 31.) According to this interpretation, Cain is a symbol for the nomadic tribe of the Kenites, who live in the desert south of Judah and who are at odds with those who live settled lives. However, there is a basic incoherence at the heart of this analysis. (Cf. Umberto M. D. Cassuto, *The Book of Genesis: Part I: From Adam to Noah; Part II: From Noah to Abraham* [Hebrew] [Jerusalem: Magnes Press, 1986 (1944)], 120–122; Claus Westermann, *Genesis 1–11* [trans. John J. Scullion; CC; Minneapolis: Augsburg, 1985], 282–284.) Which figure represents the pastoral and which the agricultural? At the start, Cain is the farmer, that is, the one leading a settled existence, and Abel the pastoralist. Then Cain is condemned to wander but settles in the land east of Eden. Furthermore, there is no indication that Cain's progeny wanders like Cain. His eldest son founds a city. (Cain himself may be the founder of this city if the name Enoch is a misreading for Irad.) Cain's condition is confined to him alone. He is not emblematic of any nomadic or agricultural group.

seemingly arbitrary evaluation of their offerings. There is only the barest of implications that Cain's offering was incorrect in the comparison of Cain's offering, "the fruit of the soil," to Abel's "choicest of the firstlings of his flock."[6] The seemingly mercurial judgment of God and the innocence of Cain in this regard are amplified by the disjunction between the events of the narrative in vv. 1–6 and God's words. We would expect God to offer criticism of Cain's offering. Rather, God mentions controlling the impulse to sin.[7] After the deed is done, the narrative then explores the inner life of the killer. When God asks obliquely about Abel's whereabouts, Cain avoids the questions and disavows knowledge, so typical of an offender who knows very well what he has done and is attempting to evade punishment. Cain's plea for mitigation of punishment borders on poignancy. This narrative shaping explores the psychology of the killer before and after the killing as an avenue for determining the responsibility of the killer for his actions.

Cain's impulse to kill is depicted as capricious and powerful, illuminating a theory of sin and personal responsibility. God cautions Cain: "Is it not true that whether you are good at being patient or not, sin is a demon at the door; toward you is its desire, but you control it" (Gen 4:7). Sin is personified as a demon, Akkadian *rābiṣu.*[8] The Akkadian word *rābiṣu* originally referred to a high official who held judicial responsibility as an examining magistrate in preliminary court investigations. Later on, it was applied to deities, reflecting their judicial role in bringing the guilty party to judgment.[9] This term was then demonized: The fearsome nature and

[6] Cf. Cassuto, *The Book of Genesis*... [Hebrew], 138.

[7] Cf. N. H. Tur-Sinai, "At the Door Sin Couches" [Hebrew], *Tarbiz* 16 (1944), 8.

[8] Hans Duhm identifies the demonological aspect in *Die bösen Geisten im Alten Testament* (Tübingen/Leipzig: J. C. B. Mohr, 1904), 8–10. Claus Westermann objects that the word רֹבֵץ could not refer to a demon because such a personification of sin was unlikely in so early a text and was simply unparalleled elsewhere in the Hebrew Bible (*Genesis 1–11,* 300). In defense of the demonological interpretation, it is in all events difficult to date this text. Although opinion on the direct dependence of Genesis 1–11 on Mesopotamian texts has waxed and waned in the last century of scholarship, even those advocating a minimalist connection recognize elements developing from a shared common tradition/culture. (Cf. Richard S. Hess, "One Hundred Fifty Years of Comparative Studies on Genesis 1–11," in *"I Studied Inscriptions from Before the Flood": Ancient Near Eastern, Literary, and Linguistic Approaches to Genesis 1–11* [ed. Richard S. Hess and David Toshio Tsumura; Sources for Biblical and Theological Study 4; Winona Lake, Indiana: Eisenbrauns, 1994], 3–26, and David Toshio Tsumura, "Genesis and Ancient Near Eastern Creation Stories," in *"I Studied Inscriptions from Before the Flood,"* 27–57, esp. 55–56.) In light of the Mesopotamian background of Genesis 1–11, a reference to a Mesopotamian concept seems a strong possibility. Gerhard von Rad's suggestion to transfer the ת from the end of חטאת to the beginning of רבץ to yield תרבץ eliminates the problem in the gender agreement between subject and verb but would necessitate the emendation of the third-person masculine suffixes in the following clauses (*Genesis* [revised edition; OTL; Philadelphia: Westminster, 1972], 105) and so in solving one problem creates an equally difficult problem.

[9] AHw, s.v. *rābiṣu,* 2.935; A. Leo Oppenheim, " 'The Eyes of the Lord,' " *JAOS* 88 (1968), 173–180; Dietz Otto Edzard and F. A. M. Wiggermann, "Maškim, Kommissar, Anwalt, Sachwalter,"

power of the official were analogized to the character of lesser divine beings, demons. These demons were not to be treated lightly, just as the officials should not be treated lightly. Like the officials, the demons possessed a dual nature, both negative and positive: They could be benevolent or malevolent. Their presence is ambivalent because of this contrast. They are found at entrances of palaces and temples in order to protect and to attack.[10]

The analogy of sin to *rābiṣu* reflects a conception of wrongdoing as a powerful impulse that can either control Cain or be controlled by him, just as the *rābiṣu* can be beneficial as well as detrimental. Its dual nature is also reflected in the use of the term חטאת, which can refer to "sin" or "purification from sin." Furthermore, the root רבץ, while referring to a demon, is also two-sided: It is not necessarily meant in a threatening sense. The root רבץ signals an animal in repose, referring mostly to domestic animals but also to wild animals.[11] Wild animals are potentially harmful but are of little immediate threat while lying down in their lair.[12] Similarly, the potent impulse to sin is subject to the commands of its master, albeit requiring a firm hand in control. The impulse to kill is also described in terms of the sexual urge.[13] Sexual desire can be powerful and capricious and can dominate the object of desire if allowed to; it can be controlled by a stronger will. In short, the impulse to kill may be capricious, it may be irrational, it may be powerful, but it can be reined in. In other words, although the impulse to kill someone may be sudden and overwhelming, the killer nonetheless bears responsibility for his action because human beings have the capacity to control this impulse.

Attention is paid to homicide because it is an event of the utmost gravity. Without a doubt, the most heinous violation of the social bond between human beings is homicide. The story of Cain and Abel highlights the seriousness by emphasizing the relationship between the brothers and by placing homicide as the first crime by a human being against another human being. Although there is no indication that the most heinous occurrence of homicide is fratricide, the relationship is foregrounded by the emphasis on the fraternal relationship between Cain and Abel: The word "brother" is repeated

RLA 7.449–455; M. L. Barré, "Rabiṣu," in *Dictionary of Deities and Demons in the Bible* (2nd edition; ed. Karel van der Toorn, Bob Becking, and Pieter W. van der Horst; Leiden: Brill, 1995), cols. 1287–1290.

[10] G. E. Closen, "Der 'Dämon Sünde,'" *Bib* 16 (1935), 436–440.

[11] John Van Seters, *Prologue to History: The Yahwist as Historian in Genesis* (Louisville, Kentucky: Westminster/John Knox Press, 1992), 138.

[12] Cf. Gen 49:9; Ezek 19:2, 29:3; Ps 104:22.

[13] The word תשוקה appears three times in biblical Hebrew, Gen 3:16, 4:6; Song 7:11. Its meaning in Song 7:11 is clearly "sexual desire; sexual urge," which would work well in Gen 3:16. However, it is unclear what sexual import this word would have in our passage, Gen 4:6. Appeal to other languages yields nothing since there are no cognates. The appearance of this rare word may be due to the construction of a parallel narrative, as we shall see, to Genesis 2–3 in Genesis 4 by the use of verbal reminiscences.

seven times within the episode, six of which are within the description and aftermath of the murder (Gen 4:2, 8 [twice], 9 [twice], 10, 11).

The killing of Abel is presented in the Bible as the first crime in human society.[14] The heinous nature of the slaying of Abel is intensified by the way the story is shaped. The story of Cain and Abel in Genesis 4 and the story of the Garden of Eden in Gen 2:4b–3:24 have been composed to form parallel narratives about human sinfulness. The narrative of Cain and Abel has an almost complete verbal parallel with the previous story: Gen 4:7b, "toward you is its desire, but you control it," echoes Gen 3:16b, "Toward your husband is your desire, and he will rule over you." There are also striking reminiscences of the story of the Garden of Eden in the story of Cain and Abel: Gen 4:9, 10, 11 ("Where is . . . What have you done . . . You are cursed . . ."), in parallel language to Gen 3:9, 13, 17 ("Where are . . . What have you done . . . You are cursed . . ."). Both narratives possess the same sequence of sin, investigation, and punishment, the equivalent use of dialogue at the climax of the narrative, and attention to psychological analysis. The "trial" takes place face to face. The pronouncement of punishment is expressed in the form of a curse. The punishment itself is expulsion, and the sentence is mitigated: God is responsible for the action that protects the transgressor from the full consequences of the crime. The intention of the author/compiler is unmistakable – to construct in Genesis 4 a narrative of crime and punishment corresponding to Genesis 3. Cain's deed is as serious a transgression as Adam and Eve's violation of God's command.

Killing is serious because the harm done cannot be undone. An amount stolen can be repaid. Embarrassment, medical fees, and lost work time can be compensated in a case of assault. But Cain's deed leaves behind permanent harm whose repair is difficult. The דמים, blood, of Abel cries out from the ground. Although a casual reader might take this as a compelling metaphor invented by a gifted writer, the image plays on a technical legal term for responsibility for homicide, דמים, "bloodguilt." This term is derived from

[14] John Van Seters argues that Gen 4:1–16 assumes an earth populated with many people, not the second generation of humanity, and therefore the story of Cain and Abel does not have a primordial valence as does the story of the Garden of Eden (*Prologue to History: The Yahwist as Historian in Genesis,* 136). By contrast, the narrative of Gen 2:4b–3:24 assumes a tone of primeval time and origins. Enmity, for example, is established between the descendants of Eve and the descendants of the serpent (Gen 3:15). Genesis 4 appears ambivalent in comparison to Genesis 2–3, and it possesses both nonprimordial and primordial elements. The nonprimordial, on the one hand, is reflected in the assumption of the institution of offerings to God in two varieties, grain and first-born animals (Gen 4:3–4). The text does not present the punishment of Cain as the practice to be established for all time (Gen 4:11–12). The occupations of Cain and Abel as farmer and shepherd appear as typical, not prototypical (Gen 4:2). On the other hand, this is in sharp contrast to Gen 4:20, where Jabal is explicitly named the first shepherd. Other elements, the founding of a city and naming it after a child (Gen 4:17) and the designation of individuals as the ancestors of people with certain occupations (Gen 4:20, 21, 22), suggest the initiation of institutions of human society.

the sense that the spilled blood of the victim has a concrete existence of its own and cannot be ignored.

The text uses other technical legal terms and institutions in the interrogation and sentence of Cain.[15] Cain denies that he is the שומר, the guardian, in equivalent English legal terminology, of his brother. Cain's sentence is banishment from his home, a punishment homologous to a forced stay in a city of refuge.

Cain's punishment is mitigated because of the assumption that all who commit homicide are liable to be killed by whomever they meet and, therefore, killers like Cain need protection. In biblical law, in fact, the number of people who have the right to kill a killer is severely limited. The statutes on homicide in the Bible give the general impression that there is anxiety over what constitutes appropriate punishment. Indeed, God's protection of a killer in Genesis 4 seems at odds with the heinous nature of the offense committed and the gravity of the punishment, yet as we shall see, it is in consonance with the treatment of the punishment of the killer elsewhere in the Bible, where protections are established for killers.

A literary text like Genesis 4 opens up the issue of the nature of literature. The presence of legal elements, such as legal institutions, technical terminology, and factors taken into account in the judicial process, in a literary text poses questions about law in literature. Is it even valid to focus on the legal elements in a literary text since it is not the intention of a literary text to describe law per se? Even if it is deemed appropriate to interpret the legal elements in a literary text, it must be asked to what extent the law and legal practice are accurately portrayed when legal elements might be exaggerated or attenuated for the sake of plot or character development or theological exposition. Furthermore, Genesis 4 poses historical questions. Genesis 4 comes across as having a historical valence for the biblical author because it purports to tell about what occurred in the most ancient of times. The issue with Genesis 4, thus, is not simply a question of how accurate it is about ancient practices but whether it is legitimate to use a literary text like this one as a document to reconstruct history.

In sum, Genesis 4 is emblematic of the issues involved in the treatment of homicide in the Hebrew Bible. The attention paid to the inner life of Cain and to the understanding of sin reflects a preoccupation with determining the responsibility of the slayer. This is expressed in Cain's story by the exposition on the impulse to sin and on Cain's psychology, while in other biblical texts, the intent of the killer is extrapolated from the manner of killing or from the

[15]David Daube, "Law in the Narratives," in *Studies in Biblical Law* (Cambridge: Cambridge University Press, 1969), 13–15. Daube also recognizes that being another person's guardian was not part of the social ethics enshrined in the Bible, but he proposes that the word שומר was being used in a metaphorical sense derived from the legal status of being a guardian of property or of a city. Cf. Paul A. Riemann, "Am I My Brother's Keeper?" *Interpretation* 24 (1970), 485–486.

prior relationship between victim and killer. The seriousness of homicide is reflected in its selection as the first crime and in the amount of space devoted to it elsewhere in the Bible. Abel's blood crying out to God is not simply a vivid phrase conjured up by an imaginative author for the tale of Cain. It is something palpable that has an existence of its own, a problem that is addressed by the biblical adjudication of homicide. And God's protection of Cain belies an anxiety over the appropriate punishment of a killer, an issue taken up by other biblical texts. Lastly, the question of the nature of literature and the debate over law and literature as well as the reconstruction of history find their touchstone in Genesis 4. The adumbration of these critical issues is not surprising considering the placement of this narrative at the beginning of the first biblical book, which orients it into a myth of origin, providing a cognitive map of sociopolitical norms.

CHAPTER TWO

Blood Feud and State Control

EACH OF the legal sources in the Pentateuch refers to homicide and assumes that the life of the manslayer was in grave danger. The Priestly law stipulates (Num 35:9–34):

> [9]The LORD spoke to Moses, saying: [10]Speak to the Israelites and say
> to them: when you cross the Jordan into the land of Canaan, [11]you
> shall make accessible[1] for yourselves cities to serve as cities of refuge
> for you, to which a slayer who strikes down a person by mistake may
> flee. [12]The cities shall be as a refuge from the avenger, so that the

[1]The use of the root קרה in Hiphil in this passage is problematic. Ibn Janah and Ibn Ezra associate it with קִירָה, "city," and Ibn Ezra renders the verb as "you shall build (cities)." Saadiah connects it with ק-ר-א, "to name," understanding it as "you shall appoint." The Targums and Rashi render it with זַמֵּן, translating it apparently as "you shall provide/prepare." (So Rashi understands Gen 27:20.) BDB defines the verb as "to cause cities to occur rightly for yourselves, i.e. select cities as suitable" (899). Although the other occurrences of the root in Hiphil in Gen 24:12; 27:20 are generally rendered "to cause/grant success," the verb in these verses more likely indicates a chance or unanticipated occurrence. Gen 24:12 would, therefore, read: "The LORD, God of my master Abraham, I beseech you, make it appear before me." In Gen 27:20, Esau explains his quick return from hunting: "for the LORD, your God, made it appear before me." The Hiphil הקרה, therefore, has the connotation of easy accessibility. See Baruch A. Levine, *Numbers 21–36* (AB; Garden City, New York: Doubleday, 2001), 554.

slayer shall not die before he has stood[2] trial before the assembly.
13 The cities which are appointed shall be six cities of refuge in total.
14 Three you shall appoint beyond the Jordan, and three you shall
appoint in the land of Canaan: they shall be cities of refuge. 15 The
six cities shall be as refuge for the Israelites and the resident alien
among them, so that anyone who kills unintentionally may flee there.
16 If a person strikes another with an iron tool so that [the victim]
dies, he is a murderer[3] – the murderer shall surely be put to death.
17 If a person strikes another with a stone tool that can kill so that
the victim dies, he is a murderer – the murderer shall surely be put to
death. 18 If a person strikes another with a wooden tool that can kill
so that the victim dies, he is a murderer – the murderer shall surely
be put to death. 19 The blood avenger himself shall put the murderer
to death: whenever he meets him he shall put him to death. 20 If a
person pushed him in hatred or aimed something at him on purpose,
21 or struck him with his hand in enmity, so that the victim dies, he is
a murderer – the blood avenger shall kill him when he meets him. 22 If
he pushed him suddenly without enmity or aimed an object at him
unintentionally, 23 or without[4] looking dropped an object of stone
that can kill, so that the victim dies – though he was not his enemy
and did not seek his harm[5] – 24 the assembly shall judge between the
slayer and the blood avenger according to these rules. 25 The assembly
shall protect the slayer from the blood avenger, and the assembly shall
return him to the city of refuge to which he fled; he shall remain there
until the death of the high priest who was anointed with the sacred
oil. 26 If the slayer ever goes outside the limits of the city of refuge to
which he has fled, 27 and the blood avenger comes upon him outside
the limits of his city of refuge, and the blood avenger kills the slayer,
there is no bloodguilt. 28 For he must remain in his city of refuge until
the death of the high priest: after the death of the high priest, the slayer
may return to his ancestral land. 29 These shall be as your ordinance
of procedure throughout the generations in all your settlements. 30 If
anyone strikes down a person, the killer shall be killed only on the

[2] The verb appears to be a legal term for trial (Num 27:2; Deut 19:17; Josh 20:6; Isa 50:8). See Jacob Milgrom, *Numbers* (The JPS Bible Commentary; Philadelphia: The Jewish Publication Society, 1989), 331.

[3] The normal order of a verbless clause is predicate-subject. Cf. Waltke-O'Connor, *An Introduction to Biblical Hebrew Syntax,* 132–134. The order is reversed here to emphasize the word רצח, "murderer."

[4] The negation of an infinitive construct is בלתי as in Gen 3:11. Here, the negation לא is part of an unusual preposition בלא, "without," which is also found in Prov 19:2. Cf. GKC, §152.

[5] The usual negation of nominal clauses, especially with a participle, is אין (e.g., Deut 4:12) – the use of לא here is apparently influenced by the circumstantial character of the verse. Circumstantial clauses are negated by לא.

> testimony of witnesses: a single witness shall not be sufficient for a
> sentence of death. [31]You shall not accept compensation for the life
> of a killer who is guilty of a capital offense, for he shall surely be
> put to death. [32]You shall not take compensation from one who has
> fled to a city of refuge to return to live at large before the death of
> the high priest. [33]You shall not pollute the land in which you are
> in, for the blood itself pollutes the land: expiation cannot be made
> on behalf of the land for the blood that was shed in it except by
> the blood of him who shed it. [34]You shall not defile the land which
> you are inhabiting, in which I dwell, for I the LORD dwell among the
> Israelites.

The book of Deuteronomy declares (Deut 19:1–13):

> [1]When the LORD your God has cut down the nations whose land
> the LORD your God is giving to you, and you dispossess them and
> settle in their cities and homes, [2]you shall set apart three cities in
> your land, which the LORD your God is giving you to inherit. [3]You
> shall determine the distance and divide the limits of your land, which
> the LORD your God has allotted to you, into three, so that any slayer
> may flee there. [4]This is the type of slayer who may flee there and live:
> whoever slays his fellow without intent and was not hostile to him in
> the past. [5]Whoever came with his fellow into the forest to cut wood:
> as his hand swings the ax to cut down the tree, the ax-head falls off
> the handle and hits the other so that he dies – that man shall flee to
> one of these cities and live, [6]lest the blood avenger pursuing him in
> his hot anger, overtakes him and slays him because the distance is too
> great, yet he was not liable to the death penalty because he was not
> hostile to him in the past. [7]Therefore, I command you to set apart
> three cities. [8]If the LORD your God extends your boundaries, as he
> swore to your fathers, and gives you all the land which he promised
> to them, [9]because you observe the instruction that I command you
> this day, to love the LORD your God and to walk in his ways at all
> times, you shall add three more cities to these three. [10]The blood
> of the innocent shall not be shed in the land which the LORD your
> God is giving to you, imputing bloodguilt upon you. [11]If a person
> is hostile to another and lies in wait and strikes him mortally so
> that he dies, and flees to one of these towns, [12]the elders of his
> town shall send and take him back from there and deliver him to the
> blood avenger so that he dies. [13]You shall not have pity on him, but
> shall make expiation of the blood of the innocent, and it will be well
> with you.

The threat of the family's agent is assumed by the statute in the Book of the Covenant, Exod 21:12–14:

> 12 Whoever fatally strikes a man shall surely be put to death. 13 If [the killer] did not lie in wait,[6] but God caused it to meet his hand, then I will appoint for you a place to which he may flee. 14 But if a man willfully attacks a man to kill him treacherously, you shall take him from my altar to be put to death.

In biblical Israel, the victim's family assumed primary responsibility for ensuring that the slayer was held accountable for his offense. A member of the family had the right and responsibility to kill the slayer and could do so with impunity under certain conditions. This agent of justice was called גאל הדם, generally translated as "the blood avenger."

It is best to understand this process as self-redress or blood feud, when the victim's kin avenges the killing by killing the slayer. This label allows us to link this process to two essential characteristics of blood feud: It is local in nature, and it is rule-bound.[7] These characteristics are interrelated because blood feud is a legal mechanism that both assures the redress of wrongs and controls the violence to a level tolerable in a community. Blood feud

[6]The root צ-ד-ה is a synonym for the more common root א-ר-ב. However, it stresses the aspect of planning and watching for an opportunity to entrap, rather than the aspect of hiding. Cf. Lam 4:18; 1 Sam 24:12; Num 35:20, 22. (Zeph 3:6 is derived from a homophonous root meaning "to lay waste".) Menahem, according to Rashi, associates it with hunting.

[7]Max Gluckman, "The Peace in the Feud," *Past and Present* 8 (1955), 1–14. An alternate version of this article is found in the author's *Custom and Conflict in Africa* (Oxford: Basil Blackwell, 1965), 1–26. The term *feud* has been used to characterize a bewildering variety of phenomena, from an individual's single act of retaliation, both lethal and nonlethal, for murder, injury, and insult to continuous acts of full-scale aggression between large groups. Cf. E. E. Evans-Pritchard, *The Nuer: A Description of Their Modes of Livelihood and Political Institutions of a Nilotic People* (Oxford: Clarendon, 1940), 151–160; Gluckman, "The Peace in the Feud," 6–9; Gluckman, *Politics, Law and Ritual in Tribal Society* (Oxford: Basil Blackwell, 1977), 111–112; Marc Bloch, *Feudal Society* (trans. L. A. Manyon; Chicago: University of Chicago Press, 1974 [1961]), 138; Jenny Wormald, "The Blood Feud in Early Modern Scotland," in *Disputes and Settlements: Law and Human Relations in the West* (ed. John Bossy; Cambridge: Cambridge University Press, 1983), 113, 115–116; Jacob Black-Michaud, *Cohesive Force: Feud in the Mediterranean and the Middle East* (Oxford: Basil Blackwell, 1975), 23; J. M. Wallace-Hadrill, "The Blood Feud of the Franks," in *The Long-Haired Kings* (Medieval Academy Reprints for Teaching 11; Toronto: University of Toronto Press, 1982 [1962]), 143; Norbert Rouland, *Legal Anthropology* (trans. Phillippe G. Planel; Stanford: Stanford University Press, 1994), 277; Bernice Calmes Caudill, *Pioneers of Eastern Kentucky: Their Feuds and Settlements* (Cincinnati, Ohio: Privately printed, 1969); Keith F. Otterbein and Charlotte Swanson Otterbein, "An Eye for an Eye, A Tooth for a Tooth: A Cross-Cultural Study of Feuding," *American Anthropologist* 67 (1965), 1470–1482; J. K. Campbell, *Honour, Family, and Patronage: A Study of Institutions and Moral Values in a Greek Mountain Community* (Oxford: Clarendon, 1964), 97, 173, 194, 196–197, 264; Joseph Ginat, *Blood Disputes Among Bedouin and Rural Arabs in Israel* (Pittsburgh: University of Pittsburgh Press, 1987), 21–27, 40–59; Thomas M. Kiefer,

is not a paroxysm of rage, careening out of control. The biblical texts that deal with homicide assume that there are constraints on the power of the victim's family to effect vengeance. The actions of the blood avenger were to be channeled into certain options: His actions were not unfettered. They were not wild justice or a step outside the law.

The rule-boundedness of blood feud was manifest in the limitation on which individuals were involved. Only the slayer was subject to action, not anyone else, whether having a connection to him or not. Only a specific member of the victim's family, גאל הדם, had the right and responsibility to kill the slayer with impunity.

Another major restriction on the actions of the avenger in the Hebrew Bible was the existence of a place of sanctuary for the killer.[8] From the

The Tausug: Violence and Law in a Philippine Moslem Society (Case Studies in Cultural Anthropology; New York: Holt, Rinehart and Winston, Inc., 1972).

Objections have been made to subsuming such varied phenomena under the rubric of feud. First, the limited violence that occurs in many societies when a murder has occurred has led to reservations about calling such events manifestations of feud. Second, some observers have hesitated to identify feud as law because of the lack of an authority imposing a settlement. Cf. Leopold Pospíšil, *Anthropology of Law: A Comparative Theory* (New Haven, Connecticut: HRAF Press, 1974), 4–5, 8–9; E. Adamson Hoebel, *The Law of Primitive Man: A Study in Comparative Legal Dynamics* (Cambridge, Massachusetts: Harvard University Press, 1954), 25–28.

Formulating a clear distinction between a chain of revenge and a single act of retribution executed on the offender is useful in highlighting the varying magnitudes of violence. However, it must be noted that prolonged violence in general is rare and, therefore, using this definition of feud removes it, at least on a semantic level, from most traditional, preindustrial societies. In fact, the word "feud" continues to be used by most anthropologists for self-redress because of the potential threat of violence without the emphasis on prolonged violence. This appears correct in my judgment.

[8]Even though I have cast this in terms of restriction, it is incorrect to posit the existence of completely unfettered blood feud. Biblical scholars have argued that originally, vengeance could be taken of any killler, whether intentional or unintentional, and was only later restricted to the intentional offender in the development of restrictions on blood vengeance in ancient Israel (cf. Brevard Childs, *The Book of Exodus* [OTL; Philadelphia: Westminster, 1974], 457, 470; Baruch Halpern, "Jerusalem and the Lineages in the Seventh Century BCE: Kinship and the Rise of Individual Moral Responsibility," in *Law and Ideology in Monarchic Israel* [JSOTSup 124; Sheffield: Sheffield Academic Press, 1991], 11–107; Henry McKeating, "Development of the Law of Homicide in Ancient Israel," *VT* 25 [1975], 46–47, and Milgrom, *Numbers,* 291). But such a stage in social development is based on theoretical assumptions about the growth of primitive societies, a type of inquiry generally abandoned by contemporary anthropologists. Most recent anthropologists have shied away from producing evolutionary theories and have concentrated on the synchronic analysis of the societies they study. Cf. Laura Nader, "The Anthropological Study of Law," in *Law and Anthropology* (ed. Peter Sack and Jonathan Aleck; The International Library of Essays in Law and Legal Theory; New York: New York University Press, 1992), 3–32; June Starr and Jane F. Collier, "Historical Studies of Legal Change," in *Law and Anthropology,* 105–110; Norman Yoffee, "Too Many Chiefs? (or, Safe Texts for the 90s)," in *Archaeological Theory: Who Sets the Agenda?* (ed. Norman Yoffee and Andrew Sherratt; Cambridge: Cambridge University Press: 1993), 60–78. The contemporary study of disputes

moment of the killing itself, the slayer was threatened by the blood avenger. The family's assumption of the initiative in remedying the wrong was the direct motivation for the existence of sanctuary and was tempered by the existence of sanctuary. The fugitive's arrival in a place of refuge put a hold on the actions of the blood avenger. He could not lay a hand on the fugitive. By having impunity to kill the slayer whatever the circumstances from the time of the killing until the slayer reached a place of sanctuary, the agent of the victim's family ensured that the slayer would go to a refuge and thereupon be judged for his actions. The violence of self-redress acted as a threat: It was an impetus to a formal trial and away from violence.

The slayer's intention was not taken into account at this stage of the process, and the only way he could attempt to claim mitigating circumstances was to seek refuge in a place of sanctuary and acknowledge that he was the killer. Ironically, only by going to a sanctuary and thereby identifying himself as the killer without any denial or dissembling on his part could the killer claim that the death was accidental.

Another major restriction was the interference of others in judging whether the accused killer was guilty. Once the slayer entered the city of refuge, he was subject to trial to determine whether he was an intentional or an accidental slayer (Num 35:24; Deut 19:12). This decision limited the ability of גאל הדם to effect vengeance because if the slayer was judged to be an accidental killer, he was permitted to stay in the city of refuge safe from the avenger. Only if the slayer was determined to be an intentional killer was he handed over to the avenger for execution. This procedure introduces an element of objectivity into the process. Other people who are not the victim's kin determine the level of culpability the accused possesses in the death. The omniscient narrator in Genesis 4 can conveniently produce an omniscient Deity to judge Cain, but human beings do not have the talent of an infallible ability to determine fault and, therefore, certain procedures to make such a determination as objective as possible must be designed.

In all the legal sources, the avenger, גאל הדם, acted as executioner. Although it may appear that his role was reduced to nothing more than carrying out the judgment of the court,[9] it was his assumption in the first place of the responsibility to avenge the killing by killing the killer that forced the killer to seek refuge. Blood vengeance was the basis of the entire process for prosecuting and punishing a killer. It was rule-bound, with a safe haven for the

has also presented a challenge to the self-help theory. The idea that fighting precedes talking in the evolution of societies is contradicted by the appearance of fighting and talking side by side in the same culture. Violence does not give way to negotiation at a certain level of social development. Rather, both are present, albeit realized in different ways in different societies. Cf. Simon Roberts, "The Study of Dispute: Anthropological Perspectives," in *Disputes and Settlements: Law and Human Relations in the West* (ed. John Bossy; Cambridge: Cambridge University Press, 1983), 8–9.

[9] Cf. Milgrom, *Numbers,* 217.

killer and procedures for determining his guilt. The places of refuge acted as a check on the right of גאל הדם to kill the slayer with impunity. He could not kill a slayer while the slayer remained within the city of refuge. Courts of various constitutions determined whether the killing was intentional or accidental. The intentional killer was handed over to גאל הדם, whereas the accidental killer was sheltered from him.

What is important to recognize is that, unlike the modern Western criminal court system, which has specialized personnel for identifying and arresting, prosecuting, judging, and punishing offenders, including killers, the legal system of ancient Israel was responsible for regulating the right of the victim's family to effect a remedy, not for initiating the prosecution of a killer or for remedying the killing, a radically different concept.[10] In such a legal system, a relative of the victim, גאל הדם, initiates the process and ensures that punishment takes place.

The legal system reflects the singular role of the family in ancient Israel's social structure. The family consisted of a family per se, בית אב, which in turn was part of a משפחה, a lineage or protective association of extended families, that operated when the family was unable to solve a problem on its own.[11] In fact, the term משפחה is a term of relationship expressing kinship, real or fictional, unconnected to ownership of land.[12] This understanding emphasizes the communal association of the members of a משפחה for their socioeconomic benefit, rather than merely a matter of blood ties. A feeling of kinship may be based on other factors in addition to genealogy. Territoriality, for example, was an important aspect of משפחה.[13] Certain towns were assimilated into lists of משפחות.[14] Names of villages were identified with ancestors (Mic 5:2;

[10]Even in the case when the victim could not be identified (and presumably his family had not come forward searching for him), a local body representing the local community, the elders of a town, not a state mechanism, would come forward on an ad hoc basis to address the problem (Deut 21:1–13).

[11]Norman K. Gottwald, in *The Tribes of Yahweh: A Sociology of the Religion of Liberated Israel, 1250–1050 B.C.E.* (Maryknoll, New York: Orbis, 1979), 267, 298–302. His primary proof that the members of a משפחה were not related by blood is that taboos of sexual relationships between cousins that operated for a kinship group are absent in the rules regulating relationships, such as in Leviticus 18: a kinship group of the next higher order above a family, one that consisted of related families, was therefore exogamous, whereas a משפחה was endogamous. Within a משפחה, permitting endogamy means that the members of a משפחה were not related. Shunya Bendor correctly recognizes that this factor did not necessarily prevent kinship (*The Social Structure of Ancient Israel* [Jerusalem Biblical Studies 7; Jerusalem: Simor, 1996], 82–86). Bendor also makes a distinction between compelling endogamy and allowing endogamy by noting that Numbers 36, by prescribing endogomy, presumed that exogamy was an alternate possibility under normal circumstances.

[12] Levine, *Numbers 21–36*, 334.

[13]C. J. H. Wright, "Family," ABD 2.762; Elizabeth Bellefontaine, "Customary Law and Chieftainship: Judicial Aspects of 2 Samuel 14:4–21," *JSOT* 38 (1987), 50.

[14]For example, the towns of Shechem, Tirzah, and Hepher (Gen 34; Josh 12:17, 24) were included in the משפחות of Manasseh (Josh 17:26; Num 26:30–33).

1 Chr 2:5 versus 4:4). Land was allotted according to משפחות (Josh 13:15; Num 33:54). Degrees of kinship were left inexact.[15] All further degrees of kinship beyond father's brother were merged; no distinctions were made between cousins.[16] Kinship was not determined in finite steps of genealogy. The term משפחה, then, refers to a group that has assumed kinship ties, even if technically a blood relationship was tenuous, even nonexistent.

Family ties in biblical Israel were not so much a matter of genealogical relations as of responsibilities. What is critical to understand about kinship is that it is a way of talking about rights and duties, about the claims individuals make on others, and about how obligations are accepted or denied, not simply a matter of blood ties. The blood avenger as a member of the victim's family takes on a duty on behalf of the victim that obviously the victim cannot.

The responsibility of the lineage in the adjudication of homicide was not anomalous. A lineage had other responsibilities in the legal arena. A גאל, redeemer, was a close male relative who was obligated to reclaim land sold by a member of his lineage (Lev 25:25; Jer 32:7–8; Ruth 3:12, 4:3–4) and to redeem a relative sold into slavery (Lev 25:47–49). He acted on behalf of a powerless person in the restoration of lost property.

In biblical law, the victim's family assumed the primary responsibility for responding to the slaying of one of its members. By contrast, the members of the victim's family did not have to assume that responsibility in Mesopotamian law. They had the right to make a claim on the slayer, but the slayer was not in mortal danger from a blood avenger waiting to strike him down. There were, of course, angry Mesopotamians who would have wanted to strike down the killer, but they did not have the legal right to do so with impunity. In some cases, the victim's family might have played a role in determining the penalty, but it must be emphasized that the members of the victim's family were not otherwise involved in the remedy.

Indeed, in Mesopotamian law, those *outside* the victim's family ensured that the offense was remedied. The right of making a charge of homicide seems to be fairly general: The initiative did not specifically devolve upon the victim's family. Anyone could initiate the legal process by informing the authorities. An official investigation would then ensue. As a result, charges could be brought up, but a trial was necessary before any punishment could be inflicted, a stark contrast to the right of גאל הדם to strike down the slayer once the homicide occurred. According to the first statute in the Laws of Hammurapi, the first of an introductory series of laws on procedure, a private person can lay a charge of homicide against another person, in this case, an unsubstantiated accusation. The relationship of this private citizen to the victim is unstated.

[15] Gottwald, *The Tribes of Yahweh*, 265.
[16] Cf. Lev 25:48–49; Num 27:11.

> LH 1
> If a man accuses another man and charges him with homicide but then cannot bring proof against him, his accuser shall be killed.

In a twenty-first century B.C.E. text (from the Ur III period), NSG 202, the victim's widow charged a particular individual with the death of her husband before the authorities. By contrast, in the Nippur Murder Trial of the early Old Babylonian period, the widow refrained from informing the authorities, which led to her conviction as an accessory. The authorities must have been notified by others, perhaps suspicious friends or neighbors. In another Ur III document, NSG 121, a man reported to the governor that he has heard a rumor about a homicide.

> [1]$^{\text{I d}}$nanna-ki-ága dumu-lugal-ad-da-ke$_4$ [2]ensí-ra [3]AN-zi-KA sa-gaz lú mu-na-<a$_5$> [4]in-na-an-dug$_4$ [5]ur-^{d}ma-mi maškim-šè in-da-an-gi$_4$ [6]^{d}nanna-ki-ága-e [7]lú a-na bí-in-dug$_4$-ga [8]mu-na-an-ḫa [9]sa-gaz-a$_5$-aš la-ba-gi-in [10]^{I}bi-da-ti [11]a-gu-za nu-bànda-ar [12]túm-mu-un ba-na-ab-dug$_4$ [13]a-gu-za ì-túmu bí-in-dug$_4$ [14]ì-lum-ma nu-bànda-ar [15]lú nag-su^{ki}-ta [16]^{d}nanna-ki-ága-da in-da-gin-na [17]túm-mu-un in-na-an-dug$_4$ [18]ì-lum-ma maškim-šè-àm nu-un-da-gi$_4$ [19]SU-nam-ÍLA.NE-àm in-da-gi$_4$ bí-dug$_4$ [20]igi-a-m[u-a]-šè [21]igi-[x x x]-šè [22]igi-n[a-x x] x-šè [23]igi-da-ti-šè [24]igi-gìri-né-i-ša$_6$-sukkala-šè [25]itu-RI mu en-eridu^{ki} ba-ḫun

> [1–4]Nannaki'aga, son of Lugaladda, told the governor that someone killed another in... [5]He sent Urmami the bailiff with him. [6–8]Nannaki'aga presented to him the one against whom he had given his statement. [9]That this one committed the murder was not ascertained. [10–12]He said to Bidati and Aguzu, the inspector: "Bring him there." [13]Aguza said: "I will bring him there." [14–17]He said to Ilumma, the collector, who came from Nagsu together with Nannaki'aga: "Bring him there." [18–19]Ilumma said [that] because he is a bailiff, he will not return with him, [but] SU-nam-ILA-NE will return with him. [20–25]Witness, Amu'a. Witness... Witness, Na... Witness, Dati. Witness, Girine'isha, the courier. The month of RI, year in which the *en*-priestess of Eridu was enthroned.

It does not appear that Nannaki'aga has witnessed the homicide but merely has come across a rumor about one. He informed the governor, who assigned a bailiff to investigate.

Neo-Assyrian law concerning homicide occupies an intermediate position between biblical law and the law of the rest of Mesopotamia – there was no threat of blood feud, but there was a group response. The slayer and his social group, the town in which he lived, initiated the process by formally assuming the responsibility for making restitution to the claimant from the victim's family before the claimant ever arrived.

ADD 618 is an acknowledgment of debt obligation: The right of the victim's family to demand compensation and the responsibility of the villagers from the killer's village to pay compensation were formally recognized.[17] The person of the killer was no longer of concern: If he died or escaped, the village was still obligated.

obv.
[1]^{na_4}KIŠIB $^{I\,d}$UTU-tak-lak [2]^{na_4}KIŠIB ^{I}ib-ta-aš!-GIŠ [3]^{na_4}KIŠIB ^{I}tab-la-a-a [4]^{na_4}KIŠIB ^{I}eri-du$_{10}$-a-a [5]^{na_4}KIŠIB ^{I}U+GUR.PAP.PAP [6]^{na_4}KIŠIB ^{I}si-lim-DINGIR [7]^{na_4}KIŠIB ^{I}mu-qa-lìl-IDIM [8]^{na_4}KIŠIB ^{I}U.PAP.PAP [9]^{na_4}KIŠIB ^{I}AŠ.GIŠ [10]^{na_4}KIŠIB ^{I}sa-a-ri-u-ni [11]^{na_4}KIŠIB ^{uru}sa-ma-na-a-a gab-bu (cylinder seal of fish man) [12]^{I}ṣi-ri-i : EN UŠ.MEŠ [13]ša ^{I}si-lim-DINGIR [14]GAZ-u-ni

rev.
[15]ina IGI-šú-nu lu-u MUNUS-šu [16]lu-u ŠEŠ-šú lu-u DUMU-šu [17]man-nu šá e-la-a-ni [18]šu-nu UŠ.MEŠ ú-šal-lumu [19]IGI ^{I}tar-di-tú-aš+šur LÚ.3-šú [20]IGI $^{I\,d}$PA.SAG-i-ši [21]LÚ.NÍ.GAB [22]IGI $^{I\,d}$NUSKU.PAP.AŠ [23]LÚ.šá UGU qa-na-te [24]IGI ^{I}man-nu-ki-^{d}10 LÚ.Ì.DU$_8$ [25]IGI ^{I}aš+šur-MU.AŠ LÚ.GAL ki-ṣir [26]šá LÚ.GAL SUM.NINDA [27]IGI ^{I}AD-ul-ZU 3-šú [28]IGI $^{I\,d}$PA-u-a A.B[A] [29]ITU.APIN UD 3 KAM [30]lim-me ^{I}NU.TEŠ

[1–11]Seal of Shamash-taklāk, seal of Ibtāsh-lēshir, seal of Tablāya, seal of Eridāya, seal of Nergal-aḫu-uṣur, seal of Silim-ili, seal of Muqallil-kabti, seal of Adad-ahu-uṣur, seal of Edu-tēshir, seal of Sariuni, seal of the entire city of Samānu. [12–15]Ṣīri, the owner of the blood, whom Silim-ili killed, is their responsibility. [15–17]Whoever appears among them [to claim compensation], whether it is his wife, his brother, or his son, [18]they themselves shall pay the blood money. [19–30]Witness: Tarditu-Assur, the third rider on the chariot. Witness: Nabu-rēsh-ishi the doorkeeper. Witness: Nusku-aḫ-iddin, the official in charge of the reeds. Witness: Mannu-ki-Adad, the doorkeeper. Witness: Assur-sum-iddin, the captain of the victualer. Witness: Abu-ul-idi, the third rider on the chariot. Witness: Nabua, the scribe. 8th month, third day, eponym of Lābāshi (657 B.C.E.).

Siri had arrived to claim compensation from Silim-ili for a homicide, but the killer Silim-ili struck again, killing Ṣiri. Since the victim was not a native, there were no relatives in the vicinity to claim compensation. Nonetheless, the

[17]A detailed study of the Neo-Assyrian texts is found in an appendix to this chapter.

village where Ṣilim-ili resided did possess corporate responsibility for compensating the victim's kinsmen. Ten of the villagers formally assumed responsibility and promised to make restitution to any claimant from the victim's family. ADD 618 represents the first stages in a case of unlawful death, when the rights of the victim's family and the obligations of the killer and his community are formally recognized, in this case by the killer's community.[18]

When the claimant did arrive, negotiations ensued, and the parties came to terms on the type and quantity of property to be handed over. Execution of the slayer was a threat only if he did not pay (ADD 321).

obv.
(beginning destroyed) (blank seal space) [1′][ú]-ma-a it-ta-at-ru-uṣ [2′][is!]-sa-ḫi-iš GEME$_2$-a-di-im-ri [3′][DU]MU.MUNUS-su šá ^{I}a-tar-qa-mu [4′][L]Ú a-na! $^{\mathrm{I\,d}}$UTU.DU.PAP DUMU-šú [5′]šá ^{I}sa-ma-ku ku-um da-me i-dan [6′]da-me i-ma-si šum-ma MUNUS [7′]la i-din ina UGU qa-bu-ri [8′]ša ^{I}sa-ma-ku i-du-ku-šu [9′]man-nu šá ina UGU man-nu BAL-u-ni [10′]10 MA.NA KUG.BAB[BAR SU]M-a[n] AN.ŠÁR ^{d}UTU [11′]a-[de-e šá MAN ina ŠU l]u-ba-[ʾi-u]...

rev.
[12′]lim-m[u...] [13′]^{I}AN.ŠÁR.DÙ.A MA[N ^{kur}aš+šur IGI ^{I}...] [14′]LÚ.GA[L...] [15′]IGI ^{I}a-da-lal LÚ.DUMU.ŠU$_{\mathrm{II}}$ šá! [DUMU.MAN] [16′]I[GI $^{\mathrm{I\,d}}$I]M-ba-ba-u ^{lú}DUMU.ŠU$_{\mathrm{II}}$ [17′]ša DUMU.MAN [18′]IGI ^{I}aš+šur-DINGIR-a-a [19′]IGI [x] [...] x x [20′][...]-ri [21′][...] x

[1′–6′]It is now mutually agreed: the one who shall give Amat-adimri, his daughter, that is of Attar-qāmu, to Shamash-kēnu-uṣur, the son of Samaku [who was killed] in place of blood[-money] and wash the blood away. [6′–8′]If he does not give the woman, they will kill him on top of Samaku's grave. [9′–10′]Whoever breaches the contract with the other party shall pay 10 minas of silver [1,000 shekels]. [10′–11′]Assur, Shamash, and the oath of the king will call him to account. [12′–21′]Eponym of...of Assurbanipal, king of the land of Assyria. Witness:..., the chief...Witness: Adalal, the *mār qātē* of...Witness: Adad-Babāʾu, the *mār qātē* of the crown prince. Witness: Assur-ilaya...

In Neo-Assyria, a number of parties assumed active roles in the process of remedying a homicide. The parties specific to the case asserted their rights and obligations and assented to the negotiations.

[18] Martha T. Roth, "Homicide in the Neo-Assyrian Period," in *Language, Literature, and History: Philological and Historical Studies Presented to Erica Reiner* (ed. Francesca Rochberg-Halton; AOS 67; New Haven, Connecticut: American Oriental Society, 1987), 362.

A role for the victim's family appears in the Middle Assyrian laws as well. MAL A 10 reserves the right of the claimant from the victim's family to choose between killing the slayer or forcing him to pay.[19]

> MAL A 10
> [If either] a man or a woman enters [another man's] house and kills [either a man] or a woman, [they shall hand over] the killers [to the head of the household]. If he chooses, he shall kill them, or if he chooses to come to an accommodation, he shall take [their property]. And if there is [nothing of value to give from the house] of the killers, either a son [or a daughter]...

The family's right is the basis of another statute, B 2:

> MAL B 2
> If a man who has not yet received his share of the inheritance takes a life, they shall hand him over to the next of kin.[20] Should the next of kin so choose, he shall kill him, or if he chooses to come to an accommodation, then he shall take his share of the inheritance.

The role of the claimant from the victim's family here is to decide on the penalty. In general, it appears, families had the right to either execution or compensation; the legal institutions of a particular society were required to preserve the rights of the family to choose. This is to be distinguished from the role of the avenger in a feud, where the avenger has the right and responsibility to take the initiative and kill the slayer on sight. In MAL A 10, other individuals have arrested the slayer and have handed him over to the victim's family. In Mesopotamia, the victim's family did not shoulder the burden of remedying the homicide but could participate in aspects of the case. The actions of the victim's family did not have to ensure that the slaying was punished.[21]

[19] If the original penalty was execution that could be mitigated to compensation, it might be expected that the killer would lose all rights that he would normally enjoy in life at the moment of conviction. Indeed, MAL B 2 addresses the right of an heir convicted of murder before taking possession of the inheritance. However, his rights are not curtailed because of his conviction. If he does remain alive because the victim's kinsman decides not to kill him, he is entitled to receive his share of the inheritance.

[20] Literally, "the owner of life."

[21] The Edict of Telepinus 49 is a special case: Although it preserves the right of the claimant from the victim's family to choose between killing the slayer or forcing him to pay, it applies only within the royal family. It is a mid-seventeenth-century text, sketching the state of affairs of the royal household at the time of Telepinus's accession. It emphasizes that the prosperity of the country and royal family depends directly upon harmony within the royal family. Above all, assassination of the royal princes by other members of the royal household must cease. (Cf. Edgar H. Sturtevant and George Bechtel, *A Hittite Chrestomathy* [William Dwight Whitney

The difference in family responsibility results in a striking contrast between the Mesopotamian and biblical materials in regard to certain technical terms for the parties involved in remedying the homicide. The Bible's term, גאל הדם, refers to a relative of the victim, who avenges the killing, whereas the Mesopotamian documents refer to *bēl damê*, a term that can refer either to the slayer or to the claimant from the victim's family.[22] The fact that the term *bēl damê,* "the owner of the blood," is used to refer to both reflects the shared responsibility manifest in the Mesopotamian process, where both parties had to participate, the party making the claim and the party obligated to discharge the claim. The biblical process, by contrast, focused on the claimant from the victim's family.

As we have seen, biblical law on homicide was based on blood feud, whereas Mesopotamian law was not. This difference between biblical law and Mesopotamian law has direct ramifications for the types of institutions involved. Because there was no blood feud and no blood avenger, cities of refuge were unnecessary and did not exist in Mesopotamia; they were an essential part of the process where feud was in effect, that is, in the Hebrew Bible.

For the same reason, the role of the monarchy and central government is different in Mesopotamian texts and the Bible. In the Hebrew Bible, their role is limited. Exod 21:12–14, Lev 24:10–23, Num 35:9–34, and Deut 19:1–13 and 21:1–9 do not portray any involvement by a central administration or the monarchy. The only reference to a central government is found in Deut 17:8–10, where a local court could appeal to the Levitical priests and the judge at the central sanctuary for clarification of the law in a difficult case; the facts of the case were then remanded to a lower court. As to the role of the king himself, only the narrative of 2 Sam 14:1–17 indicates that the king could overturn the law.[23] However, the king is portrayed as hesitant

Linguistic Series; Philadelphia: Linguistic Society of America, 1935], 200; Inge Hoffmann, *Der Erlass Telipinus* [Heidelberg: Carl Winter/Universitätsverlag, 1984], 52–53.)

> 27/19′ iš-ḫa-na-aš-ša! ut-tar ki-iš-ša-an ku-iš e-eš-ḫar i-e-iz-zi nu ku-it e-eš-ḫa-na-aš-pát 28/20′ iš-ḫa-a-aš te-iz-zi ták-ku te-iz-zi a-ku-u̯a-ra-aš na-aš a-ku ták-ku te-iz-zi-ma 29/21′ šar-ni-ik-du-u̯a nu šar-ni-ik-du LUGAL-i-ma-pa li-e ku-it-ki
>
> And a case of murder is as follows. Whoever commits murder, whatever the heir himself of the murdered man says [will be done]. If he says: "Let him die," he shall die; but if he says: "Let him pay compensation," he shall pay compensation. But to the king, he shall not pay compensation.

The Edict of Telepinus assumes a court process in which the victim's heir is called upon to decide the penalty which others carry out.

[22]Cf. the second appendix to this chapter.

[23]In general in the Pentateuch, the role of the king is ignored. While this might tell us more about the Pentateuch than legal procedures, even in Deuteronomy, the one Pentateuchal text that acknowledges the monarchy, the king's role in the legal process is submerged. The limited role of the king in adjudicating cases is reflected in texts throughout the Hebrew Bible. First, 2

as to whether he ought to become involved. The wise woman presents her case, King David equivocates, and the wise woman presses him to clarify his ruling:

> 4 The Tekoite woman spoke to the king: she flung her face to the
> ground and prostrated herself, and she said, "Help, O king." 5 The
> king said to her, "What is the matter with you?" and she said, "Alas,
> I am a widow, my husband is dead. 6 Your maidservant had two
> sons. The two of them fought in the field where there was no one
> to intervene, and one of them struck down the other and killed him.
> 7 The entire family has now come to your maidservant and said, 'Give
> up the one who killed his brother that we may put him to death for
> his brother, whom he killed, even though we kill the heir.' They will
> extinguish my last ember, without leaving my husband a name or
> remnant upon the earth." 8 The king said to the woman, "Go home.
> I will issue an order for you." 9 The Tekoite woman said to the king,
> "My lord king, may the sin be upon me and my father's house: the
> king and his throne are innocent." 10 The king said, "If anyone says
> anything to you, bring him to me, and he will not trouble you any
> more." 11 She said, "May the king remember the LORD your God
> and restrain the blood avenger from destroying so that my son not
> be killed." The king said, "As the LORD lives, not a hair of your son
> shall fall to the ground."

The widow herself admits that the king bears no responsibility: He is innocent, נקי – the clan has the responsibility – but the grieving mother argues that clan retaliation would be excessive because it would destroy not only the remaining son but also the paternal line.[24]

Sam 14:1–17, where, as we saw, the king does play a role, has, in fact, been identified as part of the Succession Narrative, a product of a court historian during Solomon's reign that was reused by the D circle of writers. A product of the royal court would most likely exaggerate the king's role, not reduce it. Second, the Chronicler's History, an alternate history to the Deuteronomistic history, presents Jehoshaphat as reorganizing the legal system but not taking part in its day-to-day operations (2 Chr 19:5–11).

A distinction must be drawn between the ideal of the king as the one who assures justice and the reality of the king's role: There is no evidence that the king acted as a court of last resort (Keith Whitelam, *The Just King: Monarchical Judicial Authority in Ancient Israel* [JSOTSup 12; Sheffield: JSOT Press, 1979], 29–37, 197–206, 219–220). The rise of the monarchy, according to Whitelam, gave rise to new legal realms, such as the royal estate and crown officials, which were outside the already established judicial system of the local communities.

[24] Levine, *Numbers 21–36*, 564–565, argues that the slaying was not premeditated and therefore the son should not be executed. This is contradicted by the wise woman's own argument in v. 7b: She assumes that her remaining son deserves to die because of his actions and, therefore, argues for his life based on other factors.

The king intervened rarely and with great reluctance into the administration of justice.[25] At the same time, it is true that the reform of Jehoshaphat in 2 Chr 19:5–11 depicts royal appointment of jurists in a judicial system in which the heads of the ancestral houses, Levites, and priests constitute a central court, while local court officials have jurisdiction in local courts.[26] Although it is unclear whether royal appointment in local courts means that locals or outsiders acted as judges, it does mean that the local community did not on its own establish a court. Texts from Deuteronomy, however, contradict the Chronicles text.[27] Deut 16:18–20 does not give the king the right to appoint judges but stipulates that local governments appoint judges. Deut 17:8–10 stipulates that the local court may appeal to the central court for a clarification of the law, but the local court retains the authority to decide the facts and the case.

The contradictions between Deuteronomy and Chronicles can be easily resolved. First, it should be noted that Jehoshaphat's reform is not found in the books of Kings and, therefore, it originates in a source that belongs only to the author/compiler of Chronicles. The question then becomes how did the Chronicler obtain this information. The key is to observe that in Chronicles, an event in a monarch's reign is connected to the meaning of his name. Jehoshaphat and judicial reform are linked because of Jehoshaphat's name, which means "the LORD judges" and contains the root ט-פ-ש, "to judge." A similar link is made in Chronicles between Asa and seeking the help of physicians because the root of Asa's name in Aramaic, י-ס-א, means "to heal" (2 Chr 16:12). Jehoshaphat's reform, with its greater centralization, is in consonance with the structure of the province of Judea in the early Second Temple period. The books of Ezra and Nehemiah purport the establishment of indigenous Jewish law by means of an authority sitting in Jerusalem (Ezra 7:25). At the same time, Ezra and Nehemiah have a great interest in records of ancestral lines, attesting to the continued importance of ancestral houses

[25]The king had limited control over his own administration. David executes the men who killed Ish-boshet, Saul's heir and David's rival (2 Sam 4:5–12), but his own military chief, Joab, is too powerful for him to do more than admonish him (2 Sam 3:39). Joab's punishment must wait until Solomon's reign (1 Kgs 2:5, 28–34).

[26]Robert R. Wilson, "Enforcing the Covenant: The Mechanisms of Judicial Authority in Early Israel," in *The Quest for the Kingdom of God: Studies in Honor of George E. Mendenhall* (ed. H. B. Huffmon, F. A. Spina, and A. R. W. Green; Winona Lake, Indiana: Eisenbrauns, 1983), 61.

[27]W. F. Albright argues that the Chronicles account is historically accurate in depicting the judicial system in the late monarchy and that the differences between the Deuteronomy texts on the judicial system and the Chronicles account of Jehoshaphat are negligible, that all these texts are describing what is essentially the same system ("The Judicial Reform of Jehoshaphat," in *Alexander Marx Jubilee Volume* [New York: The Jewish Theological Seminary, 1950], 61–82). Recent scholarship has reevaluated Albright's position. Cf. Whitelam, *The Just King,* 185–206; Wilson, "Israel's Judicial System in the Preexilic Period," 243–245, and Sara Japhet, *I & II Chronicles: A Commentary* (OTL; Louisville, Kentucky: Westminster/John Knox Press, 1993), 770–779.

(Ezra 8; Neh 7). This, too, is part of Jehoshaphat's reform, with the heads of the ancestral houses serving as part of the central court. It appears, then, that Jehoshaphat's reform reflects an early Second Temple setting. Deuteronomy represents a First Temple situation, one of less centralization and greater local control.

It seems clear, therefore, that a great deal of legal authority remained in the local community throughout the First Temple period. Justice was administered generally at the local level. Justice, however, could be sought directly from the monarchy both in the southern kingdom (2 Sam 15:2–5; 1 Kings 3) and in the northern kingdom (2 Kgs 8:3, 5). The king did possess a jurisdiction that coincided with that of the local community. The monarchy did not replace a system of local justice but actually helped in keeping the system alive, as we have seen in the case of the wise woman from Tekoa, by remedying abuses, albeit inconsistently.[28] There were reservations about appealing to a nonlocal authority. In the Elisha cycle, for example, the Shunammite woman is asked by Elisha whether he should approach the king or army commander to intervene on her behalf. The woman refuses, stating that she lives among her own people, implying that her kinsmen would take care of her (2 Kgs 4:13).[29] Furthermore, it should be noted as well that the role of the king in the system of justice is something that would not have been known except for the evidence of literary texts: Legal texts do not posit any role for the monarch. Literary texts reflect the flaws in the system that the monarch must correct.

The persistence of a local or community-based system of justice can be seen in the role of elders as administrators of justice, as well as in the threat of the blood avenger on the killer's life. The elders judge whether the accused is guilty of intentional or accidental homicide. Furthermore, the statute in Deut 19:1–13 is framed in terms of towns, not tribes, not larger administrative units, even though Deuteronomy dates from a time of urbanization.[30] At the same time, Deuteronomic statutes also recognize a court of judges in place of elders, as well as a judicial role for priests.[31] Deuteronomy appears, thus, to recognize three systems of rendering judgments, those of the elders, judges, and priests, operating simultaneously.[32] The precise jurisdiction of each is difficult to define. It is clear, though, that in cases where the law was

[28] Cf. McKeating, "The Development of the Law on Homicide," 52.

[29] Ze'ev Weisman, "The Place of the People in the Making of Law and Judgment," in *Pomegranates and Golden Bells: Studies in Biblical, Jewish, and Near Eastern Ritual, Law, and Literature in Honor of Jacob Milgrom* (ed. David P. Wright, David Noel Freedman, and Avi Hurvitz; Winona Lake, Indiana: Eisenbrauns, 1995), 420.

[30] On the urbanization of this period, see Gabriel Barkay, "The Iron Age II–III," in *The Archaeology of Ancient Israel* (ed. Amnon Ben-Tor; trans. R. Greenberg; New Haven, Connecticut: Yale University Press, 1992), 329.

[31] See Deut 19:17–18.

[32] Roland de Vaux, *Ancient Israel* (New York: McGraw-Hill, 1961), 1.153.

in need of clarification, the elders or local judges could ask a central court in Jerusalem for aid (Deut 17:8–13).[33]

Although the monarch's role in the legal system was limited, the king could have an undue influence on a court case. Biblical law holds to the principle that everyone is subject to the law and that no one, whether king, priest, prophet, or judge, is above the law, but the power relations prevailing in an actual community at a particular time restricted or distorted the actualization of this principle.[34] Extrajudicial factors affected the law, and this is reflected in narrative. In 1 Kgs 21:1–15, Ahab, king of the northern kingdom, seeks to purchase a vineyard belonging to Naboth for use as a vegetable garden for the palace. He offers Naboth a choice of a better vineyard or money, but Naboth refuses. Ahab has no choice but to return to the palace empty-handed (and dispirited). Ahab assumes that even he, the monarch, is constrained by the laws of property tenure and cannot exercise his will as he wishes. His wife Jezebel, as the well-known tale continues, manages to manipulate the legal process so as to condemn Naboth and his property: Naboth is executed and his property is transferred to the king's possession. Jezebel used royal power to influence the legal system in order to evade the restraints on such power. The crown is officially subject to the law, but the actual power relations in a society may allow it to possess the means to circumvent the law. In Naboth's case, judicial murder was the result. This was an aberration in the legal process and that is how it is portrayed in the biblical text. The crown possesses only a limited role in biblical law.

In contrast, the crown and central authority played a major role in the rest of the ancient Near East. Once the legal process had been launched by a private individual, a central authority or the monarchy assumed oversight of the situation. In Riftin 46, private individuals, a shepherd and his brother an innkeeper, intervened in a kidnapping, but the kidnapper then killed the victim. The shepherd and the innkeeper became witnesses in a homicide trial conducted by official judges:

> [1]aš-šum ^{I}ri-ba-am-ì-lí š[u]-b[a-rì-i]m [2]ša ^{I}i-din-ia-tum u-sé-pu-šu-ma [3]iš-ri-qu-šu [4]^{I}a-bu-um-ra-bi SIPA [5]i-na qá-ti-šu iṣ-ba-at [6]a-ša-ar a-bu-um-ra-bi SIPA [7]^{I}ri-ba-am-ì-lí šu-ba-ri-a-am [8]ù i-din-ia-tum mu-ṣí-pi-šu [9]i-na É a-ḫu-um ^{lú}KURUN.NA [10]i-pa-du [11]^{I}i-din-ia-tum [12]^{I}ri-ba-am-ì-li šu-ba-ri-a-am iḫ-ta-na-aq [13]i-na KÁ! ^{d}nin-mar^{ki} [14]DI.KU$_{5}$ $^{e-ne}$ di-na-am [15]ú-ša-ḫi-zu-ma [16]^{I}a-bu-um-ra-bi SIPA

[33] Bernard M. Levinson argues that the passage in Deuteronomy 17 prescribes the replacement of local justice in determining whether a homicide was intentional or unintentional by the central court (*Deuteronomy and the Hermeneutics of Legal Innovation* [New York: Oxford University Press, 1997], 128). However, he does not address the existence and import of Deut 19:1–13.

[34] Michael Walzer, "The Legal Codes of Ancient Israel," *Yale Journal of Law and the Humanities* 4 (1992), 341.

rev.
[17]ù a-ḫu-um ^{lú}KURUN.NA [18]a-na NAM.ERÍM i-di-nu-ú-ma [19]^{I}a-bu-um-ra-bi SIPA [20]ù a-ḫu-um ^{lú}KURUN.NA [21]i-na KÁ ^{d}nin-mar^{ki} [22]it-mu-ú-ma [23]^{I}i-din-ia-tum [24]i-na ÌR ḫa-na-qí-im ub-ti-ru [25]IGI ta-ri-bu-um DI.KU$_5$ [26]IGI nu-úr-^{d}MAR.TU DI.KU$_5$ [27]IGI ^{d}ZUEN-i-qí-ša-am ŠUDÚG [28]IGI ib-qú-ša ŠU.I [29]IGI ta-ri-bu-um [30]IGI ^{d}UTU-na-ṣir [31]IGI la-a-lum [32]IGI ḫa-ṣi-rum [33]IGI ḫu-na-ba-tum [34]ITU. ŠU.NUMUN.NA UD 3 KAM [35]mu dug$_4$-ga an ^{d}en-líl ^{d}en-ka-g[a-ta] [36]du-un-nu-um in-dib-ba (Seal) [1]nu-úr-^{d}MAR.TU [2]DUMU ^{d}sin-li-di-iš [3]ÌR ^{d}MAR.TU

[1–5]Concerning the Subarean Rībam-ili whom Idiniatum abducted and stole, the shepherd Abum-rabi seized [Rībam-ili] in [Idiniatum's] possession. [6–12]When the shepherd Abum-rabi locked up the Subarean Rībam-ili and his abductor Idiniatum in the house of his brother, the innkeeper, Idiniatum strangled the Subarean Rībam-ili. [13–24]At the gate of Nin-mar, the judges tried the case. They made Abum-rabi and [his] brother, the innkeeper, take an oath. Abum-rabi and [his] brother, the innkeeper, swore at the gate of Nin-mar. They convicted Idiniatum of strangling the slave (Rībam-ili). [25–34]Witness: Taribum the judge. Witness: Nur-Amurrim the judge. Witness: Sin-iqisham the priest. Witness: Ibqusha the barber. Witness: Taribum. Witness: Shamash-naṣir. Witness: Lalum. Witness: Ḫaṣirum. Witness: Ḫunabatum. The second of Tammuz, year 30 of Rim-Sin. Nur-Amurrim, son of Sin-lidish, servant of Amurrim.

Officially constituted authority intervened in the resolution of the dispute in the Old Babylonian text, CT 29 42.

[1][i-nu-ma] ip-qá-tum a-na ši-im-ti-im [i]l-li-ku-ú [2][^{I}]ib-ni-^{d}MAR-TU [ù ^{I}]DINGIR-ù-^{d}UTU DUMU.MEŠ ip-qá-tum [3]a-na ba-ši-tim ša É A.BA [di-nam] iṣ-ba-tu-ma [4]^{I}i-din-ìr-ra DUMU ta-p[í-gi-ri]-^{d}UTU [5]^{I} ^{d}NANNA-tum DUMU na-ra-am-^{d}ZUEN [6]^{I}DINGIR-šu-ba-ni DUMU SIG-^{d}IŠKUR ap-pa-an-DINGIR DI.KU$_5$ KÁ.DINGIR.RA.KI [7]^{I}im-gur-^{d}EN.ZU DUMU ṣíl-lí ^{d}IŠKUR an-na-tum DUMU a-w[i]-il-DINGIR [8]i-na pa-ni-tim di-nam i-di-nu-ni-a-ti-ma [9]iš-ša-lu-ma a-ḫu-um a-na a-ḫi-im ṭe$_4$-im-šu ú-te!-er-ma [10]a-na DINGIR-ù-^{d}UTU ù ib-ni-^{d}MAR.TU [11]ki-a-am iq-bu-ú a-li-ik [12]^{I}aš-qú-du-um i-na KÁ.^{d}NUN.GAL ki-a-am li-iz-ku!-ru [13]da-i-ik ^{I}ip-qá-tum la i-du-ú [14]a-na-ku la ú-ša-ḫi-zu ù ba-ši-tum ša [i]p-qá-tum [15]la el-qú-ú la al-pu-tu ^{I}aš-qú-du-um-m[a] [16]ù GEME$_2$-^{d}MAR.TU li-iz-ku-ru [17]di-nam an-ni-a-am ú-ul il-qú-ma [18]i-na ša-ni-im di-nim [19]^{I}ḫa-ia-ab-ni-DINGIR ^{I}i-din-ìr-ra [20]^{I}DINGIR-šu-ba-ni ^{I} ^{d}NANNA-tum [21]ù ap-pa-an-DINGIR DI!.KU$_5$ KÁ.DINGIR.RA.KI [22]i-na li-bu ka-la-ak-ki-[i]m ú-ša-ḫi-zu-šu-nu-ti [23]di!-nam ša-tu ú-ul il-qú-ú [24]i-na

ša-al-ši-im LUGAL im-ḫu-ru-ma 25 LUGAL a-na ^{d}ÍD ^{I}aš-qú-du-um ^{I}DINGIR-ú-^{d}UTU 26 ù GEME$_2$-^{d}MAR.TU iṭ-ru-da-na-ti-im-ma 27 ^{d}ÍD DI.KU$_5$ ki-it-ti[m] ni-ik-šu-ud-ma 28 ^{I}DINGIR-ù-^{d}UTU ki-a-am iq-bi um-ma 29 šu-ú-ma da-i-ik a-bi-ia i-di 30 ù GEME$_2$-^{d}MAR.TU ki!-a-am iq-bi ša a-ka-lu 31 ù ap-ra-ku ša be-li-ia-ma si-ki!-il-tam 32 [la ás]-ki-lu ^{I}lu-uš-ta-mar mu-ki-il-ka! 33 ^{I}TÚL-INANNA ra-ki-bu-ú ^{I}še-ip-ìr-ra AGA.ÚS LUGAL 34 ^{I} ^{d}ZUEN-a-ḫa-am-i-din-nam ša LUGAL 35 [. .] -pu-ut LUGAL 36 [. . . i]b-ni-šu! DUMU [. . .] 37 [. . .] x-an-ni-zi-^{d}AMAR.UTU be-el-la-nu-um 38 [. . .] x i-túr-áš-d[u-u]m DUMU e-tel-lum 39 an-nu-tum ši-bu-sú-nu 40 šá ^{d}ÍD

1–3 When Ipqatum died, Ibni-Amurrim and Ilu-Shamash, sons of Ipqatum, initiated a suit regarding the possession of the house of their father. 4–8 Iddin-Irra, son of Tapigiri-Shamash, Nannatum, son of Naram-Sin, Ilu-bani, son of Ipiq-Adad, Appan-ilu, judge of Babylon, Imgur-Sin, son of Ṣilli-Adad, [and] Annatum, son of Awil-ili rendered a decision for us in the first trial. 9 They investigated and each returned his finding. 10–16 They said as follows to Ibni-Amurrim and Ilu-Shamash: "Now, let Ashqudum[35] declare under oath at the gate of Ningal, 'I do not know the murderer of Ipqatum, I did not instigate [him], and I did not take the fortune of Ipqatum. I did not touch [it].' Ashqudum and Amat-Amurrim shall take an oath." 17–22 They [Ashqudum and Amat-Amurrim] did not accept this judgment, and in a second trial [further litigation], Ḫaya-abni-ilu, Iddin-Irra, Ilu-shubani, Nannatum, and Appan-ili, judge of Babylon, tried [?] them [Ashqudum and Amat-Amurrim] inside the storehouse. 23 They did not accept this judgment. 24–29 In a third trial, they presented [themselves/the case] to the king. The king sent us, [namely] Ashqudum, Ilu-Shamash, and Amat-Amurrim, to the River [ordeal]. We reached the River [ordeal], the true judge, and Ilu-Shamash said as follows: "I know who killed my father." 30–32 Amat-Amurrim said as follows: "What I eat and what I lie across[36] is my master's. I did not acquire [it] fraudulently."[37] 32–40 Lushtamar, the attendant, Burtu-Ishtar, the wagon-driver, Shep-Irra, the soldier of the king,

[35]P. Dhorme identifies Ashqudum as the brother of the litigants on the evidence of another tablet, "Mélanges," *RA* 8 (1914), 101–102.

[36]The meaning of the verb *parāku* is "to lie across; to obstruct, to block." Dhorme understands Amat-Amurrim's statement as "That which I eat and that which I cover" ("Mélanges," 104). Arthur Ungnad renders her statement as "What I eat and carry" (*Babylonische Briefe aus der Zeit der Ḫammurapi-Dynastie* [Leipzig: J. C. Hinrichs, 1914], 183). CAD/S s.v. *sakālu,* 68b–69a, translates it as "all that I eat and that I wear."

[37]Ungnad, in *Babylonische Briefe,* 183, suggests that this verb is from the root meaning "to trade," but CAD/S, 68b–69a demonstrates that this meaning is limited to the Neo-Babylonian period. Only in Neo-Babylonian is the semantic field of *s-k-l* equivalent to that of the corresponding Hebrew root. Otherwise, the verb *sakālu* means "to appropriate."

Sin-aham-idinnam of the king['s court]...x of the king, Adad-mansum...-ibni, son of...annazi-Marduk, Belanum...son of Etel-lum. These are their witnesses before the River [ordeal].

A number of Mari texts[38] recount the investigation launched when a corpse was found.

ARM VI 43
[1]a-na be-lí-ia [2][q]i-bí-ma [3][um]-ma ba-aḫ-di-li-im [4][ÌR]-ka-a ma [5][1 DU]MU.GABA ša ša-ad-da-ag-di-im wa-al-du [6][i-na] me-eḫ-re-et za-ka-nim BAD [7][ša] e-le-nu pí-a-tim ša-pí-il-tim [8][i-na a]-aḫ ÍD na-di-ma lúTUR šu-ú [9][i-na q]a-ab-li-šu na-ki-ìs-ma [10][x x] x ir-ti-šu a-na qa-qa-di-šu ša-ki-in [11][ù iš-tu] qa-qa-di-šu a-di še-pí-šu [12][x x x] lu-ú zi-ka-ar [13][lu-ú si]-in-ni-iš ma-an-nu-[um] [14][lu-ú i-d]e iš-tu qa-ab-li-ti-š[u] [15][a-di ša-a]p-li-iš ú-ul i-ba-aš-ši [16][i-na u$_{4}$]-mi-šu-ma ki-ma ṭe$_{4}$-ma-am ša-a-tu [17][eš-mu]-ú dan-na-tim aš-ku-un-ma [18][LÚ.ME]Š UGULA ba-ba-tim DUMU.MEŠ um-me-ni [19][ù DU]MU.MES TE.A.AB(?) ú-sà-an-ni-iq-ma [20][ú-ul be]-el lúTUR ša-a-tu ú-ul a-bu-šu [21][ú-ul um]-ma-šu ù ša ṭe$_{4}$-ma-am ša-a-tu [22][i-du-ú] ú-ul i-le-em [23][ù i-na] u$_{4}$-mi-šu-ma te$_{4}$-ma-am ša-a-tu [24][Ib]e-lí-lu-da-ri a-na ṣe-er b[e-lí-i]a [25]aš-pu-ra-am ú iš-tu UD 7 KAM [26]ša be-lí-lu-da-ri aš-pu-ra-am [27]sú-un-nu-qú-um-ma ú-sà-an-ni-iq [28]ù a[n]-x [...} [29]x [...]

[1–4]To my lord, say: thus says Baḫdi-Lim, your servant. [5–8][The body of] a child, who was born last year, was found lying on the river bank opposite the *zakānum* which is above the opening of the lower dike. [8–15]This child is cut through his waist, and...his middle is placed on his head. From his head to his feet...whether male or female, I do not know, [because] from his middle on down there is nothing left [of the child's body]. [16–22]The same day on which I heard this news, I gave strict orders and I interrogated the mayors of the quarters, the artisans, and the..., but neither the child's master nor his father nor his mother nor anyone else who knows of this matter has come forward. [23–28]The same day I sent this news via Bēli-lū-dāri to my lord, and in the seven days since I sent Bēli-lū-dāri I have continued to investigate...

ARM VI 37
[1][a-n]a be-lí-ia qí-bí-ma [2][u]m-ma ba-aḫ-di-li-im ÌR-ka-a-ma [3]a-lum ma-riki é-kál-lum ù ḫa-al-ṣum ša-lim [4]a-na še-im za-ku-tum šu-ru-bi-im a-ḫu-um ú-ul na-di

[38] Another text from Mari, ARM V 35, indicates that a killer was put on parole, but what this actually signifies is unclear.

5 [š]a-ni-tam ḫa-ab-du-IŠTAR ^{I}ba-zi-IŠTAR 6 ù ia-an-zi-ib-^{d}IŠKUR 3 LÚ.MEŠ KÁ-na-aḫ-lim$^{k[i]}$ 7 [š]a i-nu-ma ^{I}dan-nu-ta-ḫa-az a-na èš-nun-na$^{k[i]}$ 8 it-ba-lu-šu-nu-ti iš-tu ma-ḫa-ar a-tam-ri-im 9 in-na-bi-tu-nim ù e-ri-iš-ši-šu-nu-ma il-li-ku-nim 10 ^{túg}na-aḫ-ra-mi 1 i-na É-GAL-[lim a]d-di-in-šu-nu-ši-im 11 [a-na ṣ]e-er b[e-l]í-[i]a aṭ-ṭà-a[r-da-šu-nu]-ti 12 [. . . .]-šu-nu-ti 13 [. . .] x x x x

rev.
1′ [x x s]à-ḫa-ri-im 2′ a-na ia-aq-qí-im-^{d}IŠKUR ù zi-im-ri-^{d}IŠKUR 3′ dan-na-tim aš-ku-un ù ìs-ḫu-ru-ma 4′ ša-la-am-ta-šu ú-ul i-mu-ru ù ki-a-am eš-me 5′ um-ma-a-mi ša-la!-am-ta-šu i-na TÚG^{há} ú-qa-ab-ru-ma 6′ a-na ^{íd}ḫa-bu-ur i-zi-bu i-na-an-na 7′ ša-la-am-t[a-š]u ú-ul ú-ta ú qa-qa-su 8′ i-na qa-at-tu-na-a^{ki}ša-ki-in 9′ qa-qa-sú iq-qa-ab-bi-ir ù i-na a-i-im a-lim 10′ iq-qa-ab-bi-ir ù a-šar iq-qa-ab-bi-ru 11′ i-na ki-di-im i-na li-ib-bi a-lim iq-qa-ab-bi-ir 12′ ù i-nu-ma nu-qa-ab-ba-ar-šu 13′ i-na te-er-ṣí-im nu-qa-ab-ba-ru-ma a-sà-ḫi-im 14′ an-ni-tam la an-ni-tam be-lí li-iš-pu-ra-am

15′ ù e-nu-ut-sú ša i-na qa-at-tu-na-a^{ki} 16′ [ù] i-na sa-ga-ra-tim^{ki}-ma ša be-lí 17′ [i]š-pu-ra-am a-na li-ib-bi ter-qa^{ki} 18′ [l]u-še-ri-ib

1–4 To my lord, say: Thus says Baḫdi-lim, your servant. The city of Mari, the palace, and the district are well. There has been no negligence with regard to bringing in the cleaned barley.

5–13 Another matter: Ḫabdu-Ishtar, Bazi-Istar, and Ianzib-Addu, three men of Bāb-naḫlim, whom Dannutaḫaz has now brought to Eshnunna, have run away from the house of Atamrum and have arrived completely naked. I have given each one a *nāramu*-garment[39] from the palace. I have sent them to my lord. . . .

1′–14′ I have given strict orders to Iaqqim-Addu and Zimri-Addu to search . . . , but they have searched and have not seen his body. I heard thus: "They have rolled his body in a cloth and abandoned it in the Habur river." Now, I have not recovered his body, but his head is in Qattunan. Should his head be buried, and in which village should it be buried, and where should it be buried, whether inside or outside the village, and whenever we bury it, should we bury it in the regular way? I am concerned. Whether this way or that way, let my lord write to me.

15′–18′ The baggage that is in Qattunan and Sagarātim about which my lord wrote, let me bring it to Terqa.

[39] Cf. CAD/N I, 346.

In a Neo-Babylonian case, TCL 12 117, the city assembly of Uruk investigated an attempted homicide on the royal commissioner of the Eanna temple then turned the case over to the crown judges:

> [1]^{lú}ba-ni-i^{meš} ša i-na pa-ni-šú-nu [2]^{I}DÚ-^{d}15 A-šú ša ^{I}LÚ-^{d}na-na-a [3]GÍR AN.BAR ul-tu MURUB$_4$-šú a-na muḫ-ḫi [4]^{I}AN-ri-man-ni ^{lú}SAG LUGAL ^{lú}EN pi-qit-tum E-an-[na] [5]ina KÁ.GAL-i ša E-an-na is-su-ḫu [6]GÍR AN.BAR ul-tu MURUB$_4$-šú a-na muḫ-ḫi [7]^{lú}UKKIN iš-ku-šu ú ik-nu-ku

> [1–7]The citizens before whom [was presented the case of] Ibni-Ishtar, son of Amēl-Nanâ, [who] removed an iron dagger from his belt against Ilu-rîmanni, a chief official of the king, an appointed officer of Eanna, at the great gate of Eanna. The assembly bound and sealed the iron dagger which he drew from his belt.

The actual judgment was at the jurisdiction of royal judges, while the assembly was limited to the preliminary investigation. In a fifteenth-century case from Alalakh, Wiseman Alalakh 17, the slayer's property has been confiscated by the palace:

> [1]^{na}4KIŠIB ^{I}niq-me-pa (seal of Idrimi) [2]^{I}ša-tu-wa DUMU su-wa DUMU ^{uru}lu-ba [3]DUMU.SAL-šu ša ^{I}ap-ra [4]a-na É.GI.A-šu iš-al-šu [5]ù ki-ma pa-ra-as ^{uru}ḫa-la-ab^{ki} [6]ni-id-na i-za-ab-bil-šu [7]^{I}ap-ra a-na EN [8]ma-ši-ik-ti it-tu-ur

> rev.
> [9]ù ki-ma ar-ni-šu GAZ [10]ù É-šu a-na É.GAL [11]i-ru-ub ^{I}ša-tu-wa [12]it-tal-kam ù aš-šum mi-im-me- [13]-šu-ma 6 ka-qa-ru URUDU ḪI-A [14]ù 2 GÍR ZABAR il-qí-šu-nu [15]ù iš-tu UD-mi an-ni-im [16]^{I}niq-me-pa ^{I}ša-tu-wa i-[pu-ul]-šu [17]i-na EGIR-ki UD-mi di-nu-[. . .] [18]^{I}ša-tu-wa i-na mi-[. . .] [19]IGI a-pu-[. . .] [20]IGI (d) X-EN [21]IGI du-ra ŠEŠ-šu [22]IGI ir-kab-tù IGI i-ri-ḫal-pa [23]IGI LÚ-ia IGI šar-ru-wa DUB.SAR

> [1]Seal of Niqmepa (2–6) Shatuwa son of Suwa of Luba has made a payment to Apra[40] for his daughter[-in-law?] and according to the decree of Aleppo has brought a gift. [7–11]Apra has turned against a private enemy and as his punishment has killed him. Therefore his property has been confiscated by the palace. [11–14]Shatuwa has come and received what is his, namely 6 talents of copper and 2 bronze daggers. [15–16]Therefore from this day Niqmepa has satisfied Shatuwa. [17–18]In future . . . Shatuwa will [bring no further claims].

[40]Apra is mentioned in texts 139, 167, 170, but no further information about him can be gleaned from these.

> 19–23 Witness: Apu-x. Witness: x-bēl. Witness: Dura his brother. Witness: Irkabtu. Witness: Iriḫalpa. Witness: LU-ia. Witness: Sharruwa the scribe.

It can be speculated that the palace refunds the bride-price to the father because the daughter might become a slave as compensation for the slaying, and the father does not want to get involved in litigation.

Although in Neo-Assyria the private parties were required to assume greater initiative than elsewhere in Mesopotamia, the crown still maintained control. When the private parties involved asserted their rights, acknowledged their responsibilities, and assented to the negotiations, the monarchy managed them by defining the limits of their rights, serving as a mediating body for the disputants, and ensuring that the obligation was properly fulfilled.[41] There was an official recording institution of the monarchy at which outstanding homicide obligations were deposited, pending the claim of the victim's family (ADD 618 and 321). Next, the parties negotiated the amount of compensation with the intervention of a mediating authority, an officer of the crown (ADD 164). Finally, when a specific amount had been agreed upon, the obligation was paid in the presence of an official authority, a crown official (ADD 806 and PPA 95). In sum, once the state became involved, the participation of others in the process became less active. The monarchy, in essence, managed the case as it proceeded to its conclusion. It must be recognized that for Assyrians, homicide was not entirely a state crime nor was it entirely a private offense. It had first significance for the kin or community groups affected, whom the state, then, tried to manage.[42]

In Mesopotamian law in general, the king himself appeared as an actor in the judicial realm. In the Nippur Murder Trial, the case was presented before the king,[43] who then sent it back to the Assembly of Nippur for adjudication. In CT 29 42, lower courts were the appropriate venue for the first two trials, but the final appeal was made to the king, who then dispatched the case to

[41] Roth, "Homicide in the Neo-Assyrian Period," 362–363.

[42] A role for community groups in Mesopotamia exists in a single statute in the Laws of Hammurapi. Statute 24 addresses the case in which a killer has not been arrested. The mandate here is that if a person is killed in the course of a robbery, the city and governor must pay sixty shekels to the victim's kinsman if the robber is not arrested. The communal authorities must compensate the victim's family when the killer himself cannot be forced to. Otherwise, in Mesopotamia, the state managed one individual's claims against another individual.

[43] The king was in Isin even though it appeared that the homicide occurred in Nippur because Nippur was under the political domination of Isin at that time. Cf. the analysis of the situation in late 1900s B.C.E in Georges Roux, *Ancient Iraq* (3d edition; London: Penguin Books, 1992), 183.

be tried in a cultic setting. The case recounted in BBSt 9 was brought before the king: no lower court intervened:

> [1]i-na MU 2 KAM ^{d}nin-urta-NÍG.DU-URU$_3$ [2]^{I}ÌR-^{d}IMIN.BI DUMU ^{I}at-rat-taš [3][ḫar]-mi-tu šá ^{I}bu-ru-šá ^{lú}ZADIM [4]šá ^{I}EN-DINGIR.MEŠ-URU$_3$ a-na aš-šú-ti a-ḫu-zu [5]i-na šil-ta-ḫi im-ḫaṣ-ma i-duk-[ši] [6]i-na IGI ^{d}nin-ib-NÍG.DU-URU$_3$ LUGAL [7]^{I}bu-ru-šá ^{lú}ZADIM u ^{I}ÌR-^{d}IMIN.BI DUMU ^{I}at-rat-taš [8]di-na id-bu-bu-ma ^{d}nin-urta-NÍG.DU-URU$_3$ [9]LUGAL a-na ^{I}ÌR-^{d}IMIN.BI ki-a-am iq-bi [10]um-ma a-lik-ma 7 a-mi-lu-ta a-na ^{I}bu-ru-ša [11]i-din ^{I}ÌR-^{d}IMIN.BI a-mi-lu-ta na-da-[na] [12]la i-ši-ma ^{I}bu-ru-ša 7 a-mi-[l]u-t[a] [13]i-na muḫ-ḫi-šú ú-kin-ma a-na ŠÀ-bi a-m[i-lu-ti] [14]im-ru-[u]ṣ
>
> [1–5]In the second year of Ninurta-kudurri-uṣur, the king, Arad-Sibitti, son of Atrattash, attacked the *ḫarmītu*-woman of Burusha, the maker of bows and arrows, whom Bel-ilani-uṣurshu had married, with an arrow and killed [her]. [6–8]Before Ninurta-kudurri-uṣur, the king, Burusha, the maker of bows and arrows, and Arad-Sibitti, son of Atrattash, met in litigation. [8–11]Ninurta-kudurri-uṣur, the king, said to Arad-Sibitti: "Go and give 7 slaves to Burusha." [11–14]Arad-Sibitti did not complete the payment of slaves. Burusha succeeded in his claim against him for 7 slaves although he was angry about the slave woman. . . .

There is no clear pattern for determining when a case would be handled by the king or by a functionary of the central government. It appears impossible to draw conclusions about royal participation vis-à-vis a particular time period or location because of the danger of homogenizing all these cases stretched over considerable time and place. However, it is possible to measure the congruence of one king's legal function to the evidence from other monarchs. In the light of the extensive documentation of Hammurapi's participation in the judicial process, W. F. Leemans categorized the ways a king could dispose of a case: 1) The king could himself act as a court and render a judgment; 2) the king could determine the law but remit the case to local judicial authorities for the determination of the facts; 3) the king could remit the entire case to the appropriate local authorities.[44] Although Leemans dealt mostly with disputes over land tenure and revenues, the ways in which the king participated in these cases were parallel to the way in which the king participated in homicide cases. In BBSt 9, the king acted as judge. In CT 29 42, the king issued a ruling as to how the

[44]W. F. Leemans, "King Hammurapi as Judge," in *Symbolae iuridicae et historicae Martino David dedicatae II* (ed. J. A. Ankum, R. Feenstra, W. F. Leemans; Leiden: Brill, 1968), 110.

third appeal was to be handled and assigned it to a particular court. In the Nippur Murder Trial, the king assigned the case to the local assembly. Furthermore, even though this paradigm is constructed from cases involving one particular king, Hammurapi, it fits the evidence we have for lesser documented kings. The Neo-Assyrians, for example, appear to have been able to appeal to their king in person, who then disposed of the case as he wanted.[45]

In sum, the Mesopotamian documents confirm the involvement of the state in remedying homicide concomitant with the initiation of the legal process by individuals. The victim's family had the right to make a claim, but there does not seem to have been anxiety engendered by the specter of a blood avenger waiting to pounce. By contrast, feud operated in biblical law, and cities of refuge were required for the slayer's protection. The central administration and the king were generally not involved.

These differences can be attributed to the social, political, and economic differences between Israel and Mesopotamia. A pivotal characteristic of Mesopotamian society was urbanism,[46] embodying a social organization that was centralized, bureaucratic, and specialized, whereas the constituent parts of the Bible reflect a decentralized, unspecialized, mildly bureaucratic, rural society. This is so, even though the cities of Mesopotamia were highly dependent on a massive agricultural base and biblical Israel was at times a rump state centered on Jerusalem.

The essential urbanism of Mesopotamian society was pervasive.[47] Urban centers in Mesopotamia lay in sight of one another: Cities were densely concentrated. The city was the seat of culture, and by definition, nonurban life was uncultured. A bucolic countryside did not lie outside the city in Mesopotamian thought. Nomads were held in contempt.[48] The idea that urbanism was the only social structure was so persistent that the destruction of a rival political power was portrayed as the destruction of cities, even if the enemy lacked cities to destroy.[49] The great literary works reflect the climate and temper of city life, not an earlier period of preurban/tribal life.[50] The Epic

[45]Cf. J. N. Postgate, "'Princeps Iudex' in Assyria," *RA* 74 (1980), 180–182.

[46]Marc Van de Mieroop, *The Ancient Mesopotamian City* (Oxford: Clarendon, 1997), 1–19; A. Leo Oppenheim, *Ancient Mesopotamia* (rev. edition; completed by Erica Reiner; Chicago: University of Chicago Press, 1977), 79; Karel van der Toorn, *Sin and Sanction in Mesopotamia and Israel* (Studia Semitica Neerlandica; Assen/Maastricht: Van Gorcum, 1985), 3.

[47]Benno Landsberger, *Three Essays on the Sumerians* (intro. and trans. Maria deJ. Ellis; MANE 1/2; 1943; reprint, Los Angeles: Undena, 1974), 3.

[48]Toorn, *Sin and Sanction,* 155, nn. 5–8.

[49]Cf. the Assyrian campaign in 714 B.C.E. against the Mannaeans, south of Lake Urmia (F. Thureau-Dangin, *Une relation de la huitième campagne de Sargon* [TCL 3; Paris: Paul Geuthner, 1912], 16 col.i, ll. 89–90), or a campaign in the marshes at the head of the Arabian Gulf (D. Luckenbill, *The Annals of Sennacherib* [OIP; Chicago: University of Chicago Press, 1924], 35 col. iii, ll. 65–70).

[50]Toorn, *Sin and Sanction,* 3.

of Gilgamesh, for example, celebrates urban life through the acculturation of Enkidu and the exaltation of the city of Uruk.

One of the characteristics of urbanism is the substitution of a society organized politically on territorial principles for one based on ties of kinship.[51] This type of society was divided by class and ruled by an elite, whether military, religious, or political. This was certainly true for Mesopotamia. A Mesopotamian city was a society organized hierarchically along territorial or political lines, not along lines of kinship.[52] Identifying oneself as part of a lineage lessened in importance early in Mesopotamian history.[53] People acted primarily as individuals in the social and legal spheres: Lineages did not dominate economic or political life. The most basic social unit was the family, not lineage. This accounts for the absence of blood feud and the presence of the central government and crown in the Mesopotamian adjudication of homicide.

It must be noted that although urbanism and the concomitant dissolution of kinship ties were primary characteristics of Mesopotamian society, there was some variation over time and geography. Although extensive urbanism was already the norm early on, literary texts did refer to clans, *im-ru-a*, but they are rarely mentioned in administrative documents.[54] In the Old Babylonian period, there is some evidence from land sales that there were cases of joint ownership of land. The issue with these particular cases is whether this signifies that a lineage was involved or whether it was a resuscitation of family ties in order to comply with a legal requirement that was nothing more than an archaic relic of the role of the lineage.[55] There was a marked decline in urbanism in Babylonia in the late second millennium and first millennium B.C.E. By contrast, the Neo-Assyrian empire witnessed a massive expansion of cities. Undoubtedly, kinship ties in general were more significant for seminomadic people who lived outside of the settled, urban areas.[56] What is striking, though, is that with the partial exception of Assyria, variation in the extent of urbanism and kinship ties over time appears *not* to be reflected in the adjudication of homicide.

[51] V. Gordon Childe, "The Urban Revolution," *The Town Planning Review* 21 (1950), 16; Robert McC. Adams, *The Evolution of Urban Society* (Chicago: Aldine, 1966), 87, 110.

[52] Van de Mieroop, *The Ancient Mesopotamian City*, 100–104.

[53] I. M. Diakonoff, "Extended Families in Old Babylonian Ur," *ZA* 75 (1985), 52; Elizabeth Stone, "Texts, Architecture and Ethnographic Analogy: Patterns of Residence in Old Babylonian Nippur," *Iraq* 43 (1981), 19–33; Norman Yoffee, "Aspects of Mesopotamian Land Sales," *American Anthropologist* 90 (1988), 119–130.

[54] Nicholas Postgate, *Early Mesopotamia: Society and Economy at the Dawn of History* (London: Routledge, 1992), 83; Åke Sjöberg, "Zu einigen Verwandtschaftsbezeichnungen im sumerischen," in *Heidelberger Studien zum Alten Orient* (ed. D. O. Edzard; Wiesbaden: Otto Harrassowitz, 1967), 201–231.

[55] Postgate, *Early Mesopotamia*, 94–96.

[56] Samuel Greengus, "Legal and Social Institutions of Ancient Mesopotamia," in CANE, 469.

In contrast, biblical Israel is characterized by the persistence of social organization based on kinship ties.[57] It is no wonder, then, that the initiative for remedying a homicide lay with the victim's family. The lineage, the association of families, in biblical Israel acted as a mutual aid society and, therefore, in a case of homicide, blood feud ensued.

This understanding of Israelite social development contravenes the dominant models of state formation, which dictate that a kin-based society, such as that of a tribe or chiefdom, breaks down in a territorial state.[58] These theories assume that the development of society culminates in a state, a territorially defined, class-based society reflecting a fundamental change between prestate and state societies. They equate kin-based structures with prestate forms of organization. Statehood represents a fundamental reorganization of society. Controversy has arisen, therefore, over when the Israelite polity moved from stage to stage. A question that inspires heated debate is whether ancient Israel was a full-blown state during the reign of David or only a chiefdom.[59] These models of state formation make an explicit contrast between kin-based tribes and chiefdoms and territorially based states, but this distinction is insufficient.

More recent analyses have noted the striking persistence of kin-based social structures in ancient Israel, and a different developmental theory has become necessary. Israelite society, being patrimonial or segmentary, retained kin-based structures while developing a limited amount of centralization.[60] Israelite society was divided into households of extended families, that is, patrimonies or segments based on kinship ties.

In general, patrimonial authority depends on the forces of tradition and personal association. The master of a household has authority because of his personal relationship with the members of a household and because of

[57] J. David Schloen, *The House of the Father as Fact and Symbol: Patrimonialism in Ugarit and the Ancient Near East* (Studies in the Archaeology and History of the Levant 2; Winona Lake, Indiana: Eisenbrauns, 2001), 46, 51, 135–183; Bendor, *The Social Structure of Ancient Israel,* 82–86; Yigal Shiloh, "The Four-Room House: Its Situation and Function in the Israelite City," *IEJ* 20 (1970), 180–190; Gottwald, *The Tribes of Yahweh,* 267, 298–302.

[58] The reasons for the transformation differ among various theoreticians. Elman Service postulates that societies developed from tribe to chiefdom to state. As societies became more densely populated, they required stronger and more permanent coordination by a chief and his family, who thereby gained power and prestige. Morton Fried posits that deepening social stratification due to the rise of private property spawned authority structures on the level of the state. See Daniel M. Master, "State Formation Theory and the Kingdom of Ancient Israel," *JNES* 60 (2001), 123–124.

[59] Bellefontaine, "Customary Law and Chieftainship," 47–72; J. W. Flanagan, "Chiefs in Israel," *JSOT* 20 (1981), 47–73; David W. Jamieson-Drake, *Scribes and Schools in Monarchic Judah: A Socio-Archeological Approach* (The Social World of Biblical Antiquity Series 9; JSOTSup 109; Sheffield: Almond Press, 1991), 138–145.

[60] Capital cities in ancient Israel functioned as regal-ritual cities as defined by Richard G. Fox, *Urban Anthropology,* 16–57.

tradition that dictates their obedience. This model can be extended to the relationship of individual houses to the leader of a group of households. An entire society can be organized on the model of a single household. Just as members of a household would obey the master of a house, so would individual houses obey a ruler. This model can be applied to an entire state: The coalescence of a kingdom does not necessarily involve change in all levels of society. The development of a patrimonial state would add a higher level of social organization on top of the existing level of social organization. In the case of ancient Israel, what changed with the rise of the monarchy was the addition of another household, the royal household, at the next higher level of social organization. Kin-based authority systems would permeate such a society. The association of families in a lineage was the fundamental metaphor of social and political relationships. The extended household acted as the organizing model of society, and the entire social order was an extension of the ruler's household. With this model in mind, we no longer need to try to plot monarchic Israel's place on a trajectory of development that dictates that kin-based society was necessarily effaced in a state.

The social structure of biblical Israel consisted of extended kin groups or lineages, and this segmentary structure persisted through the First Temple period and reappeared in the exilic and early Second Temple periods.[61] Its recrudescence was not an invention or revival of terms dormant for half a millennium. This can be extrapolated from both textual and archaeological remains. Although these data are fragmentary and originate from a wide range of times of origin, including both evidence whose date can be fixed with some degree of precision and evidence whose date of origin must remain approximate at best, they can provide a general picture of Israelite society. Furthermore, textual and archaeological data are independent of one another: If one source is found faulty, the other is not affected.

Both First Temple and Second Temple biblical texts express the identity of individual Israelites in genealogical terms that refer to extended kin groups (Josh 7:14–18; 1 Sam 9:11; Ezra 2; 8:1–14; Neh 7:4–72; 11; 1 Chr 2–9).[62] Individuals are identified by tribe, lineage, and family, and their genealogies go back generations to ancestry remote in family history.

[61]Lawrence Stager, "The Archaeology of the Family in Ancient Israel," *BASOR* 260 (1985), 24; Avraham Faust, "The Rural Community in Ancient Israel During Iron Age II," *BASOR* 317 (2000), 17–39.

[62]Avraham Malamat, "Mari and the Bible: Some Patterns of Tribal Organization and Institutions," *JAOS* 82 (1962), 143–150; Malamat, "King Lists of the Old Babylonian Period and Biblical Genealogies," *JAOS* 88 (1968), 163–173. A useful comparison can be made to first millennium Babylonia where individuals are named "personal name 1, son of personal name 2, descendent of personal name 3," where personal name 3 is not an individual's grandfather but an ancestor or professional designation, akin to modern-day family names. (Cf. Van de Mieroop, *The Ancient Mesopotamian City,* 107–109.)

Attachment to patrimonial property remained tenacious. A number of textual examples can show this. The Priestly law in Lev 25:13–17 stipulates that patrimonial property that has been sold reverts to the family in the Jubilee year; it can never be alienated. Num 36:5–9 provides legislation preventing patrimonial estates from shifting from tribe to tribe when the only heirs are daughters, who are otherwise not entitled to the property. In the tale of Naboth's vineyard (1 Kgs 21:1–15), set in the mid-ninth century, Ahab the king wants to purchase Naboth's vineyard, but Naboth refuses to sell the vineyard, which was part of his patrimonial estate, to the king, stating: "The LORD forbid that I give you the inheritance of my fathers." The upset king realizes that he is obliged to accede to Naboth's refusal. The prophet Jeremiah, active in the late seventh and early sixth centuries, purchases the field of one of his cousins in their ancestral village of Anathoth in obedience to the law of redemption, which offered the nearest kin the first right of purchase (Jer 32:6–15).

The monarchy apparently had only a slight impact on the social structure of biblical Israel at the local level. The provincial reorganization attributed to Solomon preserved much of the premonarchic tribal boundaries intact.[63] The continuing impact of the monarchy on society did not affect kinship structures at the level of extended families. This is reflected in a variety of biblical texts. The book of Deuteronomy, at least a version of which dates from the late seventh century and which received a final redaction during the exilic period, is addressed to a villager living away from the central sanctuary in his ancestral village. Although the elders lost much of their political authority during the monarchy, they did not lose it completely and were called upon to exercise it in times of national emergency (1 Kgs 20:7; 2 Kgs 23:2), and the institution of the elders was restored in the exilic and Second Temple periods (Jer 29:1; Ezek 8:1; 14:1; 20:1, 3; Ezra 5:5, 9; and 6:7, 8, 14; Ezra 2:68; 4:2; 8:1; Neh 7:70; Ezra 1:5; 4:3).[64] The texts present a segmentary social structure reflecting the prevalent way of life, consisting of the settlement of extended families in small towns and rural settlements.

Archaeological data coincide with the textual presentation of Israelite society. Samaria ostraca of the eighth century B.C.E. record place names that also appear as names of the children of Manasseh in biblical genealogies in Josh 17:2–3 and Num 26:30–33, reflecting the continuing integrity of patrimonial structures centuries later.[65] Excavations attest to the presence of

[63] Yohanan Aharoni, *The Land of the Bible* (2d edition; trans. and ed. by Anson F. Rainey; Philadelphia: Westminster, 1979), 367; Baruch Halpern, *The Constitution of the Monarchy in Ancient Israel* (HSM 25; Chico, California: Scholars Press, 1981), 251–256.

[64] Hayyim Tadmor, "Traditional Institutions and the Monarchy," in *Studies in the Period of David and Solomon and Other Essays* (Winona Lake, Indiana: Eisenbrauns, 1982), 240, 257; Israel Eph'al, "The Western Minorities in Babylonia 6th–5th Centuries," *Or* 47 (1978), 79.

[65] Ivan T. Kaufman, "The Samaria Ostraca: An Early Witness to Hebrew Writing," *BA* 45 (1982), 229–239; Schloen, *The House of the Father as Fact and Symbol,* 156–165.

family compounds, where a lineage would dwell, well into the Iron II period at Tell Beit Mirsim, Tell Far'ahm, and Tell en-Naṣbeh and perhaps extending into later periods as well.[66] The presence of family tombs, which would be used by a lineage for a number of generations, attests to the continuing importance of kinship ties, and it is surmised that the tombs would serve as a physical claim to patrimonial land.[67]

Israelite society was agrarian, settled in small towns. Although the monarchy produced a period of urbanization, the Iron Age II cities were almost entirely given over to administrative structures and vacant of inhabitants.[68] The Israelite population lived out in the countryside in villages and farmsteads. Even Jerusalem at its greatest size of fifty to sixty hectares was only 15 percent the size of the central cities in Mesopotamia.[69]

Individuals in ancient Israel fitted into a social pattern that differed sharply from that of Mesopotamia. The overriding fact in Mesopotamian society was the state and its administrative subdivisions, whereas blood ties bound Israelite society. This distinction had other effects. Patrimonial property was not attested in Mesopotamian society because it was organized on a nongentilic pattern, although a liberal policy of the sale and purchase of land was in effect.[70] Adoption, which abrogates blood ties, became a prominent institution in Mesopotamian society; levirate marriage, which protects blood ties, never did.[71]

Assyrian law's distinctiveness confirms this argument. Assyrian legal procedure differs from other Mesopotamian law in that it posits a role for the slayer's community and for the victim's family. This variance is probably

[66] Stager, "The Archaeology of the Family in Ancient Israel," 22. Living in family compounds may be reflected in textual evidence as well; cf. the household of Micah pursuing the abducted Levite, Judg 18:22.

[67] Burial evidence has mainly been attested in Judean territory during the First Temple period. Cf. Elizabeth Bloch-Smith, *Judahite Burial Practices and Beliefs About the Dead* (JSOTSup 123; Sheffield: Sheffield Academic Press, 1992), 148–150. On the relationship between burial practices and social organization, cf. Anne Porter, "The Dynamics of Death: Ancestors, Pastorialism, and the Origins of a Third-Millennium City in Syria," *BASOR* 325 (2002), 1–36.

[68] Zeev Herzog, *Archaeology of the City: Urban Planning in Ancient Israel and Its Social Implications* (Tel Aviv: Tel Aviv University, 1997), 270, 276. Indeed, only modest remains can be dated to the United Monarchy, which biblical scholars generally consider to be a period of monumental architecture.

[69] Jamieson-Drake, *Scribes and Schools in Monarchic Judah,* 153.

[70] Malamat, "Mari and the Bible: Some Patterns of Tribal Organization and Institutions," 150. Johannes M. Renger, in "Institutional, Communal, and Individual Ownership or Possession of Arable Land in Ancient Mesopotamia from the Fourth to the End of the First Millennium B.C.," *Chicago-Kent Law Review* 71 (1995), 269–320, argues for a more cautious analysis of the documents regarding the possession and sale of arable land. He contends that in Babylonia, state control over land, owing to state involvement in irrigation, gave way gradually to the increasing control of entrepreneurs, whereas in Assyria, collective ownership over land was replaced by manorial control as the rural populace became impoverished.

[71] E. A. Speiser, "'People' and 'Nation' of Israel," *JBL* 59 (1960), 161.

due to Assyria's geographic difference from Babylonia and Sumer, and that geographic difference had an profound impact on Assyrian social structure. The fact that Assyria was assured of sufficient rainfall for dry farming meant that there were more permanent rural settlements further from cities than in Babylonia and Sumer, where permanent settlements were possible only near natural or artificial bodies of water.[72] The association of families persisted in a rural environment.

In sum, the organization of society had a profound effect upon the concept of justice and the process of law in the Bible, and the treatment of homicide in biblical Israel was directly linked to the social structure of biblical Israel. Although the most influential culture of the ancient Near East, Mesopotamia, left its mark on almost every chapter of the Bible, the Mesopotamian adjudication of homicide differed radically from that in biblical Israel because of the profound differences in social organization between the two cultures. In Israel, kinship ties were strong, and the family acted as a mutual aid society, whereas in a heavily urban and centralized Mesopotamia, a bureaucracy had control. This is striking because biblical law was based upon Mesopotamian law and yet at the same time differed so greatly. The institutions that ensured that a homicide would be investigated and remedied in biblical law were vastly different from those in Mesopotamian law. The difference originates in disparate conceptions of the organization of society.

APPENDIX ONE: THE IDENTITY OF גאל הום, "THE BLOOD AVENGER"

Biblical interpreters almost without exception hold that גאל הדם is a blood relative.[73] This is so because of the linguistic connection with the גאל, the redeemer who acted on behalf of a powerless person in the restoration of lost freedom or sold property. However, a few scholars have departed from identifying גאל הדם as a relative of the victim. Mayer Sulzberger argues that the גאל הדם was not a member of the victim's family but, rather, an official whose duty was to avenge murders.[74] Since it was the country's purity or guiltlessness that was threatened by the killing, a federal sheriff was entrusted with the duty of executing the offender. The term גאל הדם was selected because of the analogy of the positive benefit – in Sulzberger's word, "friendliness" – to

[72] Van de Mieroop, *The Ancient Mesopotamian City,* 8.

[73] Cf. S. R. Driver, *Deuteronomy* (ICC; Edinburgh: T & T Clark, 1901), 232; Moshe Greenberg, "Avenger of Blood," IDB 1.321; S. David Sperling, "Blood, Avenger of Blood," ABD 1.763–764.

[74] Mayer Sulzberger, *The Ancient Hebrew Law of Homicide* (Philadelphia: Julius H. Greenstone, 1915), 53–54, 58.

the community in warding off the danger. The establishment of an official to avenge murders was, according to Sulzberger, a Deuteronomic innovation, part of the assumption of exclusive jurisdiction by the state over all homicide cases. Another scholar, Anthony Phillips, adduced four proofs in arguing that גאל הדם was the representative of the local elders who would plead the case on their behalf at the city of refuge and then execute the killer:[75] 1) There is no evidence that blood feud was practiced against fellow Israelites: If there were blood vengeance, the Book of the Covenant would have used a formula other than the one referring to normal communal execution; that is, it would have used נקם in place of מות יומת. Furthermore, all Israel became kin by entering into the covenant and, therefore, the realm of גאל was no longer limited to blood relatives. 2) Blood was the personal property of YHWH; therefore recovering the victim's blood was not the concern of the victim's relatives but of YHWH. 3) While the term גאל הדם indicates the duty of the holder of the title, there is no such specification with regard to the גאל; therefore, it is inconceivable that they designate the same person. 4) גאל הדם only appears in connection with the cities of refuge and so must have had an intimate connection with them.

Sulzberger and Phillips both deny the existence of blood feud, the family's right to avenge the killing of one of its members. However, the motive for establishing appropriately situated cities of refuge, to prevent the blood avenger from overtaking the fugitive in hot anger, reflects the fury of a family bent on vengeance (Num 35:12, 19, 26–27; Deut 19:6). Although Exod 21:12–14 does not mention גאל הדם, it is clear that the killer flees because he is in immediate and grave danger of losing his life. If גאל הדם were a state official, it is reasonable to suppose that he would do his duty without need for restraints. Why then would a place of refuge be necessary in the first place? The basic point that underlies both Sulzberger and Phillips is, therefore, problematic. Furthermore, neither one has a satisfactory explanation of the relationship of the term גאל הדם to גאל if, unlike גאל, גאל הדם is not a relative of the victim.

In addition, other aspects of their theories are difficult to confirm. Although Sulzberger is justified in emphasizing the danger posed to the purity of the country by bloodshed, his understanding of גאל as a "friend" to the community is strained because he did not recognize that the blood of the victim as the locus of the victim's life has an objective existence of its own that requires vengeance: The use of גאל is not metaphorical or analogical but concrete.[76] Phillips's four proofs are faulty: 1) His argument that death in the course of a feud requires the use of the verb for vengeance,

[75] Anthony Phillips, *Ancient Israel's Criminal Law: A New Approach to the Decalogue* (Oxford: Basil Blackwell, 1970), 103.

[76] See the discussion in Chapter Three on the concept of blood in the Hebrew Bible.

נ-ק-ם, does not work since that verb actually refers to the punishment not of the wrongdoer himself but either the entire group he represents or selected subordinate members of that group.[77] In contrast, Exod 21:12 and 14 stipulate the punishment for the one who actually inflicted the fatal blow. Furthermore, Phillips's claim that feud did not operate within Israel because all Israel became kin by entering into the covenant requires him to posit that the hypothetical story in 2 Sam 14:4–17 does not deal with blood feud, even though גאל הדם is mentioned as being restrained by David's order. 2) In Phillips's proof that the blood belongs to YHWH, he begins with Jer 38:16, which states that the נפש, the life force, is the gift of YHWH, and basing himself on the idea that the נפש is to be found in the blood, extrapolates that blood, too, is the gift of YHWH and, therefore, belongs to YHWH. While it is true that the Israelites believed that the נפש was contained in the blood, extrapolating that since the נפש is a gift of YHWH, the blood then is also a gift of YHWH and, therefore, it belongs to YHWH contains too many questionable inductive leaps. 3) Although Phillips is correct in drawing attention to the distinction being made in the use of the term גאל הדם, instead of גאל, there may be another reason for the distinction: While the גאל was the closest relative to the victim, it is probable that in many cases the closest relative might not have the personal characteristics to serve as גאל הדם. In fact, גאל is the larger category to which גאל הדם belonged. 4) Finally, Phillips's claim that גאל הדם appears only in connection with the cities of refuge is false since he must ignore the mention of גאל הדם in 2 Sam 14:11. (Even if Phillips is correct about 2 Samuel 14, it would be logical if the two institutions were always in proximity since the sole purpose of the cities of refuge was to protect the killer from גאל הדם.)

APPENDIX TWO: THE TECHNICAL TERM *BĒL DAMÊ*

The phrase *bēl damê* refers to both the killer[78] and to the claimant from the victim's family.[79] The phrase's appearances in Šamši-Adad I, text 2, iv, 17, ABL 1109, r. 10, and ABL 1032, r. 8, clearly show that it refers to the slayer.

[77] Cf. Westbrook, *Studies in Biblical and Cuneiform Law,* 94.

[78] Cf. CAD/D, 80.

[79] Cf. Roth, "Homicide in the Neo-Assyrian Period," 363–365. Contra Ayala Mishaly, "The Bēl Dāmē's [*sic*] Role in the Neo-Assyrian Legal Process," *Zeitschrift für Altorientalische und Biblische Rechtsgeschichte* 6 (2000), 35–53, who claims that the *bēl damê* was an official, but this is based on an erroneous translation of the relative pronoun *ša* in ADD 618 13.

Šamši-Adad I, text 2[80]
col. iv
[15]^{d}UTU da-a-ia-nu [16]rab-bu-í ša AN ú KI [17]ki-ma ša-ri-ku[81] be-el da-mi [18]a-na qa-at LUGAL [19]be-el le-mu-ut-ti-šu [20]li-ma-al-⌜li-šu⌝

[15–20]May the god, Shamash, the great judge of heaven and underworld, hand him over to a king who is his enemy as *one who gives up* a killer.[82]

ABL 1109 (excerpts)[83]
rev.
[10] . . . u en-na i-qab-bu-ú um-ma EN da-me ša EN-i-nu ina UGU-i-nu
[11]ul i-rab-bi . . .

[10–11]Now, however, they are saying: "The murderer of our master shall not lord it over us."

ABL 1032[84]
rev.
[8]en-na ŠEŠ.MEŠ ša ^{I}u-tu-mu EN da-me [9]ša la-pa-an LUGAL iḫ-li-qu-u ki-i i[-qa-ab-bu]

[8–9]How can the brothers of Utumu, a murderer, who fled from the king, say . . .

The phrase's appearance in PPA 95, where the individual named as a *bēl damê* is a witness to the payment made by a father for a homicide his son committed, and in Wiseman, *The Vassal-Treaties of Esarhaddon*, where the *bēl damê* acts for wronged Esarhaddon, is clear evidence that the term can refer to the claimant from the victim's family.[85] In PPA 95, if the term

[80]Publication: Many copies are extant. Cf. A. K. Grayson, *Assyrian Rulers of the Third and Second Millennium (to 1115 B.C.)* (RIMA I; Toronto: University of Toronto Press, 1982), 51–52. Transliteration and translation: Grayson, *Assyrian Rulers of the Third and Second Millennium*, 54.

[81]This is a mistake for *ša-ri-ik*, "the one who hands over (in a legal case)." Cf. Grayson, 54, and CAD Š/II, 42–43, s.v. *šarku*, "to hand over in a legal case."

[82]Cf. Benno Landsberger, "Lexikalisches Archiv," *ZA* 41 (1933), 227.

[83]Publication: Robert Francis Harper, *Assyrian and Babylonian Letters* (Chicago: The University of Chicago Press, 1911), 11.1223–1224. Transliteration and translation: Simo Parpola, *Letters from Assyrian and Babylonian Scholars* (SAA 10; Helsinki: Helsinki University Press, 1993), 94.

[84]Publication: Harper, *Assyrian and Babylonian Letters,* 10.1131.

[85]Victor Korošec argues that only in Hittite, the expression *e-eš ḫa-na-aš-pat iš-ḫa-a-aš*, "lord of the blood," refers to the person who has the claim on the blood money (*Hethitische Staatsverträge* [Leipzig: Theodor Weicher, 1931], 38). The problem with Korošec's argument is that this phrase appears only twice in Hittite, once in the Hittite laws and once in a text where its meaning is unclear. Cf. Roth, "Homicide in the Neo-Assyrian Period," 364.

referred to the killer, then it would be applied to the son for whom the father is paying compensation, not one of the witnesses.

PPA 95
obv.
[1]^{I}še-lu-[b]u DUMU-šú [2]šal-lu-[un]-tú-šú 80 MA.NA URUDU.MEŠ [3]^{I}aš+šur-B[ÀD].PAP ina É LÚ.A.BA É.GAL [4]ú-[šal]-li-me x x x x [5]I[GI] $^{I\,d}$MAŠ.MAŠ.I LÚ qur-bu-te [6]^{uru}par-Ḫ͟A-a-a [7]IGI $^{I\,d}$PA.PAP-ir LÚ! šá UGU URU [8]IGI ^{I}ÌR-^{d}al-la-a-a [9]^{lú}ḫa-za-nu [10]IGI $^{I\,d}$PA-ú-a [11]^{lú}mu-tir-ṭè-me [12]IGI ^{I}KAM-eš-DINGIR LÚ.GAL É.GAL!

rev.
[13]IGI ^{I}ti-ni-x-x [14]^{uru}ba-da-na-a-a [15]IGI $^{I\,d}$PA-rém-a-ni [16]EN ÚŠ.MEŠ ša GUB-ni [17]IGI $^{I\,d}$PA-ú-TI.LA [18]LÚ.A.BA ṣa-bit ṭup-pi [19] I[TU.A]B UD 27 KAM [20]lim-me $^{[I]d}$PA.KAR-ir-a-ni [21][L]Ú.GAL KAŠ.LUL [22]IGI $^{I\,d}$PA.S[U] LÚ.GAL URU.MEŠ-ni [23][ša] LÚ.A.BA É.GAL

[1–4][For] Shelubu his son, Assur-duru-uṣur has paid in full his [Shelubu's] payment of 80 minas of copper in the house of the palace scribe.... [5–23]Witness: Nergal-na'id, the *qurbutu*-officer of (the city of) Parnunna. Witness: Nabu-naṣir, the city overseer. Witness: Urdu-allaya, the mayor. Witness: Nabua, the information officer. Witness: Eresh-ili, the palace overseer. Witness: Tini..., of [the city of] Badana. Witness: Nabu-remanni, owner of the blood who was present. Witness: Nabu-uballiṭ, the scribe, writer of the tablet. Tenth month, 27th day, eponym year of Nabu-eṭirani, the chief butler [740 B.C.E.]. Witness: Nabu-eriba, the city inspector of the palace scribe.

The Vassal-Treaties of Esarhaddon[86]
[576]KIMIN ki-i ša a-a-lu ka-šu-du-u-ni di-ku-u-ni [577]a-na ka-šú-nu ŠEŠ.MEŠ-ku-nu DUMU.MEŠ-ku-nu EN UŠ.MEŠ [578]lu-ka-ši-du li-du-ku-ku-nu

[576–578]ditto. Just as a stag is overtaken and killed, so may the avenger[87] overtake and kill you, your sons and your daughters.

[86]Publication, translation, and transliteration: D. J. Wiseman, *The Vassal-Treaties of Esarhaddon* (London: British School of Archaeology in Iraq, 1958), 71–74. Transliteration and translation: Simo Parpola and Kazuko Watanabe, *Neo-Assyrian Treaties and Loyalty Oaths* (SAA 2; Helsinki: Helsinki University Press, 1988), 53–54.
[87]Although Parpola and Watanabe renders *bēl damê* in the translation as "mortal enemy," the glossary in their book renders it as "avenger" (*Neo-Assyrian Treaties and Loyalty Oaths*, 86).

[582] KIMIN KIMIN ki-i šá MUŠEN ina du-ba-qi iṣ-ṣab-bat-u-ni [583] a-na ka-šu-nu ŠEŠ.MEŠ-ku-nu DUMU.MEŠ-ku-nu ina ŠU.II EN ÚŠ.MEŠ-ku-nu [584] li-iš-ku-nu-ku-nu

[582–584] Ditto, ditto. Just as one seizes a bird in a trap, so may your brothers [and] your sons place you in the hands of your avenger.

There are a number of references that are ambiguous because of the poor state of preservation of the text. In ABL 1008, it seems that a number of people were killed, and the killers fled to the mountains. The letter writer sent promises of safe passage to them. The killers then came down and made peace with the victim's kin. The good relations failed, and the killers once again fled to the mountains. The victim's kin then resumed threatening the killers.

ABL 1008[88]
rev.
[1′] [. . .]-šú-nu i-du-u-ku [. . .] [2′] [ip-ta-al]-ḫu a-na KUR-ú e-te-l[i-u] [3′] [^{Id}PA]-LAL-an-ni ina UGU-ḫi-šu-nu a-sa-ap-ra [4′] [i]t-tar-du-u-ni a-de-e is-se-e-šú [5′] i-sa-ak-nu e-tar-bu ia-mut-tú [6′] ina ŠÀ URU-šú kam-mu-su 2 URU.SE.MEŠ [7′] TA qa-an-ni-šú-nu LÚ.EN ÚŠ!.MEŠ ša a-na [8′] LÚ.GAL URU.MEŠ-ni i-du-ku-u-ni [9′] la ú-ri-du-u-ni . . .

[1′-6′] . . . They killed their . . . They became afraid and went up to the mountain. I sent [Nabû]-taqqinanni to them; they came down, concluded a settlement with him and entered into it, and [then] each was dwelling [peaceably] in his own town.

There are two problems with this text. The first is that line 7 reads LÚ.EN KUR.MEŠ, "enemies." Only if we assume that this is an error for LÚ.EN ÚŠ.MEŠ do we find the term *bēl damê* in this text. Secondly, lines 6′–9′ have difficult syntax. Martha Roth translates: "The bēl dame destroyed two villages within their borders which are in the jurisdiction of the village inspector; (they have again fled to the mountains) and have not come down." Andreas Fuchs and Simo Parpola translate it: "Two villages from their outskirts, the avengers who killed the village managers, did not come down." However, the verb *dâku* takes a direct object, not the preposition *ana* and, therefore, the action of the verb cannot be directed at the village manager(s). (The plural marker in the logogram could refer either to the manager[s] or to the

[88] Publication: Harper, *Assyrian and Babylonian Letters,* 10.1101. Transliteration and translation: Robert H. Pfeiffer, *State Letters of Assyria* (New Haven, Connecticut: American Oriental Society, 1935), 221–222; Andreas Fuchs and Simo Parpola, *The Correspondence of Sargon II, Part III: Letters from Babylonia and the Eastern Provinces* (SAA 15; Helsinki: Helsinki University Press, 2001), 67.

village[s]). It is more likely that *bēl damê* refers here to a murderer, rather than to an avenger, whose actions would be authorized and who would not need to flee.

The phrase is also found in ABL 211,[89] but it is simply too ambiguous to determine what it signifies. The letter writer claims that he is being viewed as a *bēl damê*, but this could mean that he is claiming favored status as kinsman or that he is protesting that he is being unfairly viewed as a murderer.[90] It is simply impossible to determine.

The phrase is also found in CT 53 402,[91] but the text is very broken.

There are a number of terms that have semantic ambivalence comparable to *bēl damê*. These are legal terms like *bēl dīni*, which refers to either party in a law suit, or *bēl sulummî*, which refers to either party to an agreement. It is equally plausible to argue that the meaning "owner of the blood," referring to the claimant from the victim's family, is related to *bēl napišti*, "the owner of life," the member of the victim's family who has the right to vengeance.

> MAL B 2
> If a man who has not yet received his share of the inheritance takes a life, they shall hand him over to the avenger.[92] Should the avenger so choose, he shall kill him, or if he chooses to come to an accommodation, then he shall take his share of the inheritance.

APPENDIX THREE: THE ADJUDICATION OF HOMICIDE IN NEO-ASSYRIA

There are five Neo-Assyrian legal documents that deal with homicide. Although they present unrelated cases with different victims and offenders, we can take these five texts and arrange them in the logical progression of settling a dispute.[93] They concern different phases that fit logically together and thus may be reconstructed as a single judicial process. ADD 618 reflects a preliminary stage in which the rights and obligations of the parties involved in the adjudication of homicide are formally recognized. ADD 321 represents the assistance of a mediating body in a dispute over a homicide in order to settle the issues of the rights and obligations of the parties when they are in the process of negotiating the amount of compensation for a homicide. ADD 164 reflects the further progress of the case by stating the court's

[89] Harper, *Assyrian and Babylonian Letters,* 2.213–214.
[90] Roth, "Homicide in the Neo-Assyrian Period," 364.
[91] Simo Parpola, *Cuneiform Texts from Babylonian Tablets in the British Museum* (London: British Museum, 1979), plate 105.
[92] Literally, "the owner of life."
[93] Roth arranges three of these texts in such a progression, in "Homicide in the Neo-Assyrian Period," 362–363.

confirmation of the compensation the guilty party must pay. The final two documents, ADD 806 and PPA 95, reflect the conclusion of the process: The payment is delivered to the injured party and the dispute is settled. Specifically, ADD 806 refers to land forfeited as compensation, a legal transaction conducted by government officials, while PPA 95 records a payment made in the presence of an official ensuring that the obligation was discharged properly. There is a great deal not recorded in these documents. For example, no indication of the circumstances of the homicide is offered – how was it accomplished? Was it intentional or accidental? These matters are of no concern because these documents are purely economic in nature.

ADD 618 is a formal acknowledgment by the killer's village of its obligation to pay compensation and of the right of the victim's family to demand compensation for the unlawful death. Once this formal declaration has been made, the actual killer is no longer important: No matter what happens to him, the village is still obligated. Other issues are ignored.

obv.
[1]$^{\text{na4}}$KIŠIB $^{\text{I d}}$UTU-tak-lak [2]$^{\text{na4}}$KIŠIB ^{I}ib-ta-aš!-GIŠ [3]$^{\text{na4}}$KIŠIB ^{I}tab-la-a-a [4]$^{\text{na4}}$KIŠIB ^{I}eri-du$_{10}$-a-a[94] [5]$^{\text{na4}}$KIŠIB ^{I}U+GUR.PAP.PAP [6]$^{\text{na4}}$KIŠIB ^{I}si-lim-DINGIR [7]$^{\text{na4}}$KIŠIB ^{I}mu-qa-líl-IDIM [8]$^{\text{na4}}$KIŠIB ^{I}U.PAP.PAP [9]$^{\text{na4}}$KIŠIB ^{I}AŠ.GIŠ [10]$^{\text{na4}}$KIŠIB ^{I}sa-a-ri-u-ni [11]$^{\text{na4}}$KIŠIB[95] ^{uru}[96]sa-ma-na-a-a gab-bu (cylinder seal of fish man) [12]^{I}ṣi-ri-i :[97] EN UŠ.MEŠ [13]ša ^{I}si-lim-DINGIR [14]GAZ-u-ni

rev.
[15]ina IGI-šú-nu lu-u MUNUS-šu [16]lu-u ŠEŠ-šú lu-u DUMU-šu [17]man-nu šá e-la-a-ni[98] [18]šu-nu UŠ.MEŠ ú-šal-lumu [19]IGI

[94] J. Kohler and A. Ungnad suggest that the first two signs might be an error for *URU-aš+šur*, yielding a name like *Aššurāya* (*Assyrische Rechtsurkunden* [Leipzig: Eduard Pfeiffer, 1913], 388). Nicholas Postgate reads this name as $^{\text{I d uru}}$*Ḫ̮I-a-a* and suggested with reservations that it might be *eri-du*$_{10}$-a-a (*Fifty Neo-Assyrian Legal Documents* [Warminster, England: Aris & Phillips, 1976], 170, 215), as does Theodore Kwasman (*Neo-Assyrian Legal Documents in the Kouyunjik Collection of the British Museum*, Studia Pohl: Series Maior 14 [Rome: Pontificio Istituto Biblico, 1988], 386) and Remko Jas (*Neo-Assyrian Judicial Procedures,* State Archives of Assyria Series 5 [Helsinki: The Neo-Assyrian Text Corpus Project, 1996], 63, number 41). Martha T. Roth reads it as ^{I}URU.Ḫ̮I-a-a without resolving the difficulty ("Homicide in the Neo-Assyrian Period," 352).

[95] Roth suggests removing $^{\text{na4}}$*KIŠIB* as well and replacing it with *LÚMEŠ,* since $^{\text{na4}}$*KIŠIB* could be construed as a scribal error in which the scribe after ten lines beginning with $^{\text{na4}}$*KIŠIB* automatically wrote it again ("Homicide in the Neo-Assyrian Period," 353).

[96] Postgate suggests emending the masculine determinative ^{I} to ^{uru} for two reasons: 1) The use of *gabbu,* "all," to refer to all of the prior signatories is not the normal usage, and 2) Samana is a known Neo-Assyrian toponym (*Fifty Neo-Assyrian Legal Documents,* 171).

[97] The colon indicates that *bēl damê* is in apposition to the personal name Ṣiri. See J. Krecher, "Glossen," RLA 3.431–440.

[98] This durative verb as part of a relative clause should be in the subjunctive, *ellûni,* "he rises," with a middle *-u* vowel. However, the *-a* vowel can be explained in two ways: 1) A ventive

^{I}tar-di-tú-aš+šur LÚ.3-šú [20]IGI ^{Id}PA.SAG-i-ši [21]LÚ.NÍ.GAB [22]IGI ^{Id}NUSKU.PAP.AŠ [23]LÚ.šá UGU qa-na-te [24]IGI ^{I}man-nu-ki- ^{d}10 LÚ.Ì.DU$_{8}$ [25]IGI ^{I}aš+šur-MU.AŠ LÚ. GAL ki-ṣir [26]šá LÚ.GAL SUM.NINDA [27]IGI ^{I}AD-ul-ZU 3-šú [28]IGI ^{Id}PA-u-a A.B[A] [29]ITU.APIN UD 3 KAM [30]lim-me ^{I}NU.TEŠ[99]

Before this text can be translated, a number of problems must be solved. The identity of the people described in ADD 618 is debatable. Who is the killer? Who is the victim? The subject of line 13 is ambiguous. Lines 12–13 can be translated as "Ṣiri, the owner of the blood, whom Silim-ili killed" or as "Ṣiri, the owner of the blood, who killed Silim-ili." What is the significance of calling Ṣiri "the owner of the blood"? Furthermore, who are the people mentioned in lines 1–11 and what role do they play in remedying the slaying? Finally, is it the victim's or killer's relatives who are referred to in lines 15–16, and how do they participate in settling the case?

Nicholas Postgate argues that Ṣiri is the killer and Silim-ili is the victim, and that the people of his (Ṣiri's) village, whose seals appear in lines 1–11, confirm their responsibility to deliver up Ṣiri.[100] According to Postgate, the murderer, Ṣiri, and his family, those mentioned in lines 15–16, have escaped from their own village to avoid punishment and cannot be found. The rest of the villagers, who comprise those named in lines 1–11, have assumed a corporate obligation: In the case that the killer or any of his family reappear, the villagers would be responsible for paying the blood money by handing him over to the injured party to serve as a slave in compensation.[101] Postgate appears to be reading lines 12–14 as "Ṣiri is the owner of the blood of Silim-ili [whom] he killed," and identifies the family members in lines 15–16 as members of Ṣiri's family who will be handed over to the victim's family as payment.

The identification of Ṣiri as the killer is forced upon Postgate because he believes that *bēl damê* refers only to the one who shed the blood. However, its appearance in PPA 95, where the individual named as a *bēl damê* is a witness to the payment made by a father for a homicide his son committed, is clear evidence that the term can refer to the claimant from the victim's

ending accounts for the *-a* vowel, *ellâni* (cf. Kaspar Riemschneider, *An Akkadian Grammar* (trans. Thomas A. Caldwell, John N. Oswalt, and John F. X. Sheehan; Milwaukee, Wisconsin: Marquette University Press, 1975], 234–235); or 2) the verb is ablative in Assyrian, durative *ella,* preterite *ēli,* perfect *etili* (cf. Wolfram von Soden, *Grundriss der akkadischen Grammatik* (3d edition; AnOr 33; Rome: Pontificium Institutum Biblicum, 1995],188). Here, I believe that both possibilities coalesce since with the ventive ending, the verb can be rendered "he arises," which fits the context well.

[99]Postgate (*Fifty Neo-Assyrian Legal Documents,* 171) and Roth ("Homicide in the Neo-Assyrian Period," 353) read the eponym as ^{I}NU.UR. The sign has both values.

[100]Postgate, *Fifty Neo-Assyrian Legal Documents,* 171.

[101]Cf. the slayer's daughter in the following text, ADD 321.

family. Furthermore, Postgate is of the opinion that its appearance in the phrase *bēl damê šadduni* in PPA 95 is deceiving: He argues that it should not be taken as a freestanding phrase, but rather as part of a phrase similar to frequently occurring phrases, such as *bēl eqli tadāni,* "the owner of the field being sold," or to another phrase found in the palace governor's archive in Nimrud, *bēl kaspi našê,* "the owner of the money being borrowed."[102] However, the very phrases that Postgate adduces as evidence refute his argument. In the clause *bēl eqli tadāni*, the phrase *bēl eqli* is in fact a freestanding phrase referring to "the owner of the field" who is selling his field.[103] In the clause *bēl kaspi našê*, the phrase *bēl kaspi* is a freestanding phrase referring to "the owner of the money" being borrowed.

However, Theodore Kwasman argues that Silim-ili was the killer and that Ṣiri, whose relationship to Silim-ili is not mentioned, assumed the responsibility for paying the compensation for the homicide.[104] He reads lines 12–14 as "Ṣiri is responsible for the blood money [of the person] whom Silim-ili killed." This translation is problematic because the relative pronoun *ša* cannot do double duty to denote both the possessive relationship, "of the person," and the direct object, "whom." The relative pronoun *ša* is in apposition to the personal name Ṣiri.[105] It would then be better to understand the personal name Ṣiri as either the subject or the object of the verb *GAZ-u-ni*; that is, Ṣiri is either the killer or the victim. Kwasman does agree with Postgate's rendering of the rest of the tablet. The people, therefore, enumerated in lines 15–17 are members of the murderer's family who happen to reappear in the village. They are the ones in line 18 who are to pay.[106]

Martha T. Roth, in contrast to Postgate and Kwasman, argues that the people enumerated in lines 15–17 are, in fact, claimants from the victim's family, not members of the killer's family.[107] She bases her argument on the standard pattern of a Neo-Assyrian debt-note, which she believed applied

[102]Postgate, *The Governor's Palace Archive,* 124

[103]See the multitudinous occurrences cited in CAD B, 196.

[104]Kwasman, *Neo-Assyrian Legal Documents,* 386.

[105]In Old Babylonian, what Kwasman translates would be written *Ṣiri bēl damê (ša) awīlim ša Silim-ili išgušū*. The grammatical studies of Neo-Assyrian do not treat this issue. Cf. Karlheinz Deller, "Zur sprachliche Einordnung der Inschriften Aššurnaṣirpals II. (883–859)," *Or* 26 (1957), 144–156; Deller, "Assyrische Sprachgut bei Tukulti-Ninurta II (888–884)," *Or* 26 (1957), 268–272; Deller, "Zweisilbige Lautwerte des Typs KVKV im Neuassyrischen," *Or* 31 (1962), 7–26; Deller, "Studien zur neuassyrischen Orthographie," *Or* 31 (1962), 188–196; Deller, "Neuassyrisches aus Sultantepe," *Or* 34 (1965), 457–477; Deller, "Progressive Vokalassimilation im Neuassyrischen," *Or* 36 (1967), 337–338; Riemschneider, *An Akkadian Grammar,* 228–238; von Soden, *Grundriss der akkadischen Grammatik,* 192–193.

[106]Kohler and Ungnad interpret these lines in the same fashion, as an order to the killer to compensate for the killing by handing over a member of his own family (*Assyrische Rechtsurkunden,* 388–389).

[107]Roth, "Homicide in the Neo-Assyrian Period," 352, 354–355.

here. Roth's argument that the people in lines 15–17 are claimants from the victim's family is sound because it is based on the recognition that this tablet follows the pattern of an economic text. Although the physical appearance of the tablet makes it look like a conveyance – it is a single tablet without an envelope and its writing is at right angles to its longer axis – in fact it contains the literary formulation of a debt-note or contract.[108]

This genre of document, a debt-note, almost invariably conforms to the following pattern:

Standard Neo-Assyrian Debt-Note

a) seal of obligor
b) statement of obligation
  1. commodity/object of transaction
  2. belonging to obligee
  3. at the disposal of the obligor
c) discharge of obligation
  1. date/place of discharge
  2. commodity
  3. obligor(s)
  4. obligee
  5. he/they shall make good
d) closing lines (date, witness, scribe)

According to this pattern, therefore, the people mentioned in lines 15–17 must be the members of the victim's family to whom the debt is owed. The victim and his relatives become the obligee, the one to whom the debt must be paid, and the entire village becomes the obligor, the one who must pay the debt.

The last piece of the puzzle remains: Who is the killer and who is the victim? Silim-ili's name appears among those sealing this document in line 6. None of the renderings by Postgate, Kwasman, and Roth confronts this fact. Is this the same Silim-ili referred to in line 13? If he is, then he cannot be the one who was killed. If Silim-ili was dead, it would be impossible for him to impress his seal on the document. While it is possible that two men by the name Silim-ili are mentioned in the same document, it seems odd that they are not differentiated in some way by the mention of their fathers' names or occupations. Furthermore, if the argument of Ockham's razor holds true – that the simplest explanation is preferable – then equating the Silim-ili in line 6 with the one in line 13 makes the most sense. Silim-ili, then, was the

[108]Postgate, *Fifty Neo-Assyrian Legal Documents*, 171. A debt-note or contract is written on a tablet with an envelope that carried a seal impression and a repetition of the inner tablet and with the writing at right angles to its shorter axis.

murderer of Ṣiri. His presence among those who have set their seal reflects his acquiescence in his guilt and acknowledgment of his debt.

Roth argues that the victim's family had two options: 1) They could demand payment, or if the victim's family refused to accept compensation, then 2) they might demand the life of the killer.[109] This rendering depends upon the meaning of *ina muḫḫīšunu* in line 15. According to the usage of *ina muḫḫi*-(possessive pronoun),[110] this prepositional phrase has the sense of the right to money or responsibility for money accruing to the credit or debit of someone and, therefore, should be rendered, "Ṣiri . . . is at their expense or is accrued against them." The villagers are responsible for, or at least charged with overseeing, that Ṣiri's death is remedied. The phrase should not be rendered "in their midst," that is, arrested, as Roth translates.

Since Ṣiri is identified as *bēl damê*, a term referring in this case to the claimant from the victim's family, we can extrapolate from this identification that Silim-ili had killed before and that Ṣiri was seeking to make a claim against him on behalf of the victim's family but was killed by Silim-ili. If, in fact, the opposite were true, that Ṣiri was the murderer, his killing at the hands of Silim-ili would be justified and there would be no need for this document. After the homicide, the villagers assumed the responsibility for the compensation for Ṣiri's death. If, and when, claimants from Ṣiri's family would arrive, the villagers would discharge their obligation. Hence, this text should be translated as follows:

> [1–11] Seal of Shamash-taklāk, seal of Ibtāsh-lēshir, seal of Tablāya, seal of Eridāya, seal of Nergal-aḫu-uṣur, seal of Silim-ili, seal of Muqallil-kabti, seal of Adad-ahu-uṣur, seal of Edu-tēshir, seal of Sariuni, seal of the entire city of Samānu.[111] [12–15] Ṣīri, the owner of the blood, whom Silim-ili killed, is their responsibility. [15–17] Whoever appears among them [to claim compensation], whether it is his wife, his brother, or his son, (18) they themselves shall pay the blood money. [19–29] Witness: Tarditu-Assur, the third rider on the chariot. Witness: Nabu-rēsh-ishi the doorkeeper. Witness: Nusku-aḫ-iddin, the official in charge of the reeds. Witness: Mannu-ki-Adad, the doorkeeper. Witness: Assur-sum-iddin, the captain of the victualer. Witness: Abu-ul-idi, the third rider on the chariot. Witness: Nabua, the scribe. 8th month, third day, eponym of Labashi [657 B.C.E.].

[109] Roth, "Homicide in the Neo-Assyrian Period," 354.

[110] Cf. the examples of *ina muḫḫi*-(possessive pronoun) given in CAD M/2, 175a–b, and AHw/II, 688b.

[111] Cf. the other reference to the city of Samānu in Simo Parpola, *Neo-Assyrian Toponyms* (AOAT; Kevelaer: Butzon & Bercker, 1970), 300–301.

This text tells of an odd occurrence. Ṣiri, the claimant from the victim's family, came to the village to claim compensation for a homicide, but the killer, Silim-ili, committed homicide again, killing the claimant Ṣiri. Ṣilim-ili's village assumed corporate responsibility for compensating the victim's kinsmen, and ten of the villagers formally promised to make restitution to the claimant from the victim's family whenever he or she might arrive.

The pattern can now be filled out:

Standard Neo-Assyrian Debt-Note	**ADD 618**
a) seal of obligor	seals of villagers in lines 1–11
b) statement of obligation	
1. commodity/object of transaction	Ṣiri in line 12
2. belonging to obligee	Silim-ili in lines 13–14[112]
3. at the disposal of the obligor	the villagers in line 15
c) discharge of obligation	
1. date/place of discharge	left unspecified
2. commodity	the blood (money) in line 18
3. obligor(s)	the villagers referred to in line 18
4. obligee	the kin of the victim in lines 15–17
5. he/they shall make good	line 18
d) closing lines (date, witness, scribe)	lines 19–30

The commodity, the compensation, in ADD 618 is deliberately not specified because it has yet to be negotiated. It will be determined if, and when, a member of the victim's family arrives to make a claim. The word *ÚŠ.MEŠ* in line 18 of ADD 618 is, therefore, deliberately left ambiguous. A number of options were available at the discretion of the victim's kin. They could accept compensation in various forms of payment. As can be seen in the following documents, the payment could be in the form of copper, fields, or a person. If the killer failed to pay, he and all his assets could be confiscated.

Since this document was deposited in Nineveh, it can be surmised that the villagers had this document sent to Nineveh as an official recognition of their obligation. Furthermore, since it remained in the archive, it appears that no one from Ṣiri's family came forward to make a claim. In short, ADD 618 represents the first stage in a case of homicide, when the rights of

[112]My identification of Silim-ili as the killer clears up a problem in Roth's analysis of the pattern. Because she identifies Silim-ili as the victim, the placement of his name in this part of the pattern as the obligee is, to her, merely formalistic. If, in fact, Silim-ili were the killer, identifying him as the one obliged to pay a debt fits the pattern.

the victim's family and the obligations of the killer and his community are formally recognized by the killer's community.

In ADD 321, a mediating body assists in the negotiation over the amount of compensation by proposing a solution:

obv.
(beginning destroyed) (blank seal space) **1′**[ú]-ma-a it-ta-at-ru-uṣ **2′**[is!]-sa-hi-iš GEME$_2$-a-di-im-ri **3′**[DU]MU.MUNUS-su šá ^{I}a-tar-qa-mu **4′**[L]Ú a-na! $^{I\,d}$UTU.DU.PAP DUMU-šú **5′**šá ^{I}sa-ma-ku ku-um da-me i-dan **6′**da-me i-ma-si šum-ma MUNUS **7′**la i-din ina UGU qa-bu-ri **8′**ša ^{I}sa-ma-ku i-du-ku-šu **9′**man-nu šá ina UGU man-nu BAL-u-ni **10′**10 MA.NA KUG.BAB[BAR SU]M-a[n] AN.ŠÁR ^{d}UTU **11′**a-[de-e šá MAN ina ŠU l]u-ba-['i-u] . . .

rev.
12′lim-m[u . . .] **13′**^{I}AN.ŠÁR.DÙ.A MA[N ^{kur}aš+šur IGI ^{I} . . .] **14′**Lú.GA[L . . .] **15′**IGI ^{I}a-da-lal LÚ.DUMU.ŠU$_{II}$ šá! [DUMU.MAN] **16′**I[GI $^{I\,d}$I]M-ba-ba-u ^{lú}DUMU.ŠU$_{II}$ **17′**ša DUMU.MAN **18′**IGI ^{I}aš+šur-DINGIR-a-a **19′**IGI [x] [. . .] x x **20′**[. . .]-ri **21′**[. . .] x

1′–6′It is now mutually agreed:[113] the one who shall give Amat-adimri, the daughter of Attar-qāmu, to Shamash-kēnu-uṣur, the son of Samaku [who was killed] in place of blood [money] and wash the blood away.[114] **6′–8′**If he does not give the woman, they will kill him on top of[115] Samaku's grave. **9′–10′**Whoever breaches the contract with the other party[116] shall pay 10 minas of silver [1,000

[113]Literally, "Now that [a hand] has been mutually extended." Both parties have agreed to the conditions and the tablet is, then, a statement of the agreement. The form *ittatruṣ* is a Gt perfect of *tarāṣu*, which is otherwise unattested (cf. AHw III, 1327). In fact, von Soden, in AHw, reads *i-ta-ru-uṣ*, as do Kohler and Ungnad, *Assyrische Rechtsurkunden,* 388, which would be a simple G perfect. However, there are a fair number of hapax Gt forms, and the reciprocal meaning is appropriate here.

[114]Kwasman reads lines 2–6 as follows: "Shamash-knu-uṣur, the son of Attar-qāmu, the scribe, shall give KUR-adimri, the daughter of Attar-qāmu, the scribe, in place of blood money for Samaku [who was murdered] and washes the blood away," (*Neo-Assyrian Legal Documents,* 393). However, in order to render it this way, Kwasman must separate *mārūšu* from the following phrase, *ša ^{I}sa-ma-ku,* posit that it refers back two lines to Attar-qāmu and claim that despite the single occurrence of the personal name Attar-qāmu, it is linked to both Shamash-kēnu-uṣur and KUR-adimri. Furthermore, Kwasman assumes that the first three signs in line 4′ are *LÚ.A.BA*, *ṭupšarru,* "scribe." These signs, to be sure, are given in C. H. W. Johns's copy of ADD 321 (*Assyrian Deeds and Documents* [2d edition; Cambridge: Deighton, Bell, and Co., 1924]), but Parpola has collated the line and determined that the third sign is *na,* thus *LÚ a-na* ("Collations to Neo-Assyrian Legal Texts from Nineveh," *Assur* 2/5 [1979], 49).

[115]The prepositional phrase *ina muḫḫi* is a bit ambiguous since it can mean either "on top of" or "nearby," but the sense of it, as translated here, works well in this context.

[116]Literally, "whoever transgressed before someone shall pay . . . ," meaning "to act against an agreement." Cf. the numerous attestations in Neo-Assyrian contracts, CAD N/I s.v. *nabalkutu,* 13.

shekels]. [10′–11′]Assur, Shamash and the oath of the king will call him to account. [12′–21′]Eponym of . . . of Assurbanipal, king of the land of Assyria. Witness: . . . , the chief . . . Witness: Adalal, the *mār qātē*[117] of . . . Witness: Adad-Babā'u, the *mār qātē* of the crown prince. Witness: Assur-ilaya . . .

ADD 321 conforms to the pattern of a court order:

lines 2′–6′: The guilty party is required to discharge his obligation;
lines 6′–8′: The penalty for the guilty party's failure to comply is given;
lines 9′–10′: The penalties that devolve upon either party for repudiating the agreement are stated.[118]

In the process of settling a homicide dispute, this document represents the intermediate point between the initial claim and the final disposition.[119] A third party, the crown, has mediated a proposed settlement that appears to be acceptable to both parties. The payment is said to be "in lieu of the blood" and to "wash the blood away," alluding to an idea similar to the Israelite conceptualization that the spilled blood of the homicide victim has a concrete existence that needs to be remedied. This is also reflected in the use of the term *bēl damê* to refer to the killer and to the claimant from the victim's family.

ADD 164 reflects the further progress of a case by recording the court's confirmation of the payment the guilty party must make. In ADD 164, Hani has killed shepherds in the course of stealing livestock from the crown prince. The tablet does not record the number of shepherds killed or the number of animals stolen.[120] He was ordered to pay 300 sheep and an unspecified

[117]It is unclear what type of office is held by the *mār qātē,* since there is no other reference to it.

[118]Cf. Postgate, *Fifty Neo-Assyrian Legal Documents,* 59f, and Roth, "Homicide in the Neo-Assyrian Period," 357. This penalty clause is not in conflict with that in lines 6′–8′ because the penalty in lines 6′–8′ is specific to a killer who would otherwise be subject to the death penalty if he did not pay compensation for the killing. It would appear that if the killer did not provide the slave woman, he would be killed as punishment for the killing, and then his kin would have to pay as well.

[119]Roth argues that ADD 321 contains a variation on this pattern. She holds the opinion that the court order in line 1′ is expressed as the protasis of a conditional sentence, "If it is mutually acceptable" ("Homicide in the Neo-Assyrian Period," 357). According to Roth, this raises the possibility that the settlement is dependent upon the agreement of the victim's family, who may choose not to accept it. However, her understanding of the first line as a protasis is incorrect. While a protasis may be marked or unmarked by a conditional particle (the particle *ūma* is equivalent to the Old Babylonian *inanna,* "now") and a verb in the protasis must be either in the perfect or durative, the syntax appears to be a simple declarative sentence. The perfect signifies that the action, the mutual extending of a hand signifying agreement, is occurring or has occurred.

[120]The omissions may be due to the fact that this document is the court's determination of the amount of blood money for each victim. Another document recorded the progress of the case in determining how many shepherds and sheep were killed.

fine as well, as compensation for the victims in the amount of two talents of copper per person. Hani was not able to pay and so has been arrested.

obv.
[1]de-e-nu ša ^{lú}sar-tin-nu [2]a-na ^{I}ḫa-ni-i e-mì-du-u-ni [3]3 me UDU.MEŠ a-di sa-ár-ti-ši-na [4]ša DUMU.MAN ina IGI ^{I}ḫa-ni-i [5]ÚŠ.MEŠ ša LÚ.SIPA 1-en LÚ 2 GÚ.UN URUDU.MEŠ [6]sa-ár-tu-šú[121] ^{I}ḫa-ni-i [7]a-di UN.MEŠ-šú a-di A.ŠÀ.MEŠ-šú [8]ku-um 3 me UDU.MEŠ a-di sa-ár-ti-ši-na [9]ku-<um> UŠ.MEŠ ša LÚ.SIPA.MEŠ [10]na-ši-<<na>>[122] [11]man-nu ša ú-ba-'u-šú-u-ni

rev.
[12]lu-u LÚ.GAR-nu-šú lu-u LÚ.GAL ki-ṣir-š[ú] [13]lu-u mám-ma-nu-šú-nu u-ba-'u-u-šú-ni [14]3 me UDU.MEŠ a-di sa-ár-ti-šu-na [15]ÚŠ.MEŠ ša LÚ.SIPA 1 LÚ 2 GÚ.UN URUDU.MEŠ [16]ša LÚ-ti i-da-an-nu-u-ni ^{I}ḫa-ni-i [17]ú-še-ṣa ḫur-sa-an i-tu-ra [18]IGI ^{I}tab-ni-i LÚ.A.BA [19]IGI ^{I}ṣal-mu-MAN-iq-bi [20]IGI $^{\text{I d}}$UTU.ZI.AŠ [21]IGI ^{I}am-si-i [22]ITU.ZÍZ UD 27 KAM [23]lim-mu ^{I}da-na-nu

[1–2]A court decision which the *sartinnu* imposed on Hani. [3–4]Required of Hani are 300 sheep inclusive of their fine belonging to the crown prince. [5–6]His fine is the blood money for a shepherd, 2 talents[123] copper per person. [6–10]In lieu of 300 sheep inclusive of their fine and in lieu of the blood money for the shepherds, Hani together with his people and his fields are to be taken. [11–16]Whether his governor[124] or his bodyguard captain[125] or whoever litigates for them shall give the blood money for a shepherd, 2 talents of copper per person, for his life.[126] [16–17]He shall redeem Hani. He refuses the river

[121]To what do lines 5–6 refer? Is *1-en LÚ* to be taken as the blood money and the copper as the fine, or is *1-en Lú* to be construed with the copper? Although the first possibility is supported by the fact that Neo-Assyrian can express "and" by parataxis (as translated by Kwasman, *Legal Transactions of the Royal Court of Nineveh,* 212), this may not operate here because the plural determinative in line 9 refers to additional shepherds killed by Hani. It appears more likely, then, that the two talents of copper are to be paid for each victim. CAD D, 79b, renders lines 5–6 as "his fine as blood money for the shepherds is two talents of copper per person, he will give the blood money for the shepherds – per person two talents of copper."

[122]Postgate notes that the form *na-ši-na* is impossible and that its appearance must be due to the *-ši-na* in lines 3 and 8 (*Fifty Neo-Assyrian Legal Documents*), 159.

[123]There are two weights in Neo-Assyria, a heavy and a light, which is half the weight of the heavy. Without an indication, it seems impossible to determine to which the text refers. One heavy talent is equivalent to 3,600 heavy shekels or 7,200 light shekels.

[124]Cf. CAD Š/I, especially in the Neo-Assyrian legal texts referenced on pp. 184–185.

[125]Cf. CAD K, 436–438.

[126]The meaning of *LÚ-ti* in line 16 is difficult. Postgate argues that while Neo-Assyrian usage of *aīluttu* can refer to a man in his status as a servant, it is possible that in the context of murder it refers to "human life" (*Fifty Neo-Assyrian Legal Documents,* 160). Postgate notes as well that it might not refer to the murdered man but to Hani himself while serving in debt-slavery. Kwasman argues that *LÚ-ti* was a scribal error for *sa-ár-ti-<šú>* caused by the LÚ sign in the

ordeal.[127] [18–23]Witness: Tabni, the scribe. Witness: Ṣalmu-sharru-iqbi. Witness: Shamash-napishtu-iddin. Witness: Amsî. 11th month, 27th day, eponym of Danānu.

The nature of this document and its relationship to the archive in which it was found have been debated. Postgate suggested that this was an official record rather than a legal document to be retained by one of the parties.[128] It differs from other Neo-Assyrian legal records in that it does not give a description of the progress of the case but states the court's decision. However, Kwasman argues that this text was part of the royal archives at Nineveh, which included private documents as well as state administrative and literary documents.[129] He identifies this text as constituting a single-document archive belonging to an individual, that of Hani, which was part of the larger royal archives. There are a number of difficulties with Kwasman's claim. First, although Kwasman hoped that recognition of the documents' provenance as an archive would aid in understanding their context as archives deposited for safekeeping in a royal archive, it is doubtful that the

preceding line (*Neo-Assyrian Legal Documents,* 129), but to me, this appears unlikely since it involves multiple errors.

[127]Lines 16b–17 are problematic for two reasons: 1) The verb used with the noun *ḫur-sa-an,* "river ordeal," in the phrase *ḫur-sa-an i-tu-ra* is obscure, and 2) the verbs are in a sequence of durative and then preterite. With regard to the first problem, the primary difficulty is the verb *tuāru,* "to return," and its relationship to the noun, *ḫur-sa-an,* "the river ordeal." The sign in Johns's edition is definitely *tu*. Postgate argues for the reading *tu* because of the appearance of the verb *tuāru,* "to return," in other legal documents (*Fifty Neo-Assyrian Legal Documents,* 160). Kwasman argues against Postgate's position and states that *tuāru* is never attested for *ḫursan* and that since the river ordeal needs to be completed in a legal action, a verb like *parāsu* would be appropriate (*Neo-Assyrian Legal Documents,* 129). Hence, he emends *tu* to *ba* and proposes the solution of *i-ba-ra-<as>* for *iparras*. However, he fixes one error while introducing a new error, the omission of *-as,* not known before. Furthermore, Remko Jas adduces examples of the usage of *tuāru* with *ḫursan* (*Neo-Assyrian Judicial Procedures,* 9). This phrase, therefore, does not require emendation. What is its meaning? Postgate renders it as "to refuse an ordeal" and provides many examples of this usage (*Fifty Neo-Assyrian Legal Documents,* 160, 209). [However, in Middle Babylonian legal texts, it clearly means "to be found guilty by the ordeal." (Cf. O. R. Gurney, *The Middle Babylonian Legal and Economic Texts from Ur,* 10–12). Jas argues that this connotation is found in Neo-Assyrian texts as well (*Neo-Assyrian Judicial Procedures,* 10, n. 40). The significance would be similar – the subject has not been acquitted of the offense.] The sequence of verbs and their "tenses" requires some explanation. The first verb in line 16, *ušeṣa,* is a biform of the durative (cf. von Soden, *Grundriss der akkadischen Grammatik,* 44*, 189), which is marked by the appearance of the final *-a*. It cannot be preterite with a ventive ending because that form would entail an ultralong vowel that would need to be indicated. The verb could either be *itūra,* the preterite because of the appearance of the middle *-u* vowel, or more likely *iturra,* the durative with the ventive. The subject of the first verb is the one who litigates on Hani's behalf, mentioned in line 12, while the subject of the second is the killer himself, Hani.

[128]Postgate, *Fifty Neo-Assyrian Legal Documents,* 60.

[129]Kwasman, *Neo-Assyrian Legal Documents,* 129.

large number of documents that he identifies as constituting many single-document archives is really that useful. Placing this document in a personal archive is helpful only when there are other documents in that archive. Second, Remko Jas argues that the identification of this text as part of Hani's personal archive was unlikely since Hani and his family were arrested and his possessions confiscated.[130] The winning party in the suit, the crown prince, would be the more likely archive holder. This *dēnu* text was a formal record of the permanent settlement of the case. Jas suggested as well that the texts that refer to third-party arbitration but do not mention *dēnu* seem to be ad hoc documents that were meant to be kept until a *dēnu* was issued.[131] In sum, this document, a so-called *dēnu* text, is a formal document to be kept after the affair has been settled. This particular *dēnu* text is one that includes the phrase *dēnu emādu,* "to impose a judgment," but lacks the *šulmu* clause, which states that there is now peace between the parties.[132] This may indicate that the case was not completely settled and that further litigation was expected or that the convicted party was disappointed with the outcome.

With regard to the conduct of the case, it is remarkable that the crown prince went to an official, in this case the *sartinnu*, for judgment like other Assyrians. Who is the *sartinnu*? In ABL 716, r. 11, the king himself appoints the *sartinnu* and the *sukallu*, the vizier, "to give just and equitable judgment in my land." In *Iraq* 32 132:2,[133] the *sartinnu* and the vizier serve once again as the court for those involved in a lawsuit. The *sartinnu* and the vizier own comparable estates in *Iraq* 20 187, no. 40:18.[134] The royal appointment and the status on a par with that of the vizier justify identifying the role of the *sartinnu* as chief judge and appointee of the crown.[135] In the other Neo-Assyrian *dēnu* texts, other officials acting in a judicial capacity are mentioned. Most often a *ḫazannu* presides, but a *šangû*-priest, a *sukallu*, and a *šakin māti* also hear cases. It is uncertain whether cases of a particular type were put to officials of a specific rank. In the extant Neo-Assyrian texts, a *sartinnu* is mentioned as presiding over two cases, this homicide case and another involving a dispute over a slave (ADD 163). It is unclear what these two cases have in common that would call for a judge at the rank of *sartinnu*. Unfortunately, the language of these texts is terse, a characteristic of all *dēnu* texts, and therefore the specifics of the cases are barely mentioned. However, line 17 reveals that Hani refused to undergo an ordeal, part of the procedure undertaken to ascertain the defendant's guilt.

[130] Jas, *Neo-Assyrian Judicial Procedures,* 10–11.
[131] Ibid., 2.
[132] Ibid., 6.
[133] J. N. Postgate, "More Assyrian Deeds and Documents," *Iraq* 32 (1970), 132.
[134] H. W. F. Saggs, "The Nimrud Letters IV: The Urartian Frontier," *Iraq* 20 (1958), 187.
[135] K. Deller, "Die Rolle des Richters im neuassyrischen Prozessrecht," in *Studi in onore di Edoardo Volterra VI* (Milan: A. Giuffrè, 1971), 652.

The last two texts, ADD 806 and PPA 95, originate in the final stages of a case and record payments made to discharge the debt. ADD 806, a record of the sale of a large estate, records that part of the land was forfeited as compensation. This legal transaction was conducted by government officials:

obv.
[1]10 ANŠE A.ŠÀ ina ^{uru}ni-ra-ma-a-a [2]ÌR.MEŠ ša LÚ.EN.NAM ^{kur}si-me-e [3]ku-um da-me ib-ta-at-qu . . .

[1–3]The servants of the governor of Sime took possession of 10 homers of field in Nirama in lieu of the blood money.

PPA 95 takes the form of a debt repayment record, that is, a receipt:

obv.
[1]^{I}še-lu-[b]u DUMU-šú [2]šal-lu-[un]-tú-šú 80 MA.NA URUDU.MEŠ [3]^{I}aš+šur-B[ÀD].PAP ina É LÚ.A.BA É.GAL [4]ú-[šal]-li-me x x x x [5]I[GI] $^{\text{I d}}$MAŠ.MAŠ.I LÚ qur-bu-te [6]^{uru}par-ḪA-a-a [7]IGI $^{\text{I d}}$PA.PAP-ir $^{\text{lú!}}$šá UGU URU [8]IGI ^{I}ÌR-^{d}al-la-a-a [9]^{lú}ḫa-za-nu [10]IGI $^{\text{I d}}$PA-ú-a [11]^{lú}mu-tir-ṭè-me [12]IGI ^{I}KAM-eš-DINGIR LÚ.GAL É.GAL!

rev.
[13]IGI ^{I}ti-ni-x-x [14]^{uru}ba-da-na-a-a [15]IGI $^{\text{I d}}$PA-rém-a-ni [16]EN ÚŠ.MEŠ ša GUB-ni[136] [17]IGI $^{\text{I d}}$PA-ú-TI.LA [18]LÚ.A.BA ṣa-bit ṭup-pi [19]I[TU.A]B UD 27 KAM [20]lim-me $^{\text{[I]d}}$PA.KAR-ir-a-ni [21][L]Ú.GAL KAŠ.LUL [22]IGI $^{\text{I d}}$PA.S[U] LÚ.GAL URU.MEŠ-ni [23][ša] LÚ.A.BA É.GAL

[1–4][For] Shelubu his son, Assur-dūru-uṣur has paid in full his [Shelubu's] payment of 80 minas of copper in the house of the palace

[136]Postgate reads the last three signs as *ša-du-ni* and argues that the authorities that imposed the penalty did check the payment because the tablet uses the *š*-stem, the causative, of the verb *nadānu* to refer to the payment, implying that a coercive power is causing the subject of the verb to pay the money to a third party (*The Governor's Palace Archive,* 123–124). Roth reads the last three signs as *ša GUB-ni,* in normalized form *ša izzizzuni* ("Homicide in the Neo-Assyrian Period," 359, 360, n. 20). Postgate's reading is clever but impossible. First of all, the *-a* vowel needs to be explained because the two possible forms that the verb could possibly be are the infinitive in the genitive, *šuddunī,* or the verbal adjective in the third-person masculine singular, *šuddun*. Secondly, the doubling of *d* is lacking. Third, the final -i vowel fits only the genitive infinitive, not a third-person plural verbal adjective, *šuddunū,* "they cause to be paid," but it would make sense only if the verb was in the *Št*-stem, a passive form. With regard to the first problem, the form *šadduni* does exist as a biform (cf. von Soden, *Grundriss der akkadischen Grammatik,* 27*, and the Neo-Assyrian examples in CAD N/I, 57a). However, the second and third problems remain. I would add that Roth's rendering is in consonance with the other verbs of motion used to characterize the claimant from the victim's family. This accurate understanding of this verb underscores the role of the victim's family in propelling the case toward final settlement.

> scribe.... [5–22]Witness: Nergal-nā'id, the *qurbutu*-officer[137] of [the city of] Parnunna.[138] Witness: Nabû-nāṣir, the city overseer. Witness: Urdu-allaya, the mayor. Witness: Nabua, the information officer. Witness: Eresh-ili, the palace overseer. Witness: Tini..., of [the city of] Badana. Witness: Nabu-remanni, owner of the blood who was present. Witness: Nabu-uballiṭ, the scribe, writer of the tablet. Tenth month, 27th day, eponym year of Nabu-eṭirani the chief butler [740 B.C.E.]. Witness: Nabu-eriba, the city inspector of the palace scribe.

There are two elements that separate PPA 95 from other receipts. The payment recorded in this document is made in the office of the palace scribe. The creditor is not named in the operative section of the document that mentions the repayment, possibly because the money is not paid directly to him. His name can be inferred because one of the witnesses, Nabu-remanni, is identified as *bēl damê*, "the owner of the blood," in this case the claimant from the victim's family. Otherwise, we would not know that this debt[139] has anything to do with homicide.

The money is not paid directly to Nabu-remanni but is paid into the house of the palace scribe. Although the usual practice in Neo-Assyria is to pay the fine directly to the injured party,[140] PPA 95 does not appear to be a receipt, complete with the validating seal or fingernail impression of the party being paid. PPA 95 is a record of a payment made before the authorities who had decided the case and imposed the fine and was, therefore, deposited in the public archives.[141] The *bēl damê* does not act as a party to the transaction: He is solely a witness because it is the palace that takes an active role at this point in the proceedings.

With these five documents, the outlines of the procedure put in effect in the Neo-Assyrian period when a homicide has been committed can be reconstructed. The social group to which the killer belonged took the initiative and assumed corporate responsibility.[142] First, the fact that a homicide has been committed had to be determined. Second, the identity of

[137] It is clear that the *qurbutu* is an officer of some variety, but his exact rank is unclear. Cf. CAD/Q, 315–317, and AHw II, 929.

[138] Cf. the other references to this city cited by Parpola, *Neo-Assyrian Toponyms,* 273.

[139] The large size of the debt may be an indication that it is blood money.

[140] Postgate, *The Governor's Palace Archive,* 18. However, the practice of paying a fine before the authorities is evidenced in other texts and is not limited to blood money, as can be seen in PPA 92 and 96.

[141] The governor's palace archives excavated in Nimrud are public archives and do not contain the private archives of the governor; cf. Postgate, *The Governor's Palace Archive,* 10.

[142] Roth argues that it was in the best interest of the killer to recognize the rights of the parties formally because in this way, the right of the victim's family to self-help and vengeance would be limited; negotiation between the parties would then have suspended the right of the victim's family to kill the murderer ("Homicide in the Neo-Assyrian Period," 363). However, we do not have any evidence that independent vengeance ever existed.

the responsible party had to be ascertained. Third, the killer had to be apprehended. There was an official recording institution of the monarchy at which outstanding homicide obligations were deposited, pending the claim of the victim's family. Next, the parties negotiated the amount of compensation with the intervention of a mediating authority, an officer of the crown. Finally, when a specific amount had been agreed upon, the obligation was paid in the presence of an official authority, a crown official.

CHAPTER THREE

The Development of Places of Refuge in the Bible

EACH LEGAL corpus of the Pentateuch makes reference to refuges for a killer. These sources differ on certain fundamental characteristics of such refuges, raising the question of whether these differences reflect historical development in the system of asylum.

Julius Wellhausen, whose work represents the capstone of nineteenth-century critical scholarship, argues that there were major changes in the adjudication of homicide.[1] In the earliest period, he proposes, sanctuaries were places of asylum: A fugitive would enter a sanctuary and take hold of the horns of the altar, obtaining sanctuary from an avenger in hot pursuit, according to the evidence of Exod 21:13–14 and 1 Kgs 2:28. Then, during the Deuteronomic reform in the seventh century B.C.E., in order to prevent the loss of the institution of asylum when local altars were abolished, Josiah appointed special cities of refuge (Deut 19:1–13). Wellhausen concludes that the Priestly legislator affirmed this arrangement and specified six cities of refuge, three on each side of the Jordan (Num 35:9–34; Josh 20:1–9).[2] Since four of these cities were cultic sites known from other

[1]Julius Wellhausen, *Prolegomena to the History of Israel* (preface by W. Robertson Smith; foreword by Douglas A. Knight; 1885; reprint, Atlanta: Scholars Press, 1994), 33, 162, 375.

[2]Wellhausen, *Prolegomena*, 162, asserts that Deut 4:41–43, which specifies three cities in Transjordan, could not be original. He does recognize that Joshua 20 contained a Priestly kernel

biblical texts and the cities of refuge were also Levitical cities, it seemed obvious to Wellhausen that the special status of the cities of refuge was linked to the presence of an ancient altar. He recognized, to be sure, that not every sacred site was a city of refuge. Some that became infamous as sites of pagan worship, such as Bethel, Dan, Gilgal, and Beersheba, were intentionally omitted.

Those who have followed in Wellhausen's wake have argued for minor nuances in his scheme of development. The date of the establishment of the cities of refuge has shifted back and forth. Max Löhr pushes the date back to the reign of either David or Solomon and argues that the early monarchy sought to limit blood revenge by means of the cities of refuge.[3] Roland de Vaux is of the opinion that the cities of refuge dated back to the reign of Solomon: He believes that although the texts that refer to them may be Deuteronomic, one, Josh 20:1–9, rests on older traditions because the cities it lists were under Israelite control only during Solomon's reign.[4] Milgrom agrees with a Solomonic date and argues that the cities of refuge were established by Solomon, who innovated a whole host of cultic procedures, including a type of altar that precluded altar asylum.[5]

Others have stood firm on a late-seventh-century Deuteronomic date. N. M. Nicolsky holds that the cities of refuge did not exist before the Deuteronomic revolution of the latter seventh century.[6] Henry McKeating argues that the cities of refuge were established in the seventh century when the authorities were still trying to regulate, not oust, clan-based justice.[7]

All these arguments are based on the assumption of institutional change from altar asylum to cities of refuge, whether during the first century of the monarchy or the Deuteronomic revolution. It is worthwhile, therefore, to assess the evidence for radical institutional change.

First, we will examine the argument that in the earliest stage of legal development in ancient Israel, a sacrificial altar served as a refuge for a slayer: A killer would flee to an altar and remain safe as long as he remained there. This view has been based on texts recounting the flight of Adonijah, one of David's sons, and the flight of Joab, David's army commander, to the altar in the Tent-shrine during Solomon's reign (1 Kgs 1:50–53; 2:28–34) and on the statute on homicide in the Covenant Code (Exod 21:12–14).

surrounded by Deuteronomic retouching and explains that later additions to the Pentateuch imitated Deuteronomic language (*Prolegomena*, 375). His refusal to recognize these additions as products of Deuteronomy and thereby to redate Deuteronomy after P is, no doubt, due to his belief in the late date of P. In his defense, it must be noted that passages in Deuteronomic style are found in texts, such as Jeremiah, that are certainly not part of Deuteronomy.

[3] Max Löhr, *Das Asylwesen im Alten Testament* (Halle: Max Niemeyer, 1930), 35.

[4] De Vaux, *Ancient Israel*, 162–163.

[5] Milgrom, *Numbers*, 506–507.

[6] N. M. Nicolsky, "Das Asylrecht in Israel," *ZAW* 48 (1930), 156–157.

[7] McKeating, "Development of the Law of Homicide," 64–66.

This interpretation overlooks the fact that Adonijah is not portrayed as ever having killed another person. He seeks sanctuary because he is a political offender. He attempted to claim the throne during David's reign, and as a direct result of this act, Solomon was proclaimed by David as the rightful heir. Adonijah, now fearing for his life, flees to the altar and holds on to its "horns." Solomon promises that no harm will come to Adonijah as long as he behaves. (Of course, Adonijah cannot resist and asks for one of David's concubines, a request that questions Solomon's legitimacy, another political misdeed, and he is finally put to death.) When Adonijah flees to a sanctuary, he is seeking refuge from his political predicament, not from committing a homicide.

Joab's flight has similarly been misinterpreted. Although his act has been interpreted as seeking sanctuary from the penalty for homicide, the text reflects a different motive for his flight. Joab had sided with Adonijah, Solomon's rival for the throne (1 Kgs 2:28), and when he hears the news that Solomon has executed Adonijah and has dismissed Abiathar, a supporter of Adonijah, from his post as priest, Joab realizes that it is political payback and takes refuge at the Tent-shrine. It does him little good: He is taken from the sacred precincts and killed. Joab's seeking sanctuary at an altar was politically motivated. It was not based on evading criminal culpability for a killing. Altar asylum protects from political intrigue, not from the punishment for homicide.[8]

Seeking respite from political enemies is reflected in a curious episode in Nehemiah's memoirs.[9] During the Persian period, a prophet advises Nehemiah to protect himself from those sent to kill him in the night by taking shelter in the Temple (Neh 6:10–13). Nehemiah refuses, objecting that a person in his position should not show cowardice by taking

[8] Åke Viberg, *Symbols of Law: A Contextual Analysis of Legal Symbolic Acts in the Old Testament* (Coniectanea Biblical Old Testament Series 34; Stockholm: Almqvist & Wiksell, 1992), 122ff., recognizes that Adonijah is not seeking asylum for homicide and that his action has no apparent relation to asylum for homicide. Viberg also realizes that Joab's case was problematic for two reasons: 1) Why would Joab have sought asylum since the type of homicide he committed would have allowed him to be removed from the altar? 2) If Joab committed culpable homicide, why would there have been a problem with removing him from the altar? Viberg solves this problem by arguing that Joab was appealing for some form of general asylum whereas Solomon was applying Exod 21:12–14, albeit incorrectly, since Joab was struck down at the altar without any indication that he was removed. Of course, the answer may be simpler: Joab thought that seeking asylum at the altar would or might protect him, and Solomon either thought it did not or simply killed Joab anyway. The narrator's framing of Joab's offense as the shedding of the blood of war in peacetime makes Joab's actions appear illegal. However, taking vengeance on others for what they did in war is considered acceptable, according to Judg 8: 18–21.

[9] The use of the Temple as a sanctuary from political machinations is attested for the First Temple period as well. Joash is kept hidden from his mother Athaliah within the Temple after she has killed everyone else of royal stock (2 Kgs 11:2–3).

flight.[10] As far as he is concerned, sanctuary asylum still operated in his day.

The theory that altar asylum was abrogated is also based on the reference to homicide in the Covenant Code, and it must be stated at the outset that the Covenant Code's statute is enigmatic. The evidence for the changeover from altar asylum to cities of refuge is found in the early dating of the Covenant Code and its reference to taking refuge at an altar. This evidence is in fact shaky.

Scholarly consensus identifies "the Covenant Code," Exod 21:1–23:19, as an independent collection of laws incorporated in a larger literary unit, the Book of the Covenant. Although nineteenth-century scholarship was divided on whether the Covenant Code belonged to the Pentateuchal sources J[11] or E,[12] there was a wide consensus during the past century that the Covenant Code was independent of J and E[13] and was a product of the tribal period. Since the Covenant Code does not contain any references to the monarchy and reflects the circumstances of small landholders, the period of the judges when the Israelites were settled on patrimonial estates in their tribal territories seemed appropriate.[14] The tribal period was considered

[10]Nehemiah does not object that entering the Temple precincts or the inner sanctuary would make him liable to be killed (Milgrom, *Numbers,* 507). Nehemiah does enter the Temple precincts later in the narrative in order to remove the furnishings of Tobiah's room (Neh 13:8). Those who were not cultic personnel were barred from the area of the altar in both the First and Second Temple. When concerns arose about the apparent misappropriation of money brought into the First Temple, the solution was to set aside a box for the collection on the right side of the altar (2 Kgs 12:5–12). Since the laity did not have access to the area of the altar, the Temple guards, who were priests, were made responsible for taking the money from the laity and depositing it in the collection box. 2 Chr 26:16–20 explains Uzziah's leprosy as a result of his encroachment upon the prerogative of the priests to offer incense upon the altar. However, according to 1 Kings 2, Adonijah and Joab do enter the area of the altar and take hold of it, contradicting this prohibition. The fact that the area of the altar was forbidden to the laity in the First and Second Temples may not hold true for pre-Temple shrines, like the Tent-shrine in pre-Temple Solomonic Jerusalem.

[11]Wellhausen, *Prolegomena to the History of Israel,* 12–13, 392, considers it to be an expression of a legislative element of the Jahwist, a document of the main part of the Assyrian period, ca. 800 B.C.E.

[12]Adolf Jülicher, who argues for the relationship of the Covenant Code to E, is referred to in Bruno Bäntsch, *Das Bundesbuch, Ex. XX 22–XXIII 33* (Halle: Max Niemeyer, 1892), 59–68.

[13]Bäntsch was the first to argue for the independence of the Covenant Code from the documentary sources (*Das Bundesbuch,* 73). He holds that the individual משפטים were known to J at the end of the ninth century, while the collection of them was known to E in the middle of the eighth century (*Das Bundesbuch,* 122). He also holds the opinion that the דברים were a product of the prophetic movement of the mid-eighth century (*Das Bundesbuch,* 121).

[14]Cf. Paul, *Studies in the Book of the Covenant,* 44; Childs, *The Book of Exodus,* 456. Ludger Schwienhorst-Schönberger, *Das Bundesbuch* (BZAW 111; Berlin: Walter de Gruyter, 1990), 268, distinguishes between the casuistic law of the eleventh–tenth centuries, later put together as a book in the ninth–eighth centuries, and then placed as part of divine law in the

to be the least socially differentiated period in Israelite development. Legal thought and institutions were at their least developed as well. According to this opinion, the dating of the Covenant Code to the tribal period would be the launching point for extrapolating earlier stages in the adjudication of homicide.

The consensus on the date of the Covenant Code has been undermined in recent years. One line of attack on a tribal period for its dating has focused on recognizing reformist elements within the Code. Arguments for an eighth-century date utilize three proofs highlighting a reformist tendency: 1) The amalgam of literary forms that makes up the entire complex of the Covenant Code suggests the dissolution or deliberate combination of formerly separate legal traditions.[15] 2) The presence of laws protecting the poor and regulating slavery for debt is evidence for a date well into the monarchy because there would be no need for them during the poor economic conditions of the prestate period.[16] Slavery gained significance only during the later monarchic era. 3) The Covenant Code in its attention to the alien presupposes widespread population shifts, which would fit well with the serious refugee problem dealt to Judah after the fall of the northern kingdom.[17]

However, the proofs for an eighth-century date are flawed. While it is true that the laws in the Covenant Code appear to have barely been reworked from their original formulation because texts of varying literary form had been placed side by side without any attempt to make thematic or linguistic unity, it is, however, possible to offer many different points in Israelite history when the combination of formerly separate legal traditions could have occurred. Other considerations are also equivocal. First, laws addressing social issues appear in all the legal corpora of the Bible and would be applicable in almost any period of Israelite history. Second, the social conditions that would incur debt slavery were prevalent during most of the period of the

eighth–seventh centuries. Henri Cazelles, "L'Auteur du Code de l'Alliance," *RB* 52 (1945), 188, argues for a slightly earlier date, holding that Moses is the direct source.

[15]Frank Crüsemann, *The Torah: Theology and Social History of Old Testament Law* (trans. Allan W. Mahnke; Edinburgh: T & T Clark, 1996), 165–169; Rainer Albertz, *A History of Israelite Religion in the Old Testament Period* (trans. John Bowden; 1992; reprint, Louisville, Kentucky: Westminster/John Knox, 1994), 1.183–184.

[16]One problem with this claim is the references to "slave" in biblical literature depicting the premonarchic period. Crüsemann argues that the term עבד in Joshua, Judges, and 1 and 2 Samuel was most often used as a polite designation for a subordinate speaking to a superior and, therefore, the use of the term for "slave" must date from the later centuries of the monarchy, not the tribal period nor the beginning of the monarchy (*The Torah,* 152). The real conflict during the early monarchy, according to Crüsemann, was between the king and the people, not between free and slave, according to the evidence of 1 Sam 8:16–17. However, there were slaves even during the premonarchic period, and the word used for them was עבד – there is no other term in Hebrew.

[17]Albertz, *A History of Israelite Religion*, 1.183, 336, n. 166.

monarchy as reflected in both historical texts (e.g., 2 Kgs 4:1–7) and in the social criticism of the prophets.[18] Third, poor economic conditions were not the only circumstances under which a person might be sold into slavery. A thief who could not pay the penalty for his theft would become a slave: The thief's illegal act and his inability to pay, presumably because he was poor, were the circumstances that caused him to be sold into slavery. Fourth, the absence of a king could be taken as surprising if the Deuteronomic laws, more firmly situated in the monarchic period, were replete with references to the royal establishment, but Deuteronomy makes only a few references to the institution of kingship (Deut 17:14–20). Fifth, the agrarian nature of the society reflected in the Covenant Code cannot serve as proof of an early date because Israelite society persisted in remaining agriculturally based in patrimonial estates throughout the First Temple period.[19] Lastly, the Covenant Code does not exhibit archaic language, a characteristic expected of early texts and the only sure proof of an early date.[20] In general, it is difficult to determine a specific date for the Covenant Code. It appears, then, that its date cannot be chronologically set within any specific time during the First Temple period.

The second issue is whether the refuge mentioned in the Covenant Code is an altar. In the statute, there are two references to places involved in the adjudication of homicide, one of which appears to be a safe haven, the other a place from which a killer can be taken. Exodus 21:13–14 reads, "If [the killer] did not do it by design, but God caused it to meet his hand, I will assign you a place to which he can flee. When a man schemes against another and kills him treacherously, you shall take him from my very altar to be put to death." The referent of "a place to which he can flee" in verse 13 is the crux of the matter. Does it refer to the altar mentioned in the following verse? Some have argued that the implication of taking away a killer *even* from God's altar is that the place of asylum in Exod 21:13 is identical to the altar mentioned in Exod 21:14.[21] However, if the statute in the first verse was referring to the "altar," why did it not simply state "altar"?[22] The implication, thus, is that מָקוֹם and מִזְבֵּחַ were distinct. If so, two possibilities arise: 1) מָקוֹם and מִזְבֵּחַ were two completely different places; 2) one was part of the other, the מִזְבֵּחַ being part of the מָקוֹם.

[18] Ibid., 1.183–184.

[19] See Chapter Two on the social structure of ancient Israel.

[20] The Covenant Code does contain the phrase, שארה כסתה ועֹנתה, which appears to be a legal phrase of long usage. See Shalom M. Paul, "Exod. 21:10: A Threefold Maintenance Clause," *JNES* 28 (1969), 48–53.

[21] E.g., A. Graeme Auld, "The Cities of Refuge in Israelite Tradition," *JSOT* 10 (1978), 135.

[22] Cf. Moshe Greenberg, "The Biblical Conception of Asylum," in *Studies in the Bible and Jewish Thought* (JPS Scholar of Distinction Series; Philadelphia: The Jewish Publication Society, 1995), 43; Alexander Rofé, "The History of the Cities of Refuge in Biblical Law," in *Studies in Bible* (ed. Sarah Japhet; ScrHier 31; Jerusalem: Magnes Press, 1986), 205.

The word מזבח has one meaning, "altar," but the semantic range of the word מקום is more complicated. It is the common word for "place." Sometimes, words with a general meaning have a technical meaning in specific genres of literature.[23] To see whether a specialized meaning exists for מקום in legal terminology, we need to examine the usage of the word in a legal text that contains the word enough times to indicate a specific reference. The other statutes in the Covenant Code are of no use here since מקום is found only in the passage in question. The word does appear twice in the entire complex of the Book of the Covenant, but unfortunately, it has a specific reference in one place and a general reference in the other. So in Exod 20:24, it refers to a sacred place. But in Exod 23:20, it refers to the land of Israel. These references do not allow us to extrapolate a technical meaning for מקום. If we turn to another biblical legal corpus of greater length, like Deuteronomy, מקום is used to refer to cultic sites for both the central sanctuary chosen by God (Deut 12:5, 11, 14, 18, 21, 26; 14:23, 24, 25; 15:20; 16:2, 6, 7, 11, 15, 16; 17:8, 10; 18:6; 26:2; 31:11 – these are all described as either המקום אשר יבחר... or במקום אשר יבחר...) and non-Israelite sanctuaries (singular 12:3, 13; plural 12:2).[24] This word, then, is a technical term for "sanctuary," at least as can be identified in this legal corpus.

More importantly, this specialized meaning of "sacred site" is not limited to legal terminology. The word מקום is replaced with מקדש in later biblical Hebrew texts: מקדש substitutes for the מקום of Pss 96:6, 8 in 1 Chr 16:27, 29.[25] There are several texts in Genesis that presuppose מקום to refer to a sacred site (12:6; 28:11).[26] In 2 Sam 7:10, the future sanctuary in Jerusalem is called מקום.[27] In Jer 7:12, 14, the word is used to refer to the Shiloh sanctuary and to the Jerusalem Temple, respectively. This is further confirmed by the use of *mqm* to denote a sanctuary in a number of Punic inscriptions,[28] and in the existence of jars with a dedicatory inscription to *lmqm* "[dedicated] to the

[23]Gary A. Anderson, *Sacrifices and Offerings in Ancient Israel: Studies in their Social and Political Importance* (HSM 41; Atlanta: Scholars Press, 1987), 31–33. For example, the Hebrew word מנחה generally refers to "a gift," but in the Priestly law, it signifies a particular type of sacrifice, a grain offering.

[24]Milgrom, *Numbers,* 506.

[25]A. Gelston, "A Note on II Samuel 7:10," *ZAW* 84 (1972), 92–94. Gelston also notes that 4 Q Florilegium equates מקום of 2 Sam 7:10 with the Jerusalem Temple. Japhet, *Chronicles,* 317–318, suggests that the change in the verse was made to avoid the implication that the Temple was standing in David's time.

[26]A. Cowley, "The Meaning of מקום in Hebrew," *Journal of Theological Studies* 17 (1916), 174–176.

[27]David Vanderhooft, "Dwelling Beneath the Sacred Place: A Proposal for Reading 2 Samuel 7:10," *JBL* 118 (1999), 625–633.

[28]KAI 119.7 and 173.5. Cf. J. Hoftijzer and K. Jongeling, *Dictionary of the North-West Semitic Inscriptions* (Leiden: Brill, 1995), 2.679–680. The word מקם appears in two Hebrew inscriptions from the Hellenistic period referring to a synagogue, CIJ 973, 974.

shrine/sanctuary" in Philistine sites close geographically and linguistically to ancient Israel.[29]

At the same time that this word has a specialized meaning, it is used for "place" in general. The Deuteronomic corpus uses it to indicate a sacred site, as well as to refer to a place in general without any special status (Deut 1:31 [in the land of Israel], 33 [in the wilderness]; 9:7 [the final stop in the wilderness]; 11:5 [the final stop in the wilderness]; 11:24 [territory in general]; 23:17 [a chance place to which a slave may flee]; 29:6 [in wilderness]).[30] In fact, throughout the Bible, מקום tends to be the general word for "a place," not one with specific status. It can, though not necessarily, operate as a technical word for "a sanctuary."

Furthermore, the word מקום also refers to "town." This can be proved from its use in two passages: It is in parallel with עיר in Deut 21:19, and שער מקמו is used synonymously with עיר in Ruth 4:10.[31]

To what, then, does מקום refer in Exod 21:13? Despite the evidence we have adduced, the term remains ambiguous, except in one regard. It seems safe to conclude that מקום does not refer to the altar mentioned in Exod 21:14.[32] The import of Exod 21:14 is that intentional, premeditated homicide is so heinous that the one who commits such a transgression could even be arrested at an altar, generally an area with restrictions against interlopers and encroachers who have no ritual business there.[33]

We cannot use Exod 21:12–14 as evidence for altar asylum for killers, the first part of the theory on the development of asylum. We can turn to the texts from Deuteronomy to see whether the second part of the theory, the abrogation of altar asylum, holds true. Determining what is innovative and what is assumed as existing legal practice can be based on an explicit statement of what passed for contemporary practice and what should be the norm in the future. For example, the unification of worship in Deut 12:8–14 is presented as a comparison of contemporary versus future practice. We do not

[29] Seymour Gitin, "Seventh Century B.C.E. Cultic Elements at Ekron," in *Biblical Archaeology Today, 1990* (ed. A. Biran and J. Aviram; Jerusalem: Israel Exploration Society, 1993), 251.

[30] Two references are ambiguous. Deut 12:13 may refer either to a place in general or to a Canaanite altar. Deut 26:9 may refer to the land or to the central sanctuary.

[31] Levine, *Numbers 21–36*, 567.

[32] Schwienhorst-Schönberger, in *Das Bundesbuch,* 40–41, argues that two terms, מקום and מזבח, are used for the same object because God does not erect an altar but appoints a place, where human beings erect the altar. However, this still leaves the question open as to why an altar is not mentioned in Exod 21:13. (Schwienhorst-Schönberger's theory does not even apply to Exod 20:22–26.)

[33] Cf. the execution of the unauthorized encroacher in Num 1:51; 3:10, 38; 18:7 by sanctuary guards and in Exod 28:43; 30:20–21; Lev 10:6, 9; Num 4:15, 19–20 presumably by divine means. Targum Pseudo-Jonathan and Targum Neofiti on Exod 21:14 assume that the killer to be taken from the altar was a priest, presumably because only a priest would have been authorized to be at an altar.

have an explicit comparison of present and future practice in the description of the cities of refuge in Deuteronomy 19.

Such a comparison would be the ideal type of evidence to indicate innovation, but in its absence, could other elements serve to indicate innovation? A motive clause offering a rationale for the statute is present – "The blood of the innocent shall not be shed in the land which the Lord your God is giving to you, imputing bloodguilt upon you. . . . You shall not have pity on [the intentional killer], but shall make expiation of the blood of the innocent, and it will be well with you" (Deut 19:10, 13) – but it cannot be construed as a justification for a new legal process for two reasons: 1) It does not explicitly contrast a practice to be abrogated with one to be put into effect; in comparison, the statute prescribing the centralization of worship in Deut 12:8–14 makes a clear-cut contrast between past (incorrect) worship and (correct) worship in the future. 2) The entire Deuteronomic corpus is replete with motive clauses, and it is a characteristic of Deuteronomy's general rhetorical style.

A comparison with another, presumably earlier, statute could serve as evidence. For example, the laws of the slave in Exod 21:2–6 and in Deut 15:12–18 contain many parallels in language as well as contradictions in content. These parallels and contradictions between the passages highlight the changes made in the law. First, much of the language of Exod 21:1–6 appears in Deut 15:12–18, including the rare usage of the term עברי, its only appearance in Deuteronomy. Second, the release of the slave after six years applies solely to men, according to Exod 21:2, but in Deuteronomy the provision is extended to women as well. The manner in which this transformation is expressed is, in fact, evidence for the priority of the Exodus passage. While Exodus has separate laws for a male slave (21:2–6) and for a female slave (21:7–11), the Deuteronomy passage in its opening clause, verse 12, stipulates that the law is to apply to both male and female slaves in an או formula, אחיך העברי או העבריה, "If your brother, a male Hebrew or female Hebrew." The secondary nature of the או formula is suggested by the gratuitous repetition in verse 17b of the stipulation that the law is to be applied to both male and female.[34] Third, Deut 15:13–14 dutifully takes up the next topic in the Exodus statute, the question of monetary payment. The slave leaves the master's charge without payment, according to Exod 21:2, but the Deuteronomy passages reverse the issue from a payment paid by the slave to a payment paid to the slave and requires that the slave be

[34] Michael Fishbane adds an additional reason, arguing that the use of the masculine form in the succeeding verses (vv. 12b–17a), where the interpolator failed to change the grammatical formulation of the statute, indicates an interpolation (*Biblical Interpretation in Ancient Israel* [Oxford: Oxford University Press, 1985], 171, 211, n. 99). In the same manner, Fishbane holds, the use of the masculine form subsequently in v. 18 suggests again that v. 17b is also an interpolation. However, it would have been unnecessary for the writer to change the grammatical form since the masculine is used elsewhere to apply to both male and female.

given provisions. All this suggests that Deut 15:12–18 has reworked Exod 21:2–8.

In light of this type of analysis, can such parallels and contradictions between Deut 19:1–13 and Exod 21:12–14 be found? First, the statutes on homicide lack the parallels in language that would indicate literary dependence. For example, the place of refuge is described differently: in Exod 21:13, מקום אשר ינוס שמה, versus שלש ערים... לנוס שמה כל רצח, and so on, in Deut 19:2, 3, 4. Second, the formal structures of the statutes are different. Exod 21:12–14 begins with a general prohibition of killing, followed by provisions on the procedure to be followed in accidental and intentional homicide. Deut 19:1–13, by contrast, begins with the command to establish places of refuge, with information on which acts of homicide allow a killer to gain entrance to the refuge, followed by the motive for establishing refuges and concluding with the acts of homicide for which a killer is expelled from a city of refuge to be executed. Third, the content of the laws is different. The distinctions, for example, between categories of homicide are drawn differently. Exod 21:14 defines an intentional killer as one who willfully attacks another in treachey, whereas Deut 19:11 distinguishes one who hates another and lies in wait for him as an intentional killer. Therefore, no evidence exists for the dependence of Deut 19:1–13 on Exod 21:12–14. It appears, then, that Deut 19:1–13 assumes that the cities of refuge were an institution of long standing, not an innovation.[35]

Deut 19:1–13 and its parallel tradition, Num 35:9–34, do not present the cities of refuge as something new or as a replacement. At the same time, it must be noted that the cities of refuge are nowhere mentioned in any of the texts that purport to tell about the early monarchy. An innovation can be seen as a discontinuity with the past, which is how previous scholarship has seen a change from altar asylum to cities of refuge, or as having continuity with the past. There are no texts that depict cities of refuge as a radical discontinuity. The cities of refuge are presented as having continuity with past practice.

The ambiguity of Exod 21:13 cannot be resolved completely. It refers to the refuge for an accidental homicide as מקום, a word that can have, as we have seen, the technical meaning of "sacred place" or "town." Exod 21:14 explicitly contrasts this with the declaration that the intentional killer may even be taken from the altar, the most sacred part of a sacred place. The background of the statutes in Exod 21:13–14 can either be that of a sanctuary used as a refuge or that of a city of refuge. Furthermore, because there are no texts that depict the cities of refuge as a radical innovation, we cannot determine whether cities of refuge were always part of the Israelite legal system as reflected in the Bible or whether they were a development from sanctuary refuge.

[35]Levinson argues that centralization, a Deuteronomic innovation, profoundly affected the judicial system (*Deuteronomy and the Hermeneutics of Legal Innovation*, 98–143).

There are other biblical texts that refer to refuge at a sacred place.[36] The Psalms make reference to YHWH as being a refuge and a high tower (Pss 59:17, 18; 144:2), protection in the shadow of YHWH's wings (Pss 17:8, 57:2, 61:5), dwelling in the tent of YHWH (Pss 15:1, 61:5), and hiding in the cover of his tent (Ps 27:5). While it is possible to understand these references as metaphorical, many interpreters have taken them as describing an actual situation, most likely because of the examples of taking refuge at an altar. Löhr understands these as making direct reference to altar asylum.[37] Other scholars have connected psalms to the cities of refuge. B. Dinur identifies one psalm, Psalm 27, as the ritual of admission allowing manslayers into a city of refuge.[38] L. Delekat even goes so far as to argue that the city of refuge was the *Sitz im Leben* of many Psalms: Psalms were written by and for those accused of homicide.[39] However, this identification of the speaker of the Psalms as a fugitive killer is incorrect. While it is true that the Psalms present the enemies of the speaker as wanting to kill him and that the Psalms refer to YHWH as protector and YHWH's dwelling as a place of refuge, there is no indication that the refugee has been accused of homicide. The psalms do show that a sanctuary was a refuge from a variety of enemies.

The arguments that scholars have used to prove that altar asylum for killers was abrogated and replaced by the cities of refuge has proven faulty. The documentation for seeking refuge at an altar shows that the fugitives were political offenders, not killers. The statute in the Covenant Code is obscure and does not clearly refer to altar asylum. The passages in Deuteronomy on the cities of refuge do not present them as an innovation. The evidence for radical historical change is weak.

Historical change has been based on inserting P and D into a scheme of historical development, but the evidence for prioritizing one over the other is weak. Num 35:9–34, P's set of laws on homicide, is an amalgam of the Priestly traditions P and H. These sources consist of several strata laid out side by side and result from literary activity over several centuries. Although the P source has been dated to the Second Temple period, this has been based on a scheme of cultic and social development.[40] However, the most reliable

[36]One inscription, Arad letter 18, contains an elusive reference to a person who is staying in the House of the Lord. The description of the problem is far too vague to be used as evidence for asylum for homicide.

[37]Löhr, *Das Asylwesen im Alten Testament,* 209.

[38]B. Dinur, "The Cultic Aspect of the Cities of Refuge and the Ceremony of Gaining Sanctuary in Them" [Hebrew], *EI* 3 (1954), 144–146.

[39]L. Delekat, *Asylie und Schutzorakel am Zionheiligtum: Eine Untersuchung zu den privaten Feindpsalmen* (Leiden: Brill, 1967), 11–39.

[40]Cf. Wellhausen, *Prolegomena to the History of Israel,* 34–51; Karl Heinrich Graf, "Die sogenannte Grundschrift des Pentateuchs," *Archiv für wissenschaftliche Erforschung des Alten Testaments* 1 (1869), 466–477.

determination has been made on a linguistic basis. Certain Priestly terms were not used during the postexilic period, others were replaced by synonyms in the postexilic period, and others experienced a change in meaning in the Second Temple period that contradicted their preexilic meaning.[41] According to linguistic evidence, the P source dates from the First Temple period. H, which incorporated P, can be dated by linguistic criteria as well to the exilic or early Persian period.[42]

The third main text on homicide is Deut 19:1–13. Deuteronomy as a whole is a striated book, and although scholars have been able to divide Deuteronomy into strata, they have had difficulty linking them to particular time periods. Deuteronomy has correctly been linked to the cultic reform of Josiah in the late seventh century B.C.E.[43] However, the differences between Josiah's reform and the book of Deuteronomy, as we now have it,[44] force us to admit that while the book certainly is related to the Josianic reform, it is unclear which literary accretions of Deuteronomy are directly tied to it. C. Steuernagel and J. G. Staerk separated out the layers of the text on the basis of the Israelites being addressed in the singular or in the plural,[45] but the divided text cannot be dated more precisely. The structure of Deuteronomy as a whole has many affinities to the Vassal Treaties of Esarhaddon (672 B.C.E.). Deuteronomy has a distinctive literary style, and from the seventh century onward, the historiographic and prophetic texts in the Bible exhibit many of this style's features. Deuteronomy is definitely linked to the seventh century, but whether any particular stratum of Deuteronomy predates or postdates the seventh century is sheer guesswork.

The main Deuteronomic text on the adjudication of homicide, Deut 19:1–13, can be divided into layers,[46] but these strata can be assigned a date only on a relative basis. If verses 1 and 9 are Deuteronomic, then verses 5 and

[41] Cf. Avi Hurvitz, *A Linguistic Study of the Relationship Between the Priestly Source and the Book of Ezekiel* (CahRB 20; Rome: Pontifical Biblical Institute, 1982); Hurvitz, "Dating the Priestly Source in Light of the Historical Study of Biblical Hebrew a Century After Wellhausen," *ZAW* 100 (1988), 88–99; Jacob Milgrom, *Studies in Levitic Terminology I* (Berkeley: University of California Press, 1970), 8–16, 60–87.

[42] There are some indications that H may include additions from the exilic and early Persian periods. Cf. Israel Knohl, *The Sanctuary of Silence* (Minneapolis: Fortress, 1995), 201–204; Jacob Milgrom, *Leviticus 1–16* (AB; New York: Doubleday, 1991), 27. It should be noted that the priority of P or H relative to one another has no effect on my analysis.

[43] W. M. L. de Wette, *Dissertatio critica exegetica qua Deuteronomium a prioribus Pentateuchi libris diversum, alius cujusdam recentioris actoris opus esse monstratur* (Halle, 1805).

[44] For example, in contrast to 2 Kgs 23:20, there is no indication that the priests of the *bamot* must be killed. Deut 18:6 and 2 Kgs 23:9 directly contradict each other. The title of the lawbook in Josiah's reform, ספר הברית, does not refer to Deuteronomy but to the book referred to in Exod 24:7.

[45] C. Steuernagel, *Der Rahmen des Deuteronomium* (2d edition; 1894; reprint, Halle: Max Niemeyer, 1923); W. Staerk, *Das Deuteronomium* (Leipzig: J. C. Hinrichs, 1894).

[46] A. D. H. Mayes, *Deuteronomy* (New Century Bible Commentary; Grand Rapids, Michigan: Eerdmans, 1979), 283–285, 297.

8 can be considered post-Deuteronomic, because they refer to Israel as a whole rather than to a specific community waiting to enter the land of Israel and because they use a late expression to refer to the priests, הכהנים בני לוי. There also may be pre-Deuteronomic law in verses 4–5, 11–12, assuming that casuistic formulation indicates earlier material, and post-Deuteronomic supplements in verses 8–10, a contradiction to 4:41–43.

The biblical laws on homicide, Num 35:9–34 and Deut 19:1–13, as well as Exod 21:12–14, are mutually independent sources. They do not have a common literary origin, and they stem from diverse historical and ideological/theological settings. Although previous studies of biblical law have assumed that each of the legal parts of the Pentateuch can be securely dated to different periods and have devised schemes of historical development in biblical law based on that dating, the legal portions of the Pentateuch cannot be dated with such precision and, in fact, all date from some time in the First Temple period with no clear evidence for historical priority.[47]

The legal sources in the Pentateuch, P and D, that differ on the characteristics of the places of refuge do so because they conceptualize the sanctuaries within their ideological/theological program. They disagree on the number, the sacred status, the rationale, and the existence of a technical term for the cities of refuge.

The statute in Num 35:9–34 calls for the establishment of six cities as refuges for the slayer from גאל הדם, denoting them by the technical term

[47]The narrative sources are also difficult to date. Two examples, the killing of Joab (1 Kgs 2:5–6, 28–34) and the execution of those who assassinated Joash (2 Kgs 14:5–6), can illustrate the quandary. The text of 1 Kgs 2:5–6, 28–34 forms part of the Succession Narrative (2 Sam 9–20; 2 Kgs 1–2), a product of an author in Solomon's court who collected a number of independent stories and wove them together in order to justify the new king's accession to the throne. (Cf. Leonhard Rost, *The Succession to the Throne of David* [trans. by Michael D. Rutter and David M. Gunn; intro. by Edward Ball; 1926; reprint, Sheffield: Almond Press, 1982]). The rest of Samuel is assigned to the earlier reign of David. However, can the Succession Narrative so easily be separated from the rest of Samuel? David's admonition to Solomon to kill Joab, 1 Kgs 2:5–6, a part of the Succession Narrative, depends directly on the murders of Amasa and Abner in 2 Sam 2:18–23 and 3:28–30, which are not identified as part of the Succession Narrative. More critically, the dating of these texts to the reigns of David and Solomon is problematic. It has simply been assumed that the narratives are contemporary with the events described, but there are a number of details that would indicate a later date. (Cf. David M. Gunn, *The Story of King David* [JSOTSup 6; Sheffield: JSOT Press, 1978], 32ff.) Indeed, the reigns of David and Solomon may have been an alluring setting to writers for centuries. Other narrative texts are also problematic. For example, the account of the execution of those who assassinated Joash, in 2 Kgs 14:5–6, contains a quotation of Deut 24:16. This could be used as a means of fixing the date of 2 Kgs 14:5–6. Unfortunately, I can argue for mutually contradictory dating with virtually the same reasoning. Does the quotation of Deut 24:16 by 2 Kgs 14:5–6 signify that 2 Kgs 14:5–6 must have been composed after the promulgation of Deuteronomy? Or does this show that Deut 24:16 circulated independently before the public release of Deuteronomy?

מקלט, "refuge; confines."[48] This term is not found in the other legal sections of the Pentateuch, and its appearance here reflects a characteristically Priestly concern for technical and ritual terminology.

Three cities were to be established on each side of the Jordan River, and all six were to be appointed simultaneously after the crossing of the Jordan River, reflecting P's emphasis that the Land of Canaan was to be conquered in one fell swoop and that nothing was to be established there until the conquest was complete. Canaan was not to be distributed to the tribes piecemeal, but rather was apportioned at a single official ceremony. The cities of refuge were part of a scheme of forty-eight cities assigned to the Levites. The question of whether the Levitical cities ever existed in reality has been the subject of heated debate.[49] Yet little doubt has been cast on the existence of the cities of refuge.

According to Num 35, six cities of refuge were to be established, and the number six develops from the Priestly law's endeavor to schematize Israel's antiquity.[50] God is revealed in stages and, therefore, the relationship between God and human beings is described in a series of four covenants (implicitly with Adam, Gen 1:28–2:4a; Noah, Gen 9:1–17; Abraham, Gen 17; Israelites in the wilderness, Exod 24:1–8).[51] The Israelites are divided into twelve tribes ruled by twelve chieftains. The tribes encamp in four groups of three around four standards on the four sides of the Tabernacle, the wilderness sanctuary. On the march, two standards precede the Tabernacle and two follow. Within the Tabernacle, four families serve. The priests and the Levites are given forty-eight cities, of which six are cities of refuge, three on each side of the Jordan. All these numbers are based upon the numeral 12, its multiple 48, and its divisors 2,3,4,6. The precise number of cities of refuge is therefore generated by the Priestly law's theological numerology.

The Priestly law links the cities assigned to the Levites and the places of refuge. Many scholars have, therefore, extrapolated that the reason for assigning a certain city as a place of refuge was due to its status as a sacred city and/or to the existence of an altar, presuming that the institution of asylum

[48]The choice of this term for the cities of refuge reflects the theology/criminology informing the significance of the cities of refuge for the accidental killer. See the analysis of the accidental killer's confinement in Chapter Four.

[49]E.g., W. F. Albright, "The List of Levitic Cities," in *Louis Ginzberg Jubilee Volume* (New York: American Academy for Jewish Research, 1945), 1. 49–73; Benjamin Mazar, "The Cities of the Priests and the Levites," *Congress Volume 1960* (SVT 7; Leiden: Brill, 1960), 193–204; Menahem Haran, "Studies in the Account of the Levitical Cities," *JBL* 80 (1961), 45–54, 156–165 (also *Temples and Temple-Service in Ancient Israel* [Winona Lake, Indiana: Eisenbrauns, 1995], 122–131); J. P. Ross, "The 'Cities of the Levites' in Joshua XXI and I Chronicles VI," Ph.D. diss., University of Edinburgh, 1973; John R. Spencer, "The Levitical Cities: A Study of the Role and Function of the Levites in the History of Israel," Ph.D. diss., University of Chicago, 1980.

[50]Rofé, "The History of the Cities of Refuge in Biblical Law," 225.

[51]Wellhausen, *Prolegomena*, 338–342.

developed historically from altar asylum to sanctuary in a sacred city. This begs the question as to why the status of city of refuge was not extended to all the Levitic cities: If they were sacred or possessed an altar, why did they not qualify as a city of refuge? Furthermore, a distinction must be drawn between a city for the Levites to dwell in and the location of the sanctuaries in which they performed cultic functions; there was no direct link between a Levitic city and a sacred place. A Levite might live in one place but officiate as a Levite in a different location.[52] Abiathar, for example, owns a field in Anathoth, but officiates in Jerusalem and Nob (1 Kgs 2:26).

There is another aspect to the cities of the Levites that is critical to the functioning of a refuge. They were to be distributed evenly throughout the Land of Israel and Transjordan (Num 35:8). In order to provide equal and easy access for a slayer, the cities of refuge needed to be distributed evenly throughout the territory: If each tribe had its own place of refuge, slayers from tribes with smaller territory would have easier access than those from tribes with greater territory. This is reflected in the specific language of the command, "You shall make accessible to yourselves cities of refuge" (Num 35:11). It is not the sacredness of a Levitic city that determines its status as a refuge but rather its geographic distribution.

Understanding that the cities of refuge were selected for reasons of geography clarifies a difficulty with associating the right of asylum with a function of cult sites, with an altar and sacred space. It is assumed that while one who is in the presence of God is under his protection, those who are not supposed to be in a sacred space are executed. If the Priestly statute avers that the slaying pollutes (Num 35:33–34), would a slayer be permitted to encroach upon a sacred place? Indeed, the point of the Levitic cities is that they are manned by personnel not limited by tribal geography and who had access to nonsacred aspects of sacred items. The Priestly law stipulates that the priesthood was stratified into priests, strictly defined, and Levites, service personnel limited to assigned tasks of the transport, maintenance, and handling of cultic items (Num 3–4; 8:5–22). The Levites were the corps of subordinate servitors, relegated to nonsacral functions of sacred sites and rites.[53] They assisted the priests (Num 18:2,4) and performed acts that do not pertain to the altar (Num 16:9). The functions of the Levites are outside cultic sanctity, according to the Priestly traditions (Ezek 44:11; 46:24).[54] Being divorced from the sacred and being geographically distributed, the Levites are therefore the appropriate personnel to oversee the cities of refuge. A killer was to be kept away from all that was sacred because his offense polluted the land.

[52]Menahem Haran, *Temples and Temple-Service in Ancient Israel* (Winona Lake, Indiana: Eisembrauns, 1995), 119–120.

[53]The distinction between priests and Levites may be a distinction only in Numbers. Cf. Levine, *Numbers 1–20,* 65, 81, 104–105.

[54]Haran, *Temples and Temple-Service in Ancient Israel,* 61.

Just as the theological and social program of Numbers informs the statutes establishing the cities of refuge in that book, so too does the social and theological program of Deuteronomy shape its statutes on homicide. Deuteronomy manifests anxiety over the possibility that גאל הדם might commit an accidental homicide because he could kill any slayer with impunity outside the city of refuge – "Whoever came with his fellow into the forest to cut wood: as his hand swings the ax to cut down the tree, the ax-head falls off the handle and hits the other so that he dies – that man shall flee to one of these cities and live, lest the blood avenger pursuing him in his hot anger, overtakes him and slays him because the distance is too great, yet he was not liable to the death penalty because he was not hostile to him in the past" (Deut 19:5–6). Deuteronomy is concerned with the slaying of the accidental killer and the effect it would have upon the Israelite people. In contrast to the Priestly law, where the slaying of the accidental killer does not incur culpability at all, the Deuteronomic statute evinces the belief that the killing of a fugitive who has not yet reached a refuge does. In his case, the fugitive's status as an accidental or intentional killer is not yet clear: He may potentially be an accidental killer, whose death is unwarranted. In an ironic transformation, the same term for culpability for the victim, דם נקי, "innocent blood" (Deut 19:13), is used to refer to culpability for the killer slain before he reaches the city of refuge (Deut 19:10).

If the blood avenger manages to overtake the fugitive and kill him, the Israelite people as a whole are responsible, according to Deut 19:10. The Priestly law, by contrast, avers that the land, not the people, will be polluted by the presence of the unpunished slayer, not the death of the accidental slayer. The Priestly law is concerned with the purity and the pollution of space, the Deuteronomic with that of the Israelite people. The Priestly law is concerned with the pervading presence of God in the midst of Israel, while Deuteronomy focuses on the conduct and fate of the Israelite people.[55] Indeed, Deuteronomy is completely unconcerned with the immanence of God: for Deuteronomy, the Temple in Jerusalem is not the dwelling place of God; it is the place where God causes his name to dwell. The Priestly law is concerned with the polluting effects of a slaying, whereas D is concerned with the social aspects of the law.

Like the statutes in Numbers, Deuteronomy's places of refuge are divorced from any link with the sacred or the priesthood, but this is informed by the Deuteronomic trend toward secularization and the separation of sacred and secular. This tendency is part of the larger program of Deuteronomy.[56] Warfare, for example, is stripped of its sacred ritual in Deuteronomy. There

[55] Moshe Weinfeld, *Deuteronomy 1–11* (AB; New York: Doubleday, 1991), 25.

[56] Weinfeld, *Deuteronomy and the Deuteronomic School,* 233–243. The term *secularization* may be too strong a term for this aspect of Deuteronomy's program, as Weinfeld himself notes ("On 'Demythologization and Secularization' in Deuteronomy," *IEJ* 23 [1973],

is no mention of the sounding of the priestly horns or of the plunder that is to be dedicated to the sanctuary.[57] The use of the ark and the holy vessels is missing in Deuteronomic warfare. Even the function of the priests is secularized. In P, the priests are to sound their horns so that the warriors are remembered by YHWH (Num 10:9). In D, by contrast, the priest addresses the people to inspire their courage (Deut 20:1–4). This secularization is carried through in the Deuteronomic tradition of the cities of refuge. The Levites, who are considered the Priestly class in Deuteronomy, are not connected with the cities of refuge. The high priest is not a factor in the stay of the accidental homicide in a city of refuge.

Like Numbers, the Deuteronomic refuges are established on the basis of geographic considerations: The country is to be divided up into three parts with a city of refuge established in each area so as to enable a slayer to seek refuge efficiently.

Unlike the refuges in Numbers, the tally of the cities of refuge in Deuteronomy is complex because, as the present text of Deuteronomy reads, the calculation is linked to a multistaged conquest, in contrast to the comprehensive conquest in Numbers. Three stages are indicated in the establishment of the cities of refuge. In Deut 4:41–43, Moses designates three cities after the territory east of the Jordan is conquered.[58] In Deut 19:1–7, the Israelites are commanded to designate three cities after the conquest of the Land of Israel. In Deut 19:8–9, three more cities are to be added after additional conquests. If we were to read the chapters of Deuteronomy in succession, the total number of the cities of refuge is nine. However, in Deut 19:1–7, the command to set up three cities after the conquest of the Land of Israel is presented as a new injunction without any reference to the establishment of earlier cities in the territory east of the Jordan River.[59] Indeed, in Deut 19:7–9, the text reads: "When the LORD your God enlarges your territory . . . you shall add three more cities to these *three*." If the law was to include the three cities mentioned in Deut 4:41–43 as well as the three established by Deut 19:1–7, it would have stated "these *six*." It clearly appears that the author of Deuteronomy 19 did not know of Moses' action in Deut 4:41–43. In fact, Deut 4:41–43 is placed between Moses' lengthy orations of Deut 1:1–4:40 and 4:44–26:19, an appropriate place for an insertion.

Deut 19:8–9, the command to establish three more cities after additional conquests in the land of Israel, is apparently parenthetical to the command in Deut 19:1–7.[60] Deut 19:10 does not refer back to verse 9 but to verse 7

230). Cf. Milgrom, "The Alleged 'Demythologization and Secularization' in Deuteronomy," *IEJ* 23 (1973), 156–161.

[57] Compare Num 10:9; 31:6, 50–54; Judg 7:19–20; 2 Sam 8:11; 11:11.

[58] This section and Josh 20:8 are almost identical, but it is difficult to say which has priority. Cf. Auld, "Cities of Refuge in Israelite Tradition," 138.

[59] Rofé, "History of the Cities of Refuge," 222.

[60] Ibid., 222–224.

because it deals with "the land that the LORD God is allotting to you," not to the enlarged territory. Furthermore, the motive cited by verse 10, "Thus the blood of the innocent will not be shed," is linked to verse 6, "yet he was not guilty of a capital crime." Deut 19:8–9 is a secondary layer whose purpose is to adapt the law of the cities of refuge to Num 35:9–34, which stipulates the establishment of six cities. The author of Deut 19:8–9 attempts to reconcile the two laws. However, another attempt was made to reconcile the sources, Deut 4:41–43. These texts in Deut 4:41–43 and 19:7–8 are not to be seen as connected with historical reality but as examples of intrabiblical exegesis reconciling contradictions in inherited legal literature. In fact, the original command in Deuteronomy was to establish only three cities.[61]

Both Numbers and Deuteronomy outline a specific procedure to adjudicate whether the killer committed intentional or accidental homicide. According to Numbers, once the fugitive has reached the city of refuge, the trial is conducted before the עדה, "assembly."[62] The עדה and the leaders of the עדה play an important role in the book of Numbers. The term עדה refers to the entirety of the Israelites,[63] who witness public ceremonies.[64] The term can refer more specifically to the assembly of adult Israelite males.[65] The chiefs of the עדה hold executive powers.[66] They take the initiative in dealing with certain problems and represent the entirety of the Israelites in situations where the presence of all the Israelites would be impossible.[67] When it appears in biblical literature portraying a later period, it seems to be a

[61]Rofé argues that Jerusalem was also to be included as a place of refuge even though the statute in Deuteronomy does not allude to Jerusalem ("History of the Cities of Refuge," 215, 224). Rofé understands "(geographic name) גבול ארץ" in Deut 19:3 as Israelite territory outside of Jerusalem and Benjamin which does not include Jerusalem and Benjamin. Therefore, the threefold division was established in addition to the territorial unit of Jerusalem and Benjamin. There are two difficulties with this. First, if Jerusalem were to be included as a city of refuge, why did the text not stipulate a fourfold division of the country? Second, a study of the phrase "(geographic name) גבול" indicates that when it refers to dividing territory, it includes the entire territory of a country within the actual line serving as a boundary: There is no indication that the capital city is excluded. (Cf. the dividing of the country in Num 34 and Josh 15. Also, an entire country: Gen 10:19; Exod 7:27; 10:4; Num 20:16, 17. The phrase "(geographic name) כל גבול": Exod 10:14, 19; 13:7; Judg 19:29; 1 Sam 11:3, 7; 27:1; 1 Kgs 1:3; 2 Kgs 10:32; 14:25; 1 Chr 21:12.)

[62]The term עדה can be used as proof for the First Temple date of the Priestly tradition. Cf. Avi Hurvitz, "The Use of the Priestly Term 'עדה' in Biblical Literature," [Hebrew] *Tarbiz* 40 (1970): 261–267.

[63]Exod 12:3, 6, 47; 16:1, 2, 9, 10, 19; 17:1; 35:1; Lev 4:13; 10:6; 16:5; 19:2; Num 1:53; 3:7; 8:9, 20; 10:2; 13:26; 14:1, 2, 3, 5, 7, 10, 25, 27; 15:24, 25, 26, 33, 35, 36; 16:3; 17:6, 7, 10, 11; 19:9; 20:1, 2, 8, 11, 22, 27, 29; 25:6, 7; 27:2, 3, 14, 16, 17, 19, 20, 21, 22; 31:12, 16, 43; Josh 9:19, 21; 18:1; 22:12, 16, 17, 18, 20; Ps 74:2; Jer 6:18; 30:20.

[64]Lev 8:3, 4, 5; 9:5; Num 10:3; 1 Kgs 8:5 [1 Chr 5:6].

[65]Exod 35:4, 10; Num 1:2, 18; 26:2.

[66]Num 1:16.

[67]Exod 16:22; 35:31; Lev 4:15; Num 4:34; 16:2; 31:13, 26, 27; 32:2, 4; Josh 9:15, 18, 27; 22:30.

pan-Israelite assembly. In Judg 20:1 and 21:10, 16, it has both political and judicial aspects. The עדה arbitrates between an individual and a tribe, declares war on a particular tribe, and accepts terms of peace. Its political role is otherwise vague. None of the judges is portrayed as consulting with the עדה. There is only a single reference to it in the history of the monarchy: 1 Kgs 12:20 refers to עדה as the body that crowns Jeroboam I.

It would seem very unwieldy to convene all the Israelites to judge a case of homicide, as Numbers 35 prescribes. The wilderness setting of the book of Numbers makes the judicial function of the עדה appear to be an archetype for local communities and sanctuaries. Just as the law of slaughter in Lev 17, as an example, applies to local sanctuaries, not to a central sanctuary, so too does the term עדה apply to a small local court, not a central assembly. Numbers 35 is the only reference to the judicial function of the עדה. The references elsewhere to the role of the עדה in the punishment of a violator of the Sabbath and of a blasphemer (Num 15:33, 35, 36; Lev 24:13, 16) are misleading because the עדה in these cases does not exercise any role in the adjudication. Rather, the עדה in Num 15 and Lev 24 is the entirety of the Israelites from whose midst the transgressor is extirpated. The term עדה appears to signify one meaning in almost all of the Hebrew Bible and another in Numbers 35. It appears to be a judicial body outside of the city of refuge because of the stipulation that the עדה will return the slayer to the city of refuge upon deciding that the death was inadvertent.

In Deuteronomy, the obligation for adjudicating the case devolves upon the killer's home city. According to Deut 19:12, if intentional homicide took place, the elders of the killer's city,[68] not a pan-Israelite body like the עדה, should take the killer from the city of refuge and have the blood avenger execute him. The accused must be judged in his own city *in absentia* because 1) the text describes the action of the elders as the implementation of a judgment already made, and 2) the accused is in one of the cities of refuge to which he fled in fear of the blood avenger after committing the killing. Who makes this judgment? It is likely that these elders are the ones, because 1) they are explicitly mentioned as extraditing the intentional killer, and 2) the

[68]Deut 19:12 refers to זקני עירו, "the elders of his city." Although one might argue that this refers to the elders of the victim's city, it is much more likely that the elders of the killer's city were involved. (Cf. Driver, *Deuteronomy,* 233; von Rad, *Deuteronomy,* 127; Rofé, "History of the Cities of Refuge," 228.) The elders of the offender's city are more inclined to keep one of their own safe and hold a fair trial than the victim's city with the victim's kin thirsting for revenge. If they were partial to the slayer because he was one of their own, bloodguilt would fall upon them. (Cf. Hanokh Reviv, *The Institution of the Elders in Ancient Israel* [Hebrew], [Text and Studies; Jerusalem: Magnes, 1983], 66.) Another Deuteronomic stipulation, Deut 21:1–9, contains a ceremony designed to address the guilt of the city nearest to the place where a human corpse is found. If we may call upon evidence of the role of elders from another legal action, Deut 25:5–10 stipulates that in the case of levirate marriage, the responsibility for resolving the dispute devolves upon the elders of the offender's city.

elders do exercise judicial functions in general.[69] If the fugitive is condemned as having committed homicide intentionally and with prior malice, the elders send for him and deliver him to the blood avenger.

As we have seen, Numbers 35 and Deuteronomy 19 reflect the theological and social programs of the Priestly literature and of Deuteronomy. Their conceptualization of the adjudication of a slaying coincides and diverges because their distinctive theological and social programs shape the process differently.

A new element in procedure, a hearing of admission to gain entrance into the city of refuge, is found in another tradition about the cities of refuge, Josh 20:1–9:

> [1]The Lord said to Joshua, [2]"Speak to the Israelites, saying, 'Assign
> the cities of refuge, about which I commanded you through Moses,
> [3]to which a slayer who strikes down a person by mistake unintention-
> ally may flee; they shall be a refuge for you from the blood avenger.
> [4]He shall flee to one of these cities, present himself at the entrance to
> the city gate, and plead his case before the elders of that city. They shall
> admit him into the city and give him a place to live among them. [5]If
> the blood avenger should pursue him, they shall not hand the slayer
> over to him, for he struck his neighbor unintentionally and had not
> been his enemy before. [6]He shall live in that city until he stands be-
> fore the assembly for trial, [and remain there] until the death of the
> high priest who is in office at that time. Then the slayer may return
> to his town and his home from where he fled.'" [7]They sanctified
> Kedesh in the Galilee, in the hill country of Naphtali, Shechem in the
> hill country of Ephraim, and Kiryat Arba, that is, Hebron, in the hill
> country of Judah. [8]On the other side of the Jordan, eastward, they
> assigned Bezer in the wilderness, in the steppe of the tribe of Reuben,
> Ramot in Gilead, of the tribe of Gad, and Golan in the Bashan, of
> the tribe of Menasseh. [9]These are the designated cities for all the
> Israelites and the alien who dwells among them, so that anyone who

[69]Cf. Deut 21:18–21 (although there is no explicit mention of a trial; if the child's parents did have the right to condemn him without need of official judgment, why would the parents be required to present the situation before the elders?); 22:13–21; 25:5–10; 1 Kgs 21:8–13; Ruth 4:1–12. However, Rofé suggests that if the families of the victim and the killer agree that the killing was unintentional, there is no need for the elders to be involved in any capacity ("The History of the Cities of Refuge," 229). Only if they agree on the culpability of the killer, then the elders must exercise their executive function in extraditing the fugitive. If the families of the victim and the killer do not agree, according to Rofé, the determination is made by the consensus of the local community. This solution of Rofé's seems unwieldy. A dispute cannot be resolved by an amorphous body deciding on the basis of rumors and hearsay. If a formal presentation is required for other offenses that are less serious than a charge of murder, it would be unlikely that a slaying would be adjudicated in a less organized manner. Therefore, a formal trial *in absentia* before the elders was warranted.

> kills a person by mistake may flee there and not die by the hand of the blood avenger before he has stood trial before the assembly.

In order to understand the origin of this innovation, the relationship of this tradition to the other two must be analyzed.

The presence of elements from both Numbers 35 and Deuteronomy 19 in Joshua 20 is apparent:[70]

Josh 20:2 תְּנוּ לָכֶם אֶת־עָרֵי הַמִּקְלָט אֲשֶׁר־דִּבַּרְתִּי אֲלֵיכֶם בְּיַד מֹשֶׁה, "Assign the cities of refuge" – The term עָרֵי מִקְלָט, "cities of refuge," appears only in Numbers 35 (vv. 11, 14, 25, 26, 27, 28, 32). The verb used for assigning cities here and in Num 35:13–14 is נ-ת-נ.

Josh 20:3 לָנוּס שָׁמָּה רוֹצֵחַ מַכֵּה נֶפֶשׁ בִּשְׁגָגָה בִּבְלִי־דָעַת וְהָיוּ לָכֶם לְמִקְלָט מִגֹּאֵל הַדָּם., "to which a slayer who strikes down a person by mistake unintentionally may flee; they shall be a refuge for you from the blood avenger." – The entire verse is an almost complete parallel to Num 35:11b–12a, which reads וְנָס שָׁמָּה רֹצֵחַ מַכֵּה נֶפֶשׁ בִּשְׁגָגָה וְהָיוּ לָכֶם הֶעָרִים לְמִקְלָט מִגֹּאֵל "to which a slayer who strikes down a person unintentionally may flee; the cities shall be as a refuge from the avenger." The double characterization of this type of murder, בִּשְׁגָגָה בִּבְלִי־דָעַת "by mistake unintentionally," is a conflation of the criteria of Numbers and Deuteronomy. Num 35:11b denotes this category of killing by the term בשגגה, "by mistake," while Deut 19:4 uses בבלי דעת, "unintentionally."

Josh 20:4a וְנָס אֶל־אַחַת מֵהֶעָרִים הָאֵלֶּה, "He shall flee to one of these cities." – This clause is similar to Deut 19:5b, הוּא יָנוּס אֶל־אַחַת הֶעָרִים הָאֵלֶּה וָחָי, "that man shall flee to one of these cities and live."

Josh 20:5aα וְכִי יִרְדֹּף גֹּאֵל הַדָּם אַחֲרָיו, "If the blood avenger should pursue him" – This is paralleled in Deut 19:6, פֶּן־יִרְדֹּף גֹּאֵל הַדָּם אַחֲרֵי הָרֹצֵחַ, "lest the blood avenger pursue him."

Josh 20:5b כִּי בִבְלִי־דַעַת הִכָּה אֶת־רֵעֵהוּ וְלֹא־שֹׂנֵא הוּא לוֹ מִתְּמוֹל שִׁלְשׁוֹם, "for he struck his neighbor unintentionally and had not been his enemy before." – This is paralleled in Deut 19:4b, אֲשֶׁר יַכֶּה אֶת־רֵעֵהוּ בִּבְלִי־דַעַת וְהוּא לֹא שֹׂנֵא לוֹ מִתְּמֹל שִׁלְשֹׁם, "whoever slays his fellow without intent and was not hostile to him in the past."

Josh 20:6aβ עַד עָמְדוֹ לִפְנֵי הָעֵדָה לַמִּשְׁפָּט, "until he stands before the assembly for trial." – A trial before the assembly is stipulated in Num 35:24.

Josh 20:6γ עַד מוֹת הַכֹּהֵן הַגָּדוֹל, "until the death of the priest" – The release date of the accidental homicide is the same as in Num 35:28.

Josh 20:6b אָז יָשׁוּב הָרוֹצֵחַ וּבָא אֶל־עִירוֹ וְאֶל־בֵּיתוֹ אֶל־הָעִיר אֲשֶׁר נָס מִשָּׁם.; "Then the killer may return to his town and his home from where he fled." – Num

[70] There may be another parallel, if a textual emendation is warranted. In v. 7, the cities west of the Jordan are set aside (ויקדשו), and I would argue that this is an error for ויקרו, the same verb used in Num 35:11. The error was caused by the proximity of the place name Kadesh (קֶדֶשׁ) in the same verse.

35:28 stipulates that the killer may return to his patrimonial estate, נַחֲלָה. Deut 19:12 mentions that the killer departed from "his town," עִירוֹ.

Joshua 20, however, does contain one verse that constitutes a departure from Numbers 35 and Deuteronomy 19. Josh 20:4 mandates that before the fugitive is permitted to enter the city of refuge, a hearing must take place in order to determine whether he is eligible for admission to the city at all. The accidental killer is to be stopped at the gate of the city of refuge. He can only gain admittance after he presents his case to the elders of the city of refuge that the slaying was accidental. This appears to be separate from his trial, which must still take place before the assembly (Josh 20:6). The hearing is apparently a way to prevent intentional slayers from entering the city of refuge at all.

This new element, the procedure of admission in Josh 20:4, has a relationship to certain elements in Deuteronomy. In Deut 19:12, the elders of the slayer's city play a role in determining his guilt and, if he is found culpable, deliver him to the blood avenger. City elders resolve disputes in Deut 22:13–21 and 25:5–10. In the same vein, Josh 20:4, in introducing a procedure of admission, assigns it to the elders, albeit of the city of refuge, not the elders of the killer's city, as in Deut 19:12. This is appropriate since the elders of the city of refuge are protecting it from the presence of intentional killers. In addition, the elaboration in Josh 20:5–6 that the accidental slayer will not be delivered to the blood avenger and will live in the city of refuge, ולא־יסגרו . . . וישב, uses language reminiscent of Deut 23:16–17, which mandates that an escaped slave will not be delivered over (תסגיר) to his master and will live among (עמך ישב) the Israelites.[71]

How can the presence of a new procedure in Deuteronomic language that does not appear in Deuteronomy be explained? The simplest explanation is that Joshua 20 is a Deuteronomic reworking of a Priestly kernel.[72] In fact, one manuscript of the LXX, Codex Vaticanus, contains none of the Deuteronomic additions, including Josh 20:4, and therefore provides evidence for the independent existence of a Priestly pericope. The new procedure in Josh 20:4 was worded in Deuteronomic style, although its content differs significantly. While the other versions, Numbers 35 and Deuteronomy 19, eventually restrict asylum to accidental killers, Joshua 20 limits initial entrance into the city of refuge only to accidental killers. The probability of a Deuteronomic reworking of Priestly material is further heightened by the fact that where Joshua 20 has parallels to both Numbers 35 and Deuteronomy 19, it is invariably closer to, or identical with, Deuteronomy 19. This makes sense since both are part of the Deuteronomic literature. A Deuteronomic author, later than both Numbers 35 and Deuteronomy 19, designed this new

[71]Rofé, "Joshua 20: Historico-Literary Criticism Illustrated," in *Empirical Models for Biblical Criticism* (ed. Jeffrey H. Tigay; Philadelphia: University of Pennsylvania Press, 1985), 137–138.
[72]Ibid., 141–143.

procedure to allay any anxiety over the presence of intentional killers in a city of refuge by preventing them from gaining entrance in the first place. The intentional slayer has no way of escaping the blood avenger even for a limited time in a city of refuge until he is convicted and handed over to the avenger to be killed.

The legal sources of the Pentateuch P and D differ as a direct result of their distinctive ideological and theological programs. The statute in Joshua is an attempt to reconcile these differences. I have shown that the cities of refuge were not a Deuteronomic innovation nor were they an innovation of the early monarchy. However, there may have been a development from sanctuary asylum to the cities of refuge at a glacial speed, starting with the ability of others besides killers to seek sanctuary at an altar and the indication in the Psalms that the Sanctuary was a place of refuge from danger. The development of homicide in the Hebrew Bible follows along the lines of a steady-state theory, with the recognition that even a steady-state universe experiences change from time to time.

CHAPTER FOUR

Pollution and Homicide

FOR THE ancient Israelites, the spilling of blood in a homicide was an event of profound consequence because of the blood itself, not simply because of the physical harm of the assault. The blood that was spilled polluted. One of the statutes on homicide concludes with an explicit statement of the motivation for the statute: The blood of the victim pollutes the land (Num 35:33, 34):[1]

> [33]You shall not pollute the land in which you are in, for the blood itself pollutes the land: expiation cannot be made on behalf of the land for the blood that was shed in it except by the blood of him who shed it. [34]You shall not defile the land in which you are inhabiting, in which I dwell, for I the LORD dwell among the Israelites.

[1]The viewpoint that sin defiles the land rather than affecting the sanctuary is consistent with the doctrine of H. Cf. Baruch J. Schwartz, "The Bearing of Sin in Priestly Literature," in *Pomegranates and Golden Bells: Studies in Biblical, Jewish, and Ancient Near Eastern Ritual, Law, and Literature in Honor of Jacob Milgrom* (ed. David P. Wright, David Noel Freedman, and Avi Hurvitz; Winona Lake, Indiana: Eisenbrauns, 1995), 6, and Knohl, *The Sanctuary of Silence*, 185–186. Ritual impurity and ethical impurity are treated in two discrete crystallizations of the Priestly traditions, P and H, respectively. It would, however, be incorrect to argue that only one, H, holds that ethical impurity exists, since there are many references to the polluting effects of shed blood. Cf. 2 Sam 3:28–29; Isa 26:21; Ps 106:38.

Warnings about purging evil from the midst of the Israelites appear with frequency in Deuteronomy (Deut 13:6; 17:7, 12; 21:21; 22:21, 22, 24; 24:7), but only with regard to the case of homicide does the warning specify that it is the *blood* of the innocent victim that must be removed. Deut 19:10–13, another of the statutes on homicide, warns the Israelites not to have pity upon the murderer so that the innocent blood of the victim can be purged:

> [10] The blood of the innocent shall not be shed in the land which the
> Lord your God is giving to you, imputing bloodguilt upon you. [11] If
> a person is hostile to another and lies in wait and strikes him mortally
> so that he dies, and flees to one of these towns, [12] the elders of his
> town shall send and take him back from there and deliver him to the
> blood avenger so that he dies. [13] You shall not have pity on him, but
> shall make expiation of the blood of the innocent, and it will be well
> with you.

Deut 21:1–9, a rite of absolving the community of responsibility for the death of an unknown homicide victim, specifies that the innocent blood of the victim is to be sent as far as possible from human habitation so as to be disposed of:

> [6] All the elders of the town nearest to the corpse shall wash their
> hands over the heifer whose neck was broken in the wadi. [7] They
> shall solemnly declare: "Our hands did not shed this blood nor did
> our eyes witness [it]. [8] Make expiation, Lord, for your people Israel
> whom you redeemed, and do not allow innocent blood to remain
> amidst your people Israel, and let the blood be expiated." [9] Thus,
> you will remove innocent blood from your midst, for you will be
> doing what is right in the eyes of the Lord.

In the story of Cain and Abel, it is not an accident that when God confronts Cain about Abel's murder, God speaks about Abel's blood crying out from the ground (Gen 4:10). Blood, דמים, is not simply a vivid image conjured up by a creative author for the tale of Cain. Abel's blood has a real existence of its own that must be addressed.

In the Bible, blood is a paradoxical substance: It is the most effective cleanser while being a pollutant.[2] Sacrificial blood removes pollution and sanctifies. It is the principal means of remedying impurity. The annual ceremony of atonement includes the sprinkling of the Tabernacle with blood in order to purge defilement from the Tabernacle (Leviticus 16). This allows the high priest to enter the inner sanctum without dying (Lev 16:2). Blood is used in the initial sanctification of the Tabernacle and the ordination of

[2] Gordon J. Wenham, *The Book of Leviticus* (NICOT; Grand Rapids, Michigan: Eerdmans, 1979), 188.

Aaron and his sons (Leviticus 8). Blood removes the initial impurity from the altar and sanctifies Aaron and his sons for their special station. The covenant between God and the Israelites is affirmed when Moses splashes blood on the people, signaling the change in status (Exod 24:6–8). The leper is cleansed by being sprinkled with blood (Lev 14:5–7, 14, 25).

At the same time, blood is also a powerful contaminant. A discharge of blood, whether in menstruation, in childbirth, or in recovery from childbirth, renders a woman unclean (Lev 12: 1–8). The other bodily discharge to incur impurity is semen. What the discharges of blood and semen have in common is their relationship to being the source of life.[3] Semen and blood symbolize life, and their loss is death. The other two sources of impurities are the state of death itself and scale disease, which itself manifests death as the body wastes away.[4] In Num 12:12, Aaron reacts to the sight of Miriam afflicted by scale disease by exclaiming, "Let her not be like the dead, which comes out of its mother's womb with half its flesh eaten away." Death and that which resembles death cause defilement. Blood represents both life and death and, therefore, is both a purifier and a contaminant.

Furthermore, the Hebrew Bible manifests the belief that the vitality of life is found in blood.[5] This is not simply symbolic. Blood contains human and animal life in a concrete sense. The very life of an animal is contained in its blood (Lev 17:10, 14; Deut 12:23).[6] Therefore the blood of an animal must not be eaten (Lev 17:10–14, also 7:26–27).[7] In the same concrete sense, the life of a human being is contained in his blood.[8] It has corporeality; it is not simply a metaphor.[9]

[3]Milgrom, *Leviticus 1–16*, 767, 1002.

[4]Milgrom, "The Dynamic of Impurity in the Priestly System," in *Purity and Holiness: The Heritage of Leviticus* (ed. M. J. H. M. Poorthuis and J. Schwartz; Jewish and Christian Perspectives Series II; Leiden: Brill, 2000), 31–32. This is reflected in the rabbinic statement that scale disease is tantamount to death (שהיא [צרעת] שקולה למת, b. Sanhedrin 47a). Cf. b. Nedarim 64b (תניא ארבעה חשובין כמת עני ומצורע וסומא ומי שאין לו בנים), Tanhuma 94.13; Lamentations Rabbah 3.2; Exodus Rabbah 1.34 (Margalioth 1.105).

[5]The ancient Israelites literally attributed physical and psychological functions to particular organs of the body.

[6]The presence of life in the blood may make eating blood invigorating; see David Sperling, "Blood," ABD 1.762. This may be the reason why Saul's weary soldiers consume meat with the blood in it (1 Sam 14:31–32).

[7]This concept is paralleled in other cultures. Cf. James G. Frazer, *The Golden Bough* (abridged edition; New York: Macmillan, 1951), 265.

[8]This is reflected in the rabbinic practice of burying a murdered person in his or her bloodstained clothing. See *Shulḥan Arukh,* Yoreh Deah, 364:4, and *Arukh ha-Shulḥan,* Yoreh Deah, 364:12.

[9]David H. Aaron, *Biblical Ambiguities: Metaphor, Semantics, and Divine Imagery* (The Brill Reference Library of Ancient Judaism; Leiden: Brill, 2001), demonstrates how some statements that modern critics take metaphorically would have been taken literally by readers in biblical times and proposes an innovative methodology to determine whether a text was meant literally or metaphorically or both.

Sin also possesses concreteness. Once sin is committed, it is not a past event but a real object, an odious, foul object that affects human beings and human society and that requires disposal.[10]

These factors, the polluting effect of blood and the physical inherence of life in blood, cognitively mapped with the physicality of sin, generate the belief that the spilling of the victim's blood is the physical consequence of the sin that must be rectified. Accordingly, Num 35:33–34 and Ps 106:38 warn that the blood of a murdered person pollutes. When God confronts Cain about Abel's murder, God emphasizes that Abel's blood is crying out from the ground (Gen 4:10). Abel's blood has a concrete existence, and so the blood of the victim cries out from the earth for revenge. David recoils from "the blood falling[11] on the head of Joab and his father's house" and utters a curse to ensure that the taint would fall on the murderer's descendants, not his own (2 Sam 3:28–29; 1 Kgs 2:32–33). According to a prophetic vision, when iniquity is punished, the earth will reveal the blood that has been shed on it and will not cover it up again (Isa 26:21). When the brothers of Joseph consider killing him and blaming a wild beast for his death, they speak of slaying him and covering up his blood (Gen 37:26). The sight of blood that is shed stirs God to revenge: It has been put on stone, not on earth, to prevent it from being covered up by the dust of the earth (Ezek 24:7–9). Job cries out that the earth should not cover his blood and thereby efface his cry for justice (Job 16:18). The blood has a physical existence that can be hidden by being covered, כסה, and can be shown by being revealed, גלה: Covering the blood is a means of hiding the slaying, while uncovering it brings certain punishment.

The technical term used to denote culpability for a killing is, therefore, דמים or דם, literally "blood." The singular form denotes both "blood" and "bloodguilt, culpability for death," while the plural refers to "bloodguilt, culpability for death," the responsibility for the unlawful spilling of blood. Here, the plural is used to indicate the abstract. The meaning of the plural

[10]Baruch J. Schwartz, "'Term' or Metaphor – Biblical נשא עון/פשע/חטא במקרא" [Hebrew], *Tarbiz* 63 (1994) 149–171; "The Bearing of Sin in the Priestly Literature," in *Pomegranates and Golden Bells*, 7; and *The Holiness Legislation* [Hebrew] (Jerusalem: Magnes Press, 1999), 61–63. This may be why, in both Hebrew and Akkadian, there are words that denote both sin and the punishment remedying it – עָוֹן and *arnu*. Schwartz argues that the putative meaning "punishment" is identified only in the phrase נשא עון, when in fact the word still means "sin." The phrase should still be renderd "to bear (the burden of) sin," and in this case, the sinner is forgiven when another, most usually God, bears the sin in place of the sinner.

[11]This verb is derived from חול, which is a homophonous root with three meanings, "to dance," "to fall upon," and "to tremble." While it is possible to translate the sentence as "the blood dancing about the head of Joab," it is more likely that it should be understood as "the blood falling upon the head of Joab," because the point of David's outburst is to lay the blame upon Joab. Cf. Jer 23:19 (30:23), where the verb is used to indicate the punishment falling upon the guilty and to make a play on words with the embodiment of divine anger in the form of a tempest.

form, דמים, has been extended to refer to crime in general (e.g., Isa 1:15 and the offenses enumerated in vv. 16–17). The blood of animals is always referred to in the singular.

The responsibility for knowingly committing an act for which death is the punishment is imputed in the expressions דמיו בו, דמו על ראשו, דמו בראשו "his blood is on his head." In the case of homicide, the blood of the victim attaches itself to the responsible party,[12] but when a person deserves death because of his own misdeed, his blood falls on his own head. The expression דמו בראשו is used in 1 Kgs 2:37, Josh 2:19a, and Ezek 33:4, where the offender, ignoring a warning, commited an act that subjects him to punishment, and in Josh 2:19b, where an explicit promise to protect certain individuals from death is not fulfilled and the responsibility is accepted by those who made the promise: here, the idea of clearly knowing that the act committed has made the one who acted subject to death. 1 Kgs 2:33 refers to the responsibility for murders where a royal command appears to have been ignored, more clearly for the death of Abner than for the death of Amasa (cf. 2 Sam 3:24–26). The phrase דמו על ראשו is used in 2 Sam 1:16, where the offender tells the king of his deed, for which the offender believes he will be rewarded, but the king decrees that the offender's own action and admission have condemned him to death, and in 1 Kgs 2:32 (דמו על ראשו), where the offender's own deeds have condemned him. The phrase דמיו בו is used in Lev 20:9, 11, 12, 13, 16, 27 and Ezek 18:13 to refer to a person's misdeed for which the punishment is death.

The concept that the blood of the victim has an objective existence provides the key to understanding why the avenger is called גאל הדם. The primary meaning of the verb גאל is "to restore."[13] Restoration constitutes the role of another figure in legal actions, the גאל, a close male relative who is obligated to reclaim land sold by a member of his extended family (Lev 25:25; Jer 32:7–8; Ruth 3:12; 4:3–4)[14] and to redeem a relative sold into slavery (Lev 25:47–49). He acts on behalf of a powerless person in the restoration of lost property. In the same manner, the victim's blood is lost and needs to

[12]H. Graf Reventlow, "Sein Blut komme über sein Haupt," *VT* 10 (1960), 311–327, and Klaus Koch, "Der Spruch 'Sein Blut Bleihe auf seinem Haupt' und die Israelitische Auffassung vom vergossenen Blut," *VT* 12 (1962), 396–416.

[13]Daube, "Lex Talionis," in *Studies in Biblical Law* (Cambridge: Cambridge University Press, 1969), 135.

[14]The title to the land was not retained by the redeemer but devolved to the original owner. Apparently in some cases, the redeemer purchased the property directly from the relative forced to sell it without the intermediate sale to a nonrelative (Jer 32:7–8; Ruth 3:12; 4:3–4). In Jer 32:7–8, Jeremiah assumed title to the land because he had both the right of inheritance and the right of redemption: In the end, he would have gained the title to the land. Contra Baruch Levine, "Late Language in the Priestly Source: Some Literary and Historical Observations," in *Proceedings of the Eighth World Congress of Jewish Studies, 1981, Panel Sessions: Bible Studies and Hebrew Language* (Jerusalem: World Union of Jewish Studies, 1983), 75.

be recovered.[15] The function of גאל הדם is to undo the unlawful spilling of his relative's blood by spilling the killer's blood. Blood in its capacity as a purifying agent removes the stain caused by the spilling of innocent blood, and when the killer is executed, the pollution is removed. Otherwise, the pollution persists.[16]

The use of two different titles raises the question of whether the redeemer, גאל, and the blood redeemer, גאל הדם, were one and the same person. It is likely that two titles indicate different people.[17] It appears to me that גאל is the superordinate category, of which גאל הדם is a subunit. If the גאל is the closest male relative, it would be reasonable to assume that גאל הדם is also the closest male relative, subject only to the physical strength necessary to fulfill the required task. The actual difference between the two, then, is the physical ability required of someone who must pursue and strike down the slayer. In a percentage of cases, the גאל has the capacity to act as גאל הדם; in others, another relative with the requisite characteristics must act as גאל הדם. While it is clear that the גאל is the closest relative – the story of Ruth and Boaz is based on the existence of a relative closer in degree than Boaz whose primacy must be respected – the avenger, by contrast, most likely arose from the family's consensus about which family member possessed the appropriate characteristics to pursue and strike down another person. The slayer would not meekly assent to be killed and would most likely fight back. גאל הדם had to undertake a duty that many would shy away from[18] and that many could not undertake. The existence of a special title for the גאל involved in remedying a homicide reflects the concern with the deleterious effects of spilled blood, the incurring of pollution. This גאל is given the special title of גאל הדם, the גאל for the blood whose spilling incurred pollution.

A threat of pollution is taken with great seriousness in the Bible. In the priestly tradition, the Day of Atonement is devoted to purging the sanctuary of impurity (Leviticus 16): The sanctuary requires decontamination from pollution created by bodily impurities and also from Israel's transgressions

[15] Daube, "Lex Talionis," in *Studies in Biblical Law,* 136.

[16] The implication of Num 35:33 is that execution of the killer is equivalent to purification. Cf. Jeffrey M. Tigay, *Deuteronomy* (The JPS Torah Commentary; Philadelphia: Jewish Publication Society, 1966), 473.

[17] Although, in fact, Num 35:12 refers to the גאל, not to גאל הדם.

[18] One author notes in his analysis of the machinations involved in constituting a vengeance group, as depicted in the Icelandic sagas, that most people tended to avoid being drafted and attempted to excuse themselves: "Vengeance, whether in its pure form or legitimated as the enforcement of an outlawry judgment, was a frightening prospect for avenger and wrongdoer alike. Vengeance-taking was no easy task; it involved many risks many were understandably reluctant to incur. Its difficulty and the thinly disguised averseness of avengers to undertake their grim duty is the main theme of a good portion of the saga corpus.... Settlements must have occasioned as many sighs of relief from reluctant avengers as from anxious wrongdoers and their kin" (Miller, *Bloodtaking and Peacemaking,* 299). In general, being an avenger was an unhappy business, not eagerly assumed.

penetrating the sphere of the sacred from afar.[19] The architecture of the rebuilt Temple in the vision of Ezekiel was adjusted from that of the old Temple in order to prevent ritual impurity from imperiling the new Temple: Huge gatehouses were to be built to protect the entrances, and two courtyards were to be constructed so that the laity could be banned from the inner courtyard, next to the Temple building itself.[20] In so doing, intruders would not be able to imperil the purity of the Temple.

The concept of impurity that affects ritual was extended to impurity that results from ethical violations.[21] "Ritual" impurity is incurred as a result of contact with any one of a number of natural processes and substances: the remains of dead animals (Lev 11:1–47), childbirth (Lev 12:1–8), scale disease (Lev 13:1–14:32), genital discharges (Lev 15:1–33), and human corpses (Num 19:1–22). Its effect is temporary and, in general, limited to the individual who incurred it. It is removed by bathing and by waiting for a certain amount of time to pass – a mild sanction. By contrast, "ethical" impurity is incurred by the committing of certain acts by an individual or individuals (Lev 18:24–29; 19:31; 20:1–3; Num 35:33–34; Deut 19:10). It has an effect on entities beyond the physical reach of the offense, whether the nation of Israel as a whole, the Land of Israel, or the sanctuary (Lev 18:25; 20:3; Ezek 5:11; 36:17). It desecrates without being in direct contact with the object of its desecration. Its defilement can only be removed by atonement, punishment, or exile. Ethical pollution is severe and, worse, dynamic: It is persistent, contagious, and difficult to remove.

The defiling effect of spilled blood extends beyond that of the victim's family and the duties of the blood redeemer. Homicide causes ethical pollution as well as ritual pollution.[22] It threatens the well-being of the entire

[19] Jacob Milgrom, "Israel's Sanctuary: The Priestly Picture of Dorian Gray," *RB* 83 (1976), 390–399. Baruch J. Schwartz argues that P does not hold that Israel's transgressions translate into actual defilement, whereas H and Ezekiel do. According to Schwartz, in P they do not metamorphose into defilement but infect the sanctuary in a process distinct from, though analogous to, defilement (Schwartz, "The Bearing of Sin," 17).

[20] Moshe Greenberg, "The Design and Themes of Ezekiel's Program of Restoration," *Int* 38 (1984), 192–193, 205–208. Moreover, before the Israelites can return to their land, they must be purified of both the ritual impurity and the ethical impurity that caused them to be expelled (Ezek 36:16–18, 22–25).

[21] Cf. David Z. Hoffman, *Das Buch Leviticus* (Berlin: M. Poppelauer, 1905–1906), 1.303–304; Tikva Frymer-Kensky, "Pollution, Purification, and Purgation in Biblical Israel," in *The Word of the Lord Shall Go Forth: Essays in Honor of David Noel Freedman in Celebration of his Sixtieth Birthday* (ed. Carol L. Meyers and M. O'Connor; Winona Lake, Indiana: Eisenbrauns, 1983), 399–414; Jonathan Klawans, "The Impurity of Immorality in Ancient Judaism," *JJS* 48 (1997), 1–16; Klawans, *Impurity and Sin in Ancient Judaism* (Oxford: Oxford University Press, 2000), 21–42.

[22] The idea that the blood of the victim polluted the slayer is attested in ancient Greece, but only Plato was moving in the direction of moralizing pollution. At the same time that Plato retained the concept of ritual pollution by prescribing that accidental killing required purification, he also held that the individual who used an agent to kill someone else was polluted in soul and

Israelite polity. It is the incentive for establishing the procedures to adjudicate homicide. The slayer offends not only against the victim and his family but also against God, who does not abide in a polluted place or among a polluted people. Even foreign lands, where God does not dwell, are turned into desolation because of bloodshed (Joel 4:19).

The fear of spreading pollution explains what happens to the accidental killer. According to Num 35:28, the accidental slayer is to remain in the city of refuge until the death of the high priest. If he is found to have killed accidentally, why should he be forced to remain in the city of refuge? Moshe Greenberg points out that the answer lies in the two aspects that the city of refuge has in Numbers 35.[23] It is both a refuge that protects the fugitive and a place of confinement that serves as exile. This is manifested in the technical term used in the Bible in connection to the cities of refuge, מקלט. The root of מקלט in rabbinic Hebrew means "to receive; to contain." The first meaning is the commonly used one: It is reflected in the role that the city of refuge played in protecting the killer from גאל הדם. The second meaning is also extant in the Hebrew Bible, where the root ק-ל-ט is used as an antonym to the root ש-ר-ע, "to extend"[24] in Lev 22:23. The word מקלט, therefore, may be rendered as "containment." These cities, therefore, can be understood as "confinement cities" or "prison cities."[25] This is not simply a formal exercise in philology – there is a profound difference between understanding עיר מקלט as "a refuge/sanctuary" or as "a prison." A מקלט possessed both aspects. Any killer of a human being, even accidentally, was considered guilty.[26] This is

must be dealt with exactly like the actual killer. In general in ancient Greece, the language of pollution was used to describe outrageous behavior – a misdeed made its perpetrator impure – but purification was not required. General cleanliness was required for formal, respectful behavior of any kind, whether making a sacrifice or speaking to an assembly. Homicide never incurred ethical pollution, despite the idea that pollution did not require direct contact to defile those with a connection to the dead. A death would make the relatives of the victim impure even if they were far away. When, for example, the news of a civil conflict in which 1,500 men were killed reached the Athenian assembly, a purification of the assembly was immediately carried out. Furthermore, the stain that affected a city or kingdom due to a homicide committed by its leader or one of its citizens was caused by two factors: 1) the anger of the victim and the avenging entities working on his behalf, and 2) the social isolation imposed on the killer and by extension on his associates. Neither one of these factors was defilement. Cf. Robert Parker, *Miasma: Pollution and Purification in Early Greek Religion* (Oxford: Clarendon, 1983), 5, 21, 35–36, 106–108, 112; Michael Gagarin, *Drakon and Early Athenian Homicide Law* (New Haven, Connecticut: Yale University Press, 1981), 17; Douglas M. MacDowell, *Athenian Homicide Law in the Age of the Orators* (Manchester: Manchester University Press, 1963), 145; S. C. Todd, *The Shape of Athenian Law* (Oxford: Clarendon, 1993), 140–141, 272, 274.

[23] Greenberg, "The Biblical Concept of Asylum," in *Studies in Bible and Jewish Thought,* 47.

[24] This meaning is also found in Lev 21:18; Isa 28:20.

[25] Sulzberger, *The Ancient Hebrew Law of Homicide,* 17.

[26] Greenberg, "The Biblical Conception of Asylum," 45. Even an accidental fall from a roof unprotected by a parapet incurred bloodguilt for the death, albeit on the building or household (Deut 22:8).

why he had to remain in the city of refuge, exiled from his ancestral home, family, and usual occupation. Num 35:27 explicitly states that the avenger does not incur bloodguilt if he strikes down the accidental killer outside of the city of refuge. The accidental killer is still guilty in some sense, and the blood avenger can kill him if he ventures out of the city of refuge. This idea is paralleled in other biblical texts.[27] Even Deuteronomy 19, with its concern for preventing the death of the fugitive before he reaches the city of refuge, does not regard the avenger who kills him on the way to the city of refuge to be culpable. If the city of refuge is not easily accessible, the community is responsible, not the blood avenger (Deut 19:10).

The accidental manslayer, while protected within the boundaries of the city of refuge, is still in danger if he ventures beyond them. He has to remain within the limits of the city of refuge in order to avoid meeting the blood avenger. Whether the accidental slayer waits inside the city of refuge for a short or a long period of time, the blood avenger might still be prepared to kill him. Indeed, Num 35:26–27 warns of this possibility.

If the accidental manslayer was to be confined to the city of refuge because of his guilt, why would it be possible for him to leave the city of refuge at all? Furthermore, if confinement was considered the proper punishment for accidental homicide, would not a fixed term be appropriate? A release based on the time of death of the high priest could vary greatly. The high priest might expire soon after the slayer was judged to be an accidental killer, and the killer would be freed after spending just a short time in the sanctuary. By contrast, another accidental killer might have to wait years before the high priest would die. To add to the mystery, generally a reprieve is granted at the accession of a leader, not his death; that a high priest's death should be the occasion of an amnesty is puzzling.[28]

[27]This concept is extended even further by rabbinic texts, which explicitly call the flight to a city of refuge גָלוּת, and which identify certain acts of accidental homicide as so guiltless as not to require flight to a city of refuge at all. See m. Makkot 2:1–2.

[28]Greenberg argues correctly that an amnesty extended at the death of a high priest is unusual because in general, amnesties occur at the accession of a king so that a new monarch could gain the favor of the populace ("The Biblical Conception of Asylum," 45). Generally, Mesopotamian kings proclaimed *mēšarum* decrees during their first year of rule, remitting specific types of debts and pecuniary obligations. They were not pardoning capital crimes. Cf. J. J. Finkelstein, "Ammiṣaduqa's Edict and the Babylonian 'Law Codes,'" *JCS* 15 (1961), 102. There is an exception to this, the reform of UruKAgina (Ukg. 4 xii 13–22 [= Ukg. 5 xi 20–29]; Piotr Steinkeller, "The Reform of UruKAgina and an Early Sumerian Term for 'Prison,'" *AuOr* 9 [1991], 227–233). This amnesty was promulgated at the beginning of UruKAgina's reign, ca. 2350 B.C.E., and included the release of a variety of offenders, including those who had committed homicide:

> The citizens of Lagash – the one who had lived in indebtedness, the one who had set up a [false] gur-measure [and] the one who had [improperly] filled [the accurate gur-measure] with barley, the thief, [and] the murderer – he swept their prison clean [of them and] established their freedom.

The answer lies in the status of the high priest. Many scholars have recognized the expiatory aspect of his death.[29] Only the high priest has the ability to purge guilt for others. Two examples may suffice as proof: 1) In Lev 4:13–21, he[30] makes expiation for the entire community. 2) The gold plate that the high priest wears on his forehead acts as expiation for the guilt the people incur (Exod 28:36–38).[31] The death of the high priest, whether soon upon the confinement of the accidental slayer or after many years, would serve as expiation for the killing. An animal sacrifice would not be sufficient. Only a human death can undo the killing of a human being, even if it is accidental. The accidental killer must remain in the city of refuge until the offense he has committed has been purged by the death of the high priest, who alone can expiate the guilt of others.[32] The stay of the accidental killer in the city of refuge has a cultic valence. According to Numbers 35, after the high priest's death, the accidental murderer is no longer pursued by גאל הדם, because the expiatory death of the high priest is accepted by גאל הדם.

Deuteronomy secularizes the stay of the accidental killer, a tendency that is already at work in Deuteronomy's conceptualization of the cities of refuge. There is no mention in Deut 19:1–9 of a requirement that the accidental killer be detained within the confines of the city. Yet the text does not specify that he can leave the refuge at all. Deut 19:6 identifies "the hot anger" of the blood avenger as the impetus for the fugitive's flight to the city of refuge. The implication, then, is that the accidental killer can depart when the anger of the blood avenger is appeased. S. R. Driver extrapolates from the specification of the emotions of the blood avenger that the length of the accidental killer's stay in the city of refuge depends entirely on the feelings of the blood avenger.[33] When the blood avenger calms down and reflects on what occurred, according to Driver, he will realize that it was only an accident and will no longer seek to kill the slayer. Of course, it is possible that the avenger's rage will never subside, and the accidental slayer will then be forced to remain in the city of refuge until the avenger dies or the slayer's own death.

Alexander Rofé argues that an emotional reconciliation is not sufficient.[34] After the emotions settle, he supposes, the city elders will arrange a monetary settlement. The accidental killer will not have to be concerned about the hot anger of the blood avenger once the victim's family is paid compensation. The victim's family has the power to allow the accidental slayer

[29]E.g., Erwin Merz, *Die Blutrache bei den Israeliten* (BWAT 20; Leipzig: J. C. Hinrich, 1916), 132; N. M. Nicolsky, "Das Asylrecht in Israel," 168–171.

[30]The term "anointed priest" is H's term for head priest. Cf. Lev 16:32.

[31]This concept is reflected in rabbinic sources. Cf. b. Makkot 11b.

[32]While ancient Greek culture held that the accidental killer incurred pollution, once he reached foreign soil he was purified without the need for an expiatory ritual (Parker, *Miasma,* 118).

[33]Driver, *Deuteronomy,* 232.

[34]Rofé, "History of the Cities of Refuge," 235.

freedom of movement. Although compensation is not explicitly mentioned in Deuteronomy, Rofé notes that it is assumed as part of the process of reconciliation in lesser degrees of unlawful death. Thus, ransom is explicitly preserved in the law of the goring ox, Exod 21:29–30, and the person who accidentally pushes a pregnant woman and causes harm in Exod 21:22 must pay a pecuniary mulct (as Rofé interprets the passage). The problem with Rofé's proof is that in these examples, a person redeeming himself by means of this payment is under the sentence of death. The accidental killer, by contrast, has not been sentenced to death. The implication of the other statutes on homicide is that victims' families were not permitted to take compensation at all. For Rofé to prove his claim, clearer evidence is required.

There is simply not enough evidence to fill in details about the fate of the accidental slayer according to Deuteronomy with one exception. Whatever happens to the killer according to Deuteronomy 19, he is not required to wait until the death of the high priest to leave the city of refuge. There is no religious element to his stay there. Deuteronomy and Numbers concur on the punishment of the accidental slayer, his being forced for a period of time to stay in a city of refuge, but disagree on the reason; they concur on the fate of the accidental killer, but vary on the reason for his fate and concomitantly the timing of his eventual release.

Deuteronomy as a whole evinces a general lack of interest in pollution and the sanctity of place and focuses on the holiness of the people.[35] The statutes on homicide in Deuteronomy 19 display, therefore, two concerns: 1) insuring that the intentional killer is put to death so that the evil is removed from the midst of the Israelites; and 2) protecting the accidental homicide from being killed so that his innocent blood is not spilled, imperiling the Israelites yet again.

At the same time, the polluting effects of blood itself are not ignored in Deuteronomy.[36] The rite of the elimination of bloodguilt mandated by Deut 21:1–9 reflects the perception that the blood of the victim has a physical reality that must be removed, as well as the concept that a slaying could pollute those in whose midst it occurred. The blood must be removed ritually because the killer cannot be found and executed, the usual method of elimination:

> 1 If, in the land which the LORD your God is giving to you, a corpse is found lying in open country, and it is not known who struck him

[35] Weinfeld argues that the distinction between P and D in this regard is that P is theocentric and D is anthropocentric (*Deuteronomy and the Deuteronomic School,* 189), while Eyal Regev contends that for P, holiness is dynamic and, therefore, impurity is also dynamic, in contrast to D, for which holiness is a static quality ("Priestly Dynamic Holiness and Deuteronomic Static Holiness," *VT* 51 [2001], 243–261). They are both approaching the same phenomena from different directions, illuminating different aspects of P and D.

[36] This concept is also the basis for the stipulation that the corpse of an executed criminal should not be left exposed overnight (Deut 21:23).

down, [2]your elders and judges shall go out and measure the distance
from the corpse to the surrounding towns. [3]The elders of the town
nearest to the corpse shall take a heifer which has never been worked
and has never pulled a yoke, [4]and the elders of that town shall bring
the heifer down to an ever-flowing/perennial wadi which has not been
tilled or sown and shall break the neck of the heifer in the wadi. [5]The
priests, the sons of Levi, shall come forward, for the LORD your God
has chosen them to minister to him and to bless in his name, and every
lawsuit and physical affliction is subject to their ruling. [6]All the elders
of the town nearest to the corpse shall wash their hands over the heifer
whose neck was broken in the wadi. [7]They shall solemnly declare:
"Our hands did not shed this blood nor did our eyes witness [it].
[8]Make expiation, LORD, for your people Israel whom you redeemed,
and do not allow innocent blood to remain amidst your people Israel,
and let the blood be expiated." [9]Thus, you will remove innocent
blood from your midst, for you will be doing what is right in the eyes
of the LORD.

When the animal is killed in an uncultivated area and the elders wash their hands of the blood, this act relocates the blood to an area far from human concern.[37] The drainage of the blood into the perpetually flowing brook, carrying the blood away, removes the blood even farther.[38] Washing hands is a sign of innocence,[39] and by so doing the elders demonstrate the community's blamelessness. The ceremony is undertaken because the expiation cannot be gained from executing the killer. The community nearest the spot where the corpse was found must undo the defilement and establish that it is not responsible for the crime. The representatives of the community perform the rite on its behalf in order to remove the blood and the bloodguilt. The killing of the animal is a ritual reenactment of the slaying in a place where the defilement will be least harmful.[40]

As we have seen, the biblical term, גאל הדם, manifests anxiety over the polluting effects of the blood itself. Biblical law extends the contamination of the victim's blood by conceiving of it as polluting the Israelite people or

[37]Cf. David P. Wright, "Deuteronomy 21:1–9 as a Rite of Elimination," *CBQ* 49 (1987), 387–403.

[38]The same concept is assumed by Mic 7:19 – when sins are cast into the depths of the sea, they are disposed of.

[39]Cf. Pss 26:6 and 73:13. By washing their hands over the animal after it is killed, the elders are formally displaying their innocence, not transferring their guilt to the animal. In rituals in which guilt is conveyed to an animal, such as sending a goat to Azazel (Leviticus 16), the washing of hands is done before the animal is slaughtered.

[40]Tigay, *Deuteronomy*, 472–475; Wright, "Deuteronomy 21:1–9," 393–399. Ziony Zevit, "The ʿEglâ Ritual of Deuteronomy 21:1–9," *JBL* 95 (1976), 377–390, discusses reconstructions of the pre-Israelite ritual on which the Deuteronomic ritual may have been based.

the Land of Israel. The stain is removed by blood in its capacity as purifying agent: The intentional killer is executed, and the accidental killer must wait until the death of the high priest for his release from the city of refuge. Even Deuteronomy, with its tendency toward secularization, mandates that the community in which an unsolvable slaying has occurred must perform a ritual to wash away the blood.

The Mesopotamian material contains a pale reflection of the concern with the damaging effects of the victim's blood. In ABL 753, r. 5, a petitioner implores the king not to ignore the blood of his murdered subjects:

> rev.
> [1]. . . [2]$^{I\,d}$30-ib-ni i-na me-x-x-x [3]ša UNUG^{ki} ^{lú}UNUG^{ki}-a-a i-du-ku [4]ù ḫu-bu-us-su-nu iḫ-bu-tu LUGAL be-lí-a [5]da-mu ša IR^{meš}-šu la ú-maš-ša$_8$-ar ŠÀ-ú [6]a-ga-nim-ma šad-da-giš $^{I\,d}$30-ib-ni [7]^{lú}URIM^{ki}-a-a ki-i i-du-ku man-ma [8]a-na UGU LUGAL be-lí-ia ul ú-šak-ši-du [9]ù ^{lú}NUN^{ki}-ú-a ki-i i-du-ku [10]man-ma-a-ma a-na LUGAL be-lí-a ul iq-bi [11]ù en-na ^{lú}UNUG^{ki}-a-a id-du-uk [12]LUGAL be-lí-a di-i-ni ša URU-šu ù ša ÌR^{meš}-šu [13]li-pu-uš a-na LUGAL be-lí-ia [14][al-tap]-ra LUGAL be-lí-a lu-ú i-di
>
> [2–5]Sin-ibni in the . . . of Uruk has killed the people of Uruk and plundered their goods. Let the king, my lord, not ignore the blood of his servants. [6–10]When sometime ago Sin-ibni killed the people of Ur, no one informed the king, my lord, and when he killed the people of Sippar, no one told the king, my lord. [11–14]Now, he has killed the people of Uruk. May the king my lord render justice for his city and his servants. I have sent [this message] to the king my lord so that the king my lord may know.

In ADD 321, the delivery of the compensation "washes away the blood." On rare occasions, a person is described as being "polluted with blood," *ina damê ballu*,[41] but it is not clear that this individual is even a killer:

> ARM III 18
> [1]a-na be-lí-ia [2]qí-bí-ma [3]um-ma ki-ib-ri-^{d}da-gan [4]ÌR-ka-a-ma [5]a-wa-tam mi-im-ma le-mu-ut-ta-am eš-me [6]li-ib-bi ma-di-iš iḫ-ḫi-id [7]a-ša-ar s[u-q]í-im ša-a-tu ša ^{d}da-gan [8]ú-ḫa-al-la-q[ú-š]u ṣa-bu-um i-ṣú-um [9]ú-u[l i]ṣ-ṣa-ab-ba-at [10]ṣa-bu-um [m]a-du-um-ma iṣ-ṣa-ab-ba-at [11]ù i-[na-an-na] LÚ b[e-e]l [a]r-nim [12]ša i-na [da-m]i-im ša-a-[t]u [13]ba-al-lu-ma [14]mu-ṣí-šu i-sà-aḫ-ḫu-ru [15]ù ki-ma UR.DÚR ša-gi-[e-em] [16]a-ša-ar i-na-aš-ša-ku ú-ul i-de [17]i-na-an-na as-[s]ú-ur-ri [18]be-lí i-ḫa-am-mu-uṭ-ma iš-tu é-kál-lim [19]a-na zu-qí-im it-t[a]-ṣí [20]a-di ṣa-ba-am šu-nu-ti be-lí l[a ú-s]à-an-ni-qu-ma [21]a-ia-bi-šu ù le-em-ni-[š]u

[41] See Bauer Asb. 71 (Theodore Bauer, *Das Inschriftenwerk Assurbanipals* [Leipzig: J. C. Hinrichs, 1933], 71:13), *ša ina ÚŠ.MEŠ asakku ballu.*

> [22]a-na ša-pa-al še-pí-šu [23]la iš-ku-nu-ma ù ka-la-šu-nu [24]a-na ne-pa-ri-im la ú-še-ri-bu [25]UD 3 KAM UD 4 KAM [26]b[e-lí i-na] li-ib-bi é-kál-li-šu [27]la uṣ-ṣí
>
> [1–4]To my lord, say: Thus says Kibri-Dagan, your servant. [5–10]I have heard about an evil affair, and my heart is troubled. Wherever that street [may be] which Dagan will destroy, not a small troop but a large troop should be taken prisoner. [11–16]And now, that criminal who was polluted with that blood is looking around to make his escape, and like a vicious dog, I do not know where he will bite [next]. [17–19]Now, certainly my lord will wish to leave the palace in a hurry. [20–27]As long as my lord does not put pressure on that troop, and [as long as] he has not brought his enemies and those who wish him evil into submission and has not put all of them into the workhouse, my lord must not leave his palace for 3 or 4 days.

It is equally possible that this refers to actual bloodshed or is a vivid description of a vicious offender.

There are a number of other references that might refer to the defilement caused by bloodshed, but it must be acknowledged that these references are oblique. A text from the El-Amarna archive, from the fourteenth century B.C.E., EA 8, refers to "returning the blood." In this letter, Burnaburiyash II, the Kassite king of Babylonia (Karaduniyash), dispatches a letter to Naphu'rureya (Amenophis IV/Akhenaten), the king of Egypt, demanding action on behalf of Babylonian merchants who have been killed in Canaan, an area under Egyptian rule. Burnaburiyash II offers two reasons: One is that the blood of the victims must be returned. Another text, CCT IV 30a, from the Old Assyrian period, declares that since the king in question has spilled blood, his throne is unstable:

> [1]a-na i-na-a qí-bi-ma [2]um-ma e-la-ni-ma iš-tu [3]a-li-kà-ni i-dí-ku-bu-um [4]ù ILLAT-sú U-tum ša ḫa-ḫi-im [5]ù a-na-ku a-na É.GAL-lim [6]ni-ta-na-li-ma ru-ba-ú [7]ki-ma i-ta-pu-lim i-ta-na-[pu]-lu-ni-a-ti [8]a-ma me-eḫ-ra-at [9]ma-mì-tim ša [ú-bí-lu-ni-a-tí-ni [10]a-na kà-ri-im lá-pu-ta-nim [11]ù ší-[pá-ar]-ni im-gu$_5$-ur-šu-nu-ma [12]a-wi-lu-ú i-ta-ba-al-ku-tù [13][LUGAL] da-me e-ta-pá-áš-ma [14]ku-sí-šu lá ta-aq-na-at [15]ší-ik-na-tum a-ḫu-ra [16][ru]-ba-ú i-na ba-ri-šu-nu [17][i]-ta-ṭù-lu a-bi a-ta [18]be-li a-ta ki-ma [19]DUB-pá-am ká-ru-um [20]iš-me-ú-ni mu-ḫu-ur-šu [21]té-ir-ti kà-ri-im [22]ù té-ir-ta-kà li-li-kam-ma [23]lá tal-kam a-ma-kam-ma [24]ta-ta-wa [. . .]-ma a-dá-[šu] [25]e-lá-[. . .]-id [26]a-na-ku a-na [. . .]-šu-[a] [27]ù a-di u$_4$-[me-im a-ni-im] [28]na-ak-zu-tí-ia [. . .] [29]a-ni-tám aḫ-[ta]-aḫ-[bi$_4$ . . .] [30]a-ta a-lá-[. . .]-kà ma-[. . .] [31]i-šu u$_4$-me-e ma-ší-[. . .] [32]a-ta-ša-ab a-na kà-ri-[im] [33]lá tal-kam-ma . . . [illegible]

> [1–7] To Ina say: Thus said Elani, When I came here, Idi-Kubum and his colleagues, the ten-men committee of Ḫaḫḫum, and I kept going up to the palace. Instead of answering directly, the princes repeatedly answered evasively. [8–11] Here is a copy of the oath which they brought us for writing down in the kârum and [concerning which] our envoy satisfied them. [12] The citizens have revolted. [13–14] [The king] has spilled blood and therefore his throne is unstable. [15–17] Conditions are worsening. The princes are conspiring[?] among themselves. [17–18] You are my father. You are my lord. [18–23] When the kârum has read the tablet, make an appeal to it. Let the advice of the kârum and your advice come to me. Do not come! You should talk it over there [at Kanish]. [24–29] . . . I shall give him [it] . . . I to [. . .]-shua and to [this day] my finances . . . this . . . [30–32] As for you . . . I will stay here for half a day. [32–33] Take heed of what the kârum [advises you]. . . . Do not come! . . .

This claim seems to be akin to the Israelite concept of spilled blood polluting. However, it is equally possible that this reference does not refer to pollution at all but to the general state of revolt. And even if these vague references do refer to defilement incurred by a homicide, the pollution affects only the slayer.[42] The possible defilement from a slaying is never extended to the entire country.

In a possible parallel to the rite in Deut 21:1–9, the Hittite laws contain provisions regarding a corpse found in a field when the killer presumably cannot be identified:

> HL 6
> If a person, man or woman, is killed in another[?] city, [the victim's heir] shall deduct 12,000 square meters [= 3 acres] from the land of the person on whose property the person was killed and shall take it for himself.
>
> Late version of 6
> If a man is found killed on another person's property, if he is a free man, [the property owner] shall give his property, house and 60 shekels of silver. But if [the dead person] is a woman, [the property owner] shall give [no property, but] 120 shekels of silver. But if [the place where the dead body was found] is not [private] property, but open uncultivated country, they shall measure 3 DANNA's in all directions, and whatever village is determined [to lie within that

[42] Another reference might be found in CT 51 147 24 (transliterated and translated in Erica Reiner, "A Manner of Speaking," in *Zikir šumim: Assyriological Studies Presented to F. Kraus* [Leiden: Nederlands Instituut voor het Nabije Oosten 5, 1982], 282–289): "If he keeps turning his head, he is polluted with blood." Toorn suggests that restless movements of the head were associated with the expression that blood(guilt) comes back upon the head of the perpetrator (*Sin and Sanction,* 159, n. 50).

radius], he shall take those very [inhabitants of the village].[43] If there is no village, [the heir of the deceased] shall forfeit [his claim].

The law is concerned solely with determining who must pay compensation. Indeed, the extraordinarily high penalty for a slaying in the vicinity of a village – the confiscation of the entire village – may have been intended to prevent the inhabitants of the village from shielding their own.[44] In sharp contrast to the prescription in Deut 21:1–9, no rite of purification is mandated.

The same concern with providing compensation for the victim when the killer has not been apprehended is found in a statute in the Laws of Hammurapi:

24
If a life [is lost during a robbery for which the robber is not arrested], the city and governor shall pay 60 shekels of silver to his kinsman.

LH 24 provides for a case in which the killer has not been arrested when a person has been killed in the course of a robbery. The city and governor must pay sixty shekels to the victim's kinsmen if the robber is not arrested. It appears that the communal authorities must discharge the obligation to the family against whom the act of killing was perpetrated.[45] Once again, the only concern is a financial one – there is no concern with pollution.

CTH 172, a letter from the Hittite emperor in response to the Babylonian king's demand that those who killed Babylonian merchants in areas under Hittite hegemony be executed, contains an ambiguous reference to purification:

rev.
15 [. . .] a-ka-an-na ta-aš-pu-ra um-ma-a ^{lú}DAM.GÀR.MEŠ-ia i-na ^{kur}a-mur-ri ^{kur}ú-ga-ri-it 16 [ù i-na ^{kur} . . . i-du]-uk-ku i-na ^{kur}ḫa-at-ti na-pu-ul-ta ú-ul i-du-uk-ku 17 [šum-ma i-na ^{kur}ḫa-at-ti na]-pu-ul-ta i-du-uk-ku šúm-ma LUGAL i-ši-im-me a-na a-ma-ti ša-a-ši 18 [. . . d]a-i-ka-na ša na-pu-ul-ti i-ṣa-ab-ba-tu$_4$-ma a-na ŠEŠ.MEŠ ša di-ki 19 [. . . KUG.BABBAR a-na] mu-ul-le-e ša ^{lú}di-ki ŠEŠ.MEŠ-šú i-le-eq-qu-ú ù ^{lú}da-i-ka-na 20 [. . . aš]-ra ša na-pu-ul-tu$_4$ i-na ŠÀ-šú di-ku ul-la-lu ù šúm-ma ŠEŠ.MEŠ-šú 21 [KUG.BABBAR mu-ul-le]-e ú-ul i-maḫ-ḫa-ru da-i-ka-na ša na-pu-ul-ti 22 [. . . l]i-pu-šu šúm-ma LÚ ša ḫi-tá a-na LUGAL i-ḫa-ṭu a-na KUR-ti ša-na-ti-ma 23 [. . .] ù a-na

[43] It is unlikely that this could be translated as "he shall take those very same payments [from inhabitants of the village]." Cf. Hoffner, *The Laws of the Hittites,* 173–174, n. 8, and Hoffner, "On Homicide in Hittite Law," 303–305.

[44] Hoffner, *The Laws of the Hittites,* 174.

[45] See Samuel Greengus, "Legal and Social Institutions of Ancient Mesopotamia," CANE, 469–470.

da-a-ki ú-ul par-ṣu ŠEŠ-ia ša-'a-al-ma liq-bu-ni-ik-ku [24] [. . . a]-ka-an-na ša EN ḫé-ṭi-i la-a i-du-uk-ku ^{lú}DAM.GÀR i-du-uk-ku [25] [. . . L]Ú sú-ba-ri-i a-i-ka-a i-di šúm-ma i-du-uk-ku-ma i-na-an-na ŠEŠ.MEŠ DAM.GÀR.MEŠ di-ku-ti [26] [šup-ra]-am-ma di-in-sú-nu lu-mur

[15–17] Since you wrote to me as follows: "My merchants are being killed in the land of Amurru, the land of Ugarit, [and the land of . . .]." They do not kill [as punishment] in Hatti . . . they kill. [17–18] If the king hears about it, [they investigate] that matter. They arrest the killer and deliver him to the brothers of the slain man. [19] If his brothers accept the silver as compensatory payment, [they allow] the killer [to go free]. [20] The place in which the killing occurred is purified [?]. [20–22] If his brothers do not accept the silver as the compensatory payment, they may make the killer [their slave].[46] [22–24] If a man who has committed an offense against the king escapes to another land, killing him is not permitted. Inquire, my brother, and they shall tell you thus. Now, if they do not kill an offender [against the king], would they kill a merchant? [25–26] [But in regard to] the Subareans, how am I to know if they are killing people? Now send me the brothers of the dead merchants so that I can investigate their lawsuit.

It is possible to render the phrase *[. . . aš]-ra ša na-pu-ul-tu_4 i-na ŠÀ-šú di-ku ul-la-lu* in line 20 as a command that the place in which the slaying occurred should be purified. However, it can also be understood as an order to take an oath. Harry A. Hoffner, Jr., suggests that the guilt or innocence of the inhabitants of the place is determined by whether they exonerate themselves by taking an oath.[47] This is a possibility because in Hittite, *parkunu-*, "to purify," can be understood in three distinct meanings: in the sense of cleaning something normally, in a ritual sense, and in a judicial sense of exonerating or proving innocent.

We have already noted that there is a striking contrast between Mesopotamia and the biblical materials in regard to certain technical terms for the parties involved in remedying the homicide. The Bible refers to גאל הדם, the blood redeemer, whereas the Mesopotamian documents refer to *bēl damê,* a term that can refer either to the slayer or to the claimant from the

[46]This rendering follows that of Gary Beckman (*Hittite Diplomatic Texts* [ed. Harry A. Hoffner, Jr.; SBL Writings from the Ancient World 7; Atlanta: Scholars Press, 1996], 136), and Horst Klengel ("Mord und Bussleistung im Spätbronzezeitlichen Syrien," in *Death in Mesopotamia,* 190). Albertine Hagenbuchner suggests "they give to them the killer," (*Die Korrespondenz der Hethiter* [Texte der Hethiter 16; Heidelberg: Carl Winter, 1989], 2.292), but it is unclear whether she means that the killer is executed or reduced to slavery.

[47]"Homicide in Hittite Law," in *Crossing Boundaries and Linking Horizons: Studies in Honor of Michael C. Astour on His 80th Birthday* (ed. Gordon D. Young, Mark W. Chavalas, and Richard E. Averbeck; Bethesda, Maryland: CDL Press, 1997), 305.

victim's family, as was discussed in the appendix to Chapter Two. The biblical term is unambiguous, the Mesopotamian term ambiguous. The fact that the term *bēl damê*, "the owner of the blood," can refer to both reflects the shared responsibility manifest in the Mesopotamian process and does not reflect a preoccupation with the contaminating effects of the victim's spilled blood.

Blood, in Mesopotamian thought, was not thought to be a cleansing substance. In the myth of Atrahasis, the gods purify themselves in water, a rite instituted by Enki – they do not purify themselves by the blood of the slain god, the god later used to fashion human beings.[48] After the killing, all the gods must bathe: It is more than the splattering of the blood that must be washed off. The defilement associated with the killing must be removed, even though the chief culprit has deservedly been put to death. Blood was a polluting substance and, therefore, even a lawful execution required the gods to purify themselves. The polluting effect of blood makes clear why the Mesopotamians acknowledged the need for purification. The inability of blood to purify enables the term *bēl damê*, the owner of the blood, to apply to either the slayer or the claimant from the victim's family.

It may be speculated that the Mesopotamians did not extend the polluting effects of the victim's blood to apply to a country as a whole or nation as a whole for three reasons.[49] First, impurity in Mesopotamia was of demonic origin.[50] A person who sinned or was under a sorcerer's spell became susceptible to the onslaught of demons. The goal of purification rituals was to exorcise demons and send them back to their proper homes. Committing a sin did not cause any violation of pure space, as it did in biblical thought. Committing a sin did allow a human being to come under the power of a demon and the impurity that accompanied the demon.[51]

[48] William L. Moran, "The Creation of Man in Atraḫasis I 192–248," *BASOR* 200 (1970), 51.

[49] A group has financial responsibility in the interterritorial law of the ancient Near East, but in the Hebrew Bible, there is group responsibility for the ceremony only. See the analysis of communal responsibility in Chapter Seven.

[50] For example, in the Šurpu rituals, tablet VII describes an attack of demons on a man whose god has withdrawn from him and who therefore needs to be purified, and tablets V–VI characterize a man's plight as "an evil curse like a *gallû*-demon has come upon this man" (Erica Reiner, *Šurpu: A Collection of Sumerian and Akkadian Incantations* [*AfO* Beiheft 11; Graz: n.p., 1958]). Cf. Wright, *The Disposal of Impurity,* 248–249; H. W. F. Saggs, *The Greatness That Was Babylon* (New York: Hawthorn, 1962), 302–318; Karl Frank, *Lamashtu, Pazuzu und andere Dämonen* (Leipzig: Otto Harrassowitz, 1941); Oppenheim, *Ancient Mesopotamia,* 180, 199–206; R. Campbell Thompson, *The Demons and Evil Spirits of Babylonia* (London: Luzac and Co., 1903), 1. 48–49, 75, 79, 103; Toorn, *Sin and Sanction,* 117–154; Milgrom, *Leviticus 1–16,* 1071–1079; E. Jan Wilson, *"Holiness" and "Purity" in Mesopotamia* (AOAT 237; Kevelaer: Butzon und Bercker; Neukirchen-Vluyn: Neukirchener, 1994), 45, 68–78.

[51] A god did have to be pure in order to exercise his divine functions. Cf. the statement of Ereshkigal after she has intercourse with Erra in the myth of Nergal and Ereshkigal: "I am

Second, in biblical thought, impurity had an effect on national institutions and concerns because the Israelites conceived of themselves as a holy people. The concept of ethical pollution made the defiling effects of spilled blood a grave threat to that status. Therefore, the rituals meant to offset the damage of impurity had a common goal, to remove pollution from the Israelite body politic. This concept shaped the disposal of ritual impurity. Mesopotamian and Hittite rituals used numerous means to dispose of impurity – burial, sealing in containers, throwing in sea or river, sending to and depositing in foreign lands, burning – whereas the Priestly sources used a limited repertoire. The reason for this is clear – the nonbiblical rites have no common goal, whereas the Priestly rites in the Hebrew Bible have a single common goal – to protect the sanctuary's holiness and the community's purity.[52] Even Deuteronomy with its secularizing tendencies mandates a rite to safeguard the community from the deleterious effects of spilled blood. In contrast, the well-being of the sanctuary is protected in the Mesopotamian *akītu* festival, the well-being of society is protected in the Hittite plague rituals, and the well-being of the suffering patient is protected in the Mesopotamian purification rituals with no larger social goal. Impurity in P is solely impersonal, with no connection to the underworld, nor does impurity have any connection to mythology.

Third, the Mesopotamian pantheon was remote for the average worshiper. An individual's religious sentiment was focused on his personal gods.[53] In contrast, the single Israelite God claimed the exclusive adoration of both individual and nation.[54] Therefore, the action of a single individual could imperil all. The effect of sin was limited to an individual in Mesopotamia, whereas sin could have an impact on an entire nation in ancient Israel.

While the biblical concepts of pollution retained the valence of defilement, the language of purification was utilized in Mesopotamia in the legal realm without any miasma attached. The verbs *zakû*, "to become clean; to become free from specific claims or obligations,"[55] and *ebēbu*, "to become purified; D to clear a person from legal claims,"[56] refer to freedom from legal claims.

sexually defiled, I am not pure, I cannot execute the judgment of the great gods" (O. R. Gurney, "The Sultantepe Tablets VII: The Myth of Nergal and Ereshkigal," *AnSt* 10 [1960], 122, ll. 7′ and 23′) and the description: "The pure god who is suited for kingship" (W. G. Lambert, "The Gula Hymn of Bullutsa-rabi," *Or* 36 [1967], 127, l.157).

[52] Wright, *The Disposal of Impurity*, 273–274.

[53] Thorkild Jacobsen, *The Treasures of Darkness* (New Haven, Connecticut: Yale University Press, 1976), 155–164.

[54] Toorn, *Sin and Sanction*, 4–5, 114. Even though a personal god for a Mesopotamian could be one of the great cosmic powers, like Shamash or Sîn, the relationship remained on the level of an individual and a god and was never extended to an entire nation.

[55] Cf. CAD/Z, 25–28.

[56] Cf. CAD/E, 4–6.

Just as a purified person was freed from the control of demons, a person purified in the legal sense was freed from obligations. Obstructions, whether demons or debts, were removed.

The divergence between biblical and Mesopotamian conceptualizations of homicide is not surprising. Cultures living in close proximity to one another can understand a legal issue differently. Let a New World example suffice. Although the Comanche and the Cheyenne Indians of the North American plains were neighbors, their treatment of homicide differed greatly.[57] The Comanche strongly held to the belief that only a killing could redress a killing. They did not distinguish between types of killing – even the blood avenger could be killed by the offender's kin. At the same time, this belief meant that only the actual killer was affected by the deed and only he could be dispatched in revenge. Homicide was a secular affair. The Cheyenne, in contrast to their neighbors the Comanche, did conceive of a religious effect of law, although it was limited to homicide. Homicide was a sin: It polluted the killer, the tribal sacred objects, and the well-being of the tribe as a whole. Disgrace befell all the Cheyenne when a murder occurred. They would have difficulty finding food. Game would disappear. Even war fell under the pall. The chiefs, whose authority devolved from the sacred, had jurisdiction over homicide, whereas the military associations, really men's clubs, solved other disputes.[58] The rest of Cheyenne law was secular.

The Israelites may have even been aware of the difference between their law and the law of other people. In 2 Sam 21:1–14, the Gibeonites demand Saul's sons as recompense for Saul's extermination of the Gibeonites:

> [1]There was a famine in the days of David for three years, year after year. David inquired of the LORD, and the LORD said, "There is bloodguilt on Saul and on his house because he put the Gibeonites to death." [2]The king summoned the Gibeonites and said to them – now, the Gibeonites were not Israelites but were a remnant of the Amorites, with whom the Israelites made an oath, but Saul sought to wipe them out on account of his zeal for the people of Israel and Judah. [3]David said to them, "What shall I do for you? How shall I make expiation so that you bless the LORD's portion?" [4]The Gibeonites said to him, "We cannot have any claim on silver or gold with Saul or his house nor can we have any claim to put to death any person in Israel." He replied, "Whatever you say, I will do for you." [5]They [then] said to the king, "The man who consumed us and planned to destroy us so

[57] Hoebel, *The Law of Primitive Man,* 156–169.

[58] Hoebel speculates that the Cheyenne originally had a sacred conception of homicide (*The Law of Primitive Man,* 263). Then, in the course of establishing sacred tribal objects, the Cheyenne utilized the idea of pollution to stamp out feud. Hoebel singles out the Cheyenne for their creativity in fashioning such an effective end that so many other peoples at their level of social and economic development missed.

> that we should have no place in the territory of Israel – [6]let seven of
> his sons be given to us and we will impale them before the LORD in
> Gibeah of Saul, chosen of the LORD." The king replied, "I will do so."
> [7]The king had compassion on Mephiboshet son of Jonathan son of
> Saul because of the oath of the LORD that was between them, between
> David and Jonathan son of Saul. [8]The king took Armoni and Mephi-
> boshet, the two sons that Rizpah daughter of Aiah bore for Saul, and
> the five sons of Michal daughter of Saul whom she bore for Adriel
> son of Barzillai the Meholathite. [9]He gave them to the Gibeonites;
> they impaled them on the mountain before the LORD, and all seven
> died together. They were put to death in the first days of the harvest,
> the beginning of the barley harvest. [10]Rizpah daughter of Aiah took
> sackcloth and spread it on a rock for herself from the beginning of the
> harvest until rain fell upon them from the sky: she did not allow the
> birds of the sky to rest upon them or the beasts of the field by night.
> [11]David was told what Rizpah daughter of Aiah, concubine of Saul,
> had done. [12]David went and took the bones of Saul and the bones of
> Jonathan his son from the citizens of Jabesh-Gilead, who stole them
> from the square of Beth-Shean, where the Philistines had hung them
> when the Philistines had struck down Saul at Gilboa. [13]He brought
> up the bones of Saul and the bones of Jonathan his son from there and
> gathered the bones of those who had been impaled. [14]They buried
> the bones of Saul and of Jonathan his son in the territory of Benjamin
> in Zela, in the tomb of Kish his father. They did everything the king
> commanded. Thereafter God accepted prayers for the land.

The king asks the Gibeonites how the defilement could be expiated, assuming that the killings incurred pollution. The Gibeonites' diplomatic suggestion that they could not demand compensation from any Israelite or the death of any Israelite indicates that they would accept either as the just punishment for the deaths of their fellow countrymen. Understanding the hint, the Israelite king indicates to the Gibeonites that he will agree to whichever penalty they prefer. The writer of the story, in formulating the negotiating positions, assumes that the Israelites conceived of homicide as defiling while the non-Israelites (in this case, the Gibeonites) do not and would accept either monetary payment or execution (albeit in the end, they prefer the death of those associated with the culprit).[59] Although we do not know what the

[59]McKeating argues that the Israelites put curbs on blood feud under the influence of a Canaanite sacral conception of homicide ("The Development of the Law on Homicide in Ancient Israel," 46–68). According to McKeating, the Gibeonites as well as the rest of the Canaanites already had a sacral conception of homicide, regarding it as a pollution of the land, a defilement to be expiated. Therefore, the Gibeonites rejected monetary payment, even though they were aware that this was the Israelite way. The Canaanite conception inspired the Israelites to assume a sacral conception of homicide. In order for the defilement to be expiated their way,

neighbors of the Israelites actually thought, in the mind of the writer of this biblical story the Israelites conceived of homicide differently. This is even the case here, which reflects a characteristic of political killings, in which those who have not killed but who are associated with the killer are liable to be executed.

Both in Mesopotamian texts and in the Bible, the spilled blood itself was perceived to have a real existence that was dangerous and needed to be remedied. However, only in the Bible was it conceived to affect more than the killer himself. The nation as a whole or the land of Israel would be contaminated. In contrast, in Mesopotamia, there was no indication that the larger community need be concerned about possible contamination from the spilled blood. The references to the victim's blood in Mesopotamian texts indicate that the spilled blood is conceived to have a concrete existence of its own that requires the attention of the parties involved, but no one else.

the Gibeonites in fact asked for a sacrifice (2 Sam 21:4–6) but worded it in such a way as to allow their demand to be interpreted as a killing for a killing. However, this seems to be what David is doing. McKeating's explanation would work if the Gibeonites had used David's words and David had used their words. The Israelites assumed a sacral conception of homicide, not the Canaanites. McKeating has the polarities reversed: It is David who represents the "older" sacral conception of homicide, and the Gibeonites the monetary.

CHAPTER FIVE

Typologies of Homicide

IN THE story of Cain and Abel, an omniscient narrator explores Cain's responsibility for Abel's death by constructing conversations between God and Cain, in which God explains the capricious and potent impulse to murder and Cain reacts to God's reference to Abel and to the declaration of his punishment. In contrast, three biblical legal texts, Exod 21:12–14, Num 35:9–34, and Deut 19:1–13, analyze the responsibility of the killer by extrapolating the intent of the killer from the manner of killing or from the prior relationship between victim and murderer. They do not have the luxury of omniscience as does the author of Genesis 4.

These three legal texts manifest the intent to articulate more precisely and accurately a distinction between intentional and unintentional killing.[1] They provide conflicting typologies of homicide, probably for two interrelated reasons: 1) Without direct access to a person's thoughts, it is fiendishly

[1] In modern Western society, premeditated homicide is taken as the gravest offense, much more than intentional homicide without prior planning. Yet it is doubtful whether it is better for society to contain members who fly into a murderous rage without premeditation than members who, taking their time to devise a plan, might lose interest in carrying out the slaying or who might be discovered and prevented from carrying out their plan. In any case, in contemporary American law, premeditation, the length of time spent in prior thought, has been eroded to include the shortest possible duration necessary to design a plan. See Joshua Dressler, *Understanding Criminal Law* (2d edition; Legal Text Series; n.p.: Richard D. Irwin, 1995), 474.

difficult to know what he intended; and 2) although the positing of ground rules is easy, the difficulty comes in applying these rules to actual persons and events. At the same time, the legal texts share the principle that only intentional killing by direct action is culpable, and they divide acts of homicide into two categories, one for which the penalty is death and the other for which it is not.

Accidental homicide is defined in Exod 21:12–14 as "if [the killer] did not do it by design, but God caused it to meet his hand" (Exod 21:13). The connection is made between what a person does with his hands and what occurred. Similarly, Hittite Laws 3–4[2] characterizes accidental homicide as "only his hand is at fault,"[3] making a distinction between the action of the offender with his hand and the intention of the offender in the seat of his intellect. There is thus a qualitative difference between an act and a physical event. Legal responsibility is attributed to the most direct cause of death,[4] a physical act that causes death. Although a distinction is drawn between a physical act intended to kill and a physical act that happens to kill, in both cases the offender must flee (Exod 21:13–14). Ultimately, greater legal culpability is imputed to the killer who lies in wait – "But if a man willfully attacks a man to kill him treacherously, you shall take him from my altar to be put to death" (Exod 21:14). Nonetheless, the direct physical act subjects the killer to legal action. The offender can see the connection between his hand and the corpse and knows to flee.

Limiting legal action to direct physical contact is not a sign of an inability to grasp a less direct connection but stems from an eminently practical concern.[5] A death can be clearly linked to a direct physical injury. The legal process can take such evidence with certainty. Less direct causation, such as poisoning, means greater doubt and less certainty about the identity of the offender.

Limiting legal action to direct physical action is a principle followed in narrative as well. In the story of Joseph, Joseph's brothers plan to kill him and dump the corpse in a pit:

> They saw him from afar, and before he drew near them, they conspired to kill him. They said to one another, "Here comes this dreamer." Now, let us kill him and throw him into one of the pits; we can say,

[2]The most recent edition and translation of the Hittite Laws, used here, is that by Harry A. Hoffner, Jr., *The Laws of the Hittites: A Critical Edition* (DMOA 23; Leiden: Brill, 1997). These particular statutes are on p. 18.

[3]Although the Hittite verb *waštai* is often rendered "to sin," it does not have the element of moral depravity associated with the English verb. Hence, the translation adopted here is "to be at fault." Cf. Harry A. Hoffner, Jr., "On Homicide in Hittite Law," in *Crossing Boundaries and Linking Horizons*, 297.

[4]David Daube, "Direct and Indirect Causation in Biblical Law," *VT* 11 (1961), 246–247.

[5]Ibid., 247.

> 'a savage animal ate him'; we will see what becomes of his dreams." (Gen 37:18–20)

Reuben objects to their plan and suggests that Joseph be left alive in the pit to perish without anyone dealing the fatal blow:

> When Reuben heard it, he tried to save him from them; he said, "Let us not take his life." Reuben said to them, "Don't shed blood. Throw him into this pit here in the wilderness, but don't lay your hand against him." (Gen 37:21–22)

Reuben makes a contrast between killing Joseph directly and indirectly.[6] If they kill him directly, the brothers would be fully culpable. If they kill him indirectly by casting him into a pit out in the wilderness and leaving him to die, they would be less culpable, if not immune. Joseph's brothers readily agree to this subterfuge.

The same principle is followed in the narrative of David and Bathsheba, 2 Samuel 11–12. David is deemed guilty for taking Uriah's wife, not for causing his death. For the latter offense, he is not culpable because he did not directly shed Uriah's blood.[7] This is seen clearly in Nathan's parable. Its point is the theft of the poor man's ewe by the wealthy man. The death of the poor man is not even mentioned. The purpose of Nathan's parable is not to condemn David for Uriah's death, but rather for commandeering Uriah's wife. David reacts to the parable by ordering the wealthy man to pay for a stolen ewe (2 Sam 12:5–6).[8] In Nathan's explication of his parable, he holds David responsible for Uriah's death – "Why did you treat the word of the LORD with contempt, doing what is evil in his sight, by smiting Uriah the Hittite with the sword, taking his wife as your own, and killing him with the sword of the Ammonites?" (2 Sam 12:9) – but Nathan bases David's

[6]Daube, "'Lex Talionis,'" in *Studies in Biblical Law,* 111.

[7]This strategem is used by Saul, who promises David his daughter's hand if David would battle the Philistines (1 Sam 18: 17–27). Saul hopes that in the process of killing the Philistines, David would be killed but Saul himself would not be responsible – "... now Saul thought: Let my hand not be upon him but the hand of the Philistines" (1 Sam 18:17).

[8]Although David's first words are "[I swear] as the LORD lives, that man deserves to die," David then orders the man to pay. The first reaction, "[I swear] as the LORD lives, that man deserves to die," is an expression of moral approbation, not law. The judgment to pay is law. Further, the penalty for adultery is death (Lev 20:10), and after David confesses it, the penalty is transferred to the son who is to be born. Some have suggested that the term בן מות is not a juridical term, but an emphatic expression, based on analogy with the term איש מות and the use of מות in emphatic expressions. This argument is faulty: The correct analogy is to the technical legal term בן הכות, "one who deserves a lashing," in Deut 25:2. The phrase בן מות is a juridical term. Cf. Anthony Phillips, "The Interpretation of 2 Samuel xii 5–6," *VT* 16 (1966), 243–245; P. Kyle McCarter, *II Samuel* (AB; Garden City, New York: Doubleday, 1984), 299; H. Seabass, "Nathan und David in II Sam 12," *ZAW* 86 (1974), 203–204; D. Winton Thomas, "A Consideration of Some Unusual Ways of Expressing the Superlative in Hebrew," *VT* 3 (1953), 219–220; Svi Rin, "The מות of Grandeur," *VT* 9 (1959), 324–325.

punishment solely on the sin of taking Uriah's wife – "And now, the sword shall never depart from your house because you have despised me and taken the wife of Uriah the Hittite to be your wife" (2 Sam 12:10). Nathan does not subject David to legal action for Uriah's death because he did not actually deal the fatal blow. David's punishment reflects his transgression – "Thus says the LORD: I am going to make trouble for you out of your own house. I am going to take your wives before your very eyes and give them to someone else, and he will lie with them in the light of the sun itself, because although you acted in secret, I am going to do this in front of all Israel, in front of the sun" (2 Sam 12:11–12). David's punishment is a transfiguration of his crime, the affair with Bathsheba. What he did in secret will be done to him in public.

At the same time, a distinction is drawn in narrative texts between responsibility and culpability. To return to the case of Joseph's brothers, when they descend to Egypt and are treated harshly, they link this to their harsh treatment of Joseph. Reuben reproaches his brothers for the responsibility they bear for Joseph's fate (Gen 42:22), although they did not directly cause his death: "Reuben answered them, 'Did I not say to you, 'Do not wrong the boy,' but you did not listen, and now his blood is being requited.' "

The same distinction lies behind a series of killings and counterkillings among David's retainers. The killing of Asahel (2 Sam 2:18–23) is depicted as the first link in a chain of events. Abner slays Asahel in battle. Asahel's brother, Joab, then ambushes Abner and kills him in revenge. David, in turn, reacts emphatically, horrified by "the blood falling on the head of Joab and his father's house." He utters a curse upon Joab and his patrimonial house to ensure that the taint would fall on the killer's descendants, not his own (2 Sam 3:28–29). David orders Joab and the army to display outward signs of mourning, and David himself walks before Abner's bier and intones a dirge. These formal acts of grieving constitute a public declaration that David did not intend the death of Abner. The presumption, however, is that the king *is* responsible for the actions of one of his men. This same presumption lies behind David's deathbed scene, where he instructs Solomon to kill Joab for the slaying of Abner and the slaying of Amasa, commander of the army of Judah (1 Kgs 2:5). After David's death, when he sees Solomon settling David's unfinished business, Joab flees to the Tent-shrine and takes hold of the horns of the altar. Joab's action is of no avail. Solomon instructs Benaiah to kill Joab in order to remove bloodguilt for the deaths of Abner and Amasa from David and his house (1 Kgs 2:31). David and his house bear moral responsibility for their subordinate's deed, not actionable culpability.[9] The

[9] An analogous case is that of Rahab, who is warned by the spies that she will bear the bloodguilt if her family ventures out of doors during the conquest of Jericho. The spies will bear it if her family remains indoors and is not protected (Josh 2:17–20), even though neither Rahab nor the spies deal the fatal blow.

fact that a person could be held morally responsible but legally exempt for what he did not do is a phenomenon we would not be aware of if it were not for narrative texts. Legal texts, by contrast, are concerned with actionable killings, that is, with offenses for which there are legal consequences. These are limited to certain acts of killing.

Although biblical law requires that death be the result of direct physical assault in order for the slayer to be subject to legal action, that requirement is not sufficient. Intent to kill is necessary as well. Exod 21:14 defines intentional homicide as premeditated. Its cause is the direct physical act of the killer who treacherously lies in wait. On the other hand, the cause of the other grade of homicide signaled in Exod 21:13 is ascribed as God.[10] By attributing to God the responsibility for accidental homicide, the Covenant Code holds the view that visible agents of the killing – implements of wood, stone, or metal – are equally directed by the ultimate mover.[11] Accidental killing is equated with an accident without a human cause.

The emphasis in the Covenant Code is on the distinction between the two types of homicide, one for which sanctuary is legitimate, the other for which no place offers respite, not even an altar. The typology is based on intentionality.

The definition of intentional and unintentional homicide is a critical issue for the other biblical statutes on homicide in Num 35:9–34 and Deut 19:1–13. Num 35:16–24 contains two distinct definitions of the categories of homicide:

> [16]If a person strikes another with an iron tool so that [the victim]
> dies, he is a murderer – the murderer shall surely be put to death. [17]If
> a person strikes another with a stone tool that can kill so that the vic-
> tim dies, he is a murderer – the murderer shall surely be put to death.
> [18]If a person strikes another with a wooden tool that can kill so that
> the victim dies, he is a murderer – the murderer shall surely be put to
> death. [19]The blood avenger himself shall put the murderer to death:
> whenever he meets him he shall put him to death. [20]If a person pushed
> him in hatred or aimed something at him on purpose, [21]or struck
> him with his hand in enmity, so the victim dies, he is a murderer –
> the blood avenger shall kill him when he meets him. [22]If he pushed

[10] Exod 21:13 may have other parallels in ancient Near Eastern statutes. LH 266 attributes the death of sheep to *lipit ilim*, "a plague (lit. a touching) of the god," while LH 249 attributes the death of a rented ox to a god. These phrases signify an event that has no human cause. Karel van der Toorn notes that this phraseology emphasizes the fortuitousness of an accidental and fatal action (*Sin and Sanction,* 71). Cf. Paul, *Studies in the Book of the Covenant,* 63–64, and Daube, "Direct and Indirect Causation," 255. However, the biblical usage is a radical extension of the phrase since it refers not to an otherwise inexplicable illness but to a fatal assault directly done by human hands. The Hittite conception, in HL 3–4, has also been radically extended in the Bible by linking the activity of human hands to the direction of God.

[11] Daube, "Direct and Indirect Causation," 255.

> him suddenly without enmity or aimed an object at him unintentionally, [23] or without seeing dropped an object of stone that can kill, so that the victim dies – though he was not his enemy and did not seek his harm – [24] the assembly shall judge between the slayer and the blood avenger according to these rules.

The first definition is in Num 35:16–18, which bases capital murder on the instrument involved, an iron tool,[12] a stone hand-tool of the type that can kill, or a wooden hand-tool of the type that can kill. Against this, Num 35:20–23 introduces the idea of intent in the three examples of capital murder it offers: shoving[13] someone in enmity, hurling something on purpose, or striking in enmity with one's hand. Three examples of unintentional homicide according to this typology are given in contrast.[14] The killer shoved the victim suddenly without enmity, or hurled something unintentionally, or caused a deadly stone implement to fall upon the victim without seeing him. Num 35:20–23 explains these examples by correlating them to the relationship between the killer and the victim – "[the killer] was not his enemy and did not seek his harm." The criterion at work in verses 16–18 is fundamentally distinct from that in verses 20–23. That in verses 16–18 defines the categories of homicide formally: The extent of culpability depends on the type of object that caused death. The criterion in verses 20–23, on the other hand, depends on determining the state of mind of the slayer.[15]

[12] It appears that iron tools in any form are assumed to be capable of causing death. Cf. Rashi.

[13] The verb ה-ד-פ signifies direct pushing in 2 Kgs 4:27 and Ezek 34:21.

[14] No corresponding list of unintentional homicide according to the criteria of vv. 18–20 is offered.

[15] This divergence is a sign that vv. 9–34 underwent a complicated history of redaction. There is other evidence for redactional activity. Vv. 16–18 use the term רוצח to denote someone guilty of capital homicide, in contrast to the use of the term to denote any killer in the rest of the chapter, vv. 11, 12, 25, 26, 27. (It is impossible to determine whether the verse in the Decalogue, Exod 20:13, refers to any slaying or solely to intentional homicide.) In addition, the definition of culpable homicide in vv. 20–21 is most likely interpolated material because it is encased in a *Wiederaufname* that may indicate interpolation and because it contradicts the definition in vv. 16–18. Lastly, vv. 33–34 appear to be doublets: V. 33 has a parallel in the P material in Gen 9:6, while v. 34 contains H wording (cf. Knohl, *The Sanctuary of Silence*, 99).

I would propose the following redaction history of vv. 9–34 that takes into account the divergent denotations of the term רוצח, the differing definitions of capital homicide, and the doublet of vv. 33–34. First, the priority of vv. 9–14 and 24–29 seems clear. Then, a number of additions were made. A definition of culpable homicide was added, vv. 16–19, which included a technical term, רוצח, for capital homicide. Vv. 30–33 use רוצח to denote culpable homicide and may belong to the same layer, but it is difficult to provide any definitive timetable for the addition of vv. 30–33. Another definition of capital homicide was added, vv. 20–21, to the definition in vv. 16–19. Later, a corresponding definition to vv. 20–21 of noncapital homicide and legislation regarding the stay of the accidental homicide in the city of refuge was added, making up vv. 22–23. Vv. 15 and 34 are additions originating from a H editor (on v. 15, cf. Knohl, *The Sanctuary of Silence*, 99), but the timing of this is difficult to determine. This redaction history points to a number of redactional layers, reflecting different historical periods and their views of evidence.

Determining intentionality lies behind both criteria. However, verses 16–18 derive it from the instrument of killing, an "objective" definition. The use of particular instruments of deadly force presumes intent by the sheer fact of their use. In contrast, the categories in verses 20–23 are predicated upon a witness analyzing the occurrence.

The statute on homicide in Deut 19:1–13 utilizes a different element to provide the understructure to a typology of unlawful deaths:

> 4 This is the type of slayer who may flee there and live: whoever slays his fellow without intent and was not hostile to him in the past. 5 Whoever came with his fellow into the forest to cut wood: as his hand swings the ax to cut down the tree, the ax-head falls off the handle and hits the other so that he dies – that man shall flee to one of these cities and live.

The previous relationship between the killer and the victim is now a factor. Deuteronomy stipulates two criteria for those seeking refuge: 1) The assault must have been done unintentionally; and 2) there must have been no malice before the killing between the killer and his victim. Two examples, each showing the criteria for accidental and intentional homicide, are given. In one example, a person enters a stand of trees with another person to chop wood. When he swings his ax to cut the wood, the ax-head flies from the handle[16] and strikes his neighbor. This accidental killing incurs no culpability. The other example given is that of the act of the culpable murderer (Deut 19:11):

> 11 If a person is hostile to another and lies in wait and strikes him mortally so that he dies, and flees to one of these towns, 12 the elders of his town shall send and take him back from there and deliver him to the blood avenger so that he dies.

A person hates another person and prepares an ambush in order to strike him down. These two examples show that both elements, intention and prior malice, are necessary for capital murder according to Deuteronomic law.

The criterion of the relationship between the killer and the victim in Deuteronomy – "this is the type of slayer who may flee there and live:

[16] There is confusion over the referent of העץ in the clause ונשל הברזל מן העץ. If we connect the word העץ in the previous clause to this one, it would appear that the text describes a case in which the ax-head, being attached to the ax, bounced off the tree to strike the other man. In contrast, the case where the ax-head flew off the handle should be expressed: ונשל הברזל מן עצו, strictly, "the ax head flies off *its* wood." However, the case of an ax-head flying off the handle seems much more likely than the rebound from the tree. Indeed, there may be problems in general with keeping an ax-head on its handle (cf. 2 Kgs 6:5, where one of Elisha's miracles is to recover an ax-head that came off its handle and fell into the Jordan River). Information on the shape and composition of axes is available (cf. J. D. Muhly, "Metals," in *OEANE* 4.1–5), but little is known of the means of their use outside of warfare (cf. Rupert Chapman, "Weapons," in OEANE 5.334–339).

whoever slays his fellow without intent and was not hostile to him in the past" – is radically different from its use in Num 35:23 – "though he was not his enemy and did not seek his harm" – for two reasons: 1) Deut 19:4,6, by using the adverb מתמל שלשם, "previously," focuses on the relationship between the victim and the killer prior to the murder, while Num 35:23 is concentrating on the character of the relationship at the time of the murder; and 2) Deut 19:4–5, 11–12 defines incidences of accidental slaying by this criterion, while Num 35:23 uses the relationship as an explanation as to why certain fatal events are not intentional.

Although few details about the use of witnesses are provided, the typologies of homicide presume their use, and the definitions shed light on the testimony elicited from witnesses. The formal typology in Num 35:16–18 requires them to identify the instrument of murder. The typology based on the state of mind of the murderer in Num 35:20–23 requires the witnesses to make judgments on the murderer's internal motivation. The typology of homicide in Deut 19:1–13 requires, in addition to information on the actual crime, knowledge of events prior to the murder in order to prove prior malice between victim and killer. This may require additional witnesses or lines of inquiry.

Examination of matters extraneous to the act itself is not without parallel in other legal systems. In modern France, for example, courts investigate the *personnalité* of the accused: Inquiry is made into his or her personal history and family life, schooling, work record, military service, financial situation, leisure interests, and character traits without any restrictions as to their influence on the criminal act itself.[17]

There is also a formal requirement about the number of witnesses. Num 35:30 stipulates that the number be more than one in order to condemn the killer:

> Any killer – the murderer shall be killed on the testimony of witnesses:
> a single witness shall not be sufficient for a sentence of death.

However, Num 35:9–34 does not indicate whether the killer is released without prejudice from the city of refuge if there is only one witness. Deut 17:6 and 19:15 contain a general provision that for any transgression, two or more witnesses are required.

Furthermore, in the adjudication of homicide, judicial action relies on the testimony of witnesses, not on physical evidence. Witnesses may report on the manner of killing (Exod 21:13–14; Num 35:20–23), the instrument of killing (Num 35:16–18), or the prior relationship between the murderer and the victim (Deut 19:4), depending on the statute. There is no indication that

[17] Bron McKillop, "Anatomy of a French Murder Case," *American Journal of Comparative Law* 45 (1997), 541–543, 551–554, 579–582.

the body or other physical evidence must be produced in the proceedings.[18] An exception proves the rule. In Deut 21:1–9, the unknown human corpse found with indications of foul play becomes, in lieu of witnesses, the evidence for a murder that must be dealt with.[19] Rarely does physical evidence play a significant role in biblical law. One such instance concerns shepherds, who must produce the remains of the animal under their care that had been taken by a predator in order to be released from compensating the owner (Exod 22:12).

Without witnesses, the offense cannot be remedied. An admonition against one who commits homicide in stealth appears in a list of forbidden acts committed in secrecy (Deut 27:24):

> "Accursed is the one who strikes down another in secret," and all the people shall say, "Amen."

A homicide has been committed in such a way that it is difficult to prove who did it. The culprit cannot be apprehended and punished. By anathematizing acts committed clandestinely, their punishment becomes God's responsibility, thereby discouraging would-be perpetrators who might assume that they could escape a penalty for their transgression.[20]

Two other cases of killing are defined in the Book of the Covenant, but are not included in the laws of homicide. In the course of treating theft, Exod 22:1–2 stipulates that killing a thief who is tunneling in during the night is justifiable homicide, while killing him during the day is not and incurs bloodguilt. The issue at hand is that at night in the dark, the thief's intention cannot be determined. He has illegally entered a home, and whether he intends to steal or to kill cannot be easily determined. The presumption is the worst-case scenario – that he is trying to kill someone. During the day, it can be seen that he is just a thief, not a killer.

Intention is also a factor in holding the master of a slave culpable for the slave's death. According to Exod 21:20–21, the deciding factor is the time in which the slave's death occurs. If it is immediately upon a beating, the master is punished. If the slave lingers for a day or two before dying, the master is not punished. What lies behind this distinction is determining the intention of the master. If the slave dies immediately, the master appears to have intended his death. If the slave lingers, the master's intention becomes murky and, therefore, the principle that takes precedence is the master's ownership of the slave and his right to impose discipline on that slave.

[18]Victor H. Matthews and Don C. Benjamin, *Social World of Ancient Israel, 1250–587 BCE* (Peabody, Massachusetts: Hendrickson, 1993), 129.
[19]The showing of the tattered remains of Joseph's embroidered tunic to Jacob by his sons reflects, to a certain extent, this exception (Gen 37:32–33).
[20]Tigay, *Deuteronomy,* 253.

Narrative also recognizes that intention is critical. In 1 Kgs 3:16–27, the two prostitutes appeal to King Solomon because one killed her child by lying on him. However, there is no hint that the mother who killed her son was considered culpable or responsible. Apparently, the killing of the child was not actionable because there was an element of lack of human intent: Certainly, the mother did not intend to kill her child.[21] Moreover, there was nothing inherently dangerous in her act: She did not swing an ax or other dangerous implement that could kill if used in a hostile manner. Accidental homicide covers acts that the actor should have known could potentially cause harm.

The biblical legal texts clearly express an anxiety over articulating a distinction between intentional and accidental homicide. They are trying to provide concrete illustrations of the distinction. The best proof of this is to compare the biblical statutes to those of the rest of the ancient Near East.

The cuneiform law collections fail to provide criteria for determining whether a slaying was intentional or accidental. In general, they lack information on the procedures set into motion when a homicide occurred. How was it determined that a homicide in fact occurred? How was the identity of the killer ascertained? How was the killer apprehended? These matters are ignored.[22]

Only the statutes in the Laws of Hammurapi provide some insight into how a case might have been initiated. LH 1 is the first in an introductory series of laws on procedure and addresses an unsubstantiated accusation of homicide. According to LH 1, a private person can lay a charge of homicide against another person.[23] The relationship of this private citizen to the

[21]Daube, "Direct and Indirect Causation," 256–257.

[22]In general, archaic codes, whether Eastern or Western, lack provisions on procedure. Cf. F. L. Attenborough, *The Laws of the Earliest English Kings* (Cambridge: Cambridge University Press, 1922), and Wallace Johnson, *The T'ang Code* (Vol. 2; Princeton Library of Asian Translations; Princeton: Princeton University Press, 1997).

[23]Roth argues that the first and last statutes in LH are intended to bear a political message for Hammurapi's vassals, as do the prologue and epilogue ("Mesopotamian Legal Traditions and the Laws of Hammurabi," *Chicago-Kent Law Review* 71 [1995], 18–19). Both LH 1 and 282 deal with verbal utterances that are not substantiated. LH 1, punishing a false accusation of murder, translated into the political realm is equivalent to a warning about treasonous utterances, especially as it follows the glorification of Hammurapi's military power in the preamble. LH 282, punishing a slave's denial of his subservience to his master, would be understood as rebellion, especially in light of the curses against anyone who would disrespect the stela in the epilogue. Roth argues that these two statutes, in conjunction with the rest of the composition, were intended to reinforce Hammurapi's superior position and to remind his contemporaries of the consequences of treasonous and rebellious behavior. It seems to me that this hypothesis fits LH 1 better than it fits LH 282. LH 1 and the three following provisions all mandate the remedy for unsubstantiated charges in the legal arena. This would seem to reinforce a message to vassals to cease political jockeying among themselves, rather than be disloyal to their overlord. Roth herself notes that the political message was certainly not the sole message conveyed by the placement of these particular statutes.

victim is unstated. There was no public official who held the responsibility of charging a person on behalf of a private citizen, nor was the right to make such an accusation limited to the victim's family. What happens in the rest of the process is omitted. For example, the critical role of the crown, so pronounced in the other Mesopotamian documents we have analyzed in Chapter Two, is simply not mentioned explicitly. It may be implicitly assumed in the ascription of so many of the law collections – LL, LU, LH, and the Edict of Telepinus – to kings.

To be sure, the adjudication of homicide was considered important elsewhere in the ancient Near East. Six out of seven law collections contain statutes on homicide. Homicide provisions were placed at the beginning of law collections, and what is striking is that all but one of the cuneiform law collections for which the beginning of the statute section is preserved start with a statute on some aspect of homicide, whether a general rule, a rule about a specific type, or a matter of legal procedure.[24]

> The first statute in the Laws of Ur-Nammu:
>
> LU 1
> If a man commits a homicide, they shall kill that man.
>
> The first statute in the Hittite Laws:
>
> HL 1
> [If] anyone kills [a man] or a woman in a [quarr]el, he shall [bring him] [for burial] and give 4 persons [lit. heads], male or female respectively, and he shall look [to his house for it.]
>
> The first statute in the Laws of Hammurapi:
>
> LH 1
> If a man accuses another man and charges him with homicide but then cannot bring proof against him, his accuser shall be killed.

A homicide statute is placed at the beginning of the Laws of Ur-Nammu, the Laws of Hammurapi, and the Hittite Laws, but not the Laws of Eshnunna.[25] With regard to the Laws of Lipit-Ishtar, unfortunately, there is a sizable gap between the preamble and statute section. Indeed, the beginning of the statute section of LL is missing and, therefore, we cannot know whether LL commenced with a statute on homicide.[26] Homicide as the first item

[24] Martha T. Roth, *Law Collections from Mesopotamia and Asia Minor* (contribution by Harry A. Hoffner, Jr.; SBL Writings from the Ancient World Series; Atlanta: Scholars Press, 1995), 72.
[25] LE contains other differences from the other law codes, such as the lack of an apologetic preamble, and may originate in another literary tradition, that of the *mīšarum* edict, which has been welded to that of the codes. See J. J. Finkelstein, "Ammiṣaduqa's Edict and the Babylonian 'Law Codes,'" *JCS* 15 (1961), 102.
[26] No statute regarding homicide appears at the beginning of the Middle Assyrian Laws (MAL). However, MAL do not appear to be a unified collection of statutes.

demonstrates the importance of statutes against homicide. It also seems to be part of the style of the law collections.

The law collections share other stylistic elements: The remedy for the killing of free persons is equally likely to be either compensation or execution, depending on the circumstances, but there is striking uniformity across the law collections for particular groups of cases. Thus, a fine is the remedy for unintended death caused in the course of an assault, such as a miscarriage or a death caused by an animal. However, this uniformity is not necessarily the case within a single code. For example, the penalties in LH for similar cases are not congruent. The circumstances in LH 207, the death of a member of the free class from an assault, have an affinity to the circumstances in which a pregnant woman of the free class dies from an assault (LH 210):

> 207
> If [a free man] dies from his beating, he shall also swear ["I did not strike him intentionally"]. If [the victim] is a member of the free class, he shall pay 30 shekels of silver.
>
> 210
> If [a free man strikes a woman of the free class and] that woman dies, they shall kill his daughter.

The penalties in these similar cases are different: A fine is mandated in the first case, while in the second case, an execution is prescribed. This is so because death caused in the course of a brawl is punished by a fine in other law collections, while the remedy for the death of a pregnant woman is capital punishment, as is reflected in other law collections.[27]

The cuneiform law collections draw a distinction between intentionality and unintentionality on the part of the offender in a number of related cases. LE 47A is located at the conclusion of a series of statutes on bodily injuries and mandates a fine for a death occurring during a *risbatum,* "a brawl." The term *risbatum* is the third of three terms mentioned in these provisions, the other terms being *sūqum,*[28] literally "street" (LE 44), and *šigištum,* "a fight" (LE 47). These terms specify the circumstances in which the injury

[27]There may be a discernible reason for this difference: In LH 207, the accused swears that he did not do the action intentionally. Nothing like this is noted in LH 210.

[28]The reading here is difficult. Rykle Borger ("Der Codex Eschnunna," in *Rechts- und Wirtschaftsurkunden Historisch-chronologische Texte* [Texte aus der Umwelt des Alten Testament, Band 1/1; Gütersloh: Gütersloher Verlagshaus Gerd Mohn, 1982], 20), and CAD S, 70, s.v. *sakāpu,* read *ina sūqim.* In his original publication, Emile Szlechter restores it to *ina [ṣa-al-tim],* "in the course of a fight" (*Les lois d'Eshnunna* [Publications de l'Institut de Droit Romain de l'Université de Paris 12; Paris: Centre Nationale de la Recherche Scientifique, 1954], 28), but rereads it as *[i]k-l[u-i-tim],* "in darkness," omitting *ina,* in his 1978 publication ("Les lois d'Eshnunna," *RIDA* 25 [1978], 138). This reading is also held by Landsberger, "Jungfraulichkeit," 101. Albrecht Goetze suggests that from the context, the missing signs should indicate something along the lines of "altercation," *The Laws of Eshnunna* (New Haven, Connecticut: American Schools of Oriental Research, 1956), 120.

was inflicted, factors that mitigate or aggravate the culpability of the guilty party.[29] LE 44 indicates that the injuries treated in LE 44–46 occurred while the victim was passing by innocently on the street. LE 47 indicates that an injury took place in a *šigištum*, "a fight." The injured was himself involved in aggressive behavior, and therefore his injury merits a lesser penalty, only ten shekels, in comparison to the fines ranging from twenty to thirty shekels in LE 44–46. By contrast, LE 47A specifies that injuries resulting in death took place in a *risbatum*, "a brawl:"

> 44
> If a man knocks down another in the street and breaks his hand, he shall weigh out 30 shekels of silver.
>
> 45
> If he should break his foot, he shall weigh out 30 shekels of silver.
>
> 46
> If a man strikes another man and breaks his collarbone, he shall weigh out 20 shekels of silver.
>
> 47
> If a man should injure [?] another man in the course of a fight, he shall weigh out 10 shekels of silver.
>
> 47A
> If a man in a brawl caused the death of a member of the *awīlu*[free]-class, he shall weigh out 40 shekels of silver.

These statutes allude to the mitigating circumstance – the injury indirectly resulted in the victim's death. LE 47A goes beyond the other statutes, 44–47, on bodily injuries since it treats a category of killing. However, the lack of intention to cause death in the case dealt with in 47A has affinities to the cases of injuries addressed in statutes 44–47.

Other statutes use similar logic to associate accidental homicide to injuries incurred in the course of a brawl, LH 207–208 treat death during a brawl immediately after the statutes on bodily injuries, LH 206:

> 206
> If a free man has struck another man in a brawl and has injured him, that man shall swear, "I did not strike him intentionally." He shall satisfy [i.e., pay] the physician.
>
> 207
> If [a free man] dies from his beating, he shall also swear ["I did not strike him intentionally"]. If [the victim] is a member of the free class, he shall pay 30 shekels of silver.

[29] Roth, "On LE 46–47A," *NABU* 3 (1990), 70.

208
If [the victim] is a member of the client/common class, he shall pay 20 shekels of silver.

LH 206 provides the rule for an injury incurred without premeditation. The offender must pay the victim's medical expenses. LH 207–208 indicate that if the injury resulted in death, the compensation is thirty shekels if the victim is a free man and twenty shekels if he is a dependent/commoner.

Three types of cases involving negligence are presented in cuneiform law collections. A mistake by a physician is found in LH 218, the fatal attack of a goring ox is found in LH 250–253 and LE 53–55, and the miscarriage of a pregnant woman caused by an assault is found in LH 209–214, SLEx 1′–2′, LI d–f, MAL A 21, 50–52, and HL 17–18.

LH 218 mandates that if a patient dies at a physician's hands, the hand of the physician is cut off:

218
If a physician performs major surgery with a bronze lancet upon a free man and causes the free man's death or opens a free man's temple with a bronze lancet and blinds the free man's eye, they shall cut off his hand.

This type of negligence is mentioned only in the Laws of Hammurapi.

The statutes on the goring ox assume that liability for the death of a human being[30] is operative only when the ox is known to be a habitual gorer whose behavior had already warranted a formal warning by the ward authorities. If an ox who has never gored previously kills, no legal action, it is implied, can be taken against the owner.

The Laws of Eshnunna:

53
If an ox gored [another] ox and killed it, both [ox owners] shall divide the value of the live ox and the carcass of the dead ox.

54–55
If an ox [was] a gorer and the ward [authorities] have had [it] made known to its owner, but he did not guard his ox and it gored a man and killed [him], the owner of the ox shall weigh out 40 shekels of silver.
If it gored a slave and killed [him], he shall weigh out 15 shekels of silver.

[30] Although it may appear that LE presents ambivalent rules on the necessity of intention on the part of the responsible party – in LE 53, the owner of the ox has absolute liability, while in LE 54–58, the owner has been warned of the danger posed by his possession – this is not so. LE 53 applies to the death of another ox, when one ox causes the death of another ox, not a human being.

The Laws of Hammurapi:

250
If an ox gores a free man to death while it is passing through the streets, that case has no basis for a claim.

251
If a free man's ox is a known gorer and the authorities of his city quarter notify him but he does not pad[?] its horns or control his ox and that ox gores to death a member of the free class, he shall give 30 shekels of silver.

252
If it is a free man's slave, he shall give 20 shekels of silver.

The statutes in LE on the goring ox are accompanied by rules on analogous cases, death caused by an aggressive dog (LE 56–57) and a tottering wall (LE 58). In all of these, liability is dependent on a formal warning of the dangerous circumstances to the owner, and the statutes provide for the remedy when the duly forewarned owner did not take precautions. The formal warning by the ward authorities obviates any claim by the owner that he was unaware of the danger.

The case of the aggressive dog[31] occurs only in LE, but it does not appear to be substantially different from the case of the vicious ox, and so it is placed next to the statute on the goring ox:

56–57
If a dog [was] aggressive and the ward [authorities] have had [it] made known to its owner, but he did not guard his dog and it bit a man and

[31]The rendering of *kalbum šegûm* has been debated. The lexica are self-contradictory: AHw/I, 424b, and CAD N/ii, 54a, render *šegûm* as "rasend, tollwütig," ("rabid, mad"), while AHw/III, 1208b, translates it as "aggressiv," ("wild, aggressive,") and CAD K, 69a, renders it as "vicious." CAD /II 260b refers to two meanings, listing "to rage, be rabid" under the G-stem and "to become rabid" as the ingressive to the G-stem. G. R. Driver argues for the rendering of *kalbum šegum* as "rabid dog" because the statute specifies that the victim dies: While a person bitten by a vicious dog might on occasion die from his wounds, the victim of a rabid dog would certainly die ("Review of R. Yaron, *The Laws of Eshnunna,*" *Journal of the Royal Asiatic Society* [1972], 57). However, Yaron argues that a rabid dog would be immediately destroyed and not be kept for any reason (*The Laws of Eshnunna*^{2}, 300). If, in fact, LE 56–57 were treating the situation of a rabid dog, they would represent a radically different situation from that of LE 54–55, which, as noted, would fail to explain the same penalties in LE 54–55 and in 56–57. An aggressive ox in the habit of goring, if kept under control, is still of use, but a rabid dog would serve no useful purpose. Furthermore, while there are numerous incantations against dog bites in which the dog is described as having spittle dripping from its mouth, which is a sign of rabies, the only one that instructs the dog to be taken into confinement does not describe it as rabid (this incantation is found in M. Sigrist, "On the Bite of a Dog," in *Love and Death in the Ancient Near East: Essays in Honor of Marvin H. Pope* [ed. John H. Marks and Robert M. Good; Guilford, Connecticut: Four Quarters Press, 1987], 85). It is clear, then, that the adjective *šegûm* means "wild, aggressive."

caused [him] to die, the owner of the dog shall weigh out 40 shekels of silver.

If it gored a slave and caused him to die, he shall weigh out 15 shekels of silver.

This is not a series of situations of increasing gravity.[32] The case of the aggressive dog is not more dangerous than that of the goring ox, and the penalties are of the same gravity.[33]

LE 58 addresses another case that is not mentioned in the other collections, death caused by the collapse of a tottering wall:

58
If a wall was about to fall and the ward authorities have made it known to the owner of the wall but he did not reinforce his wall and the wall collapsed and killed a member of the *awīlu* [free] class, it is a case concerning life – it is a decree of the king.

Comparing this statute to ones in LH (such as 229–233) that deal with collapsed structures is instructive. The statutes in LH ascribe the death to shoddy workmanship and the responsibility to the builder. By contrast, LE 58 addresses the responsibility of the owner for the upkeep of his property, an issue in consonance with LE's laws on the goring ox and aggressive dog.

In contrast to the other provisions on negligence next to which it is placed, LE 58 treats an offense that is specifically and explicitly denoted as a capital case. What differentiates this case from the others? It has been suggested that a legal principle is at work. For Albrecht Goetze, this principle is that of predictability.[34] The common element in the cases of a vicious animal is that its behavior, whether an ox or dog, is unpredictable, whereas the danger incurred by a sagging wall is always predictable – a sagging wall will collapse. The owner should have known to repair the wall and, therefore, the more severe punishment is warranted. Goetze's principle, however, does not fit the situation envisioned: The statutes on the ox and dog refer to an animal whose owner has already received a warning about its previously demonstrated bad temper because the dangerous behavior exhibited by the animal is likely to recur.[35] Richard Haase attempts to salvage Goetze's theory by focusing on the responsibility the victim holds for his own injury: He argues that a person

[32] Finkelstein, *The Ox That Gored, 22.*

[33] Yaron, *The Laws of Eshnunna*^{2}, 302.

[34] Goetze, *The Laws of Eshnunna,* 140.

[35] Dieter Nörr followed a similar line of reasoning to that of Goetze and argued that there is a difference in the level of the owner's responsibility between LE 54–57 and LE 58, which can account for the difference in penalties ("Zum Schuldgedanken im altbabylonischen Strassrecht," *ZSS* 75 [1958], 11–13). An animal has a will of its own, which an owner can curb but not excise. An animal to an extent is independent of its owner. The owner's responsibility for the consequences of the animal's action is, therefore, lessened. However, the situation articulated in the statute emphasizes that the owner has been reminded of his responsibility.

would know to avoid animals owned by others.[36] According to Haase, then, the victim in the situations treated in LE 54–57 would have contributed to his own demise by his lack of care. In contrast, a sagging wall might be a less obvious danger. A serious objection can be raised against Haase's viewpoint. An aggressive animal may come upon a person suddenly: No precautions he could have undertaken would have prevented the tragedy.[37] In contrast, the location of a dangerous wall is stationary. If such a wall comes to the knowledge of the local authorities, it is probably well known in the area. It is probable that it even looks unstable. The person who still passes underneath it has contributed through lack of care to his own death. A sagging wall is a predictable danger.

Yaron adds another explanation for the difference in sanction in LE 58. He contends that the difference is due to the origin of LE 58. LE 58 refers to *ṣimdat šarrim*, "a decree of the king." Yaron argues that this phrase indicates that the source of this particular ruling is a decree of the king in a specific case.[38] This concurs with the use of the phrase in other Akkadian texts: It refers to specific decrees already issued.[39] By the use of this phrase, this statute shows that it incorporates an actual ruling, perhaps handed down after a particularly egregious case. The fact that the penalty, capital punishment, is out of proportion to its neighboring cases, LE 54–57, is due to the prerogative of the monarch.

The laws on another variety of negligence, striking a pregnant woman, are found in LL d–f, SLEx 1′–2′, LH 209–214, and HL 17–18:

> LL d--f
> If [a . . .] strikes the daughter of a man and causes her to lose her fetus, he shall weigh and deliver 30 shekels of silver. If she dies, that male shall be killed.
>
> If a . . . strikes the slave woman of a man and causes her to lose her fetus, he shall weigh and deliver 5 shekels of silver.
>
> SLEx 1′–2′
> If he jostles the daughter of a man and causes her to miscarry her fetus, he shall weigh and deliver 10 shekels of silver.
>
> If he strikes the daughter of a man and causes her to miscarry her fetus, he shall weigh and deliver 20 shekels of silver.

[36] Haase, "Die Behandlungen von Tierschäden in den Keilschriftrechten," *RIDA* 14 (1967), 51.
[37] ARM III 18:15f reads: *kīma kalbim šegêm ašar inaššaku ul idi,* "like an aggressive dog, where he will bite I do not know." It is in the nature of an aggressive dog that it bites unexpectedly.
[38] Yaron, *The Laws of Eshnunna*², 302–303.
[39] Cf. Maria deJ. Ellis, "Taxation in Ancient Mesopotamia: The History of the Term *miksu*," *JCS* 26 (1974), 215. This phrase does not refer to the transfer of a case to the king's court, as some would render it. Cf. CAD Ṣ, 194–196, and G. R. Driver and John C. Miles, *The Babylonian Laws* (Ancient Codes and Laws of the Near East; Oxford: Clarendon, 1952), 1.17–20.

LH 209–214
209
If a free man strikes a woman of the free class and causes her to miscarry her fetus, he shall pay 10 shekels of silver for her fetus.

210
If that woman dies, they shall kill his daughter.

211
If he causes a woman of the client/common class to miscarry her fetus by the beating, he shall pay 5 shekels of silver.

212
If that woman dies, he shall pay 30 shekels of silver.

213
If he strikes a free man's slave woman and causes her to miscarry her fetus, he shall pay 2 shekels of silver.

214
If that slave woman dies, he shall pay 20 shekels of silver.

HL 17–18
17
If anyone causes a free woman to miscarry, [if] it is in her tenth month,[40] he shall pay 10 shekels of silver; if it is her fifth month, he shall pay 5 shekels of silver. He shall look to his house for it.

Late version of 17
If anyone causes a free woman to miscarry, he shall pay 20 shekels of silver.

18
If anyone causes a female slave to miscarry, if it is her tenth month, he shall pay 5 shekels of silver.

Late version of 18
If anyone causes a female slave to miscarry, he shall pay 10 shekels of silver.

SLEx 1′–2′ make a distinction between involuntarily jostling a pregnant woman and striking her intentionally. Both LH 209–214 and LL d–f mandate different remedies based on the consequence to the person injured, whether she suffers miscarriage or death, as well as on social status. The consequences are independent of the intention of the offending party. A particular woman may survive a miscarriage, while another woman, having less robust health

[40]The nine months of pregnancy would be counted in ten calendrical months.

or just bad luck, may not. The offender is at fault, even though his action is just one of a number of factors leading to the bad outcome. There is a distinction between fault and cause, but this is of little import to the accidental killer, who must pay in all events.

In general, the presentation of the process by which homicide is adjudicated in the cuneiform law collections is sketchy.[41] If we compare the elements that can be adduced from legal records analyzed in Chapter Two, such as the role of the crown, the activities of the involved parties, and the possibility of negotiation in a settlement, elements necessary in the remedy of actual cases, the law collections contain serious omissions. Only certain situations, such as negligence or death of a slave in contrast to a free person, are addressed. Other situations are not treated at all. Moreover, important variants to cases are omitted. Why is this so? Two theories, both involving literary considerations, can account for these characteristics of cuneiform law collections. The first is based on the development of a scribal tradition: Certain cases and punishments are standardized. The second explanation stems from the principles of composition of the cuneiform laws. The paucity of detail is due to the manner in which the statutes are used within the structure of the texts as a whole. These two postulates operate together.

Any theory must explain the striking fact that cuneiform law collections share a great deal of material. A number of cases occur again and again. Thus, the cases of the goring ox, the pregnant woman being injured, and assault unintentionally leading to death all appear in a number of texts. Other cases dealing with other matters also appear again and again. Five characteristics of these shared cases must be taken into account:

1. There are statutes whose wording is exactly or nearly exactly the same in a number of law collections.[42]

[41]Cf. Barry Eichler, "Murder" [Hebrew], *Encyclopaedia Miqra'it,* 7.420–429. The exception to this is HL 1–6, which devotes attention to the social status, gender, and age of both the victim and the perpetrator and to the conditions under which the homicide occurred. These provisions systematically treat intentional and accidental homicide of and by free men and women and male and female slaves, in Hatti, nearby lands with ties to Hatti, and remote lands without diplomatic connections to Hatti, both when the slayer has been identified and when he has not. However, the acts that constitute intentional and accidental homicide are not defined in these statutes. Other statutes in HL provide examples of intentional homicide, whose penalties are drastically different from the ones provided in HL 1–6. Thus, HL 43 mandates that if a man, while crossing a river holding his ox's tail, is pushed off the tail by another and drowns, the deceased man's heirs claim the other person as a slave. HL 44a provides that if a man pushes another person into a fire so that the other person dies, he must give up his son as punishment. These penalties in which the perpetrator or his son is enslaved differ from the penalties in HL 1–4. Although HL 1–4 mandate payment in persons, it is not required that the perpetrator or his son themselves be enslaved. Cf. Hoffner, "On Homicide in Hittite Law," 294, 306–312.

[42]Provisions on unlawful death: LL d, e, f // (are parallel to) LH 209, 210, 213. Provisions on other issues: LL 9 // LE 12; LE 13 // LH 21 // HL 93; LL 10 // LH 59. The examples of parallels for other topics are far from exhaustive.

2. There are statutes whose content is nearly the same but whose wording is substantially different in a number of law collections.[43]
3. There are statutes addressing the same topic but whose content is substantially different.[44]
4. The order of the parallel statutes is the same in a number of law collections.[45]
5. The order of the parallel statutes is the same in two law collections but is different in a number of law collections.[46]

These characteristics are not limited to the statutes on unlawful death but apply across the board to statutes treating a variety of cases.

What can account for these phenomena? The issue of the goring ox is instructive. Each code contains one case about this issue not treated in the other. LE 53 deals with the case of an ox goring another ox, a case not addressed in LH. LH 250 deals with an ox not known as a gorer that does in fact gore a human being, a case not dealt with in LE. Both LE 54–55 and LH 251–252 treat the ox that is a serial gorer; the ward authorities notified the owner, but the owner has failed to take the necessary precautions. Although the circumstances are the same, the wording of the statutes is not the same. The penalties are different: sixty shekels for the free person in LE and thirty shekels in LH, fifteen shekels for a slave in LE and twenty shekels in LH. The relationship between the statutes cannot, therefore, be an act of simple word-for-word copying. Rather, in my opinion, it appears to be generated from a scribal tradition in which certain types of cases make up the repertoire, but the author composes his own variations on the theme.

The existence of a scribal tradition was made possible by the fact that law collections were known to later generations. The tablets that make up the LU do not date from the Third Dynasty of Ur; they are from a later period. One tablet is from Nippur and was inscribed in the time of Hammurapi.[47] LH became a didactic composition copied in schools and scribal centers for over a thousand years. Copies of LH have been excavated in Ur, Larsa,

[43]Provisions on unlawful death: LL 24 // LH 167. Statutes on other issues: LL 28 // LH 148; LL 29 // LH 160 // LE 25 // LU 15; LE 26 // LH 130 // MAL A 12; LE 28 // LH 129 // MAL A 15 // HL 197–198.

[44]Statutes on homicide: LU 1 // LH 1 // HL 2; LU 3 // LE 22–24 // LH 114–116; LI d, e, f // SLEx 1′–2′. Statutes on other issues: LL 25 // LH 170–171; LL 31 // LH 105; LU 18–22 // LE 42–46 // LH 196–201 // HL 7, 11–16.

[45]Statutes on unlawful death: LL d, e, f // LH 209, 210, 213; LE 53–55 // LH 250–252. Statutes on other issues: LL 24–25 // LH 167, 170–171; LL 31–32 // 165–166.

[46]LU 19, 20, 22 // LE 36, 42 // HL 12, 13, 7 // LH 197, 201; LU 18–22 // LE 42–46 // LH 196–201 // HL 7, 11–16; LL 24–27 // LOx 3, 1, 2, 4 // LH 247–248; LE 26–30 // LH 130, 128, 129, 135, 136.

[47]S. N. Kramer, "Ur-Nammu Law Code," *Or* 23 (1954), 40.

Nippur, Sippar, Babylon, Borsippa, Assur, Nineveh, and Susa. Texts of the complete LH as well as epitomes of LH, commentaries on LH, and even a bilingual Sumerian-Akkadian extract have been found. Some were made contemporary to Hammurapi. Others were drafted a millennium later. MAL are found in a group of tablets most of which are eleventh-century B.C.E. copies of fourteenth-century originals.[48] These tablets were excavated at the Assyrian capital Assur. Only one tablet, MAL A, contains an exact date: It contains a date formula referring to the eponymy of Sagiu, an official during the reign of Tiglath-Pileser I, who ruled from 1114 to 1076.[49] It is debated whether these tablets were intended for Tiglath-Pileser's royal library[50] or for the personal library of later scribes.[51] It is striking to consider what remained the same in these law collections despite the variety of social, linguistic, ethnic, economic, and political changes during the span of two millennia. Certain topics were to be treated, others omitted. Each law code contained some but not a great deal of variation. (MAL is the exception, and it appears not to be part of this scribal tradition.)[52]

The second reason for the sketchiness in the treatment of homicide is due to the principles of literary composition used. Within the law collections as a whole, there appear to be topical groupings. Certain legal cases appear to be bridges between these groupings. Within a single grouping, two principles

[48]Roth, *Law Collections,* 154.

[49]H. Freydank dates this official to the reign of Ninurta-apil-ekur, who ruled from 1191 to 1179 ("Fernhandel und Warenpreise nach einer mittelassyrische Urkunde des 12 Jahrhunderts v.u.Z," in *Societies and Languages of the Ancient Near East: Studies in Honor of I. M. Diakonoff* [Warminster, U.K.: Aris & Phillips, 1982], 66).

[50]Ernst F. Weidner, "Die Bibliothek Tiglatpilesers I," *AfO* 16 (1952), 197–215.

[51]W. G. Lambert, "Tukulti-Ninurta I and the Assyrian King List," *Iraq* 38 (1976), 85–86 n. 2.

[52]It must be noted that the Middle Assyrian Laws look different from the others in that the twenty-odd tablets that contain them do not constitute a single document. Furthermore, the unusual composition of a tablet, such as Tablet A, which deals with various offenses committed by or against women, militates against the fact that a tablet could be a section of a larger corpus, since these offenses would have to be treated again with respect to other persons. Because of these characteristics, Paul Koschaker argues that Tablet A of the Middle Assyrian Laws, at least, is in fact the product of a jurist who has supplemented an earlier text with additional laws on a particular subject and explanations for his private use, and is not the product of a legislator who has amended and redrafted earlier laws for practical use as enactments (*Quellenkritische Untersuchungen zu den 'altassyrischen Gesetzen'* [Mitteilungen der Vorderasiatisch-aegyptischen Gesellschaft 26; Leipzig: J. C. Hinrichs, 1921], 79–84). Koschaker calls the Middle Assyrian Laws a *Rechtsbuch,* comparing it to the Digest of Justinian. Additional evidence for Koschaker's position is found in the repetition in MAL O of some but not all of the provisions in MAL B. Furthermore, although he restricts his remarks to Tablet A, it does apply to the other tablets, which consist of statutes treating a particular subject, as if the intent of the scribe was to collect various rulings on that subject. For example, just as MAL A deals with women as perpetrators or victims in a wide variety of situations – ranging from theft, blasphemy, bailment, assault and battery, sexual assault and sexual offenses, homicide, false accusations, inheritance, and marriage and marital property to veiling, witchcraft, pledges and debts, and abortion – MAL B deals with land issues involving inheritance as well as agriculture and irrigation.

of arrangement appear to be operative.[53] One is the placement side by side of a group of cases in which the variants are maximal.[54] These polar cases provide a clear statement of the just laws in extreme cases but leave a gray area in the middle where some but not all the criteria are fulfilled.[55] The other principle of arrangement in cuneiform law collections is the creation of a legal statement by the juxtaposition of one legal case with another. The relationship between one case and its neighbor creates the context in which the cases ought to be understood.

LE can illustrate the use of these principles vis-à-vis the statutes on unlawful death (LE 23–24, 47A, 54–58). LE 22–24 discuss the laws of distraint, a case in which a loan has fallen due and the creditor has distrained a person from the debtor's household:

> 22
> If a man had no claim against a free man yet distrained the man's slave woman, the owner of the slave woman will swear by a god, "You have no claim upon me," and he shall weigh out as much silver as the value[?] of the slave woman
>
> 23
> If a man had no claim against a free man yet distrained the man's slave woman, detained the distrainee in his house, and caused [her] to die, he shall replace 2 slave women to the owner of the slave.
>
> 24
> If he had no claim against him yet distrained the wife of a commoner/dependent or the son of a commoner/dependent, detained the distrainee in his house, and caused him/her to die, it is a case of life; the distrainer who distrained shall die.

The first case, LE 22, deals with illegal distraint in which the distrainee is not harmed. The second and third cases, LE 23–24, treat illegal distraint in which the creditor has caused the death of the distrainee. LE 23 discusses the detention of a slave belonging to a member of the *awīlu* (free) class, whereas LE 24 treats the detention of a member of the *muškēnu* class. If the deceased distrainee is a slave, the statute prescribes compensation; if the deceased distrainee is a member of the debtor's family, the distrainor suffers capital punishment. The cases in the middle, such as illegal distraint in which the

[53] Barry L. Eichler, "Literary Structure in the Laws of Eshnunna," in *Language, Literature, and History*, 71–72.

[54] Besides Eichler in his article, this is also discussed by J. J. Finkelstein, "Sex Offenses in Sumerian Law," *JAOS* 86 (1966), 368, and Kraus, "Ein zentrales Problem des altmesopotamischen Rechtes," 286.

[55] This principle of arrangement is significantly different from that of other legal texts. For example, a chapter of Mishnah appears to be intentionally arranged in such a way as to explore the gray areas in the middle, where the variations between cases are minimal.

creditor has injured but not killed the distrainee or illegal distraint in which the creditor has detained a person of the *awīlu* class, are neglected.

LE 22–24 act as a bridge combining elements of the previous series of laws with elements of the next series of laws, linking the laws of contract with the laws of marriage.[56] LE 22–24 focus on the unlawful deprivation of one's rights over another because of a claim of an unpaid loan. LE 22–24 are located at the conclusion of a grouping of legal cases: LE 14–21 deal with financial obligations, such as contracts, loans, and interest payments, while the laws that follow, LE 25–30, deal with a person's legal rights over another person through the relationships of betrothal and marriage. Because LE 22–24 act as a bridge, they include elements that serve as linkages: financial obligations and one person's legal rights over another. Other information is superfluous. In contrast, the parallel laws in LH, 115–116, treat lawful detention because they are embedded in a series dealing with financial obligations and repayments, 112–119.

LE 47A acts as an extreme case indicating how far bodily injury can be taken before it becomes a capital offense. It appears at the penultimate position in the series of laws on bodily injuries incurring fines, LE 42–47. The following statute, LE 48, acts as a summary statement making explicit a distinction between cases that incur a fine, which are adjudicated by judges, and capital cases, which are decided by the king:

> 44
> If a man knocks down another in the street and breaks his hand, he shall weigh out 30 shekels of silver.
>
> 45
> If he should break his foot, he shall weigh out 30 shekels of silver.
>
> 46
> If a man strikes another man and breaks his collarbone, he shall weigh out 20 shekels of silver.
>
> 47
> If a man should injure [?] another man in the course of a fight, he shall weigh out 10 shekels of silver.
>
> 47A
> If a man in a brawl caused the death of a member of the *awīlu* [free] class, he shall weigh out 40 shekels of silver.
>
> 48
> And for a case involving a fine of silver ranging from 20 shekels to 60 shekels, the judges shall determine the judgment against him. A capital case is for the king only.

[56] Eichler, "Literary Structure in the Laws of Eshnunna," 78.

LE 47A serves as the maximal variant and, as such, requires the inclusion of material pertinent to the extreme situation and the exclusion of extraneous material.

LE 53 in the context of LE 54 deals with an ox whose vicious disposition was not known before:

> 53
> If an ox gored [another] ox and killed it, both [ox owners] shall divide the value of the live ox and the carcass of the dead ox.
>
> 54
> If an ox [was] a gorer and the ward [authorities] have had [it] made known to its owner, but he did not guard his ox and it gored a man and killed [him], the owner of the ox shall weigh out 40 shekels of silver.

LE 54 presents the polar opposite of the ox in LE 53. The ox of LE 54 is an ox whose vicious disposition was so well known as to be known to the ward authorities. They, in turn, warned the owner, who in spite of the warning did not restrain his ox. The muddy middle is not touched, that is, the case of a vicious ox that breaks out of his enclosure or who leaves his enclosure after thieves have destroyed part of the fence. In these latter cases, the responsibility of the owner is less certain because he has restrained his ox. Unfortunately, because of circumstances beyond his control, the ox gets free and causes damage.

Literary structuring can, thus, account for the omission of critical variants in much of the Mesopotamian material. The scribal tradition that informs the genre of cuneiform law collections provides the types of cases. Each code contains improvisations on these types.

If we compare the Mesopotamian law collections to the legal records from Mesopotamia, the contrast between them is striking: The content of legal records is far more varied. This is so for two reasons. The legal records are directly linked to the details of individual cases. Furthermore, they are not part of a single literary tradition, which constrains variations to a great degree.

Legal documents, legal records, letters, and treaties are clearly related to actual practice, to what was in fact undertaken in the case of homicide. But when we turn to the so-called cuneiform law collections, their relationship to real cases is not so clear, and, in fact, is a subject of great debate. Although the collections differ widely in date and place of composition, they constitute a distinct class of texts in cuneiform literature. The statutes in the collections at least did not develop out of the particular social and political circumstances of their time. They were part of a scribal tradition independent of their historical situation. The introductions, the epilogues, and the impetus for writing a code at all were probably linked to particular needs of the king to whose name the code was linked.

A different array of elements in the treatment of homicide present themselves in the law collections when compared to the other material we have analyzed. For example, in contrast to the cuneiform legal records analyzed earlier, where the penalty is predominately pecuniary, in the law collections the penalty seems to be equally divided between capital punishment and monetary compensation. In the the cuneiform legal records, the manner in which the victim was killed was omitted because these documents are only concerned with the monetary payments involved. By contrast, the law collections present a wide range of possibilities, from intentional homicide to unlawful death resulting from negligence.

Two specific cases of homicide, the case of injury to a pregnant woman (LI d–f, SLEx 1′–2′, LH 209–214, MAL A 21, 50–52, and HL 17–18) and the case of a goring ox in cuneiform law (LE 53–55 and LH 250–253), are treated in cuneiform laws because they are conventional cases. Similar cases appear in the Covenant Code. A pregnant woman has become involved in a scuffle and has been injured with fatal results in Exod 21:22–25. An owner is held responsible for the actions of his goring ox in Exod 21:28–32. These cases are about negligence, a different type of homicide from the accidental and intentional homicide of Exod 21:12–14, Num 35:9–34, and Deut 19:1–13. In the latter, a variety of specific cases are offered to illustrate principles applied to a variety of actual situations.

The statutes on the goring ox in LE contain the closest parallel in literary formulation and substance to any biblical law. LE 53 reads, "If an ox gores another ox and thus causes its death, the two ox owners shall divide the value of the living ox and the carcass of the dead ox." Exod 21:35 reads, "If someone's ox gores his fellow's ox so that it dies, they shall sell the living ox and divide its price and the carcass of the dead ox." How can this similarity be explained?

Raymond Westbrook asserts that the biblical writer possessed a concrete knowledge of cuneiform law.[57] He argues that the biblical formulation was made with the statute in LE in mind. The identity of Exod 21:35 with LE 53 would then serve as proof of the existence of LE as a school text far beyond the borders of Eshnunna and far later than its time of promulgation. Otherwise, there are no attestations of copies or sections of LE beyond the borders of Eshnunna. We do know that cuneiform scribal schools were established in Canaanite cities prior to the Israelites.[58] According to Westbrook, cuneiform law collections were literary works used as school texts in Canaanite scribal workshops and, by implication, were used the same way during the Israelite

[57] Raymond Westbrook, "Biblical and Cuneiform Law Codes," *RB* 92 (1985), 257, and *Studies in Biblical and Cuneiform Law,* 2–3. Also, Paul, *Studies in the Book of the Covenant,* 104.
[58] Westbrook, *Studies in Biblical and Cuneiform Law,* 3.

period. However, to my mind, if there were actual dependence, would it not be visible in the same striking type of correlation in more than one statute?

Reuven Yaron argues that the biblical provisions regarding the goring ox may have been derived from a common Near Eastern legal tradition and practice, rules that were widely used but only sporadically put into writing.[59] He compares the solution of LE and Exod 21:35 to Greek and Roman legislation. First, the Laws of Gortyn, the earliest Greek code, do not contain any law comparable to LE 53 and Exod 21:35. Second, Roman law, which does address the case of the goring ox, holds the owner of the ox that gored responsible. If the surviving ox was the one that gored, its owner is liable to make good the damage. If the surviving ox was the one that was gored, the owner of the goring ox need not make good the damage. In contrast, LE and Exodus divide the loss, regardless of which ox survives. In the latter situation, the owner of the aggressive ox and the owner of the victimized ox are equally likely to lose or gain, depending on the respective values of their oxen. If the two animals are of roughly the same value, both owners have neither lost nor gained by the incident. However, if the animals are of differing value, one owner will be more greatly compensated than the other. The owner of the aggressive ox may come out ahead or behind. The owner of the victimized ox may come out ahead or behind. In a sense, this is grossly unfair to the owner of the ox that was gored, who may suffer a loss, even though he and his ox were not responsible. This no-fault principle[60] differs sharply from the at-fault ruling of Roman law. It was the rule for goring oxen used in the ancient Near East that by chance was recorded in LE and Exod 21:35. It was not an innovation of either text. There is a commonality in a single legal principle between LE and the Hebrew Bible.

Unfortunately for Yaron's view, the rest of the statutes on the goring ox differ greatly. The topic may be the same, but the details are not. According to Exod 21:28–29, if an ox kills a human being, whether it has gored (animals) before or not, the ox must be killed and its flesh may not be eaten. This is not a concern of LE or of any other cuneiform law collections, which are not interested in the fate of the goring ox; for these nonbiblical collections, if an ox known to gore animals kills a human being, the owner must pay according to what is determined at the time. Even the biblical law that has such a striking parallel in LE, Exod 21:35, is followed by a statute addressing the case of a known gorer killing another animal, a case not mentioned in cuneiform law collections. Furthermore, the statutes on the goring ox

[59] Reuven Yaron, *The Laws of Eshnunna*^{2}, 294–295.

[60] This no-fault principle assumes that the two animals were roughly the same value, and it does not take into account where the encounter occurred. Yaron infers that the ruling might be different if they were not approximately equal in value or if the circumstances of the assault were considered. For example, the penalty might be different if the goring took place in the public domain, the field of the aggressor ox, or the field of the victimized ox. However, the ruling here might be aimed at the lowest common denominator of all such cases.

in Exodus are in association with statutes about an animal falling into an uncovered pit (Exod 21:33–34), cases not found in cuneiform law. The fact that Exodus prescribes the stoning of an ox that gores a human being and the death penalty for the owner of the ox requires explanation.[61]

The same phenomenon occurs with the other shared topic between biblical law and cuneiform law, the statutes on injury to a pregnant woman, Exod 21:22–25. The biblical statutes demand the death penalty for the unintentional death of the woman. They do not mandate a fixed sum of compensation for the death of the fetus. They do not mention a distinction between the death of a free woman and a slave woman in this situation.[62] These differences have inspired scholars to focus on the divergences between biblical law and cuneiform law.

Moshe Greenberg argues that law was "an expression of the underlying postulates or values of culture," and distinguishes between the characteristic principles of the Hebrew Bible and those of Mesopotamia, especially with regard to the laws of homicide.[63] He argues that the concept

[61]Paul, *Studies in the Book of the Covenant,* 81.

[62]However, the biblical statutes do distinguish, it appears, the treatment of nonfatal injuries to a slave from those to a free person.

[63]Greenberg, "Some Postulates of Biblical Criminal Law," 18–37, and "More Reflections on Biblical Criminal Law," 1–18. Others deny that the concepts informing law can be isolated so easily, indeed, that this type of analysis is valid altogether. Bernard S. Jackson rejects the broad use of abstraction from biblical and cuneiform law codes by arguing that it is misguided both theoretically and methodologically. First of all, he argues that the law in ancient Israel and the rest of the ancient Near East was conceived in terms of cases rather than principles (*Essays in Jewish and Comparative Legal History,* 29, 32ff). If the ancients did not make these principles explicit, then they probably were not felt by the ancients to exist. At the same time, Jackson argues that generalizing from a small number of written laws and assuming that they reflect implicit principles is misguided because individual scholars may select for emphasis different aspects of the text and thereby (re)construct different principles. Jackson also warns that there is grave danger in importing modern abstract and sophisticated concepts to ancient documents. Israelite and related societies did have principles of law, but that methodologically, for us as modern interpreters, we are unable to gain access to them if they are not explicitly articulated. Jackson acknowledges that principles may lie under the surface, being expressed only in concrete situations, but that we can be confident of their existence only when they are explicitly articulated, are presented as valuable, and are defined as operating within specific parameters.

Against Jackson, however, simply because a society was not capable of or did not articulate such a principle or abstract method does not mean that such a principle or method did not exist (Richard A. Posner, *The Economics of Justice* [Cambridge, Massachusetts: Harvard University Press, 1981], 17). Jean Bottéro compares the Laws of Hammurapi to Mesopotamian scientific treatises, in which principles are expressed through examples: Nonetheless, we can articulate the principle behind the example even if the ancient authors did not choose to articulate it (*Mesopotamia: Writing, Reasoning, and the Gods,* 169–184). In extrapolating from individual laws to principles, we must keep two mutually contradictory generalizations in mind: 1) Like cases were judged alike, and 2) individual laws, while seemingly similar to other regulations, may resist analogical comparisons. This may be compared to rabbinic legal reasoning that often makes analogies from one situation to another yet warns that with regard to certain

that human life is the ultimate value was the principle by which the legislators of ancient Israel reworked Mesopotamian law.[64] The necessary implication of this principle, according to Greenberg, is that the punishment of homicide must be the execution of the offender. The leniency of biblical law in dealing with property offenses comcomitant with its severity in the case of homicide is in stark contrast with nonbiblical law. Greenberg finds the catalyst for the transformation in an ideal that the value of human life reigns supreme over any other value, whether money or other type of property.

On purely logical grounds, the implications of the concept that human life is the ultimate value are not so clear. While Greenberg concludes that the necessary implication of this concept is that the only appropriate penalty for taking human life is capital punishment, others would hold that the necessary implication is that no human life should be taken under any circumstances.[65] In truth, the necessary consequence of the concept that human life reigns absolute over any other value is a matter of instinct on the part of the person making the connection, rather than strict logic. Affirming that it means that the killer must be executed is, in fact, based on an assertion that human life is not fungible and cannot be translated into pecuniary terms. So, too, is the opposite conclusion. The concept that human life is the ultimate value can also lead to the conclusion that no human life should be taken under any circumstances. This, too, is a matter of personal belief *rather than* of necessity in inductive or deductive logic.

Furthermore, even in the Hebrew Bible, human life can be, in certain cases, fungible. Certain statutes in the Hebrew Bible itself do hold that human life can be redeemed in monetary terms. The statute addressing the death of a human being caused by a serial goring ox prescribes the death penalty for the owner of the ox, which can be commuted to a mulct apparently by

rules, "the laws are without roots and are not to be learned from one another" (b. Moed Katan 12a). All synthetic methodologies, including the extrapolation from individual laws to underlying concepts, have been questioned; it seems to me that so long as the inherent problems are articulated and the conclusions recognized as tentative pending new evidence, they are legitimate. This same reasoning applies to the recognition of concepts that inform other genres of biblical literature. In the end, Jackson's strictures are important: He is not, in fact, being self-contradictory in what he wants to assert, but rather he is being cautionary, arguing for greater circumspection in the conclusions drawn from case law.

[64] Greenberg, in "Some Postulates of Biblical Criminal Law" and in "More Reflections on Biblical Criminal Law," implies that the lawmakers of ancient Israel were reformulating earlier laws. He states this more clearly in "Crimes and Punishments," *Interpreter's Dictionary of the Bible*, 1.737.

[65] This has been one of the arguments made in the debate over the abolition of capital punishment in the United States. Cf. Thomas Upham, 51, John O'Sullivan, 52–53, and Gerald Gottlieb, 123, in *Capital Punishment in the United States: A Documentary History* (ed. Bryan Vila and Cynthia Morris; Primary Documents in American History and Contemporary Issues; Westport, Connecticut: Greenwood Press, 1997).

the victim's family (Exod 21: 29–30).[66] In this case, the owner of the ox is permitted to extract himself from the death penalty – it is the owner's life that is evaluated in financial terms, not the victim's. Most importantly, what is considered the appropriate penalty for any crime is culturally determined. For example, imprisonment for theft, which is the norm in our contemporary American culture, would be incomprehensible to an ancient Israelite, who would expect his stolen sheep to be repaid fourfold and his stolen cow fivefold.

It is unclear how the single postulate isolated by Greenberg can account for the major differences we have isolated in our study between Israelite and cuneiform law.[67] In this study, we have seen elements in the treatment of homicide throughout the Hebrew Bible directly linked to specific characteristics of Israelite society and biblical literature – the role of the victim's family in instigating the remedy of a slaying in the guise of feud; the cities of refuge as refracted through the ideology of the legal sources of the Pentateuch; the relationship between concepts of pollution and the treatment of the killer. All of these represent a trajectory to achieve justice that cannot be subsumed under a single principle.

In a similar vein to that of Greenberg, J. J. Finkelstein argues that the conceptual universe of the Mesopotamian statutes on the goring ox is vastly different from the biblical statutes on the same topic.[68] An Israelite author appropriated an ancient Near Eastern legal theme, but by fitting it into a distinctly different framework, he in effect transformed it in the most profound sense, even while retaining much of the original form and language. The biblical thought-world was hierarchical in nature: God has complete dominion over human beings, who in turn have complete dominion over nature. Therefore, an attack by an ox on a human being is a category error, an assault against the hierarchy. The ox, whether it had gored before or not, had to be destroyed by stoning, a particular type of execution applied to offenses that compromise the integrity and essence of the entire Israelite community. (An ox that gores another ox is sold, not stoned.) In contrast, Mesopotamian thought on the role of humanity vis-à-vis nature and the gods was not hierarchical.[69] Humanity was, in fact, of secondary importance, created after

[66] These two cases, death caused by a serial goring ox and death caused to a pregnant woman, are clearly borderline cases, hedging on the indirectness of intention, as Greenberg notes in "More Reflections on Biblical Criminal Law," 10.

[67] Greenberg's article "Some Postulates of Biblical Criminal Law" was clearly polemical. Indeed, Greenberg did not mean that outside of ancient Israel, human life was considered valueless. People were not killed indiscriminately outside of ancient Israel. What Greenberg was advocating in his article is attention to the content of biblical law and its relation to an Israelite worldview.

[68] Finkelstein, *The Ox That Gored*, 5.

[69] Perhaps this should be qualified somewhat as being not so stringently hierarchical. One could argue that there is a hierarchy in Mesopotamia as exemplified by the position of human beings as workers for the gods in Atrahasis and Enuma elish.

the gods had built the great cities of Sumer and Babylon. Humanity was not to have dominion over nature. An attack by an ox on a human being did not pose the cosmic threat in Mesopotamia that it did in ancient Israel. The fate of the ox is of no concern and, therefore, is not mentioned in LE 54–55 and LH 250–252.[70] In my opinion, Finkelstein's argument about the distinct conceptual universes from which the biblical and cuneiform statutes originate is valid because it is narrowly focused on a single case in biblical law and its Mesopotamian antecedents and the differences between them.

Finkelstein further argues that the biblical statutes must be part of a scribal tradition, because the actual occurrence of an ox goring is so unlikely that it is improbable that such an incident occurred in Israelite experience to be the source of the biblical laws. He bases this argument on the few legal records about goring oxen that he found: This implies that actual occurrences were extremely rare. This rarity applies as well to the case of a woman's miscarriage resulting from becoming entangled in a scuffle: It seems so improbable – common sense dictates that pregnant women would avoid being involved in fisticuffs – that it appears to be proof of a common legal tradition between the cuneiform law collections and the Hebrew Bible.[71] In my opinion, Finkelstein's argument is faulty. An ox goring in an agro-pastoralist society seems probable: An ox is usually a docile animal, but considering the number of oxen in use, the case of an ox going berserk would occur from time to time.[72] Furthermore, an argument on whether an occurrence is probable on the basis of its presence in documents of actual cases is faulty simply because so few legal documents mention anything other than the sale of barley, slaves, donkeys, or orchards of date palms. To put it in statistical terms, out of the approximately twenty-five hundred legal documents I surveyed, I found four cases of theft, one case of slander, one case of assault, and one case involving a dispute over the responsibility for a prisoner.[73]

The key, in my opinion, to decoding the relationship between the biblical and cuneiform sources is to recognize that the nature of the differences between the biblical and cuneiform sources is already familiar to us from our analysis of the cuneiform law collections themselves. While it is true that there are significant differences between the Mesopotamian versions and the biblical, the same sort of divergences between the biblical material and the Mesopotamian material on fatal assault are found in the Mesopotamian

[70]Although the ox may well have been dealt with in some manner.

[71]Finkelstein did not find any records about an assault on a pregnant woman. I could not find any case earlier than the Hellenistic period (*Corpus papyrorum Judaicarum* [ed. Victor A. Tcherikover; Cambridge, Massachusetts: Harvard University Press, 1957], 1.246–247).

[72]Cf. the statute in the Chinese law code, *The T'ang Code,* article 207, 2.193–195.

[73]This is not as odd as it seems. The vast bulk of legal documents in our contemporary society is also devoted to recording economic transactions, such as the sale of merchandise, automobiles, and homes.

material itself. Thus, between the biblical and cuneiform sources, there are four differences: 1) The biblical statutes are concerned with the fate of the ox, while the cuneiform ones are not. 2) The biblical statutes recognize only two social categories, free and slave, for the ox's victim and none at all with regard to the pregnant woman, while the cuneiform statutes vary in this regard. 3) The biblical statute provides a penalty that could be changed – it mandates the death of the owner of a serial gorer with the qualification that his punishment could be converted to compensation – whereas the cuneiform statute prescribes a penalty without any mention of any alternative. 4) The biblical statutes on the fatal assault on a pregnant woman make a distinction between intentional and unintentional. With regard to assault on a pregnant woman, LH recognizes three social categories (209–214), whereas LL recognizes only two (d, e, f). MAL does not mention the assault on a slave at all but makes distinctions based on marital and maternal status (A 50–52). HL 17–18, SLEx 1′–2′, LH 209–214, and LL d, e, f mandate a single penalty for each offense, whereas MAL A 21 requires a multiple penalty. SLEx reflects a distinction between intentional and unintentional not found in the other cuneiform law collections (1′–2′).

In the context of the divergences among cuneiform law collections, the biblical statutes in the Book of the Covenant appear to be part of a scribal tradition represented in the cuneiform law collections. The scribal tradition provides the types of cases, and each code contains improvisations on these types. Their variation is one of quantity, not magnitude. The cases of the goring ox and a miscarriage caused by a pregnant woman intruding into a scuffle are traditional literary themes by which a scribe would show his legal flair and even test his larger assumptions about the world.[74] The influence of this tradition appears to be limited to the Book of the Covenant and does not extend to the other treatments of homicide in the Bible. This is significant for identifying what has influenced the Book of the Covenant. It is also significant for what it has failed to influence, the other statutes on homicide in the Bible.

These other biblical texts, in their self-presentation, reflect an apprehension about which slayings fall under which rubric of homicide.[75] They are eager to articulate more precisely and accurately a distinction between intentional and unintentional killing. It may be speculated that this specificity allays a need to provide practical guidance to actual legal cases: The biblical legal texts were intended to offer directives to an actual court. The use of

[74]Although in regard to the scribe's worldview, one need not generalize as far as Greenberg does.

[75]This trend is carried to the nth degree in the Mishnah, which draws finer and finer distinctions between instances of homicide (Makkot 2:1–2). For example, a distinction is drawn between a death caused by a jar, being let *down* from a roof, falling on someone, and killing him; and a death caused by a jar, being drawn *up* to a roof by a rope that breaks, falling on someone and killing him.

cases like the goring ox and a pregnant woman involved in a scuffle in the Covenant Code originates in a scribal tradition, not in what is necessary to the process of remedying a homicide.

In sum, certain features of the adjudication of homicide in the Bible are characteristic of traditional cultures similar in economic and social development to ancient Israel and are therefore reinvented independently by disparate societies. Indeed, there are features of homicide in ancient Israel that are present virtually everywhere, such as the basic division of homicidal acts into intentional and accidental or the death penalty as the appropriate punishment for murder. This holds true for many legal institutions: Human beings can and do have the same basic response to a situation.[76] However, in the context of the similarities on the specific cases of a goring ox and a miscarriage caused by assault, the statutes in the Book of the Covenant and the statutes from the rest of the ancient Near East have a genetic relationship.

APPENDIX ONE: THE PUTATIVE HISTORICAL DEVELOPMENT OF INTENTIONALITY IN HOMICIDE IN BIBLICAL LAW

Albrecht Alt argues that the fact that two apodictic statutes, Exod 20:13 and 21:12, do not make a distinction between intentional and unintentional homicide signified that Israelite law originally did not make such a distinction.[77] At some point later in Israelite history the distinction was reintroduced, as reflected in the poorly drafted casuistic formulation in Exod 21:13–14.

Alt bases his argument on the striking differences in the literary style of biblical statutes.[78] Some of them exhibit the distinctive formal characteristic of casuistic law by being drafted in conditional sentences. They preserve the invariable use of an ordered series of specific particles in the protasis of a conditional sentence. Initial conditions are introduced with כי or וכי, "(and) when." Additional conditions are introduced with אם or ואם, "(and) if." In sharp contrast, other statutes lack these particular markers and are far more

[76] Alan Watson, *Legal Transplants: An Approach to Comparative Law* (Charlottesville: University of Virginia Press, 1974), 12–13.

[77] Alt connects these laws to the absolute prohibition of killing in Gen 4:10 and 9:6, where the demand of a stern Deity for strict retribution is reflected ("The Origins of Israelite Law," 141–142).

[78] Much work has been done in recent years on the compositional integrity of the Book of the Covenant as reflected in its literary structure. Despite the expected disagreements among scholars, there is large agreement as to the basic structure. Cf. Jörn Halbe, *Das Privilegrecht Jahwes* (Göttingen: Vanderhoeck & Ruprecht, 1975), 413–421; Yuichi Osumi, *Das Kompositionsgeschichte des Bundesbuches Exodus 20,22b–23,33* (Orbis Biblicus et Orientalis 105; Freiburg, Switzerland; Gottingen: Universitätsverlag Freiburg Vanderhoeck & Ruprecht, 1991), 155; Ludger Schwienhorst-Schönberger, *Das Bundesbuch*, 23. A detailed discussion of the structure of the Book of the Covenant is beyond the scope of this study.

varied in form. These laws exhibit an apodictic style alien to the conditional sentences of the casuistic laws.[79] For example, Exod 21:12 contains a circumstantial participle in place of the protasis and an infinitive absolute in the apodosis – "Whoever fatally strikes a man shall surely be put to death." Statutes with parallel linguistic structure can also be found elsewhere in the Covenant Code (Exod 21:15–17; 22:17–19). This group of statutes (Exod 21:12, 15–17; 22:17–19) has a similar form to the list of offenses put under a curse in Deut 27:15–26. Each sentence in the Deuteronomic list contains the same predicate and a subject in the form of a participle. This suggests that Exod 21:15–17 + 22:17–19 also form a series, one in which casuistic statutes (Exod 21:13–14) have been inserted. The Decalogue appears to be another list of statutes, albeit exhibiting another noncasuistic style. These noncasuistic formulas are denoted as apodictic.

Alt argues that the varying syntactic formulations are indications of disparate sources stemming from different origins.[80] He notes that the casuistic statutes in the Covenant Code exhibited a grammatical form strikingly similar to the literary form of other ancient Near Eastern statutes. This is apparent even though only a few of the statutes exhibit a pure casuistic form. Exod 21:2–11 contain the use of the second person in place of the third person commonly used in the casuistic statutes found elsewhere in the Bible and ancient Near Eastern literature. Alt surmises that the casuistic statutes of the Book of the Covenant stemmed from Canaanite law, the local embodiment of ancient Near Eastern law, the pre-Israelite legal source that the Israelites adopted. He argues that apodictic law, in contrast, originated in the Israelite circles. Indeed, the apodictic statutes were distinctively and uniquely Israelite in origin and essence. The apodictic laws were part of a list of behavioral norms recited in the cult. The use of these lists are clear from their context, a cultic ceremony in which behavioral norms are recited.[81] In short, there is an equivalence between the different styles of the statutes and the different settings from which they originated.

Alt maintains that these different settings represented different temporal stages, not only different social origins. Casuistic law stemmed from a pre-Israelite stage, while the apodictic came from an Israelite period. Isolating apodictic from casuistic law allowed him to reconstruct Israelite law in opposition to the common legal tradition of the ancient Near East. The

[79] However, many of these statutes bear an uncanny resemblance to casuistic form. Exod 21:12, for example, contains a circumstantial participle in place of a finite verb in the protasis. Its apodosis contains an infinitive absolute complementing a finite verb, the same form found in the casuistic statutes of Exod 21:36 and 22:5, 13. Both this form and the pure casuistic form are in the third person.

[80] Alt, "The Origins of Israelite Law," 103–171.

[81] This is not to say that this list necessarily originated in the cult. The present form of the Decalogue is a result of a complex history of development, whose individual steps cannot be reconstructed with precision. See Raymond F. Collins, "Ten Commandments," ABD 6.383–387.

apodictic statutes reflect the changes Israelites had made to Canaanite practice. Scholars before Alt had produced a catalog of legal forms but had not gone beyond the literary realm to posit a connection between literary form and the life of a community.[82]

Alt argues that the presence of an apodictic statute regarding homicide, an excerpt from a cultic list, indicated what was specifically Israelite. The apodictic statute was later transformed by a statute phrased in an acquired literary form, the casuistic form.

However, Alt's contention is flawed because it does not take into account the disparate institutional settings of apodictic and casuistic statutes. Drafting legislation or recording legal decisions requires the specification of details and, therefore, casuistic statutes contain a magnitude of detail not found in liturgical recitations. For example, in the case of theft, the penalty may vary on the basis of the kind of item stolen, whether the thief had sold the item or was caught with it, or whether the thief was caught in the process of stealing. In contrast, expressing behavioral norms in cultic recitations does not require such detail.[83] The cultic lists from which the apodictic laws originated use a more absolute and unqualified form of expression in refraining from naming individual cases.[84] They lay down principles. This mode of expression is made more emphatic in the Decalogue, which omits the penalty for the offense. Cultic recitations are not concerned with the circumstances of mitigating and aggravating factors. Therefore, Alt's reasoning here is faulty because stages in legal history cannot be extrapolated by comparing the

[82]Cf. Bäntsch, *Das Bundesbuch*, 28–33, who argues that there was a distinction drawn in Exod 24:3 between the משפטים drafted in casuistic form and the דברים put into apodictic form. This distinction extended to their content: The משפטים dealt with secular social order while the דברים treated ethical and cultic affairs. Anton Jirku, *Das weltliche Recht im Alten Testament* (Gütersloh: T. Bertelsmann, 1927), makes finer distinctions within the categories of casuistic and apodictic law.

[83]Volker Wagner argues that the apodictic laws belong to a series of ten delicts (Exod 21:12, 15–17, and 22:18; Lev 20:10–14) that incur the death penalty in the intertribal court of nomadic society and were not related to Israelite religion (*Rechtssätze in gebundener Sprache und Rechtsatzreihen im israelitischen Recht* [BZAW 127; Berlin: Walter de Gruyter, 1972], 23–31). He bases his argument on the view that the delicts involved were not related to the cult but pertained to the legal arena. Gerhard Liedke argues that the apodictic laws represent the legislation of the paterfamilias in a noncultic setting (*Gestalt und Bezeichnung alttestamentlicher Rechtssätze* [WMANT 39; Neukirchen-Vluyn: Neukirchener, 1971], 101–135). Hermann Schulz argues that the apodictic laws ending in מות יומת belonged to the sacred court of a tribe (*Das Todesrecht im Alten Testament* (BZAW 114; Berlin: Walter de Gruyter, 1969], 99–113). However, the recitation of a list in a cultic recitation in Exod 20:1–14 and Deut 27:15–26 is a much stronger proof of the social setting of these laws than the more implicit evidence that Wagner, Liedke, and Schulz present. Cf. the arguments for a cultic setting by John Bright, "The Apodictic Prohibition: Some Observations," *JBL* 92 (1973), 185–204.

[84]Alt recognizes this feature of apodictic law but does not see its implications when he used the cultic recitations to reconstruct the innovations of Israelite law ("The Origins of Israelite Law," 157).

content of apodictic statutes and casuistic statutes. They are two distinct styles that coexisted.

Furthermore, in light of the extensive documentation of individual responsibility in ancient Near Eastern societies of all levels of social development, it is difficult to understand why such a concept should elude the Israelites. Indeed, all our texts assume individual responsibility for homicide except for those which involve political killings, such as 2 Sam 21:1–14 or 2 Kgs 14:5–6. Corporate responsibility was an important issue in Israelite society – a contentious issue as witnessed by Ezekiel 18 and Jer 31:29–30[85] – but it was not an issue in the adjudication of homicide.

APPENDIX TWO: DIRECT CAUSATION OF HOMICIDE IN CUNEIFORM LAW

In the Neo-Assyrian documents, the killer's community took the initiative in acknowledging the obligation. It would appear, then, it did so because it was also considered liable. To what extent are those who did not inflict the fatal blow considered responsible elsewhere in Mesopotamia? At issue in two of the cases in other Meopotamian documents is the culpability of such a person in a homicide. In CT 29 42, the person who instigated a slaying is being sued by the victim's sons. The content of the charges made can be extrapolated from the oaths to be taken by Ashqudum and his wife Amat-Amurrim. Although Ashqudum is accused of instigating the death of Ipqatum, the issue under contention is that of the illegal possession of Ipqatum's property. The victim's sons have accused Ashqudum of causing the death of their father, albeit at the hands of another, in order to acquire Ipqatum's fortune. However, Ashqudum is not being prosecuted for the unlawful death itself. Although he bears part of the responsibility, he is not culpable for it.[86] Only the actual killer, who dealt the coup de grace, is subject to legal action for homicide. Ashqudum, however, is legally responsible if he fraudulently acquired Ipqatum's property. This case is purely a dispute over property.[87] The

[85] Compare as well Deut 5:9–10 and 24:16.

[86] The final outcome of the case is left vague. However, since Ilu-Shamash averred in an oath that he could identify his father's murderer and Amat-Amurrim denied complicity in illegally appropriating Ipqatum's property, it is probable that the charge that Ashqudum instigated Ipqatum's murder was affirmed. Cf. J. G. Lautner, *Die richterliche Entscheidung und die Streitbeendigung im altbabylonisichen Prozessrechte* (Leipziger rechtswissenschaftliche Studien 3; Leipzig: Theodor Weicher, 1922), 84.

[87] Dhorme notes that the oaths taken are similar to one made by the person who has possession of disputed property averring that property is his, according to LH 9 ("Mélanges," 105). However, there are significant differences from LH 9: 1) The person claiming the property must make a statement declaring that the property is his, whereas in CT 29 42, the plaintiff is claiming that Ashqudum instigated Ipqatum's death; 2) in LH 9, the person who has possession must name the person who sold it to him and the people who served as witnesses for the transaction. The

issue of homicide is brought in solely as an aside, to explain how Ashqudum allegedly acquired possession of Ipqatum's property.

However, other pieces of evidence indicate that a person other than the one who dealt the fatal blow can be subject to legal action. Indeed, in the account of the Nippur Murder Trial, the issue that is debated is the culpability of the victim's wife:

> [6]u$_{4}$ lú-^{d}inanna dumu lugal-uru$_{4}$-du$_{10}$-ke$_{4}$ [7]ba-úš-a-ta [8]^{I}nin-da-da dumu-munus lú-^{d}nin-urta [9]dam lú-^{d}inanna-ra [10]lú-^{d}inanna dam-a-ni [11]al-gaz-za [12]in-na-an-ne-eš [13]^{I}nin-da-da dumu-munus lú-^{d}nin-urta [14]ka nu-un-ba TÚG ba-an-dul . . . [35]^{I}šu-qa-li-kum ERÍN-GAL-GAL uku-uš ^{d}nin-urta [36]^{I}u-bar-^{d}en-zu nu-giri$_{11}$ [37]igi-ne-ne in-gar-re-eš-ma [38]nin-da-da dumu-munus lú-^{d}nin-urta [39]dam-a-ni ḫé-en-gaz [40]munus-e a-na bí-in-ag-e [41]al-gaz-e-dè bí-in-eš [42]pu-uḫ-ru-um nibru^{ki}-ka [43]igi-bi bi-ib-gar-ma [44]munus dam-a-ni nu-un-kal-la [45]lú-kur-ra-a-ni hé-en-zu-àm [46]dam-a-ni ḫé-en-gaz [47]dam-a-ni al-gaz-za [48]giš ḫa-ba-an-tu ku-àm [49]a-na-aš-àm KA u-gù-na li-bi-in-si [50]e-na-àm dam-a-ni in-gaz [51]nam-tag-ga-a-ni lú-in-gaz-eš-am [52]a-ab-diri bí-in-eš
>
> [6–14]After Lu-Inanna, son of Lugal-uru-du, had been put to death, they told Nin-dada, daughter of Lu-Ninurta, wife of Lu-Inanna, that Lu-Inanna, her husband, was killed. Nin-dada, daughter of Lu-Ninurta, did not open her mouth and covered it up.... [35–41]Shuqalilum, the *Erin-gal-gal,* sergeant of Ninurta, and Ubar-Enzu, the orchard man, addressed [the assembly] as follows: "Nin-dada, daughter of Lu-Ninurta, may have killed her husband, but what can a woman do in [such a matter] that she is to be killed?" they said. [42–52]In the Assembly of Nippur, [the assembly] addressed them as follows: "A woman who does not support her husband may give information to his enemy and thus [the enemy] may [be able to] kill her husband. That her husband is killed, [the enemy] may let her hear – why should he not thus make her keep silent about him? – she [more than anyone else] killed her husband. Her guilt is greater than [of those] who killed a man," they said.

Even though the victim's wife did not take part in the assault, she is adjudicated as guilty, if not more guilty, than the ones who actually struck the blow. This is a radicalization of the concept of guilt. The accused in CT 29 42

differences may be due to the circumstances of this case in CT 29 42 in which the sons of the deceased claim that his property appears to be in the possession of the person who instigated his death. That is, the differences really amount to a different focus for CT 29 42, which deals specifically with the homicide, but also with the property.

had knowledge of the crime before it happened and assuredly could have acted to prevent the tragedy; indeed, he was the one who instigated the homicide. In contrast, the victim's wife in the Nippur Murder Trial participated in the cover-up after the crime. A possible role for her before the killing is imputed to her solely because she is the victim's wife and could have betrayed him.[88] Although there is no evidence for her participation in the homicide, her position as the victim's wife, possessing thereby special access to him, is sufficient. What is at work here is the application of a different and harsher standard to the woman because of the assumption that a woman is inherently dangerous.[89] Her most minor infraction will lead to an escalating series of offenses: If she does not support her husband, she will betray his right to exclusive sexual access[90] and commit adultery, leading her to ask for her husband's death. Her lover will then kill her husband and tell her, in a relationship of trust that she did not have with her husband. In the trajectory posed by this scenario, it does not matter whether she actually dealt the coup de grace: Because she could have violated her husband's trust, her guilt exceeds that of those who actually killed her husband.

The concept that a person is liable for punishment even though he did not deliver the fatal blow is also reflected in NSG 41. The wife and daughter of the killer are enslaved because their husband and father was a killer. Indeed, he was executed for his crime,[91] but that penalty was not sufficient. However, it must be noted that self-defense is recognized as justifiable in the second case recounted in NSG 202. The linking of the fatal blow with culpability is not absolute.

[88]LH 153 addresses the case of a woman who has had her husband killed and mandates the penalty of impalement. In the Nippur Murder Trial, the wife is brought under the jurisdiction of the law in a consideration of her role as accessory, whereas in LH 153, the wife's role is defined as a discrete crime, associated with other family offenses, for which a distinctive penalty is effected. These differences indicate that there is no direct connection between the Nippur Murder Trial and LH. Cf. Jacobsen, "An Ancient Mesopotamian Trial for Homicide," 213.

[89]Martha T. Roth, "Gender and Law: A Case Study from Ancient Mesopotamia," in *Gender and Law in the Hebrew Bible and the Ancient Near East* (ed. Victor H. Matthews, Bernard M. Levinson, and Tikva Frymer-Kensky; JSOTSup 262; Sheffield: Sheffield Academic Press, 1998), 175–181.

[90]Note that in the original presentation of the case, the verb used to express that the killers told Nin-Dada in l.12 is *e*, "to say" in an informational sense; in contrast, when the Assembly of Nippur describes her act in l.45, the verb used is *zu*, "to know; to learn," which can have a sexual connotation.

[91]Adam Falkenstein believes that the death of Kuli had nothing to do with the murder he committed, and he argues that it cannot be extrapolated from the language used to describe the death of Kuli that he was killed as part of a vendetta (*Die neusumerischen Gerichtsurkunden* [Munich: Bayerische Akademie der Wissenschaften, 1956], 1.133). However, the form of the verb *ku-li ba-gaza* (line 5) is passive and should be rendered "Kuli was executed," not as Falkenstein translates, "Kuli died."

A master is not liable for the acts of his slave, but he is paid compensation if his slave is killed. In the Nippur Murder Trial, two of the accused are free men, but the third is a slave. No special consequences of his status as slave are noted in the account. He was tried in exactly the same manner as the free men were. His owner did not participate in the trial nor is any legal responsibility imputed to the owner because of the actions of his slave.

CHAPTER SIX

Lex Talionis

IN THE Hebrew Bible, an individual found guilty of intentional killing was subject to the most severe penalty, execution.[1] In our analysis of the polluting effects of homicide, we observed that the only means of removing the defilement caused by a homicide was the execution of the intentional killer or the death of the high priest in the case of an accidental killer. The execution of the intentional killer is warranted for another reason, and in order to illuminate this aspect of the punishment, we must turn to another legal text.

[1]Although the remedy for premeditated murder is execution (Exod 21:12, 14), Martin J. Buss holds the view that the same texts that have been read as proof of capital punishment for homicide need to be understood differently. He argues that the phrase מות יומת, generally rendered as "[the murderer] shall be killed," should be understood as "he may be killed" or "he is liable to be killed" in light of the permissive sense of the imperfect ("The Distinction between Civil and Criminal Law in Ancient Israel," *Proceedings of the Sixth World Congress of Jewish Studies 1973* [Jerusalem: World Congress of Jewish Studies, 1973], 1.55–56). Buss would have, in fact, sharpened his argument if he had relied upon the nuance of potentiality inherent in Hophal verbs because the imperfect can also express the sense of obligation as well as that of permission. (Cf. the discussion on the modal nuances of Hophal in Waltke and O'Connor, *An Introduction to Biblical Hebrew Syntax,* 445, 452.) Whether this clause expresses permissivity or obligation depends on its context. In this case, the legal context would militate against the permissive sense because of the point of a statute – it directs a particular course of behavior. Otherwise, the sense of permissibility would be found in many legal apodoses, rendering them contentless. Therefore, it is clear that the penalty for premeditated homicide is death.

The sole focus of Lev 24:17–21 is to highlight the punishment for assault and for killing, whether the victim is a human being or an animal:

> If a man strikes another and kills him, he shall surely be killed. The one who strikes an animal and kills it shall make restitution, a life for[2] a life. If a man maims his fellow, as he has done so shall it be done to him, a fracture for a fracture, an eye for an eye, a tooth for a tooth, as he maims a man so shall it be done to him. The one who strikes an animal [and kills it] shall make restitution, and the one who strikes a man [and kills him] shall be killed. You shall have one law for both resident alien and citizen, for I am the LORD your God.

In order to understand Lev 24:17–21, we must analyze its literary form. First of all, the homicide laws in Lev 24:17–21 are embedded in an oracular response to a case of blasphemy, recounted in 24:10–12. The juxtaposition of blasphemy and deadly assault can be explained on two levels, conceptual and formal/linguistic. Both are to be applied to the Israelite citizen and to the alien. Both are capital cases whose statutes contain the formal sentence of מות יומת. Thus, there are two linkages, a conceptual and a formal/linguistic.

Second, the oracular response in this episode is similar to the response in two of the three other episodes of cases brought to Moses whose law is unknown – Num 9:6–14 and 27:1–11, but not 15:32–36 – in that the ruling issued is more comprehensive than one solely addressing the case that initially required a response.[3] Num 9:6–14 deals with those who were impure at the time of the paschal offering. The response contains the law pertaining to that particular case, as well as the law for those who were ritually pure at the time of the feast who refused to take part. Num 27:1–11 treats the question of the inheritance of the daughters of Zelophehad. The response not only deals with them but also provides a complete list of inheritors in order of priority: son, daughter, brother, paternal uncle, nearest clan relative. In contrast, the law in the fourth episode, Num 15:32–36, is confined to the case of a man gathering wood on the Sabbath.

These four ad hoc legal situations present adjustments to covenantal law. Moses is unable to decide them on the basis of given covenantal law and

[2]The meaning of תחת in this verse and in the following verses is "in place of, in lieu of, instead of," expressing exchange (e.g., Gen 22:13; cf. Ronald J. Williams, *Hebrew Syntax: An Outline* [2d edition; Toronto: University of Toronto Press, 1976], 59, but compare Waltke and O'Connor's understanding of this as an abstract locational use, *An Introduction to Biblical Hebrew Syntax*, 220). This preposition is used in Deut 22:29 with a noun clause, תחת אשר ענה, "in lieu of having forced her."

[3]Fishbane, *Biblical Interpretation in Ancient Israel*, 103. The oracular response is an H framework for P material. Cf. Knohl, *The Sanctuary of Silence*, 121.

must receive new information.[4] What judicial difficulty underlies the case in Leviticus 24? The description provides only a few details: During the course of a fight with an Israelite, a person of mixed parentage blasphemed the Israelite God, YHWH. The restatement of the case in casuistic form presents the rule that all who blaspheme YHWH are subject to the jurisdiction of Israelite law without regard to the ethnic status of the offender. Blaspheming YHWH is punishable whether the offender is Israelite without question or is of mixed parentage whose covenantal status is unclear. The ruling in this case is that the law is to be applied to the citizen and alien alike.[5] The point of the law on assault being appended to the blasphemy law is that penalties for killing an animal and for killing a person *also* apply to citizen and alien alike. (We can extrapolate from this statement the recognition that biblical differs from nonbiblical law on penalties for killing.)

The emphasis on the same law applying to citizen and alien is integral to the passage whether or not the assault law was original to the passage. The start and conclusion of this pericope contain similar wording: Lev 24:17, וְאִישׁ כִּי יַכֶּה כָּל־נֶפֶשׁ אָדָם מוֹת יוּמָת וּמַכֵּה נֶפֶשׁ בְּהֵמָה יְשַׁלְּמֶנָּה נֶפֶשׁ תַּחַת נָפֶשׁ; and 24:21, וּמַכֵּה בְהֵמָה יְשַׁלְּמֶנָּה וּמַכֵּה אָדָם יוּמָת. This phenomenon, denoted by the technical term *Wiederaufname,* often indicates interpolated material.[6] Although this phenomenon is present in Lev 24:17–21, this does not eliminate an organic connection between the attached material and that to which it is attached. There is an indistinct boundary here between authorial and scribal activities, if indeed authorship and scribal transmission are separate at all.[7]

The substance of the section dealing directly with homicide is reflected in its literary structure (Lev 24:17–21):

a. (v. 17) ואיש כי יכה כל נפש אדם מות יומת
  b. (v. 18) ומכה נפש בהמה ישלמנה נפש תחת נפש
    c. (v. 19) ואיש כי יתן מום בעמיתו כאשר עשה כן יעשה לו
      d. (v. 20a) שבר תחת שבר עין תחת עין שן תחת שן
    c′. (v. 20b) כאשר יתן מום באדם כן ינתן בו

[4]Lev 24:10–23 does not take into account the principle that a person may only be punished for conduct defined as criminal before he acted, a concept termed *legality* in American law. Cf. Dressler, *Understanding Criminal Law,* 29.

[5]The equality of alien and citizen is a major theme of H (Knohl, *The Sanctuary of Silence,* 21). Cf. Lev 17:8, 10, 12, 13, 15.

[6]The significance of *Wiederaufnahme* for literary criticism is discussed by Curt Kuhl, "Die 'Wiederaufnahme' – ein literarkritische Prinzip?" *ZAW* 65 (1952), 1–11. An alternate use of the term is discussed in Shemaryahu Talmon and Michael Fishbane, "Issues in the Ordering of Selected Chapters of Ezekiel" [Hebrew], *Tarbiz* 42 (1972–1973), 35–38 (a translation of this article is "The Structuring of Biblical Books: Studies in the Book of Ezekiel," *Annual of the Swedish Theological Institute in Jerusalem* 10 [1976], 143–146); and Talmon, "The Presentation of Synchroneity and Simultaneity in Biblical Narrative," in *Literary Studies in the Hebrew Bible: Form and Content* (Jerusalem: Magnes Press, 1993), 112–133.

[7]Fishbane, *Biblical Interpretation in Ancient Israel,* 86.

b′. (v. 21a) ומכה בהמה ישלמנה
a′. (v. 21b) ומכה אדם יומת

a. If a man strikes another and kills him, he shall surely be killed.
b. The one who strikes an animal and kills it shall make restitution, a life for a life.
c. If a man maims his fellow, as he has done so shall it be done to him,
d. a fracture for a fracture, an eye for an eye, a tooth for a tooth,
c′. as he maims a man so shall it be done to him.
b′. The one who strikes an animal (and kills it) shall make restitution,
a′. and the one who strikes a man and kills him shall be killed.

The chiastic structure of the passage reveals its trifurcated content: 1) *Lex talionis* applied to nonfatal bodily injuries; 2) the differentiation between the penalty for killing a man and for killing an animal; and 3) the equivalence of lex talionis applied to the death of an animal, in the form נפש תחת נפש, and ישלמנה, compensation.

The problem of lex talionis is revealed most acutely in this passage. The statute makes a clear distinction between the remedy for the killing of a human being and that for killing of an animal – execution in contrast to compensation. What is striking is that the principle enunciated for the killing of an animal is "a life for a life," a statement usually understood as forbidding compensatory payments, but the remedy for killing an animal is compensation. The penalty for slaying a human being is death, but lex talionis is *not* used as the reason. Moreover, the principle of punishment for nonfatal bodily injury is "a fracture for a fracture, an eye for an eye, a tooth for a tooth." At first glance, it would appear that there is a relationship between "a life for a life" and "a fracture for a fracture, an eye for an eye, a tooth for a tooth" simply on the basis of linguistic similarity: Both are formulations of lex talionis and both make an equivalence between injuries. However, the first is applied to the death of an animal, the second to the nonfatal injury of a human being, and *neither* is applied to the death of a human being. What, then, is the significance of lex talionis?

First of all, the polarity between retaliation and compensation vis-à-vis a fatality is not as complete as may initially be thought. Certainly, in Leviticus, lex talionis is set in a context in which the authors felt that talionic punishment involved compensation.[8] Secondly, the remedy for killing an animal is that the animal must be replaced in kind – the object lost is replaced by an object of the same species, not in money.[9] There is a cognitive distinction between repaying in kind and paying in currency. Lex talionis, then, expresses

[8]Exod 21:23; Lev 24:18.

[9]Daube, "Lex Talionis," 135–139. The verb שלם means "to restore," to be distinguished from paying a pecuniary mulct (Exod 21:36, 37; 22:2, 3, 4, 5, 6, 8, 10, 11, 12, 13, 14). With one

a principle of legal symmetry, of repaying in kind.[10] Those guilty of physical assault are made to suffer the exact harm they inflicted on others. This is in sharp contrast to fines, a fixed amount to be paid in particular circumstances. In the case of killing an animal, lex talionis means replacing the particular animal killed instead of paying a fine. In the case of killing a person, lex talionis means the killer is killed. The act of punishment must be similar to the offense in the aspects in which the original act was wrong.[11] In a sense, it is a reversal of roles: The original agent of harm becomes the recipient of the same action of the type that constituted the offense. The killing of animals is treated in the same way as the killing of humans.

Lex talionis appears in two other statutes, Deut 19:16–21 and Exod 21:23b–25. In the law on false witnesses in Deut 19:16–21, lex talionis emphasizes that the penalty applied to the false witness must be the same penalty that would have been applied to the accused. The false witness suffers what the victim of his lie would have suffered (or did suffer). Lex talionis articulates a concept of equivalence.

The principle of equivalence comes across even more strongly in Exod 21:23b–25: This statute concludes in the distinctive formulation of lex talionis, a contrast to the casuistic style in which these provisions commence. The talion formula in verse 23b exhibits a different construction from the casuistically formulated statutes because there is no attempt to arrange the cases in conditional clauses within a series of main and subordinate conditional

exception (Exod 21:34), wherever payment in currency is required, the verb used for "to pay" is נתן (Exod 21:19, 22, 30, 32; 22:16).

[10]Tikva Frymer-Kensky, "Tit for Tat: The Principle of Equal Retribution in Near Eastern and Biblical Law," *BA* 49 (1980), 230–234. Some have argued that the term, *lex talionis,* is correctly applied only to nonfatal bodily injuries and to punishing the offender by making him subject to the same injury as he inflicted. Cf. Jackson, *Essays in Jewish and Comparative Legal History,* 281, n. 1; Yaron, *The Laws of Eshnunna*², 262.

[11]Jeremy Waldron, "Lex Talionis," *Arizona Law Review* 34 (1992), 34–35, 42–43. Lex talionis should not be interpreted as imputing strict liability without any consideration of the intention of the offender because it is presented as a principle of determining punishments for offenses. It is not put forward as a principle treating accidental deaths in the same way as intentional homicide. Some have argued that this literary structure should be isolated as a remnant of a stage in which the intentions of a killer were not considered. Alt argues that since lex talionis does not take into account the subjective guilt of the offender, it exacts a strict penalty based on the external aspects of a crime ("The Origins of Israelite Law," 135). Alt was unable to shed light on the origin of lex talionis ("Zur Talionsformel," in *Kleine Schriften zur Geschichte des Volkes Israel* [Munich: C. H. Beck'sche Verlagsbuchhandlung, 1953 (1932)], 1.341–344). Frank Crüsemann argues similarly and adds that a contemporary book of law may contain technical terms and formulations and refer to legal institutions created hundreds of years earlier (*The Torah: Theology and Social History of Old Testament Law,* 113). The presence of these fixed forms in a contemporary book of law cannot invalidate its interpretation as a self-contained lawbook of its time. However, lex talionis is not applied as anything other than a principle of equivalence in particular cases, and there is no evidence that it would be applied as an articulation of specific punishments for injuries.

sentences. Lex talionis is meant here to be of general application – it is not limited to the single case, fatal injury to a pregnant woman, to which it now applies. It mentions many injuries, none of which are fatal assault on a pregnant woman. Indeed, the principle of talionic retribution contradicts the statutes on injury because in a case of assault according to Exod 21:18–19, the offender must pay compensation. Why then is a talionic formula used in a statute on injuries not mentioned in the talionic formula? In biblical law, principles are expressed in specific terms. The talionic formula does not refer to "a burn for a burn" as a particular punishment. Rather, it uses specific injuries to articulate equivalence as a principle of punishment.

This principle of equivalence applies to homicide in general. Execution as the penalty is to be understood as an equivalence. The penalty is similar to the slaying in the aspect in which the original slaying was wrong. It is a reversal of roles: The original agent of harm, the killer, becomes the recipient of the same action of the type, killing, that constituted the offense. This is the principle underlying execution as the penalty for intentional homicide.

Gen 9:5–6 is an expression of lex talionis in a literary context:

> 5 But your own lifeblood I will require; of every beast I will require it;
> of man for his fellow man, I will require human life. 6 Whoever sheds
> the blood of man by man shall his blood be shed, for in his image did
> God make man.

The death penalty expresses an equivalence between the offense and the manner in which the remedy is carried out. The punishment is the embodiment of lex talionis: The killer is himself killed. Other dimensions of the punishment are also reflected in this text. Emphasis is placed on the importance of blood as the life force of the victim: The only way that the spilling of blood can be undone is for the blood of the offender to be spilled as punishment. Moreover, God takes a particular interest in the punishment of homicide. It is an offense against God because the divine image is reflected in human beings, and the elimination of homicide occupies a central place in the re-creation of society after the Deluge.

Cuneiform law operates differently because the killer may be subject to two radically different punishments, being forced to pay compensation or being killed. These punishments are the means of undoing the wrong, but not in the same way that biblical punishment operates because the biblical punishment uses the same means in punishment as was used in the offense. The loss is made good in cuneiform law, but not through the same action as the offense. Rather, the cuneiform laws on homicide reflect concern with the status of the victim and how that status affected the individual suffering the loss and the type of loss involved.

First, the lowest status is that of slave. Although in general, the statutes in cuneiform law collections may be divided into delicts against property and against persons,[12] the status of slave straddles the distinction – he is a person who is property. Whenever a slave is injured, this is conceived as an offense against the owner of the slave because the slave is the property of his master. Therefore, the penalty for the death of a slave is always in terms of property:

LL f
If a . . . strikes the slave woman of a man and causes her to lose her fetus, he shall weigh and deliver 5 shekels of silver.

LE 23
If a man had no claim against a free man yet distrained the man's slave woman, detained the distrainee in his house and caused [her] to die, he shall replace 2 slave women to the owner of the slave.

LE 55
If it gored a slave and caused [him] to die, he shall weigh out 15 shekels of silver.

LE 57
If it gored a slave and caused him to die, he shall weigh out 15 shekels of silver.

The master's loss must be made good. This is, of course, in partial contrast to the statute in Exod 21:20–21, which stipulates that an Israelite master who, in the course of disciplining his slave, causes his immediate death is subject to the same punishment as the killer of any other individual. If the slave dies sometime later, this is not considered homicide but an unforeseen effect of a beating, and the death of the slave is the master's loss. If a slave is gored, his master receives compensation. The slave in Israelite law occupies an intermediate position, generally considered chattel, sometimes not.

Since a slave is property, compensation can be paid in two forms, a fixed amount or a replacement of the slave. The fixed amount is the general rule, while the replacement of the slave appears in only two statutes on unlawful death, LE 23 and LH 231. The penalty in LE 23 is based on the issue of wrongful appropriation rather than of unlawful killing:

LE 23
If a man had no claim against a free man yet distrained the man's slave woman, detained the distrainee in his house and caused [her] to die, he shall replace 2 slave women to the owner of the slave.

The sanction here is a penalty in kind. Two slave women are to be returned in place of the one taken wrongfully and killed. In similar logic, misappropriation of a slave requires the return in double of the lost property in other

[12]Szlechter, *Les Lois d'Ešnunna*, 117; Yaron, *The Laws of Eshnunna*^{2}, 256–257.

provisions of LE. So, in LE 49, two slaves are to be returned as a penalty for harboring one as a fugitive: "If a man should be seized with a stolen slave or slave woman, a slave shall lead a slave, a slave woman shall lead a slave woman."[13]

The same principle also informs varied statutes in LE, such as LE 25, where the bride-price must be returned in double: "If a man comes to claim [his bride] at his father-in-law's house but his father-in-law refuses [?] him and then gives his daughter to another, the father shall return twofold the bride-wealth he received." However, in LE 34–35, the wrongfully taken child of the equivalent status is to be given back alone: "If a slave woman of the palace gives her son or her daughter to a commoner/dependent for rearing, the palace shall remove the son or daughter whom she gave. But the one who takes the child of the slave woman of the palace in adoption shall restore [another slave of] equal value for the palace." This penalty is imposed on the commoner/dependent, not on the slave woman who gave the child to the commoner, presumably because the slave woman did not have the means to possess or buy a slave herself. In LE 33, "If a slave woman acted to defraud and gives her child to a woman of the *awīlu* [free] class, when he grows up, should his master locate him, he shall seize him and take him away": Doubling is not imposed here because the child has now grown up and is no longer in the care of another who can be forced to pay the double penalty. Since the adult is in fact a slave, he is taken as a slave.

By contrast, the penalty of replacing a slave in LH 231 is generated by the logic of the remedies in the adjoining cases:

> 231
> If [the house that collapses] causes the death of a slave of the householder, he shall give to the householder a slave of similar value for the slave.

Thus, if a slave is killed, a new slave is provided. This follows the logic of the previous statutes, LH 229–230:

> 229
> If a builder constructs a house for a free man but does not make his work sound and the house that he constructs collapses and causes the death of the householder, that builder shall be killed.
>
> 230
> If it causes the death of a son of the householder, they shall kill a son of that builder.

[13] Although the wording of the apodosis in LE 49 is cryptic, it is probable that *ÌR ÌR* $GEME_2$ $GEME_2$ *i-re-ed-de*, "a slave shall lead a slave, a slave woman shall lead a slave woman," indicates that the original slave is to be returned along with an additional slave. See Roth, *Law Collections*, 70, n. 26.

Whatever is lost from the point of view of the head of the household must be replaced. In LH 229, thus, if a builder fails to construct a sound building and the head of the household dies in its collapse, the builder is executed. In LH 230, if a son is killed, the builder's son is executed.

The slave's inferior status has another effect. Since the remedy for the unlawful death of a person other than a slave may be either pecuniary or capital, the relationship between the sanction for the death of a nonslave and a slave operates in two modes. In some statutes, when a slave is killed, the penalty to be paid by the offender follows along the same lines as the penalty for killing a free person in that the penalty for killing a slave is simply some amount less than that for killing a free person. This occurs when the penalty is purely pecuniary. The penalty in LL d for causing a woman of free status to abort her fetus is thirty shekels; in LL e, it is reduced to five shekels for a female slave. LE 54–57 mandates lower penalties for the death of slave caused by a goring ox or vicious dog, fifteen shekels as opposed to forty shekels for a free person. However, in other statutes, when a slave is killed, the penalty is of a different species from the penalty for killing a human being. The killer is executed for the death of a nonslave but is forced to pay compensation for the death of a slave. In LE 23–24, the illegal distrainer, a creditor who makes an illegal seizure as payment for a debt, compensates the owner for the death of his female slave by replacing her with two new slaves, but if he seizes the wife or son of a commoner/dependent and they die in his custody, he is executed. In LE, the penalty for the illegal distrainer of a slave is equivalent to the penalty for stealing a slave (LE 49) – the owner obtains two slaves in place of one.

Slaves are property, and this status shapes how their slaying is punished. The second characteristic of cuneiform law is to recognize gradations among those who are not slaves. LH makes a distinction between two ranks in the nonslave class, the *awīlum,* the free person, and the *muškēnum,* the commoner/dependent.[14] In LH 207–208, if a free person is killed unintentionally, the penalty is thirty shekels. It is reduced to twenty shekels in the death of a commoner/dependent:

> 207
> If [a free man] dies from his beating, he shall swear ["I did not strike him intentionally"]. If [the victim] is a member of the free class, he shall pay 30 shekels of silver.
>
> 208
> If [the victim] is a member of the client/common class, he shall pay 20 shekels of silver.

[14]The debate over the nature of the status of the *muškēnum* has been heated. See M. Stol, "Muškēnu," *RLA* 8.492–493. For the sake of this study, the sole critical point is the recognition that the *muškēnum* is of lower rank.

In the case where a miscarriage occurs, a compensatory death is mandated in the death of a free woman, but the statute assesses a monetary penalty in the death of a woman in the commoner/dependent class (LH 209–212):

> 209
> If a free man strikes a woman of the free class and causes her to miscarry her fetus, he shall pay 10 shekels of silver for her fetus.
>
> 210
> If that woman dies, they shall kill his daughter.
>
> 211
> If he causes a woman of the client/common class to miscarry her fetus by the beating, he shall pay 5 shekels of silver.
>
> 212
> If that woman dies, he shall pay 30 shekels of silver.

Monetary penalties are also assessed for nonlethal injuries to a commoner/dependent, but physical punishment is mandated when the victim is of the free class (LH 196–201). Even within the same rank, notice is taken of whether the offender and victim are of differing or equal status (LH 202–203).[15] It is clear, then, that social categories inform the assessment of penalties.

Despite the strict recognition of social gradations, it is possible to speculate that the categorization allowed for leniency in LH.[16] According to LH 210 and 212, the vicarious death penalty is imposed if the victim is a woman of the free class, but the death penalty for the killing of a woman of the client/common class is excluded. The penalty imposed is thirty shekels of silver, identical to the penalty imposed in LH 251 in which class gradations are not recognized. In LH 208, the penalty for the death of a member of the client/common class is equal to that imposed in the death of a slave in LH 252.

In contrast to LH, the statutes in LE are far less consistent in distinguishing between the free person and the commoner/dependent. LE 47A specifies the penalty for killing a member of the free class in a brawl but does not indicate the penalty for a commoner dependent:

> 47A
> If a man in a brawl caused the death of a member of the *awīlu* [free] class, he shall weigh out 40 shekels of silver.

[15] See Roth, "Mesopotamian Legal Traditions and the Laws of Hammurabi," 13–37.
[16] Reuven Yaron, "Enquire Now About Hammurabi, Ruler of Babylon," *Tijdschrift voor Rechtsgeschiednis* 59 (1991), 235–236.

LE 54, 56, and 58 provide the remedy for the death of a free person but not for the commoner/dependent:

> 54
> If an ox [was] a gorer and the ward [authorities] have had [it] made known to its owner, but he did not guard his ox and it gored a man and killed [him], the owner of the ox shall weigh out 40 shekels of silver.
>
> 56
> If a dog [was] vicious and the ward [authorities] have had [it] made known to its owner, but he did not guard his dog and it bit a man and caused [him] to die, the owner of the dog shall weigh out 40 shekels of silver
>
> 58
> If a wall was about to fall and the ward authorities have made it known to the owner of the wall but he did not reinforce his wall and the wall collapsed and killed a member of the *awīlu* [free] class, it is a case concerning life – it is a decree of the king.

Similar omissions occur in other statutes in LE that address other offenses. LE 12–13 address the compensation to be paid if a person trespasses on a field of a commoner/dependent but do not mention trespass on a field belonging to a member of the free class. Similar lacunae appear in two statutes treating the case of a slave woman giving away her child. That child, if given to a free person, is always subject to seizure, even when the child becomes an adult, according to LE 33. LE 34 mandates that if a slave woman belonging to the palace gives her child to a *muškēnum* for rearing, that child must be returned. The variables in these cases are too incongruous for an accurate comparison to be made between LE 33 and 34. The parallel case to LE 33, the case of a slave woman's child having been given to a free person and now grown up, would be a child given to a person not belonging to the free class and now grown up, that is, either a *muškēnum* or another slave, but those situations are ignored. The parallel case to LE 34, the case of a child of a palace slave woman being given to a *muškēnum*, would be the case of a slave woman of a palace giving her child to either a free person[17] or another slave for rearing, but that is not mentioned.[18] Furthermore, it is unclear whether the possibility of seizure in LE 33 correlates to forced return in LE 34.

[17]The difference between this case and LE 33 is that in LE 33, the child has become an adult.
[18]Since the parallel cases are not included, it must be asked whether omissions signify that the offense in question would not be punished if done to a member of the omitted class. Yaron argued that in LE, the free classes were not differentiated, except in those cases where they were directly contrasted (*The Laws of Eshnunna*[2], 138–139). Omissions in LE constitute a special situation in which the logic of the entire composition is based on the presentation of maximal variants. This issue was discussed in greater detail in the previous chapter.

In contrast to LH and LE, MAL is less consistent on the importance of rank. MAL A 10 does not base the remedy for homicide in general on gradations of social status.

> A 10
> [If either] a man or a woman enters [another man's] house and kills [either a man] or a woman, [they shall hand over] the killers [to the head of the household]. If he chooses, he shall kill them, or if he chooses to come to an accommodation, he shall take [their property]. And if there is [nothing of value to give from the house] of the killers, either a son [or a daughter] . . .

However, in the case of a fatal assault on a pregnant woman, two statutes provide contradictory distinctions. MAL A 21 mandates the remedy on the basis of a woman's status in the free class, while the penalties in MAL A 50–52 are based on the maternal status of the woman:

> A 21
> If a man strikes a woman of the *a'īlu* class causing her to abort her fetus and they prove the charges against him and find him guilty, he shall pay 9,000 shekels of lead; they shall strike him 50 blows with rods; he shall perform the king's service for one month.

> A 50
> [If a man] strikes [another man's wife causing her to abort her fetus, . . .] a man's wife [. . .] and they shall treat him as he treated her. He shall make full payment of a life for her fetus. And if that woman dies, they shall kill that man; he shall make full payment of a life for her fetus. And if there is no son of that woman's husband and his wife whom he struck aborted her fetus, they shall kill the assailant for her fetus. If her fetus was a female, he shall make full payment of a life only.

> A 51
> If a man strikes another man's wife who does not raise a child causing her to abort her fetus, it is a punishable offense. He shall give 7,200 shekels of lead.

> A 52
> If a man strikes a prostitute causing her to abort her fetus, they shall assess him blow for blow. He shall make full payment of a life.

According to MAL A 50, if the pregnant woman has no son from a prior pregnancy, the assailant is executed, except if the fetus was female. In that case, the offender pays the appropriate compensation for a life. According to MAL A 51, if the assailant causes a woman who has not adopted a child to miscarry, a penalty of 7,200 shekels of lead is assessed. In the context of statutes that base punishment on the maternal status of a woman, it might be questioned whether an assault on a prostitute, that is, on no man's wife, would be subject to legal action. MAL A 52, however, makes the fatal assault on a prostitute an offense for which compensation is required.

HL 17–18 take a different tact and base the penalty on the developmental stage of the fetus:

> HL 17
> If anyone causes a free woman to miscarry, [if] it is in her tenth month, he shall pay 10 shekels of silver; if it is her fifth month, he shall pay 5 shekels of silver. He shall look to his house for it.
>
> Late version of 17
> If anyone causes a free woman to miscarry, he shall pay 20 shekels of silver.
>
> HL 18
> If anyone causes a female slave to miscarry, if it is her tenth month, he shall pay 5 shekels of silver.
>
> Late version of 18
> If anyone causes a female slave to miscarry, he shall pay 10 shekels of silver.

The length of pregnancy was considered to last ten months, counting the set month of the year in which the infant was conceived as the first month. (The nine months of pregnancy would end in the tenth calendrical month.) If the miscarriage occurs in the tenth month, the penalty is doubled from what it would be in the fifth month.

In the law collections, the status of the victim affects the penalty. The slave's status as property means that compensation for his death, whether in kind or in money, is paid to his master. Other gradations in rank prompt gradations in penalty.

The pecuniary penalties in the law collections are fixed amounts. No regard is taken of the inevitable variations in an individual's net worth – the size of one's estate or the success of one's business.[19] Group characteristics, such as whether a person is a member of the free, *muškēnum*, or slave class, are taken into consideration, while individual variables are ignored. Every person had a standard "worth" based on social status and gender. Factors such as the emotional suffering and social loss encountered by the victim's family are disregarded. (By contrast, it would appear, at least from the Neo-Assyrian documents, ADD 321 and 164, and from the MAL, A 10, that in Assyria the parties negotiated the amount to be paid with the assistance of the crown – the amount is not fixed.)

[19] Hoffner, "On Homicide in Hittite Law," 295.

As we review the penalties for homicide in cuneiform law, we realize that the execution of the killer is not based on the principle of lex talionis.[20] According to lex talionis, the penalty must be similar to the offense in the aspects in which the original offense was wrong. It is a reversal of roles: In the case of homicide, the original agent of harm, the killer, becomes the recipient of the same action of the type, killing, that constituted the offense. In cuneiform law, the victim's loss is made good, but the penalty inflicted on the transgressor is realized in many different ways, sometimes capital punishment, sometimes monetary compensation, sometimes compensation in kind. The offender does suffer a loss, but it is not the same as the loss suffered by the victim. Social categories imposed their qualifications on the law, and there is general inconsistency.

It is most important to recognize that although there are statutes on unlawful death whose remedy is death, leading us to suppose that the penalty is to be identical to the offense,[21] these are purely coincidental. They are not instances of lex talionis because they fall under the rubric of serious offenses punished by death. Therefore, capital punishment for homicide is not an example of lex talionis. The principle of lex talionis does not operate as the foundational principle of the statutes on homicide in the cuneiform law collections.

This does not mean that lex talionis, retaliation in kind, was not a principle in cuneiform law. It was imposed on a false witness in LL 17 and LH 3:

> LL 17
> If a man, without grounds, accuses another man of a matter of which he has no knowledge, and that man does not prove it, he shall bear the penalty of the matter for which he made the accusation.

> LH 3
> If a man comes forward to give false testimony in a case but cannot prove his accusation, if that case is a capital case [lit. "a case of life"], that man shall be killed.

It was imposed on nonfatal bodily injuries when certain classes of society were involved.

LH 196–201 can be compared to LE 42–43:

> LE
> 42
> If a man bites the nose of another man and cuts it off, he shall weigh and deliver 60 shekels of silver; an eye, 60 shekels; a tooth, 30 shekels;

[20] As against, for example, Sick, who argues that the death penalty for the homicide provision was a result of an imposition of lex talionis (*Die Tötung*, 306).

[21] Herbert Petschow, "Neufunde zu keilschriftlichen Rechtssammlungen," *ZSS* 85 (1968), 18, n. 64.

an ear, 30 shekels; a slap on the cheek, he shall weigh and deliver 10 shekels of silver.

43
If a man should cut off the finger of another man, he shall weigh and deliver 20 shekels of silver.

LH
196
If a free man should blind the eye of another man of the free class, they shall blind his eye.

197
If he should break the bone of another free man, they shall break his bone.

198
If he should blind the eye of a palace dependent/commoner, he shall weigh and deliver 60 shekels of silver.

199
If he should blind the eye of a free man's slave or break the bone of a free man's slave, he shall weigh and deliver one-half of [the slave's] value.

200
If a free man should knock out the tooth of another free man of his own rank, they shall knock out his own tooth.

201
If he should knock out the tooth of a palace dependent/commoner, he shall weigh and deliver 20 shekels of silver.

The imposition of the death penalty in particular cases of homicide is not based on lex talionis, but as the penalty in severe cases:

LL e
If she dies, that male shall be killed.

LE 24
If he had no claim against him yet distrained the wife of a commoner/dependent or the son of a commoner/dependent, detained the distrainee in his house and caused him/her to die, it is a case of life; the distrainer who distrained shall die.

LH 14
If a free man should kidnap the young child of another man, he shall be killed.

LH 15
If a man should enable a palace slave or slave woman, a palace dependent's slave or slave woman to leave through the main city gate, he shall be killed.

LH 210
If that woman dies, they shall kill his daughter.

LU 1
If a man commits a homicide, they shall kill that man.

LU 2
If a man acts lawlessly [?], they shall kill that man.

The death penalty was imposed when the offense was severe. Homicide was just one of those offenses.

Although death was imposed as vicarious punishment in particularly heinous cases, it was not a form of lex talionis. It is critical to recognize that Mesopotamian society was organized by status, and when in a specific case the damage is to be remedied in terms of the loss, the remedy has to be in the same quality as that which was damaged. If the free man kills a free man's son while detaining him for distraint, his son is to be killed (LH 116). If he strikes and kills a woman of the free class, his daughter is to be killed (LH 210). If he builds an unsound structure and the building's collapse kills the son of the owner, his son is to be killed (LH 230). Putting the builder to death for the loss of a minor would be a gross imbalance of justice: A minor is equal only to another minor.[22] This principle is adumbrated in LE 49 in the penalty of paying for the death of a slave by providing two slaves in return – the free person who killed the slave is not killed. The status of the offender and the victim generates the penalty. Sometimes the penalty that is imposed is death, and only sometimes is the death penalty a result of lex talionis.

The principle of lex talionis can be used in a variety of ways. If we refer to the law that gave the name to this principle, we see that lex talionis is not meant as a concept of punishment but is entirely another matter. This law is the second provision in Table VIII of the XII Tables, which reads, *Si membrum rup[s]it, ni cum eo pacit, talio esto,* "If anyone has broken another's limb and does not come to an agreement with him, there shall be retaliation in kind (*talio*)."[23] Lex talionis is meant as a threat, not as a

[22]Finkelstein, *The Ox That Gored,* 34.
[23]The Latin text of the XII Tables is to be found in S. Riccobono, *Fontes iuris romani anteiustiniani* (2d edition; vol. 1; Florence: Barbera, 1941). A translation and commentary on the XII Tables is found in Allan Chester Johnson, Paul Robinson Coleman-Norton, and Frank Card Bourne, *Ancient Roman Statutes* (The Corpus of Roman Law II; Austin: University of Texas Press, 1961), 9–18.

principle of punishment.[24] It is a way in Roman law of forcing the offender to come to terms with the victim. For more minor injuries, a series of fixed monetary penalties is prescribed in the XII Tables.

An intriguing term appears in a number of cuneiform texts. The term *dīn napištim*, literally "the punishment in a capital case," appears in the Laws of Eshnunna and in the Laws of Hammurapi and in some letters.[25] Does this term shed light on cases of homicide?

> LE 24
> If he had no claim against him yet distrained the wife of a commoner/dependent or the son of a commoner/dependent, detained the distrainee in his house and caused [him/her] to die, it is a capital case [lit. a case of life]; the distrainer who distrained shall die.
>
> LH 3
> If a man comes forward to give false testimony in a case but cannot prove his accusation, if that case is a capital case (lit. "a case of life"), that man shall be killed.

A variation on the term appears in other statutes of LE:

> LE 48
> And for a case involving a fine of silver ranging from 20 shekels to 60 shekels, [the judges] shall determine the judgment against him. A capital case is for the king only.
>
> 58
> If a wall was about to fall and the ward authorities have made it known to the owner of the wall but he did not reinforce his wall and the wall collapsed and caused a member of the *awīlu* [free] class to die, it is a case concerning life – it is a decree of the king.

In the law collections, the term signifies a capital case for which the penalty, it appears, is death, but it is understood differently in the letters.

[24] Alan Watson, *Rome of the XII Tables: Persons and Property* (Princeton: Princeton University Press, 1975), 123. There are statutes in cuneiform law that appear to be applications of lex talionis because they entail meticulous attention to the exactness of retribution, leading to statutes resulting in punishments that may appear grotesque; see LH 209/210, MAL A 55. However, the remedy in these provisions is not based on *talio* but on the status of the son or daughter of a free person.

[25] The phrase appears in some other texts. ARM V 12:4 is too broken for analysis. (Georges Dossin, *Lettres* [TCL 26; ARM V; Paris: Paul Geuthner, 1951], no. 12; *Correspondance de Iasmaḫ-Addu* [ARMT V; Paris: Imprimerie Nationale, 1952], no. 12). The phrase appears in an incantation describing how the supplicant has infuriated his goddess, and among the misdeeds he has committed, he has taken an oath in a capital case. (Cf. Reiner, *Šurpu,* 2.86, 15.) It is unclear, though, whether this particular transgression is more serious than the other sins listed.

ARM VIII 1

[1]ia-ḫa-at-ti-ìl [2]DUMU ḫi-il-la-lim [3]ù DUMU ^{f}a-li-tum [4]da-ma-qí-šu-nu i-da-mi-iq [5]li-mi-ni-šu-nu i-li-mi-in [6]šum-ma ḫi-il-la-lum a-bu-šu [7]ù ^{f}a-li-tum um-ma-šu [8]a-na ma-r[i-šu-nu] ia-ḫa-at-ti-ìl [9]ú-ul ma-ri-ni at-ta i-qa-bu-ma [10]i-na É ù e-nu-tim [11]i-ta-al-lu-ú [12]šum-ma ia-ḫa-at-ti-ìl [13]a-na ḫi-il-la-lim a-bi-šu [14]ù ^{f}a-li-tum um-mi-šu [15]ú-ul a-bi at-ta [16]ù ú-ul um-mi at-ti i-qa-bi-ma [17]ú-ga-la-bu-šu-ma [18]a-na KUG.BABBAR i-na-ad-di-nu-šu [19]^{I}ḫi-il-la-lum [20]ù ^{f}a-li-tum

rev.

[21]ma-ri ma-du-tim ma-li ir-[šu]-ú!-ma [22]^{I}ia-ḫa-at-ti-il-ma ap-lu-um [23]i-na É ḫi-il-la-lim a-bi-šu [24]ši-it-ti-in i-li-qí-ma [25]aḫ-ḫu-šu ṣé-ḫe-ru-tum [26]a-ḫu-um ki-ma i-za-az-<zu> [27]ba-qí-ir i-ba-qa-ru-šu [28]a-sa-ak ^{d}UTU ^{d}i-túr-me-er $^{I\,d}$UTU-ši-^{d}IŠKUR [29]ù ia-ás-ma-aḫ-^{d}IŠKUR i-ku-ul [30]ù 3 1/3 MA.NA KUG.BABBAR di-in na-pí-iš-tim [31]i-na-ad-di-[i]n [32]IGI ú-ṣur-a-wa-sú [33]IGI ^{d}NANNA-ìl [34]IGI DINGIR-šu-a-bu-šu [35]IGI ú-ma-an-ni-su-ta [36]IGI ik-šu-ud-ap-pa-šu [37]IGI i-din-ì-lí ku-um-rum [38]IGI ia-ar-i-ip-ìl ku-um-rum [39]IGI ak-ka-ba-ni ku-um-rum [40]IGI šu-^{d}nu-nu DUMU ^{I}da-gan-nu-pa-ra-ia [41]IGI i-din-^{d}nu-nu DUMU ^{I}da-gan-ma-lik [42]IGI ^{d}da-gan-aš-ra-ia [43]DUMU ^{I}da-gan-ga-am-li [44]IGI šu-INANNA DUMU GISSU-lí-INANNA ku-um-rum [45]IGI ḫa-da-ta-an [46]DUMU la-ri-im-lu-ú [47]IGI wa-ri-ki-ma [48]IGI ^{f}an-nu-aš-ri [49]DUMU.MUNUS GISSU-lí-ak-ka [50]IGI ṣa-pur-sà-lim ^{lú}MÁ.LAḪ$_4$ [51]IGI za-ki-ri-im [52]IGI a-ḫi-im DUBSAR [53]ITU ḫi-bi-ir-tim UD 28 KAM [54]li-mu às-qú-du-um

[1–5]Yahatti-el is the son of Hillalum and Alitum. He shall rejoice in their joys and commiserate in their miseries. [6–11]Should Hillalum, his father, and Alitum, his mother, say to their son Yahatti-el: "You are not our son," they shall forfeit house and belongings. [12–18]Should Yahatti-el say to Hillalum, his father, and Alitum, his mother: "You are not my father, you are not my mother," they shall have him shaved and shall sell him for money. [19–26]As for Hillalum and Alitum, regardless of how many sons they have, Yahatti-el is primary heir, and he shall take a double share of the estate of Hillalum, his father. His younger brothers shall divide the remainder in equal shares. [27–31]Whichever [among the brothers] shall enter a claim against him will [be considered to] have infringed on a taboo of Shamash, Itur-Mer, Shamshi-Adad, and Yasmah-Adad, and shall pay three and one-third minas of silver, the penalty in a capital case. [32–52]Witnesses. [53–54]Month of Hibirtum, 28th day, eponym of Asqudum.

If the brothers contest the status of the adopted son as the eldest, especially in regard to inheritance, they will pay three and one-third minas of silver, which is identified as *dīn napištim,* the penalty in a capital case. A set amount is recognized as the compensation in a capital case, but the particular circumstance in which it is paid is not a capital case. The penalty for contesting a legal transaction in other tablets, taking this volume of ARM as an example, is one mina in ARM VII 5.9 and ten minas in ARM VII 8.9, 11.28, 12.7. The expression *dīn napištim,* employed mainly in LE, is taken to mean the imposition of the death penalty without any mitigation. However, here it refers to a financial penalty, and it is in fact a moderation of the more common amount in a penalty clause:[26]

ARM XIII 145
(1)[a-n]a be-[lí-ia] (2)qí-bi-ma (3)um-ma ia-wi-[AN] (4)ÌR-ka-a-ma (5)DUMU.MEŠ ši-ip-ri-im ù lúŠU.GI (6)ša ia-ar-ki-ba-dIŠKUR a-na- ṣe-r[i-ia] (7)il-li-ku-nim-ma ki-a-am iq-bu-nim [um-ma-mi] (8)it-ti-ka ú-ul na-ak-ra-ku (9)ù a-na a-wa-at bu-nu-ma-dIŠKUR ú-ul [a-qú-ul] (10)ù a-na-ku ki-a-am a-pu-ul-šu-nu-[t]i (11)um-ma a-na-ku-ma na-ak-ra-at ù sa-al-ma-at (12)ma-an-nu-um i-di-ka la wa-ta-ar (13)na-ka-ar-ka uš-te-ed-di (14)[at-t]u-nu-[m]a na-ka-ar be-lí-ia zi-im-ri-li-im (15)[it-ti-ia-m]a na-ak-[ra-a]t (16)[ù a-na-k]u ÌR be-lí-i[a zi-im-ri-li-im] (17)[x x ad-b]u-bu-šu-nu-t[i-ma] (18)[ar-ḫi-i]š a-wa-sú-nu ki-a-a[m iš-ku-nu]

rev.
(19)[um]-ma-a-mi šum-ma bu-nu-ma-[dIŠKUR] (20)di-in na-pí-iš-tam id-di-[in] (21)ù na-pí-iš-tam um-ta-al-[la] (22)ta-s[a-l]i-[im-ma an]-ni-tam iq-[bu-nim] (23)ù ki-a-am [a-pu-ul-šu]-nu-ti (24)um-ma a-na-[ku-ma zi-im]-ri-li-im be-lí (25)i-na a-lim t[a-al-ḫ]i-yi-im wa-ši-ib (26)ba-lum be-lí-ia mi-im-ma e-pé-ša-am (27)ú-ul <e>-li-im i-na-an-na be-lí a-wa-tam (28)li-na-ṭì-la-am-ma ša [qa-bé-e] (29)be-lí-ia lu-p[u-úš aš-šum x x x x] (30)an-ni-im ba-[lum be-lí-ia mi-im-ma] (31)e-pé-ša-[am ú-ul e-li-i]... (32′)[ma]-a-tum šu-tam-ma-at (33′)[ù] wa-ar-ki be-lí-ia (34′)i-la-k[u] (35′)x x

(1–4)To my lord, read: Thus says Iawi-ila your servant. (5–9)The messengers and elders of Iarkiba-Addu have come to me and have said: "We are not hostile to you. Do not pay attention to the matter of Bunuma-addu." (10–16)I responded to them thus: "You are (both) hostile and conciliatory. Who knows you? It is too much. You have made known your hostility. You are an enemy of my lord Zimri-Lim, and with me you are hostile, and I am a servant of Zimri-Lim." (17–22)Thus I said to them. Quickly they decided thus: "If Bunuma-Adda has been accused in a capital case and has paid [the value of] a life, then he will be reconciled." (22–27)They said thus to me, and I responded to them: "Zimri-Lim is my lord, who resides in Talhiyum. Without the

[26]Georges Boyer, *Textes juridiques et administratifs* (TCL 29; ARM VIII; Paris: Paul Geuthner, 1957), 168.

> authorization of my lord, I cannot do anything." [27–31] Now, may my lord look favorably upon the matter which I have done according to my lord's order.... Without my lord's authorization, I cannot do anything. [32′–34′] ...

Here again, *dīn napištim* signifies a pecuniary penalty. It is not only these letters from Mari that assume that the penalty is a fine. In the legal records from Mesopotamia as well, the penalty for a homicide is financial.[27]

We have come across many different penalties for homicide. Recourse to compensation in place of capital punishment has inspired theories on the historical development of the treatment of homicide in the ancient Near East. G. R. Driver and John C. Miles suggest a historical process in which a blood feud ensued when a member of one family injured another: The community, which could be affected by the loss of fighting men, limited the vendetta by ending it when the killer himself was killed or by providing an alternate remedy in compensation.[28] This principle was then extended to limit liability to the actual injury incurred. Eventually, compensation became the preferred penalty.[29]

Driver and Miles base their explanation upon one of the most influential theories of legal evolution, the self-help model developed in the late eighteenth and the nineteenth centuries.[30] This theory attempted to answer the question of whether there were evolutionary patterns in law, by which societies move from one definable stage with particular institutions to another definable stage with particular institutions. The self-help model presumed that in the earliest period of human existence, violence was prevalent but not chaotic. Violence was organized by a rule-bound system of vengeance. The earliest states were established in an effort not to eliminate this violence but to supervise and institutionalize it. There were four stages postulated in

[27] E.g., NSG 41, Wiseman Alalakh 17, BBSt 9, ADD 618, ADD 321, ADD 164, ADD 806, PPA 95.

[28] Driver and Miles, *The Babylonian Laws,* 1.501–502.

[29] Marian San Nicolò, "Rechtsgeschichtliches zum Gesetze des Bilalama von Ešnunna," *Or* 18 (1949), 261; Goetze, *The Laws of Eshnunna,* 261.

[30] J. D. Michaelis, one of the most prominent proponents of biblical criticism in the eighteenth century, was among the first to argue against the prevailing theory, the social contract model, and for a rule-bound system of vengeance. The self-help model received new impetus in the nineteenth century when it was championed by G. W. F. Hegel in *Philosophy of Right* (trans. T. M. Knox; Oxford: Oxford University Press, 1952 [1821]), and by the preeminent legal historian Rudolf von Jhering in *Geist des römischen Rechts auf den verschiedenen Stufen seiner Entwicklung* (Aalen: Scientia Verlag, 1968 [1898]). The most widely read proponent of this model today is Max Weber, *Economy and Society: An Outline of Interpretive Sociology*, ed. Guenther Roth and Claus Wittich, trans. Ephraim Fischoff (Berkeley: University of California Press, 1978 [1922]). A recent analysis of the self-help model from the viewpoint of Law and Economics was written by James Q. Whitman, "At the Origins of Law and the State: Supervision of Violence, Mutilation of Bodies, or Setting of Prices," *Chicago-Kent Law Review* 71 (1995), 41–84.

this process. In the first stage, the "state of nature," kin groups or individuals exacted vengeance when injured by other kin groups or individuals in the form of talionic reparations, "an eye for an eye, a tooth for a tooth." In the second stage, the early state supervised the existing system of vendetta by forcing the parties to have recourse to the state for a formal hearing in order to exact talionic vengeance. In the third stage, the early state assumed the role of enforcement and took the responsibility from the injured party to exact vengeance. Only the state could legitimately have recourse to violence. Finally, the state eliminated violence by substituting monetary damages for talionic reparations.

However, the discovery of early law collections that prescribe pecuniary penalties for injury and homicide has inspired scholars to reverse the historical process: They argue that the law developed from compensation to talionic punishment. According to A. S. Diamond, this development was a sociological advance as certain wrongs were no longer considered private: They were no longer civil wrongs covered by civil law but public wrongs covered by criminal law, because the state had advanced to a level of complexity that could police these occurrences.[31] The difficulty with this proposal is that pecuniary punishment is found in later law collections as well as in earlier ones: The explanation that the law collections preserving monetary compensation originated in less advanced societies is strained.

J. J. Finkelstein attempts to salvage this theory by proposing that corporal punishment in terms of lex talionis in the Laws of Hammurapi reflected an innovation in jurisprudence, not social development.[32] What was formerly covered by civil law, a legal realm in which the penalties are purely pecuniary, was subsequently covered for the injury of a member of the upper class by criminal law, in which corporal sanctions can be imposed. According to Finkelstein, this was clearly an innovation, when protection was granted to the upper class. Others, of inferior status, had to be content with compensation. However, it appears to me that it is difficult to understand why this innovation was not sociologically determined. More importantly, there may not have been a sharp distinction between civil and criminal law, and if corporal punishment is the characteristic of criminal law – Finkelstein's definition of criminal law – then it was already introduced in the Laws of Ur-Nammu (LU 1, 2, 6, 7). LE makes attempted theft part of criminal law: In LL 9 the penalty is a fine; in LE 12–13 the penalty is a fine if attempted during the day and death if attempted during the night; in LH 21 the penalty is death. In general, in cuneiform law a financial penalty is the remedy for theft (LL 9, 10; SLHF iii 13–15; MAL A 5, C 5, 8; HL 63–70, 93–97, 108,

[31]A. S. Diamond, "An Eye for an Eye," *Iraq* 19 (1957), 51–55; Diamond, *Primitive Law Past and Present* (London: Methuen & Co., 1971).

[32]Finkelstein, "Ammiṣaduqa's Edict and the Babylonian 'Law Codes,'" 96–99, and *The Ox That Gored,* 59, n. 13.

110, 119–143), except for LH, where death is the punishment (LH 6, 7, 8, 9, 10). LH makes death the punishment for anyone bringing a false charge that necessitates a trial by ordeal for the accused (LU 13–14; LH 2). LE 28 mandates death for the wife caught *in flagrante delicto*, whereas LH 129 allows the husband to forgo the death penalty. Harboring a fugitive slave results in a fine in LL 12, whereas the same act results in execution in LH 16. The imposition of the death penalty is a recurring refrain of the Laws of Hammurapi (1–3, 6–11, 14–16, 19, 21–22, 25–26, 33–34, bb, 108–110, 116, 129–130, 133b, 143, 153, 155, 157, 210, 229–231). Corporal and capital punishment are found in law collections both early and late.

In sum, lex talionis is a flexible concept. In biblical law, it is used as a principle expressing equivalence. The penalty must be equivalent to the harm inflicted. In the case of a human death, the offender must be killed, and in the case of an animal death, the animal victim must be replaced. The penalty for homicide in cuneiform law is death, but it is not an expression of lex talionis. The death penalty is the penalty for serious offenses. The concern manifest in cuneiform law is on the fixing of the status of the victim in certain categories and how that status affects the punishment. Lex talionis was a principle in cuneiform law for cases of false witness or nonfatal bodily injuries. In early Roman law, lex talionis is not a principle of punishment but a threat to force the offender to come to settle with the victim.

Lex talionis in biblical law restricts the punishment to the offender himself. Lex talonis makes rich and poor equal in biblical law.[33] More than that, status, with the exception of the slave, is simply not a factor in biblical law.

The question is, therefore, whether lex talionis is a manifestation of Israelite culture other than the fact that it is found in ancient Israel. In order to answer this question, we must compare this penalty to other penalties. The principle of the penalty for intentional homicide is based on the reversal of roles: The original agent of harm becomes the recipient of the same action of the type that constituted the offense. Therefore, the appropriate punishment is execution: The killer is subject to being killed. This concept of equivalence appears to be at work with regard to stealing a sheep: Just as the thief has taken a particular type of animal away from its owner, a particular type of animal is demanded from the thief. He does not simply return the stolen animal but suffers a loss in the same "coinage," sheep.

What is seen as equivalent depends on the culture. A particular human being was not seen as fungible in the way a particular animal was viewed. In cuneifom law, human life was considered fungible in pecuniary terms. This was not valid in Israelite culture, at least according to what is presented as legitimate in the Hebrew Bible. However, what is striking about the law in Num 35:31–32 is its insistence that a monetary indemnity should not be accepted in any case, whether for intentional or accidental homicide. This

[33]Paul, *Studies in the Book of the Covenant,* 40, 76–77.

stipulation implies that compensation was accepted in practice, albeit not legal according to this statute.

APPENDIX: ALTERNATE PENALTIES IN THE LAWS OF ESHNUNNA

Emile Szlechter argues that alternate penalties also exist in LE because of the differences in the way capital punishment is formulated in LE.[34] In LE 24/26, the formula is *dīn napištim ... imât,* "it is a case of life ... he shall die." In LE 58, the formula is *napištim ṣimdat šarrim,* "[it is a case concerning] life: decree of the king." In LE 12, 13, and 28, the formula is *imât ul iballaṭ,* "he shall die, he shall not live." Szlechter interprets the first two as indicating differences in the administration of the penalty, that the punishment could be mitigated and that the punishment could be imposed by the offended party immediately upon discovering the offense. He argues that *dīn napištim ... imât* indicated that the death penalty was applicable only in the absence of a settlement between the perpetrator and the victim's family, whereas the emphatic expression *imât ul iballaṭ* indicated that the death penalty was mandatory and that the offended party could resort to it immediately in a self-help mode. Benno Landsberger and Ulrich Sick agree with Szlechter's first thesis but not with his claim about self-help.[35] Szlechter himself omits the self-help thesis in his 1978 publication. Yaron argues for the opposite conclusion – although the emphatic nature of the phrase *imât ul iballaṭ* implies that the death penalty is mandatory, its mandatory use in these particular cases appears out of line because LE 12, 13 and 28, where this formula appears, share a common element in that the offender was caught *in flagrante delicto.*[36] This is reflected in the use of *naṣbutum,* "to be seized, caught," in all three provisions. In LE 12 and 13, trespass, an offense that generates the lowest penalty, ten shekels, the most minor amount to be paid as a fine, becomes greatly aggravated when it occurs in the nighttime. When trespass occurs at night, the penalty is death, not a fine. The owner reacts violently to the intrusion and kills the intruder, justified in fearing for his life. In LE 28, the husband, outraged by catching his wife in the lap of another man, kills her. The offended party may kill in the moment of fear or fury, but once that moment has passed, normal judicial procedures come into play.

[34] Szlechter, *Les lois d'Ešnunna* (Publications de l'Institut de Droit Romain de l'Université de Paris 12; Paris: Centre National de la recherche scientifique, 1954), 110–11, and "Les lois d'Ešnunna," *RIDA* 25 (1978), 197–198.

[35] Landsberger, "Jungfraulichkeit," in *Symbolae Iuridicae et Historicae Martino David Dedicatae II,* 72; Ulrich Sick, *Die Tötung eines Menschen und ihren Ahndung in den keilschriftlichen Rechtssammlungen unter Berücksichtigung rechtsverglechender Aspekte* (Ph.D. diss., Eberhard-Karls-Universität, 1984), 150.

[36] Yaron, *The Laws of Eshnunna*^{2}, 260.

The statutes provide a license for immediate punishment, but the remedy effected when matters calm down is different.

In my opinion, it is questionable whether intrusion during the night is so heinous as to exclude a lesser penalty. If adultery is pardonable in other ancient Near Eastern law collections, LH 129, MAL A 15, HL 197–198, there is no reason to assume that it was otherwise in LE. However, it is critical to note that the phrase *imât ul iballaṭ* is not extant elsewhere in Akkadian legal formulations. The phrase fits the style of the other formulations of the death penalty in LE, each of which contains two clauses. The formulation *dīn napištim . . . imât* contains clause 1) *dīn napištim*, and clause 2) *imât*. The formulation *napištim ṣimdat šarrim* contains clause 1) *napištim*, and clause 2) *ṣimdat šarrim*. The formulation *imât ul iballaṭ* also contains two clauses, *imât* and *ul iballaṭ*. The emphatic nature of this formula is more apparent than real. Yaron himself suggests that the purpose of the double clauses was to present a smooth literary style in place of a curt and abrupt one-word decree of the death penalty.

CHAPTER SEVEN

Interterritorial Law: The Homicide of a Foreign Citizen

WE HAVE seen that at the same time certain statutes in biblical law were part of the tradition of cuneiform legal traditions, many other aspects of biblical law differed radically from cuneiform law. There is little in the way of shared assumptions between biblical law and cuneiform law. We have determined that cuneiform law collections share a common tradition and that the legal records from Mesopotamia diverge and converge with other legal records and with the law collections. Another way of testing the commonality of the legal traditions of the ancient Near East is to ask whether there were basic ground rules about the treatment of homicide beyond a general assumption that the unlawful killing of a human being is wrong.

One method of answering this question is to analyze the case of a citizen of one territory slain in another. There are a number of ancient Near Eastern documents that address this case. This group of texts allows us to examine the question of whether there was generally accepted international law that governed such occurrences or whether one country attempted to impose its law upon another. Serendipitously, these texts all come from about the same time period, from the mid–fourteenth century B.C.E. to the mid–thirteenth century B.C.E., granting us the opportunity to observe legal procedures that might have operated concurrently.[1]

[1]There is an earlier text from Mari, ARM II 123, in which the death of caravaneers is reported, but the remedy is not mentioned.

The texts fall into two sets. The first consists of two letters, an Amarna letter from the king of Babylonia to the Egyptian king (EA 8) and a letter from the Hittite emperor to the Babylonian king mentioning the death of merchants while abroad (CTH 172). EA 8 is a letter in Akkadian from Burnaburiyash II of Babylonia to Amenophis IV/Akhenaten of Egypt. It dates from circa 1349–1334 B.C.E. (the overlap between the reigns of the two kings). CTH 172 is a letter in Akkadian from Hattusili III, the Hittite emperor, to Kadashman-Enlil II of Babylonia. It dates from approximately 1260 B.C.E. The second set consists of a dozen texts on this topic that have been excavated at Ugarit, including treaties stipulating the responsibilities and obligations of the countries in an occurrence in the future in which a foreign merchant will have been killed (RS 17.146, 17.230, 18.115), and actual cases in the form of records of settlements (RS 17.234, 17.251, 20.22) and records of trials (RS 17.299, 17.229, 17.158, 17.42, 17.145, 17.337). RS 17.369B + RS 17.69 is too fragmentary to classify. The treaties outline the procedure to be followed in cases of slaying in the future, while the legal records reflect how homicides that have already occurred were remedied.

In a letter unearthed in the El-Amarna archive (EA 8), Burnaburiyash II, the king of Babylonia (Karaduniyash), demands action from Naphu'rureya (Amenophis IV/Akhenaten), the king of Egypt, on behalf of certain Babylonian merchants who have been slain.

obv.
(1)[a]-na na-ap-ḫu-'u-ru-ri-[ia . . .] (2)LUGAL ^{kur}mi-iṣ-ri-i ŠEŠ-ia q[i-bi-ma] (3)um-ma bur-ra-bu-ri-ia-aš LUGAL ^{kur}ka-ra-[du-ni-ia-aš] (4)ŠEŠ-ka-ma a-na ia-a-ši šu-ul-mu (5)a-na ka-ša KUR-ka É-ka GEME.MEŠ-ka DUMU.MEŠ-ka (6)^{lú}GAL.MEŠ-ka ANŠE.KUR.RA-ka ^{giš}MAR.MEŠ-ka (7)da-an-ni-iš lu šu-ul-mu

(8)a-na-ku ù ŠEŠ-ia it-ti-a-ḫa-mi-iš (9)ṭa-bu-ta ni-id-da-bu-ub (10)ù an-ni-ta ni-iq-ta-bi (11)um-ma-a ki-i ab-bu-ni it-ti a-ḫa-mi-iš ṭa-a-bu[2] (12)ni-i-nu lu ṭa-ba-nu (13)i-na-an-na DAM.GÀR.MEŠ-ú-a (14)ša it-ti ŠEŠ ṭa-a-bu te-bu-ú (15)i-na ^{kur}ki-na-aḫ-ḫi a-na ši-ma-a-ti it-ta-ak-lu-ú (16)ul-tu ŠEŠ-ṭa-a-bu a-na mu-uḫ-ḫi ŠEŠ-ia i-ti-qu (17)i-na ^{uru}ḫi-in-na-tu-ni ša ^{kur}ki-na-aḫ-ḫi (18)^{I}šu-um-ad-da DUMU ^{I}ba!-lum-me-e (19)^{I}šu-ta-at-na DUMU ^{I}ša-ra-tu-um ša ^{uru}ak-ka (20)LÚ.MEŠ-šu-nu ki iš-pu-ru ^{lú}DAM.GÀR-ia (21)id-du-ku ù KUG.BABBAR-šu-nu it-tab-lu (22)[^{I}az-z]u a-na pa-[ni-k]a ki-i [ka-al-li-e][3] (23)al-ta-ap-ra-a[k-k]u ši-ta-[al-šu-nu] (24)li-iq-ba-ak-[ku] (25)[^{kur}ki-]na-aḫ-ḫi KUR-ka ù LUGAL!-[ša ÌR.MEŠ-ka] (26)i-na

[2]This word is actually found on the reverse: See Otto Schroeder, "Zur Amarnatafel VAT 1704," *Orientalistische Literaturzeitung* 18 (1915), col. 175.

[3]This reconstruction follows William L. Moran, *The Amarna Letters* (Baltimore: The Johns Hopkins University Press, 1992), 17, n. 5.

KUR-ka ḫu-um-mu-ṣa-ku su-ni-iq-[šu-ni-ti-ma] [27]KUG.BABBAR ša it-ba-lu šu-ul-l[i-im-šu] [28]ù LÚ.MEŠ ša ÌR.MEŠ-ia i-[du-uk-k]u [29]du-uk-šu-nu-ti-ma da!-mi-[šu-n]u te-e-er [30]ù šum-ma LÚ.MEŠ an-nu-ti ul ta-ad-du-uk [31]i-tu-ur-ru-ma lu-ú KASKAL at-tu-ú-a [32]ù lu $^{\text{lú.meš}}$DUMU.MEŠ i-du-ku-ú-ma [33]i-na bi-ri-ni DUMU si-ip-ri ip-pa-ar-ra-as [34]ù šum!-ma i-na-ak-ki-ru-ka [35]1 LÚ at-tu-ú-a ^{I}šu-um-ad-da [36]GÌR.MEŠ-šu ki-i ú-na-ak-ki-su [37]i-tu-šu ik-ta-la-šu [38]ù LÚ ša-na-a ^{I}šu-ta-at-na ak-ka-a-a-ú [39]i-na re-ši ki-i ul-zi-iz-zu [40]a-na pa-ni-šu iṣ-ṣa-bat LÚ.MEŠ ša-šu-nu [41]l[i-i]l-[k]u-ni-ik-ku-um-ma a-mu-ur-ma [42]k[i mi-t]u[4] ša-al-ma lu ti-i-di [43][a-na šu-ul-m]a-ni 1 MA.NA ^{zá}ZA.GÌN uš-te-bi-la-ak-ku [44][DUMU ši-ip-]ri-ia ḫa-mu-ut-ta ku-[uš-šid-š]u [45][ṭe-e]-ma ša ŠEŠ-ia lu i-d[i-ma] [46][DUMU] ši-ip-ri-ia la ta-ka-a[l-la-šu] [47][ḫ]a-mu-ut-ta li-it-ta-a[l-ka]

[1–7]Say to Naphu'rureya, the king of Egypt, my brother: Thus Burna-Buriyash, the king of Karaduniyash, your brother. For me all goes well. For you, your country, your household, your wives, your sons, your magnates, your horses, your chariots, may all go very well.

[8–12]My brother and I made a mutual declaration of friendship, and we said this: "Just as our fathers were friends with one another, so will we be friends with one another." [13–21]Now, my merchants who were on their way with Ahu-tabu were detained in Canaan on business matters. After Ahu-tabu went on to my brother, in Hinnatuna of Canaan, Shum-adda, son of Balumme, and Shutatna, son of Sharatum of Akka, having sent their men, killed my merchants and took away their money. [22–27]I send Azzu to you posthaste. Inquire from him so that he can inform you. Canaan is your country, and its kings are your servants. In your country I have been despoiled. Bring them to account and make compensation for the money they took away. [28–29]Execute the men who put my servants to death, and so return their blood. [30–33]If you do not execute these men, they are going to kill again, whether a caravan of mine or your own messengers, and then messengers between us will be cut off. [34–42]If they try to deny this to you, Shum-adda, having blocked off passage [lit. cut off the feet] to a man of mine, retained him in his company, and another man, having been forced into service by Shutatna of Akka, is still serving him. These men should be brought to you so you can investigate, inquire whether they are dead, and become informed. [43–47]As a greeting gift, I send you 1 mina of lapis lazuli. Send off my messenger immediately so that I may know my brother's decision. Do not detain my messenger. Let him be off to me immediately.

[4]This reconstruction follows Moran, *The Amarna Letters,* 17, n. 11.

In the case of citizens sent on royal business, the king intervenes to avenge their deaths and protect his interests. Since the homicides took place outside the realm of Babylonia, the king, not the victims' families, must take the active role in avenging the homicide. The king of Babylonia contacts his counterpart, the king of Egypt. Although the killing occurred in Canaan, the duly authorized authority is the king of Egypt since the kings of Canaan are his vassals and he is their overlord. Therefore, Burnaburiyash holds the king of Egypt responsible. At the level of international diplomacy, the parties involved must be of the equivalent political status.[5] A king cannot hold negotiations with a vassal/dependent of another territory's dominant ruler without speaking to the overlord himself. In other words, contact can only take place between two overlords or lesser rulers, but not between an overlord and a lesser ruler not under his aegis. Therefore, the king must assume the initiative because he is the only one possessing the status high enough to contact the appropriate person in the foreign territory. As we will see, this contrasts with the Ugaritic documents, from a territory under Hittite overlordship, where responsibility is assumed by the citizens of each country or locality as a collective body. In a sense, the locations under Hittite hegemony share a concept of corporate responsibility not recognized between the land of Babylonia and the land of Egypt. In contrast, the case in EA 8 is between two realms, two sovereign states.

Indeed, the claim made by Burnaburiyash II in EA 8 is predicated upon the alliance already established between the kings personally. Each dominant regional power exercises jurisdiction over its territory. If a wrong occurs to its citizens in a foreign territory, a regional power can only contact the dominant power in its region and ask for satisfaction, based on alliance, not on a general sense of what is just. Burnaburiyash II must cajole Naphu'rureya into acting by recounting the positive relations between them. Beyond that, he appeals to Naphu'rureya's own interests by emphasizing the consequences to Naphu'rereya's own men.[6] Burnaburiyash II warns that if the killers are not killed, they will strike again and are as equally likely to kill Naphu'rureya's own men as his own. Burnaburiyash also sends a gift, one mina of lapis lazuli, to reinforce friendly relations.

Burnaburiyash II demands two actions from Naphu'rureya, compensation for the money stolen and the execution of the men responsible. Compensation for the missing money is reasonable, but why does the Babylonian king demand that the killers be executed? Would he not benefit more from compensation? When Burnaburiyash II demands the execution of the killers, he provides two reasons: first, that the blood of the victims be returned, and second, that if the killers are not executed, they will surely strike again.

[5]Mario Liverani, *Prestige and Interest: International Relations in the Near East ca. 1600–1100 B.C.* (History of the Ancient Near East/Studies I; Padua: Sargon, 1990), 97.
[6]Liverani, *Prestige and Interest,* 98.

The second reason originates in practical concerns: Burnaburiyash II must protect his merchants if he wants to preserve his country's international trade.[7] Moreover, political considerations underlie this second reason – the king of Egypt may be more likely to act if his own interests are at stake. The first reason is elusive and difficult to understand. It may be akin to an Israelite concept, which holds that the blood of the victim is lost and needs to be returned: This concept is reflected in the usage of the word *te-er* (line 29).[8] Whatever the conceptual underpinning, Burnaburiyash's first demand implies that death is the only appropriate penalty, but the personal stake Naphu'rureya has in protecting his own men is the most effective motive Burnaburiyash can provide to Naphu'rureya for the execution of those who killed his men.

CTH 172 is instructive in regard to the appropriate punishment for homicide. In this letter, Hattusili III, the Hittite emperor, tells Kadashman-Enlil II, the king of Babylonia, that there is a distinction between the penalty for homicide in his land and in the neighboring land of the Assyrians (called here Subareans).[9] No capital punishment, not even for lèse-majesté, is ever used in the Hittite realm:

rev.
[15][. . .] a-ka-an-na ta-aš-pu-ra um-ma-a ^{lú}DAM.GÀR.MEŠ-ia i-na ^{kur}a-mur-ri ^{kur}ú-ga-ri-it [16][ù i-na ^{kur}. . . i-du]-uk-ku i-na ^{kur}ḫa-at-ti na-pu-ul-ta ú-ul i-du-uk-ku [17][šum-ma i-na ^{kur}ḫa-at-ti na]-pu-ul-ta i-du-uk-ku šúm-ma LUGAL i-ši-im- me a-na a-ma-ti ša-a-ši [18][. . . d]a-i-ka-na ša na-pu-ul-ti i-ṣa-ab-ba-tu$_4$-ma a-na ŠEŠ.MEŠ ša di-ki [19][. . . KUG.BABBAR a-na] mu-ul-le-e ša ^{lú}di-ki ŠEŠ.MEŠ-šú i-le-eq-qu-ú ù ^{lú}da-i-ka-na [20][. . . aš]-ra ša na-pu-ul-tu$_4$ i-na ŠÀ-šú di-ku ul-la-lu ù šúm-ma ŠEŠ.MEŠ-šú [21][KUG.BABBAR mu-ul-le]-e ú-ul i-maḫ-ḫa-ru da-i-ka-na ša na-pu-ul-ti [22][. . . l]i-pu-šu šúm-ma LÚ ša ḫi-tá a-na LUGAL i-ḫa-ṭu a-na KUR-ti ša-na-ti- ma [23][. . .] ù a-na da-a-ki ú-ul par-ṣu ŠEŠ-ù-ia ša-'a-al-ma liq-bu-ni-ik-ku [24][. . . a]-ka-an-na ša EN ḫé-ṭi-i la-a i-du-uk-ku ^{lú}DAM.GÀR i-du-uk-ku [25][. . . L]Ú sú-ba-ri-i a-i-ka-a i-di šúm-ma i-du-uk-ku-ma i-na-an-na ŠEŠ.MEŠ DAM.GÀR.MEŠ di-ku-ti [26][šup-ra]-am-ma di-in-sú-nu lu-mur

[15–17]Since you wrote to me as follows: "My merchants are being killed in the land of Amurru, the land of Ugarit, [and the land of . . .]." They do not kill [as punishment] in Hatti . . . they kill. [17–18]If the king

[7]The vassal kings Shum-adda and Shutatna, who killed the merchants of Burnaburiyash, do not appear to have killed them themselves. Shum-adda and Shutatna sent their own men to kill Burnaburiyash's merchants.

[8]Burnaburiyash does not demand the return of his servants forced into the service of Shum-adda and Shutatna.

[9]On the identification of the Subareans, see Ignace J. Gelb, *Hurrians and Subareans* (Studies in Ancient Oriental Civilizations 22; Chicago: University of Chicago Press, 1944), 44, 49, 85.

> hears about it, [they investigate] that matter. They arrest the killer and deliver him to the brothers of the slain man. [19]If his brothers accept the silver as compensatory payment, [they allow] the killer [to go free]. [20]The place in which the homicide occurred is purified. [20–22]If his brothers do not accept the silver as the compensatory payment, they may make the killer [their slave]. [22–24]If a man who has committed an offense against the king escapes to another land, killing him is not permitted. Inquire, my brother, and they shall tell you thus. Now, if they do not kill an offender [against the king], would they kill a merchant? [25–26][But in regard to] the Subareans, how am I to know if they are killing people? Now send me the brothers of the dead merchants so that I can investigate their lawsuit.

Different countries have different sanctions. There is no single remedy used throughout the ancient Near East.[10] Although the Babylonian king has demanded that the killers be executed, the Hittite emperor cannot and will not execute them. The Hittite laws are in agreement with the Hittite emperor's claim: The penalty is compensation, albeit very high in the case of a merchant in statute 5, 100 minas in contrast to 3 minas in the documents from Ugarit:

> HL 1
> [If] anyone kills [a man] or a woman in a [quarr]el, he shall [bring him] [for burial] and give 4 persons (lit. heads), male or female respectively, and he shall look [to his house for it.]
>
> HL 2
> [If] anyone kills [a male] or female slave in a quarrel, he shall bring him [for burial] [and] shall give [2] persons [lit. heads], male or female respectively, and he shall look to his house for it.
>
> HL 3
> [If] anyone strikes a free [man] or woman so that he dies, with only his hand at fault, he shall bring him [for burial] and shall give 2 persons [lit. heads], and he shall look to his house for it.
>
> HL 4
> If anyone strike a male or female slave so that he dies, with only his hand at fault, he shall bring him [for burial] and shall give one person [lit. head], and he shall look to his house for it.

[10]Raymond Westbrook's argument that capital punishment and compensation for homicide were part of the common law of the ancient Near East and were in effect simultaneously is contradicted by the evidence of the international documents analyzed here (*Studies in Biblical and Cuneiform Law,* 45–46).

> Late version of 3–4
> [If anyone . . .]s[?] [a woman,] so that she dies, but it is an accident, [he shall pay 4? minas of silver]. But if the woman is a slave, he shall pay 2 minas [= 80 shekels] of silver.
>
> HL 5
> If anyone kills a merchant, he shall pay 4,000 shekels [lit. 100 minas] of silver, and he shall look to his house for it. If it is in the lands of Luwiya [= Arzawa] or Pala, he shall pay the 4,000 shekels of silver and also replace his goods.[11] If it is in the land of Hatti, he himself shall [also] bring the aforementioned merchant [for burial].
>
> Late version of 5
> [If] anyone kills a Hittite [merchant] in the midst of his goods, he shall pay [. . . minas of silver], and shall replace his goods threefold. But [if] [the merchant] is not in possession of goods, and someone kills him in a quarrel, he shall pay 240 shekels of silver. If it is only an accident, he shall pay 80 shekels of silver.

The Hittite laws reflect the Hittite emperor's refusal to execute the Babylonian merchants' killers, as the Babylonian king demands. Hittite law and Babylonian law differ on the penalty for homicide, and the Babylonian king must use diplomatic means to prevent his merchants from being denied justice according to the standards of Babylonian law. He attempts to have Babylonian law applied extraterritorially.

A king assumes responsibility for remedying the slaying of his merchants in a foreign land. Assigning responsibility for initiating the process of remedying the homicide is one of the major issues in the three treaties, RS 17.146, 17.230, and 18.115, between Ini-Teshub, king of Carchemish, and the citizens of Ugarit, which address the death of merchants while engaged in trade abroad.[12] RS 17.146 is as follows:

> [1] ^{I}i-ni-^{d}tešub LUGAL KUR ^{uru}kar-ga-miš [2] DUMU-šu ša ^{I}ša-ḫu-ru-nu-wa DUMU DUMU-šu [3] ša ^{I}LUGAL-^{d}30 UR.SAG [4] ri-kíl-ta i-na be-ri ša KUR ^{uru}kar-ga-miš [5] ù be-ri ša kur ^{uru}u-ga-ri-it a-kán-na ir-ku-us [6] ma-a šum-ma-me-e $^{lú.meš}$DAM.GÀR ma-an-da-ti [7] ša LUGAL kur ^{uru}u-ga-ri-it i-na ŠÀ-bi KUR ^{uru}kar-ga-miš [8] i-du-ku-mì ù LÚ.MEŠ da-i-ku-šu-nu iṣ-ṣa-ba-tum-mì [9] ù DUMU.MEŠ KUR ^{uru}kar-ga-miš NÌ.GA^{meš}-šu-nu [10] ú-nu-te-MEŠ-šu-nu gab-ba ki-i ša ŠEŠ-šu-nu [11] i-qa-ab-bu-ni a-kán-na ú-šal-la-mu-ni [12] ù mu-ul-la ša 1-en LÚ-lim [13] 3

[11]It would appear the special rule for a slaying committed in Luwiya and Pala, countries east and north, respectively, of Hatti in Asia Minor, was due to their political connections with Hatti. This special rule is reflected in statutes 19–21 and 23, which prescribe special remedies for offenses committed in or against a citizen of those countries.

[12]Even though the wording in RS 17.230, l. 4, refers to *LÚ,* "a person [in general]," it is clear that the treaty deals with a merchant because of the attention paid to the goods that were in the victim's possession.

ma-na KUG.BABBAR.MEŠ DUMU.MEŠ KUR ^{uru}kar-ga-miš [14]ú-šal-la-mu-ni ù DUMU.MEŠ [15]ša KUR ^{uru}u-ga-ri-it aš-šum NÌ.GA^{meš}-šu-nu [16]aš-šum ú-nu-te-MEŠ-šu-nu i-tam-mu-ni [17]ù DUMU.MEŠ KUR ^{uru}kar-ga-miš NÌ.GA^{meš}-šu-nu [18]ú-nu-te-MEŠ-šu-nu a-kán-na ú-šal-la-mu-ni [19]ù šum-ma LÚ-ma UZU ka-a-ma i-ṣa-ba-tu$_4$-ni [20]ù da-i-ku-ti-šu-nu la-a i-ṣa-ba-tu$_4$-ni [21]DUMU.MEŠ KUR ^{uru}kar-ga-miš il-la-ku-nim-ma i-na [22]KUR ^{uru}u-ga-ri-it i-na NAM.ERIM$_2$ i-tam-mu-ni [23]ma-a šum-ma LÚ.MEŠ da-i-ku-ti-šu-nu ni-di-mì [24]ù ša LÚ.MEŠ DAM.GÀR ša-a-šu-nu NÌ.GA^{meš}-šu-nu [25]ú-nu-tu-MEŠ-šu-nu i-ḫal-li-iq [26]ù DUMU.MEŠ KUR ^{uru}kar-ga-miš 3 ma-na KUG.BABBAR.MEŠ [27]mu-ul-la-a ša 1-en LÚ-im ú-šal-la-mu-ni [28]ù šum-ma LU.MEŠ DAM.GÀR ša LUGAL KUR ^{uru}kar-ga-miš [29]ša ma-an-da-ti i-na ŠÀ-bi KUR ^{uru}u-ga-ri-it i-da-ku [30]ù da-i-ku-šu-nu i-ṣa-ab-ba- tu$_4$-ni [31]DUMU.MEŠ KUR ^{uru}u-ga-ri-it NÌ.GA^{meš}šu-nu [32]ú-nu-te-MEŠ-šu-nu ki-i ša ŠEŠ.MEŠ-šu-nu [33]i-qa-ab-bu-ni a-kán-na ú-šal-la-mu-ni [34]ù ša 1-en LÚ 3 ma-na KUG.BABBAR.MEŠ mu-ul-la-a [35]ša BE^{meš} DUMU.MEŠ KUR ^{uru}u-ga-ri-it ú-ma-al-lu-ni [36]ù šum-ma LÚ.MEŠ da-i-ku-šu-nu la-a iṣ-ṣa-b[a]-tu [37]ù DUMU.MEŠ KUR ^{uru}u-ga-ri-it il-la-ku-nim-ma [38]i-na ^{uru}nu-ba-an-na ù šum-ma i-na ^{uru}gur-a-ta [39]a-na pa-ni ŠEŠ.MEŠ ša $^{lú.meš}$DAM.GÀR šu-nu-ti [40]i-na NAM.ERIM$_2$ i-tam-mu-ni <ma-a.šum-ma LÚ.MEŠ da-i-ku-šu-nu ni-di-mi> [41]ù ša LÚ.MEŠ DAM.GÀR NÌ.GA^{meš}-šu-nu ú-nu-te-MEŠ-šu-nu [42]i-ḫal-li-iq ú DUMU.MEŠ KUR ^{uru}u-ga-ri-it [43]3 ma-na KUG.BABBAR.MEŠ mu-ul-la-a ša 1-en LÚ.MEŠ [44]ú-ma-al-lu-nim-ma [45]^{I}i-ni-^{d}tešub LUGAL KUR ^{uru}kar-ga-miš DUMU-šu [46]ša ^{I}sá-ḫu-ru-nu-wa DUMU DUMU-šu ša ^{I}LUGAL-^{d}30 [47]UR.SAG ri-kíl-ta an-ni-ta [48]ma-an-nu-me-e ša ri-kíl-ta an-ni-ta [49]ú-ša-aš-na-a ^{d}IM AN ^{d}UD AN [50][^{d}]NIN ku-ba-ba GAŠAN KUR ^{uru}kar-ga-miš [51]^{d}nin-gal GAŠAN ^{uru}nu-ba-an-ni [52][^{d}]nin-gal GAŠAN ^{uru}gur-a-ti [53]lu-ú be-lu ma-mi-ti-šu

[1–5]Ini-Teshub, king of the land of Carchemish, son of Shahurunuwa, grandson of Sharrukushuh, the warrior, made a treaty between the land of Carchemish and the land of Ugarit as follows: [6–18]If merchants in the service of the king of Ugarit are killed in the land of Carchemish and the men who killed them are arrested, the citizens of the land of Carchemish will ask for any property or goods of their brothers thus and will pay in full. The citizens of the land of Carchemish will pay the full compensation per person, 3 minas[13] of silver. The citizens of the land of Ugarit will take an oath concerning the property or goods, and the citizens of the land of Carchemish will deliver safely the property

[13]The value of a mina was sixty shekels in Babylonia but apparently was fifty shekels at Ugarit (see de Vaux, *Ancient Israel,* 203–204) and forty shekels at Hatti (see H. Otten, "Zum hethitischen Gewichtssystem," *AfO* 17 [1954–56]: 128–131).

> or goods. [19–27] If they take hold of the body of a man but do not arrest those who killed them, the citizens of the land of Carchemish will go to the land of Ugarit and will take an oath thus: "We do not know the men who killed them, and the property and goods of those merchants are missing." The citizens of the land of Carchemish shall pay 3 minas of silver, the full compensation per person. [28–35] If merchants in the service of the king of Carchemish are killed in the land of Ugarit and the men who killed them are arrested, the citizens of the land of Ugarit will ask for any property or goods of their brothers and will pay in full. The citizens of the land of Ugarit will pay the full compensation for the blood, 3 minas of silver. [36–44] If they do not arrest those who killed them, the citizens of the land of Ugarit will go either to Nubanna or to Gurata[14] before the brothers of those merchants and will take an oath thus: "We do not know the men who killed them, and the property and goods of those merchants are missing." The citizens of the land of Ugarit shall pay 3 minas of silver, the full compensation per person. [45–53] Ini-Teshub, king of the land of Carchemish, son of Shahurunuwa, grandson of Sharrukushuh, the warrior, made this treaty. Whoever changes this treaty, may Adad of heaven, Shamash of heaven, Lady Kubaba lady of Carchemish, Ningal lady of Nubanni, Ningal lady of Gurati, be the masters of its curse.

According to RS 17.146, if a merchant in the service of the king of Ugarit is killed in the land of Carchemish and his killers are arrested, the citizens of Carchemish are to confiscate the property of the killers, that is, their fellow citizens who committed the homicide, and return the stolen goods[15] as well as pay compensation for the death. Likewise, if a merchant in the service of the king of Carchemish is killed in the land of Ugarit and his killers are arrested, the citizens of Ugarit are to seize the killer's property and return the stolen goods[16] as well as pay compensation for the death. If, however, the identity of the killers is not known, the citizens of the land in which the murder occurred must travel to the country of the dead merchant(s) in order to take an oath attesting to the fact that the killers have not been identified and that the property of the merchants is missing. The other treaties, RS 17.230 and 18.115, follow the same pattern of assigning responsibility for initiating the legal process:

> RS 17.230
> [1] ^{I}i-ni-^{d}tešub LUGAL ^{kur}kar-ga-miš [2] i[t-t]i LÚ.MEŠ ^{kur} ú-ga-ri-it [3] ri-ik-ša an-ni-ta ir-ku-us [4] šum-ma LÚ.MEŠ ša ^{kur}kar-ga-miš [5] i-na ŠÀ

[14] W. Röllig speculated that Gurata was perhaps identical with the city of Qarāti ("Gurata," RLA 3.703).
[15] Presumably the stolen goods are returned to the king of Ugarit.
[16] Presumably the stolen goods are returned to the king of Carchemish.

^{kur}ú-ga-ri-it [6]id-da-a-ak [7]šum-ma ša i-du-ku-šu [8]i-ṣa-ab-ba-tu$_4$ [9]LÚ 3-šú ú-ma-al-la [10]ù ú-nu-te^{meš} [11]ša it-ti-šu [i-]ḫal-li-qu [12]3-šú-ma ú-ma-a[l]-la [13]ù šum-ma ša i-du-ku-šu [14]la-a im-ma-ru ZI 3-šú ú-ma-al-lu-ú [15]ú ú-nu-te^{meš} ša it-ti-šu [16]i-ḫal-li-qu [17]ma-la ša i-ḫal-li-qu [18]SAG.DU-šu-nu-ma [19]ú-ma-al-lu-ú [20]ù šum-ma LÚ ^{kur}ú-ga-ri-it [21]i-na ŠÀ ^{kur}kar-ga-miš [22]id-da-a-ak [23]mu-ul-la-a a-kán-na-ma

[1–3]Ini-Teshub, king of Carchemish, made this treaty with the people of Ugarit. [4–12]If a person of Carchemish is killed in Ugarit, and those who killed him are arrested, they will pay a triple compensation per individual, and [if] the goods which were with him [the deceased] are missing, they will pay triple. [13–19]If those who killed him are not seen, they [the people of Ugarit] will pay triple compensation per person, and [if] the goods which were with him are missing, they will pay simple compensation for whatever is missing. [20–23]If a person of Ugarit is killed in Carchemish, the compensation is as follows . . .

RS 18.115

[1]^{I}i[-ni-^{d}tešub LUGAL KUR ^{uru}kar-ga-mis DUMU ^{I}ša-ḫu-ru-nu-wa LUGAL KUR ^{uru}kar-ga-miš] [2]r[i-kil-ta i-na be-ri ša KUR ^{uru}kar-ga-miš ù be-ri ša KUR ^{uru}u-ga-ri-it] [3]a-kán[-na ir-ku-us ma-a šum-ma-me-e $^{LÚ.MEŠ}$DAM.GÀR ma-an-da-ti] [4]ša LUGAL kur ^{ur}[^{u}u-ga-ri-it i-na ŠÀ-bi KUR ^{uru}kar-ga-miš i-du-ku-mi] [5]ù DUMU.MEŠ KUR ^{uru}[kar-ga-miš $^{LÚ.MEŠ}$da-ku-ti-šu-nu] [6]iṣ-ṣa-ba-tum-mì ù [DUMU.MEŠ KUR ^{uru}u-ga-ri-it qa-du LÚ.MEŠ ša ba-bi-šu-nu] [7]il-la-ku-nim-ma [i-na KUR ^{uru}u-ga-ri-it li-it-mu-ma] [8]aš-šum ŠEŠ.MEŠ-šu-[nu KUG.BABBAR.MEŠ-šu-nu LU.MEŠ-šu-nu gab-ba ki-i] [9]ša ŠEŠ.MEŠ-šu[-nu i-qa-ab-bu-ni DUMU.MEŠ KUR ^{uru}kar-ga-miš a-kán-na ú-šal-la-mu-ni] [10]ù KUG.BABBAR.MEŠ mu[-ul-la-a ša ZI.MEŠ 3 ma-na ša 1-en LÚ [11]DUMU.MEŠ KUR ^{uru}kar[-ga-miš ú-šal-la-mu-ni . . .] [12]ù šum-ma $^{lú.meš}$[UZU ka-a-ma i-ṣa-ba-tu-ni ù $^{lú.meš}$da-ku-ti-šu-nu] [13]la i-ṣa-ba-tu[m-mì ù DUMU.MEŠ KUR ^{uru}kar-ga-miš qa-du LÚ.MEŠ ša ba-bi- šu-nu] [14]il-la-ku-nim-ma [i-na KUR ^{uru}u-ga-ri-it i-na NAM.NE.RU li-it-mu] [15]ma-a šum-ma-mi LÚ.MEŠ [d]a-[ku-ti-šu-nu ni-di-mi] [16]ù ša $^{lú.meš}$DAM.GÀR an-nu-ti K[UG.BABBAR.MEŠ LU.MEŠ gab-bu mim-mu šu-nu i-ḫal-liq] [17]ù KUG.BABBAR.MEŠ mu-ul-la-a ša ZI.[MEŠ 3 ma-na ša 1-en LÚ] [18]ú-šal-la-mu-ni DUMU.MEŠ KUR ^{uru}kar-ga-[miš ù KUG.BABBAR.MEŠ LU.MEŠ] [19]ša $^{lú.meš}$DAM.GÀR la-a ú-maš-ša-ru[. . .] [20]ù šum-ma $^{lú.meš}$DAM.GÀR ša ma-an-da-t[i ša LUGAL KUR ^{uru}kar-ga-miši-na KUR ^{uru}u-ga-ri-it] [21]i-du-ku-ni ù $^{lú.meš}$da-ku-ti-šu-nu [i-ṣa-ba-tum-mì ù] [22]DUMU.MEŠ KUR ^{uru}kar-ga-miš qa-du LÚ.MEŠ š[a ba-bi-šu-nu il-la-ku-nim-ma] [23]i-na KUR ^{uru}u-ga-ri-it li-it-mu-ma [aš-šum ŠEŠ.MEŠ-šu-nu LU.MEŠ-šu-nu . . .] [24]ù DUMU.MEŠ KUR

^{uru}u-ga-ri-it KUG.BABBAR.[MEŠ-šu-nu LU.MEŠ-šu-nu gab-ba mim-mu-šu-nu] [25]a-kán-na ú-šal-la-mu-ni ù [mul-la-a ša ZI.MEŠ] [26]3 ma-na KUG.BABBAR.MEŠ ša 1-en LÚ-lim [a-na DUMU.MEŠ KUR^{uru}kar-ga-miš ú-šal-la-mu-ni] [27]ù šum-ma DUMU.MEŠ KUR ^{uru}kar-ga-miš LÚ.MEŠ [da-ku-ti-šu-nu iš-tu DUMU.MEŠ] [28]KUR ^{uru}u-ga-ri-it la-a ú-še-el-l[u-ú DUMU.MEŠ KUR ^{uru}u-ga-ri-it il-la-ku-nim-ma] [29]qa-du LÚ.MEŠ ša ba-bi-šu-nu i-na ^{uru}[nu-ba-an-na ù šum-ma i-na ^{uru}gur-a- ta] [30]li-it-mu-ú ma-a šum-ma-mi $^{\text{lú.meš}}$da-[ku-ti-šu-nu ni-di-mi] [31]ù ša $^{\text{lú.meš}}$DAM.GÀR ša LUGAL KUR ^{uru}ka[r-ga-miš KUG.BABBAR.MEŠ] [32]LU.MEŠ gab-bu mim-mu-ú-šu-nu i-[ḫal-liq ù DUMU.MEŠ KUR ^{uru}u-ga- ri-it] [33]mu-ul-la-a ša ZI.MEŠ 3 ma-[na KUG.BABBAR.MEŠ ša 1-en LU ú-šal-la- mu-ni] [34]ù ^{lú}DAM.GÀR a[-n]a? $^{\text{lú.meš}}$š[i]-b[u-ti?] [35] . . . [36]x . . .

[1–3]Ini-Teshub, king of the land of Carchemish, son of Shahurunuwa, king of the land of Carchemish, made a treaty between the land of Carchemish and the land of Ugarit as follows: [3–11]If merchants in the service of the king of Ugarit are killed in the land of Carchemish and the citizens of land of Carchemish arrest the men who killed them, the citizens of the land of Ugarit together with the men of their gate will go and take an oath concerning their brothers, their silver, and their sheep. They will ask for anything of their brother. The citizens of the land of Carchemish will pay as follows: the full compensation per person, 3 minas of silver for one person. [12–19]If they are in possession of the body of a man but do not arrest those who killed them, the citizens of the land of Carchemish together with the men of their gate will go to the land of Ugarit and will take an imprecatory oath: "We do not know the men who killed them, and that which belongs to those merchants, their silver, their sheep, anything of theirs, is missing." They shall pay the full silver per person, 3 minas of silver per person. If the citizens of the land of Carchemish do not release the silver and the sheep of the merchants . . . [20–26]If merchants in the service of the king of Carchemish are killed in the land of Ugarit and the men who killed them are arrested, the citizens of the land of Carchemish together with the men of their gate will go and take an oath in the land of Ugarit and . . . concerning their brothers, their silver, their sheep . . . the citizens of Ugarit will repay in full their silver, their sheep, and anything of theirs thus. They shall pay the full compensation for persons, 3 minas of silver per person, to the citizens of the land of Carchemish. [27–36]If the citizens of the land of Carchemish do not take away the men who killed them from the citizens of the land of Ugarit, the citizens of the land of Ugarit will go and will take an imprecatory oath together with the men of their gate either in Nubanna or in Gurata: "We do not know the men who killed

> them, and that which belongs to the merchants of the land of Carchemish, their silver and their sheep, whatever is theirs, is missing." The citizens of the land of Ugarit shall pay the full compensation for persons, 3 minas of silver per person. The merchants ... to the witnesses ...

Thus, the citizens in the country in which the homicide took place must take the initiative to remedy the slaying. They ascertain whether a homicide in fact took place, and if possible, they determine the identity of the killers and apprehend them. In the event that the killers cannot be identified, they commission a delegation of their own to appear in the victim's country in order to acknowledge their obligation formally and then discharge it. In short, they do not wait for a claim to be made by the king in whose service the merchant belonged. They are the ones who must play the active role, not the victim's king nor the victim's family. They initiate the process of redressing a homicide of a foreigner since the individuals who are responsible for the victim, such as his superior or his family, who would otherwise assume the initiative for remedying the killing, are not present in the place where the unlawful death took place.

The nature of the group named as the citizens of the country is left vague. Is it an assembly that has been already constituted, or is it specially commissioned by the ruler or administrator of the country? One of the treaties between Ini-teshub and Ugarit provides more information on the composition of the delegation sent from one country to another, and it is from this evidence that we can extrapolate the identity of the "citizens of the country." RS 18.115 specifies that the citizens of both countries act in conjunction with *LÚ.MEŠ ša ba-bi-šu-nu*, "the men of their gate" (lines 6, 22). The "men of their gate" are elders who perform judicial functions.[17] It is possible, then, to assume with some degree of certainty that reference to the citizens of the country reflects some sort of assembly. If they were commissioned by a ruler, would they not have been designated, as the merchants were, as linked to the king of their country?

Although in Ugarit there were three social classes, "servants of the king," "servants of the servants of the king," and "the citizens of Ugarit,"[18] besides

[17]Although CAD B, 23b, translates "the people of Ugarit together with the aliens [Akk. *LÚ.MEŠ*] living within their gates," it seems more plausible to recognize the judicial function of these men because the gate was a place at which legal functions would take place. This holds true for Mesopotamian material (cf. CAD B, 19b–20a) and for the Bible (cf. Ruth 4:1–12). While for Ugarit there are few references to gates in general, there is one that clearly indicates their role as a judicial forum. In Aqhat (KTU 1.17.6–8), Daniel sits by the gate and ensures justice for the widow and orphan. Furthermore, one of the titles of the Ugaritic king was *mlk ṯǵr*, "king of the gate," which may refer to the king in his role as dispenser of justice. Cf. Cyrus H. Gordon, *Ugaritic Textbook* (AnOr 38; Rome: Pontifical Biblical Institute, 1965), 505.

[18]Michael Heltzer, *The Rural Community in Ancient Ugarit* (Wiesbaden: Dr. Ludwig Reichert, 1976), 5.

slaves, references are made in these documents to the citizens of Ugarit or of a particular local or rural community within the kingdom of Ugarit without any social distinction. It is important to recognize that the citizens were treated as a collective body in the legal arena.[19]

The delegation undertakes certain actions in the country to which it travels. It must perform a formal legal act, the taking of an oath, for the claim to be valid. If the killers are not identified, the citizens of the country in which the homicide occurred must take an oath attesting to the fact that they cannot determine the identity of the killers. If the killers are arrested, the citizens of the victim's country, who are claiming the property, must take an oath.[20] The delegation also acts as the official body that disburses or accepts compensation.

The records of legal cases reflect concern with certain aspects of legal procedure assumed by the treaties. Collective responsibility is assumed by the place in which the victim was killed. Delegations are dispatched from one country to another to file a suit. In RS 17.234, the citizens of Shatega lay a claim on the citizens of Ugarit because a number of citizens of Shatega were killed in Ugarit.

> RS 17.234
> [12][. . . KUG.BABBAR].MEŠ mu-ul-la-a [13][a-na DUMU.MEŠ ^{uru}ša-t]e-ga id-dá-an-nu [14][ur-ra še-ra i-na EGIR U]D-mi DUMU.MEŠ ^{uru}ša-te-ga [15][aš-šum ZI.MEŠ š]a i-na ^{kur}ú-ga-ri-it [16][di-i-ku a-na muḫ-ḫ]i DUMU.MEŠ ^{kur}ú-ga-ri-it [17][la-a i-ra-gu-mu ù] DUMU.MEŠ ^{kur}ú-ga-ri-it [18][a-na muḫ-ḫi DUMU.MEŠ ^{uru}š]a-te-ga aš-šum mu-ul-li-i [19][ša id-dá-an-nu la-a] i-ra-gu-mu [20][ša i-ra-gu-um ṭup-pu] an-nu-ú i-le-'e-e-šu
>
> [12–13]the silver as full compensation shall be given to the citizens of Shatega. [14–19]In the future, the citizens of Shatega shall not sue the citizens of Ugarit on account the people who were killed in Ugarit, and the citizens of Ugarit shall not sue the citizens of Shatega on account of the compensation which was given. [20]Whoever sues, this tablet will prevail against him.

In RS 17.299, Qadidu brings a case against the citizens of the town in which his brother was killed:

[19]Heltzer, *The Rural Community in Ancient Ugarit,* 18–47. They were also considered as collective bodies for conscription, corvée, and taxes by the royal authorities. Heltzer believes that this evidence reflects the persistence of rural structures of authority in both Ugarit and Carchemish.

[20]If we extrapolate from the details about the oath taken when the killers are *not* arrested, the oath taken when the killers *are* arrested probably consists of swearing to their identification as the killers.

obv.
(1)[a]-na pa-ni ^{I}ba-ba (2)[^{I}]qá-di-du it-ti DUMU.MEŠ ^{uru}ḫal-pí-DAGAL-ši (3)[a]-na di-ni iš-ni-qu (4)[ù] ^{I}qá-di-du [a-k]án-na [i]q-[bi] (5)ma-a ŠEŠ-ia [i-na ^{uru}ḫal-pí-DAGAL-ši] (6)dì-ik-mi [...] (7)ù DUMU[.MEŠ ^{uru}ḫal-pí-DAGAL-ši] (8)[ma-a] ^{I}qá-[di-du...

rev.
(1)[...] x x [...] (2)[^{I}]x-taḫ-mu [DUB.ŠAR]

(1–3)Before Baba, Qadidu and the citizens of Ḫalpi-rapshi engaged in legal proceedings. (4–6)Qadidu said as follows, "My brother was killed in Ḫalpi-rapshi." (7–8)The citizens of Ḫalpi-rapshi [said:] "Qadidu ..." .... (rev. 2) X-taḫmu, the scribe...

Although RS 17.369B + 17.69 are in fragments, the sense that one town is suing another because the inhabitants of the first were killed in the second is clear:

RS 17.369B
rev.
(1)[^{d}]ḫé-bat ^{uru}a-ri (2)[š]a-mé.e (3)[^{d}UTU]-ši LUGAL GAL LUGAL ^{kur}ḫa-at-ti (4)[...] $^{lú.meš}$DAM.GÀR ^{kur}[...] (5)[...] LÚ[...]...

RS 17.69
rev.
... (6′)[DU]MU.MEŠ m[u...] (7′)[^{uru}i-r]i-ma-aš DUMU[...] (8′)[...-na] ù DUMU.MEŠ na[...] (9′)[i-na ^{uru}ap-s]ú-na i-du-ku-mi (10′)[x]-ma DUMU.MEŠ ^{uru}ap-sú-[na] (11′)[...]-din a-na ŠU ^{I}pur-š[i...] (12′)[...]a ša ^{d}UTU-ši LUGA[L GAL (13′)[...Š]U ^{I}tu-ta-[...] (14′)[...] ŠU ^{f}ia-ar-[...] (15′)[...^{uru}i-]ri-ma-aš[...]

obv.
(1)[...] x x LÚ iš-tu LÚ-l[um...] (2)[...] mim-mu ga-mi-ir a-di da-[ri-ti] (3)[iš-t]u UGU DUMU.MEŠ ^{uru}ap-sú-na[...] (4)[...p]a-ni ^{d}ḫé-bat ^{uru}a-ri[...] (5)gam-]ri-šu-nu šum-ma-mi LÚ[...] (6)[...m]i ŠEŠ.MEŠ[...]

(RS 17.369B rev. 1–5)Ḫebat of Ari...of the heavens. The Sun, the great king, king of Ḫatti...merchants...

(RS 17.69 rev. 6′–9′)citizens of Mu...of Irimash, son of...and the sons of Na...killed in Apsuna...the citizens of Apsuna...

(10′-obv. 2)in the hand of Pur...of the Sun, the great king...hand of Tuta...hand of Iar...the city of Irimash...one from the other...all is finished. (3–6)In the future from the citizens of Apsuna...before Ḫebat of Ari...completely. If one...the brothers...

In RS 17.158 and 17.42, the citizens of Ugarit are sued by Arshimiga, the representative of the king of Tarhudashshi, for the death of a merchant in the service of the king of Tarhudashshi and the concomitant loss of his goods:

RS 17.158
(1)[a-na pa-n]i ^{I}i-ni-^{d}tešub LUGAL ^{kur}kar-ga-miš (2)[^{I}ar-ši-]mi-ga ^{lú}DAM.GÀR ÍR ša LUGAL ^{kur}tar-ḫu-da-aš-ši (3)[it-ti] DUMU.MEŠ ^{kur}ú-ga-ri-it a-na di-ni (4)[iš-ni-q]u ^{I}ar-ši-mi-ga a-kán-na iq-bi (5)[ma-a ^{lú}]DAM.GÀR ša LUGAL ^{kur}tar-ḫu-da-aš-si (6)[DUMU.MEŠ ^{kur}]ú-ga-ri-it i-du-ku-ú-mi (7)[ù ^{I}]ar-ši-mi-ga ú-nu-te-MEŠ-šu mi-im-ma (8)[ša ^{lú}]DAM.GÀR ša i-na ^{kur}ú-ga-ri-it (9)dì-i-ku ú-ul ú-še-li ù LUGAL (10)DI-šu-nu a-kán-na ip-ru-us ma-a ^{I}ar-ša-mi-ga (11)^{lú}DAM.GÀR ša LUGAL ^{kur}tar-ḫu-da-aš-si (12)li-it-mi-ma ù DUMU.MEŠ ^{kur}ú-ga-ri-it (13)mu-ul-la-a ša ^{lú}DAM.GÀR ša-a-šu (14)ša i-na ^{kur}ú-ga-ri-it dì-i-ku (15)li-šal-li-mu i-na-an-na ^{I}ar-ša-mi-ga (16)it-ta-ma ù DUMU.MEŠ ^{kur}ú-ga-ri-it (17)1 me-at 80 GÍN KUG.BABBAR mu-ul-la-a (18)a-na ^{I}ar-ša-mi-ga ÍR ša LUGAL ^{kur}tar-ḫu-da-aš-ši (19)ú-šal-li-mu i-na EGIR-ki UD-mi ^{I}ar-ša-mi-ga (20)a-na muḫ-ḫi DUMU.MEŠ ^{kur}ú-ga-ri-it aš-šum ^{lú}DAM.GÀR (21)ša dì-i-ku la-a i-ra-gu-um (22)ù DUMU.MEŠ ^{kur}ú-ga-ri-it aš-šum 1 ME 80 GÍN KUG.BABBAR (23)mu-ul-li-šu-nu a-na muḫ-ḫi ^{I}ar-ša-mi-ga (24)la-a i-ra-gu-um ša i-ra-gu-um (25)[ṭ]up-pu an-nu-u i-le-'e-e-šu

(1–4)Before Ini-Teshub, king of Carchemish, Arshimiga, a merchant [and] a servant of the king of Tarhudashshi, and the citizens of Ugarit met in trial. (4–9)Arshimiga said as follows: "The citizens of Ugarit killed a merchant of the king of Tarhudashshi." Arshimiga had not recovered any of the goods of the merchant who was killed in Ugarit. (9–15)The king decided their case as follows: "Arshimiga, merchant of the king of Tarhudashshi, shall take an oath, and the citizens of Ugarit shall pay the full compensation for that merchant who was killed in Ugarit." (15–19)Then Arshimiga took the oath, and the citizens of Ugarit paid the full compensation of 180 shekels of silver to Arshimiga, servant of the king of Tarhudashshi. (19–25)In the future, Arshimiga shall not sue the citizens of Ugarit on account of the merchant who was killed, and the citizens of Ugarit shall not sue Arshimiga on account of the 180 shekels of silver of their compensatory payment. Whoever does sue, this tablet will prevail against him.

RS 17.42
(1)^{I}SUM-^{d}UTU-ga ÌR LUGAL ^{kur}tar-ḫu-da-aš-ši (2)[a-n]a DUMU.MEŠ ^{kur}ú-ga-ri-it a-kán-na iq-bi (3)[ma]-a ŠEŠ-ia ^{lú}DAM.GÀR ša LUGAL ^{kur}tar-ḫu-da-aš-ši (4)tá-dú-ka-a ù ú-nu-te^{meš} mim-ma (5)ša ŠEŠ-šu ša ^{I}SUM-^{d}UTU ša dì-i-ku (6)^{I}SUM-^{d}UTU iš-tu ŠU-ti DUMU.MEŠ

^{kur}ú-ga-ri-it [7]la-a ú-še-li DUMU.MEŠ ^{kur}ú-ga-ri-it [8]^{I}SUM-^{d}UTU ú-tam-mu-ú-ma [9]1 ME 80 GÍN KUG.BABBAR mu-ul-la-a [10]ša ŠEŠ-ia id-di-nu-uš-šu [11]i-na EGIR-ki UD-mi [12]^{I}SUM-^{d}UTU aš-šum ŠEŠ-šu [13]ša dì-i-ku a-na muḫ-ḫi [14]DUMU.MEŠ ^{kur}ú-ga-ri-it [15]la-a i-ra-ag-gu-um [16]ú DUMU.MEŠ ^{kur}ú-ga-ri-it [17][a]š-šum 1 ME 80 GÍN KUG.BABBAR [18][m]u-ul-la-a ša a-na ^{I}SUM-^{d}UTU [19][id]-dì-nu a-na muḫ-ḫi ^{I}SUM-^{d}UTU [20][la-a] i-ra-gu-mu [21][ša] i-ra-gu-um ṭup-pu an-nu-ú [22][i]-le-'e-e-šu [23]^{zá}KIŠIB ^{I}SUM-^{d}UTU ^{zá}KIŠIB ^{I}SUM-^{d}UTU

[1–7]Arshimiga, a servant of the king of Tarhudashshi, said as follows to the citizens of Ugarit: "You have killed my brother, a merchant of the king of Tarhudashshi." Arshimiga did not recover any of the goods of the brother of Arshimiga who was killed from the hands of the citizens of Ugarit. [7–10]The citizens of Ugarit made Arshimiga swear an oath and gave him the full compensation of 180 shekels of silver. [11–20]In the future, Arshimiga shall not sue the citizens of Ugarit on account of his brother who was killed, and the citizens of Ugarit shall not sue Arshimiga on account of the 180 shekels of silver of their compensatory payment. [21–23]Whoever does sue, this tablet will prevail against him. Seal of Arshimiga.

Arshimiga is not the actual brother of the victim, but he acts as the representative for the merchants of the king of Tarhudashshi. It is not appropriate for Arshimiga to make a claim on the actual killer, even if the identity of the actual killer is known. Legal responsibility for the death of a foreigner is assigned solely to the citizens of the country in which the homicide took place.[21] This is not to say that the killer would not be penalized in some way by his fellow citizens. It is reasonable to assume that he would have to reimburse his community, but holding the citizens of the country responsible ensures that the payment would be made in any and all circumstances.

According to the treaties, the delegation from the victim's country comes to the country where the homicide occurred only when the killers have been identified. However, it is not clear whether the legal records follow this principle because the actual killer is named in only a single legal record. In RS 17.229, Talimmu, a manager of foreign merchants, brings a claim in Apsuna against the citizens of Apsuna because one of Talimmu's merchants was killed there:

RS 17.229
obv.
[1]^{I}ta-li-im-mu ^{lú}DAM.GÀR [2]a-kán-na iq-bi [3]ma-a $^{lú.meš}$DAM.GÀR-ia [4]i-na ^{uru}ap-sú-na-a dì-ku$_{8}$-ú-mi [5]ù ^{I}ta-li-im-mu [6]it-ti DUMU.MEŠ

[21] Reuven Yaron, "Foreign Merchants at Ugarit," *Israel Law Review* 4 (1969), 76.

^{uru}ap-sú-ú-na [7]a-na di-ni iq-ri-bu [8]di-na iš-ni-qu-ú-ma [9]ša BE e-te-ep-šu [10]ù DUMU.MEŠ ^{uru}ap-sú-ú-na [11]1 GUN KUG.BABBAR

rev.
. . . [2]ur-r[a še-ra] [3]šum-ma ^{I}ta-l[im-mu] [4]tup-pu kán-ku ša [da-ki] [5]an-ni-i ša ú-še-el-la-a [6]i-bá-aš-ši ṭup-pu an-nu-ú [7]i-le-'e-e-šu

[1–4]Talimmu, the merchant, said as follows: "My merchants were killed in Apsuna." [5–8]Talimmu with the citizens of Apsuna drew near for judgment and engaged in legal proceedings. [9–11]Those who spilled the blood and the citizens of Apsuna [will pay] 1 talent of silver . . .

[rev. 2–7]In the future, if it happens that Talimmu does not produce a sealed tablet about the murder, this tablet will prevail against him.

Although the killers appear to have been identified according to their mention in line 9, Talimmu has traveled to Apsunu to make the claim. The citizens of Apsuna as well as the killers are required to assume the responsibility to pay one talent of silver.

According to two of the treaties, RS 17.146 and RS 18.115, if the killers have not been identified, compensation for the death is paid but not compensation for the missing property. According to the third treaty, RS 17.230, compensation is to be made for both the death and the missing goods. The single legal record that treats a case in which the killers have not been identified, RS 20.22, notes that no compensation is to be paid at all.

[40]ù aš-šum di-ni GEME^{ti} [41]ša ^{lú}mu-ut-ši it-ti DUMU ^{I}ḫu-ti-i[a] [42]ša i-na ^{uru}ar-zi-ga-na i-du-ku [43]ša tàš-pu-ra i-na-an-na LÚ.MEŠ ^{uru}ar-zi-ga-na [44]i-na ^{uru}a-ar-ru-wa li-it-mu-ú [45]a-kán-na li-iq-bu-ú ma-a šum-ma [46]^{lú}mu-ut-ši ša GEME-ti [47]ù áḫ ^{I}ÌR-a-na-tum [48]i-na URU-lim ni-id-du$_4$-ku [49]ia-nu-ma ša id-d[u$_4$]-ku-šu [50]ni-de$_4$-mi li-it-mu-ú-ma [51][di]n? GEME-tím ša-a-ši qa-ta li-i-l[i] [52]ù šum-ma DUMU.MEŠ LÚ.MEŠ ^{uru}ar-zi-ga-na iš-tu ma-mi-ti [53]i[-n]a-aḫ-s[ú] ù ki-i [m]u-ul-la-a DUMU.MEŠ ^{uru}ar-z[i-g]a-na [54]a-na DUMU ^{I}ḫu-t[i]-ia um-tal-lu-ú ù a-na GEME-ti š[a-a-ši] [55]mu-[u]l-la-a a-n[a ŠU-ši ù] lu-ú-[m]ál-[li-ni-ši][22]

[40–43]Regarding the matter of the woman's husband who was killed in Arzigana [and the matter of] the son of Ḫutiya [who was also killed there][23] about which you wrote: [43–51]Now, let the people of Arzigana take an oath and let them say, "We have not killed the husband of

[22] P.-R. Berger, "Zu den 'akkadischen' Briefen Ugaritica V," *Ugarit Forschungen* 2 (1987), 287.

[23] Although the text is somewhat ambigous as to whether Ḫutiya or his son was the one slain, it is clear from the reference to the compensation paid to the son of Ḫutiya that Ḫutiya was the one killed in Arzigana, not the son. Otherwise, the son would not be alive to accept the payment.

> this woman, the brother of Abdianatum, nor do we know who killed him." [52–55] If the sons of the men of Arzigana withdraw from the oath, they will pay to that woman the same amount the people of Arzigana paid to the son of Ḫutiya.

The oath alone is sufficient to release the people of Arzigana from the obligation.

As assumed by the three treaties, the oath is a formal requirement for the completion of the case in the legal records. There is no mention of any requirement that either physical evidence, such as a corpse, or testimony from witnesses to the crime be produced.

The remedy for the homicide is conceived solely in financial terms. The treaties differ on the compensation to be paid.[24] In RS 17.146 and 18.115, the compensation for each decedent is three minas. In RS 17.230, triple compensation for each victim is prescribed, but the specific amount is not given. In RS 17.146, when the killers have not been identified, compensation for missing property is not to be paid,[25] whereas in RS 17.230, simple compensation is the rule for missing property.[26] The amounts mentioned in the legal records differ from the ones recorded in the treaties as well as from each other. The compensation for the death of the merchant of the king of Tarhudashshi, according to RS 17.158 and 17.42, is 180 shekels of silver. In RS 17.145, the people of Ugarit pay 1,200 shekels of silver. The penalty in RS 17.229 is one talent of silver. These amounts may depend on details of the homicide or of the status of the victim that are not recorded in the documents we have. Moreover, the fact that we have three treaties between the

[24] These three texts do not appear to be copies of the same treaty. While RS 17.230 contains a fragment of a treaty between Carchemish and Ugarit, it is not the same treaty as RS 17.146 or 18.115 because the wording and content of its provisions are very different. RS 17.146 and 18.115 overlap far more. Nonetheless, they, too, are not identical.

[25] RS 18.115 is broken at the points where the compensation for missing property would have been mentioned.

[26] At first glance, it may appear that RS 17.146 and 17.230 are addressing different kinds of cases. RS 17.146 specifies that the killers are not identified, while RS 17.230 specifies that the killers are not seen. Does this mean that there are no witnesses who can identify them and, therefore, they are not known? Or is it, rather, that the killers have been identified but have not been seen and located and, therefore, have not been arrested? The first possibility appears to be the more plausible because of the varied terminology in RS 18.115. The case in which the slayers are not arrested is described in the following terms in the third treaty, RS 18.115: lines 12–13, "If they are in possession of the body of a man but do not arrest those who killed him," and lines 27–28, "If the citizens of the land of Carchemish do not take away the men who killed them [the merchants from Carchemish] from the citizens of Ugarit." In neither case is the fact that the killers have not been identified mentioned. Although it might be extrapolated that the killers are known but have not been arrested or extradited for some reason, the oath to be taken according to RS 18.115 specifies that the killers are not known to the citizens of the country in which the slayings happened. Therefore, it is improper to posit that these treaties are dealing with different kinds of cases. The treaties deal with only two cases: 1) The killers are known and have been arrested, and 2) the killers are not known and, therefore, cannot be arrested.

same countries with differing amounts of compensation may reflect a dispute over the appropriate amount: It may be speculated that new treaties were negotiated in order to solve the diplomatic impasse over compensation since the amounts of compensation were not standardized.[27] There was no call for the execution of the killer. There was no requirement that the merchants who were in the service of a foreign king be replaced by equivalent personnel. This is striking in light of the legal records RS 17.251[28] and 17.337,[29] which record the substitution of servants in the case of kidnapping, embodying a concept of the fungibility of persons as compensation. In the case of homicide, however, only monetary compensation is required.

In contrast to the treaties, the legal records recount that the cases are brought before an outside party. In RS 17.299, the case of Qadidu against the citizens of Ḫalpi-rapshi is brought to trial before Baba.[30] In addition, Ini-Teshub, king of Carchemish, presides over a number of trials. Thus, in RS 17.145, Aballa and the citizens of Ugarit appear before Ini-Teshub. The trial recorded in RS 17.158 and 17.42, treating the death of a merchant in the service of the king of Tarhudashshi in Ugarit, does not take place in either Ugarit or Tarhudashshi but before Ini-Teshub in Carchemish.

It is likely that the outside party was selected because of his political or social power to enforce the judgment. This was the case with Ini-Teshub, who possessed political power in the region. After the conquest of Carchemish by Suppiluliuma I, who installed his son Piyassili (throne name Sharrikushuh) as king, the kings of Carchemish acted as the Hittite viceroys of Syria. Their power in relationship to the Hittite empire can be illustrated in the legal documents found at both Ugarit and Boghazkoy.[31] These legal texts are drafted as judgments or contracts made by kings and ratified by their seals: In

[27]Unfortunately, these treaties are not dated and, therefore, we cannot reconstruct the negotiations.

[28]Text: DO 4641 = Ras es-Shamra 17.251. Publication: Nougayrol, *Le Palais Royal d'Ugarit IV/II*, plate XXXIII; *Ugaritica* 3 (1956), 41, fig. 55. Transliteration and translation: Nougayrol, *Le Palais Royal d'Ugarit IV/I*, 236–237.

[29]Text: DO 4678 = Ras es-Shamra 17.337. Publication: Nougayrol, *Le Palais Royal d'Ugarit IV/II*, plate XLVI. Transliteration and translation: Nougayrol, *Le Palais Royal d'Ugarit IV/I*, 168–169

[30]Baba's status is not mentioned in this tablet, nor can it be determined from other sources, since he is not mentioned elsewhere.

[31]J. D. Hawkins, "Karkamiš," RLA 5.430. On the power of the king of Carchemish vis-à-vis the Hittite king, see also Hawkins, "Kuzi – tešub and the 'Great Kings' of Karkamiš," *Anatolian Studies* 38 (1988), 99–108, esp. 104, nn. 27 and 28, and "'Great Kings' and 'Country-Lords' at Malatya and Karkamiš," in *Studio Historiae Ardens: Ancient Near Eastern Studies Presented to Philo H. J. ten Cate on the Occasion of his 65th Birthday* (ed. Theo van den Hout and Johan de Roos, Uitgaven van het Nederlands Historisch-Archaeologisch Instituut te Instanbul 74; Leiden: Nederlands Historisch-Archaeologisch Instituut te Instanbul, 1995), 73–85. As a reflection of Ini-tešub's power, it is to be noticed that while the titles "Great King, Hero," (*LUGAL.GAL qarrādu*) were reserved for the Hittite king, Ini-teshub occasionally assumes the title "Hero," *qarrādu*. Cf. RS 17.352.3, 17.68.4, 17.108.3 (PRU IV/I, 121, 164ff). Even a minor case of theft

some, the Hittite king takes the lead and the king of Carchemish assumes the secondary role; in some, they act together without any clear distinction between overlord and viceroy; and in others, the king of Carchemish acts on his own authority. Presenting a case to a higher authority is simply not an issue in the treaties because of the status of one of the signatories, Ini-Teshub, the king of Carchemish.[32] There is no one of greater prominence in the region. To say it in another way, the Syrian vassals apparently had to go through Carchemish; they could not avoid the viceroy of Carchemish by making a direct appeal to the Hittite sovereign.

The legal records also show that the parties to a case may come to an agreement outside of court even when a decision has already been rendered. In RS 17.145, Aballa, the manager of a group of foreign merchants,[33] has made a claim against the citizens of Ugarit because one of the merchants in his charge was killed in Ugarit:

> [1]a-na pa-ni ^{I}i-ni-^{d}tešub LUGAL ^{kur}kar-ga-miš [2]^{I}a-bal-la-a ù DUMU.MEŠ ^{kur}ú-ga-ri-it [3]a-na di-ni iš-ni-qu ^{I}a-bal-la-a [4]a-kán-na iq-bi ma-a $^{\text{lú.meš}}$DAM.GÀR ša ŠU-ia [5]i-na ^{kur}ú-ga-ri-it dì-ku-u-mi ù LUGAL DI.<KU$_5$>-šu-nu [6]a-kán-na ip-ru-us ma-a ^{I}a-bal-la-a li-it-ma-mi [7]ù LÚ.MEŠ ^{kur}ú-ga-ri-it mu-ul-la-a [8]ša $^{\text{lú.meš}}$DAM.GÀR a-na ^{I}a-bal-la-a [9]li-ma-al-lu-mi ^{I}a-bal-la-a ù LÚ.MEŠ ^{kur}ú-ga-ri-it [10]i-na bi-ri-šu-nu im-tág-ru ù ^{I}a-bal-la-a [11]iš-tu ma-mi-ti ut-te-er-ru LÚ.MEŠ ^{kur}ú-ga-ri-it [12]1 li-im 2 me-at GÍN KUG.BABBAR.MEŠ a-na ^{I}a-bal-la-a [13]um-te-el-lu-ú i-na EGIR UD-mi [14]^{I}a-bal-la-a aš-šum mu-ul-li-i ša $^{\text{lú.meš}}$DAM.GÀR [15]a-na muḫ-ḫi LÚ.MEŠ ^{kur}ú-ga-ri-it [16]la-a i-ra-gu-um ù LÚ.MEŠ ^{kur}ú-ga-ri-it [17]aš-šum 1 li-im 2 me-a[t KUG.BABBAR] a-na muḫ-ḫi [18]^{I}a-bal-la-a la-a [i-ra-gu-m]u [19]ša i-ra-gu-um ṭ[up]-p[u a]n-nu-ú [20]i-le-’e-e-šu

> [1–3]Before Ini-Teshub, king of Carchemish, Aballa and the citizens of Ugarit engaged in legal proceedings. [3–5]Aballa said as follows: “Merchants in my charge were killed in Ugarit.” [5–9]The king decided their case as follows: “Let Aballa take an oath, and the people of Ugarit shall [then] pay in full the compensation for the merchants to Aballa.” [9–10]Aballa and the people of Ugarit came to an agreement. [10–11]They released Aballa from the imprecatory oath. [11–13]The people of Ugarit paid Aballa in full 1,200 shekels of silver. [13–18]In the future, Aballa shall not sue the people of Ugarit on account of the compensation for

by a foreign merchant in Ugarit must be tried before Ini-Teshub in Carchemish, not locally in Ugarit (Yaron, “Foreign Merchants at Ugarit,” 79).

[32]Ini-Teshub’s higher status has no effect upon his countrymen’s duty to pay compensation. The rights and responsibilities of his country and of Ugarit are equal. Only in the matter of form, not susbstantive law, is Ini-Teshub given prominence. Cf. Yaron, “Foreign Merchants at Ugarit,” 76.

[33]Their country of origin is not specified.

> the merchants, and the people of Ugarit shall not sue Aballa on account of the 1,200 shekels. 19–20 Whoever sues, this tablet will prevail against him.

Ini-Teshub has rendered a verdict, putting pressure on the two parties to settle out of court. Aballa and the citizens of Ugarit then came to an agreement, forestalling the need for Aballa to take an oath. However, the citizens of Ugarit do agree to pay 1,200 shekels of silver as per Ini-Teshub's order. It is unclear why the citizens of Ugarit would release Aballa from the oath if they would have to pay compensation in any case.[34]

Documentation was important. Many texts conclude *ša iraggum ṭuppu annû ile"ešu,* "whoever does sue, this tablet will prevail against him" (RS 17.234, 17.158, 17.42, 17.145, 17.337). Indeed, RS 17.229 shows that a tablet could abrogate other tablets. RS 17.229 specifies that (rev. 2–7) *ur-ra še-ra šum-ma* ^{I}*ta-l[im-mu] ṭup-pu kán-ka ša [da-ki] an-ni-i ša ú-še-el-la-a i-bá-aš-ši ṭup-pu an-nu-ú i-le-e-e-šu,* "In the future, if [in regard to] Talimmu, there is a sealed tablet about the murder which he [is able to] produce, this tablet will prevail against him." RS 17.229 negates the possibility that another tablet pertaining to the homicide may be produced: It takes precedence over any other tablet (possibly forged?) that purports to record a settlement of the case. In addition, the legal records do provide evidence for legal procedures that could produce multiple documents. RS 17.158 and 17.42 are two documents that deal with the same case, the homicide of a merchant of the king of Tarhudashshi in the land of Ugarit. RS 17.158 records the verdict of the judge, Ini-Teshub, and contains the impression of his seal. RS 17.42 is a record of the discharge of the obligation of the citizens of Ugarit and contains the seal impression of Arshimiga, the representative of the king of Tarhudashshi, who received the payment. These two tablets were deposited in the archives at Ugarit. The corresponding tablet with the seal of the citizens of Ugarit was probably taken by Arshimiga back to Tarhudashshi and deposited in the archives there.

Let us sum up what we have seen in the texts from Ugarit. The legal process prescribed by the treaties is congruent with, but does not overlap, the process reflected in the legal records. First, corporate responsibility in both sets of texts is assumed by the place in which the slaying was committed. It is so pervasive that it is the rule even when the killers have been identified and apprehended. Despite the fact that an individual actually dealt the fatal blow, it is a corporate body that assumes the debt and pays. Second, the remedy for homicide is financial compensation, not the execution of the killer. Third, the taking of an oath is an indispensable element in validating the claim.

[34] It is possible that the 1,200 shekels might be less than the amount they would otherwise be obliged to pay. Unfortunately, this text does not indicate how many merchants were killed and, therefore, we cannot compare the amount paid according to this text to the amounts mentioned in the other texts from Ugarit.

However, an outsider presided over the cases in the legal records, whereas the treaties did not require this provision because the individual with the most political power in the region was a party to the treaty. It would be an infringement on him to submit his case to a lesser figure.

In the international documents from Ugarit, the killer's community takes the initiative in assuming corporate responsibility.[35] A similar principle informs one statute in the Laws of Hammurapi and one in the Hittite Laws. Statute 24 in the Laws of Hammurapi provides for the case in which the killer has not been arrested. The mandate here is that if a person is killed in the course of a robbery, the city and governor must pay sixty shekels to the victim's kinsman if the robber is not arrested. It appears that the communal authorities must discharge the obligation to the family against whom the act of killing was perpetrated when the killer himself cannot be apprehended. Otherwise, in Mesopotamia, legal institutions managed the affairs of individuals. The same kind of corporate responsibility is evident in the Hittite Laws as well. The responsibility for paying compensation is imputed to the person on whose land the homicide occurred:

> HL 6
> If a person, man or woman, is killed in another[?] city, [the victim's heir] shall deduct 12,000 square meters [= 3 acres] from the land of the person on whose property the person was killed and shall take it for himself.

This statute was later emended:

> Late version of 6
> If a man is found killed on another person's property, if he is a free man, [the property owner] shall give his property, house and 60 shekels of silver. But if [the dead person] is a woman, [the property owner] shall give [no property, but] 120 shekels of silver. But if [the place where the dead body was found] is not [private] property, but open uncultivated country, they shall measure 3 DANNA's in all directions, and whatever village is determined [to lie within that radius], he shall take those very [inhabitants of the village]. If there is no town/village, [the heir of the deceased] shall forfeit [his claim].

This extraordinarily high penalty for a village – the confiscation of the entire town – may have been intended to prevent the inhabitants of the villages from shielding their own.[36] Despite the presence of corporate responsibility

[35] A parallel concept is reflected in Deut 21:1–9, where in the case of the killer not being identified, the elders of the town closest to the spot in which the corpse was found perform a ceremony in which they deny any involvement in the slaying.

[36] Hoffner, *The Laws of the Hittites,* 174.

in Babylonian and Hittite law,[37] it was never expanded to the national level. The concept of corporate responsibility on the part of the territory in which the homicide occurred is not reflected in either EA 8 or CTH 172. The kings whose men have been killed must take the initiative to protect their citizens abroad and force a foreign government to comply with their demands.

In EA 8 and CTH 172, in which a citizen of one territory is killed in another, the law of one political entity is set over and against that of another. One ruler attempts to impose the law of his realm upon another, and the only way he can do so is by diplomatic means. This contrasts with the documents from Ugarit, where the areas under Hittite hegemony share certain legal concepts and institutions, such as corporate responsibility, compensation as the appropriate remedy for homicide, and an oath as an indispensable element of the legal process, not recognized between Babylonia and Egypt or between Babylonia and the Hittite empire. Yet even this shared set of legal procedures and principles must either be specified in a treaty or invoked by appealing to an overlord with enough influence to impose a settlement.

International law, in the sense of law that states feel obliged to observe,[38] which has evolved after a long historical process, does not appear to have existed, but that which might best be called interterritorial or interstate law did. Each territory had its own law, but in the case of a citizen killed in a foreign territory, the law of one territory might be contradicted by that of another. In some cases, the leaders of the territories involved attempted to devise ad hoc resolutions to a particular situation.[39] Sometimes the disjunction could not be resolved, as in CTH 172. However, where there was

[37] Although one could object that the laws and the letters are not close in date, it should be noted that while the Laws of Hammurapi was written 500 years before these letters, it was extant in many copies for over a millennium, and that the new version of the Hittite Laws dates from the same period of Hittite history, the New Hittite period (the New Hittite recension dates from ca. 1350 to ca. 1200 B.C.E.), as these letters.

[38] Cf. J. G. Starke, *Introduction to International Law* (10th edition; London: Butterworths, 1989), 3–6, 18–20.

[39] The attempts of one country to impose its law on another persist in contemporary times. A case making headlines at the time this book was being written is that of an American convicted of murdering his lover in the United States who escaped from there and was captured in France twenty years later. The French authorities insisted that French law regarding capital punishment be applied to his case in the United States in order for him to be extradited from France to the United States. Cf. Steven C. Kiernan, "Extradition of a Convicted Killer: The Ira Einhorn Case," *Suffolk Transnational Law Review* 24 (2001): 353–385. A recent case in which foreign authorities have attempted to apply elements of another system of law in their own court as a response to the demands of another government is treated in Renee Lettow Lerner, "The Intersection of Two Systems: An American on Trial for an American Murder in the French Cour D'Assizes," *University of Illinois Law Review* 2001: 791–856.

a power that held sway over the territories involved, this power could be called upon to adjudicate a specific dispute between them, similar to forced arbitration. In other cases, these territories followed a specific set of procedures agreed apon in advance by the parties involved. This set of procedures operated like a contract between the territories for their exclusive use, rather than commonly accepted international law the parties felt constrained to follow.

Conclusion

HOMICIDE IS an occurrence that is viewed as heinous in every human society. However, it embodies the social, religious, and intellectual characteristics of a particular culture. In the Hebrew Bible, the adjudication of homicide typified aspects of Israelite culture and society. The organization of society shaped the process. The victim's family had the right and responsibility to ensure that justice was done. The process, blood feud, was always rule-bound and intrinsically part of the legal process. By contrast, in cuneiform law, the central government exerted control over the process, and the victim's family could participate only in a late stage of the process. In Israel, kinship ties persisted; the lineage, the association of families, was responsible for the protection of family members in the legal arena, and in general, a community-based system of justice prevailed, whereas in Mesopotamia, a bureaucracy had control. This is because ancient Israel perceived itself to be and was in fact a rural, decentralized society with only mild bureaucratic interference and little in the way of specialized professions. Mesopotamia was urban and centralized, with the disintegration of extensive family ties and the rigid control of bureacracy. Biblical law was not lagging behind the rest of society. Blood feud was not an archaic or outmoded institution retained for an offense like homicide. It fit the contours of biblical culture.

Cultic considerations were also a significant factor. Measures had to be taken to prevent the very real effects of spilled blood. The contamination incurred by the shedding of blood originated in the concept of ritual purity and impurity in biblical religion: Blood was both a contaminant and a cleanser. An unlawful death was linked to ethical impurity: Certain acts were so heinous that they generated severe impurity that affected the nation as a whole. The blood of a slain person caused defilement, and the way to undo that defilement was through blood. Since the contamination incurred by homicide operated as both ritual and ethical impurity, the remedy did not necessitate physical application of blood to remove impurity, as the sanctification of the altar, to offer an example, did. Rather, the slaying of the intentional killer, the death of the high priest as the representative of the Israelite people in the case of accidental homicide, or the ceremonial removal of the contagion of blood in the case of a victim whose killer cannot be found was sufficient to defer the consequences of unlawful slaying. No such concern with the ill effects of slain blood is found in cuneiform law. Mesopotamian religion was not concerned with the contaminating effects of spilled blood, nor were the actions of individuals the source of peril for a nation as a whole.

Concomitant with the concern over the defiling effects of unlawful killing, the principle of *lex talionis* caused the death penalty to be imposed on the slayer in biblical law. Capital punishment for homicide in cuneiform law is an example of the proper punishment for serious crimes and was not an actualization of lex talionis. Lex talionis was used in cuneiform law as a principle in determining the punishment for nonfatal bodily injuries.

The differences in the characteristics of the cities of refuge in the Priestly traditions and in Deuteronomy reflect the ideology and theology characteristic of each Pentateuchal source, rather than historical development. Historically, asylum did operate for others besides killers. Political offenders could seek respite from their enemies at a sanctuary.

Certain phenomena, such as the cities of refuge, appear in ancient Israel due to the confluence of factors specific to ancient Israel. The cities of refuge existed there and nowhere else in the ancient Near East. It may be speculated that the emphasis on communal solidarity of the Israelites as a nation apart[1] may have served as one impetus for the creation of refuges within Israelite borders, so that avoiding a blood avenger would not necessitate flight to a foreign territory. Adding to this impetus is the concept in ancient Israel that the danger posed by impurity affects the entire nation and that steps need to be taken as a preventative. Therefore, even an accidental homicide

[1]See Peter B. Machinist, "The Question of Distinctiveness in Ancient Israel: An Essay," in *Ah, Assyria . . . : Studies in Assyrian History and Ancient Near Historiography* (ScrHier 33; ed. Mordechai Cogan and Israel Ephᶜal; Jerusalem: Magnes Press, 1991), 203–207, and "Outsiders or Insiders: The Biblical View of Emergent Israel and its Contexts," in *The Other in Jewish Thought and History: Constructions of Jewish Culture and Identity* (ed. Laurence J. Silberman and Robert L. Cohn; New York: New York University Press, 1994), 41–54.

is dangerous because although the death was accidental, the shed blood is still polluting: A city of refuge, then, has dual aspects, both protection and confinement, and the accidental slayer must wait until the death of the high priest for the stain to be neutralized. In contrast, while cities in the Late Assyrian and Babylonian periods had the right of *kidinnūtu,* a privilege of autonomy in certain matters, that theoretically prevented royal officials from executing anyone who had entered a city's precincts, this was not limited to, or even meant for, killers.[2] In the Old Babylonian period, certain persons and any property placed into their care or any other person enjoying their hospitality were immune from the interference of others. This was most likely intended to protect economic and commercial interests.[3]

The biblical treatment of homicide differed radically from that of cuneiform law despite Mesopotamia's profound political, economic, and cultural influence on the ancient Near East because biblical law was linked to aspects of biblical society, religion, and ideological traditions. There are only two specific statutes of biblical homicide law, the goring ox and the fatal assault on a pregnant woman, that appear to have been drawn from cuneiform legal tradition. The parallels to Mesopotamian law occur in the Covenant Code, a legal corpus that has another affinity to Mesopotamian law collections: Most of the Covenant Code is written in casuistic style, the style of most of the Mesopotamian law collections.

Certain Israelite scribes, in order to produce business or diplomatic documents that could be used further afield throughout the ancient Near East, must have learned Akkadian, the lingua franca of the ancient Near East, and among the school texts used for training native Akkadian scribes were legal collections and texts composed of legal formulas. It is reasonable to suppose that such material was available in the education of Israelite scribes. Probably not all Israelite scribes had this training, but a percentage did. Some educated individuals, not necessarily scribes by profession, may also have been exposed to this type of training.

In this study, we have addressed the question of whether we can tell if a phenomenon has been borrowed or independently invented. An element that is very general, we must assume, was independently invented, but something unusual calls attention to itself as something parallel. Here, our argument that it is borrowed is buttressed by the parallels within cuneiform law: Just as an unusual case was repeated in cuneiform legal collections, so too was it repeated in another legal collection, that is, the Covenant Code.

The mode of analysis used to answer this question has been comparative, and it is clear that the comparative method is useful if used judiciously. It

[2]Amélie Kuhrt, *The Ancient Near East* (Routledge History of the Ancient World; London: Routledge, 1995), 614–616.

[3]J. J. Finkelstein, "On Some Recent Studies in Cuneiform Law," *JAOS* 90 (1970), 253, esp. n. 46.

throws the characteristics of each society into sharper relief. At the same time, it highlights the links between societies, while acknowledging the differing contours of each. It shows that even when certain aspects of one culture's law are transplanted from another culture, they may appear differently because when a legal institution or statute takes root in alien soil, it acquires native characteristics. What is so striking about the biblical adjudication of homicide is that in two cases it parallels cuneiform law and yet is otherwise so different. Biblical law incorporated a few elements from nonbiblical law and yet produced so much that was not dependent at all.

This study has shown that the analysis of narrative texts in the Bible that touch on law is essential to the study of biblical law because narrative texts manifest critical aspects of the law not incorporated in legal texts. For example, although biblical texts agree that only killing by direct action is subject to legal review, individuals might be held ethically responsible for causing a death indirectly. This is reflected only in narrative texts, and we would not be aware of it were it not for them. Literature is a lamp onto the law. Biblical narrative illuminates what happens in the interstices of the law. It does not portray a world in which the law is carried out as prescribed and whose goals are accomplished perfectly, but focuses on the imperfections and tensions. Narrative texts cannot be analyzed innocently. The genre of narrative shapes and selects what it represents.

This is no less true for other genres. Each of the cuneiform records of actual cases fails to contain the complete spectrum of elements that could have been utilized in a trial. Thorkild Jacobsen argues that the absence of a detailed establishment of the facts of the case in the Nippur Murder Trial through the testimony of witnesses, the killer's confession, the taking of oaths, or the like, in contrast to the contents of a civil trial record, signified that such an establishment did not take place.[4] Simply because they are absent from the tablet, according to Jacobsen, they did not occur. Rather, the Nippur Murder Trial was part of a procedural tradition in which the facts and guilt of the accused were taken for granted by the community, which had been aroused to punish the offender in the emotionally highly charged situation of lynch justice. In effect, the Assembly of Nippur was to render its verdict on the basis of its members' personal convictions, rather than on facts proven in court. In Jacobsen's view, the facts of the case were already determined by the king, who in turn dispatched the case to the Assembly so that it could act out its part in this tradition. Jacobsen reconstructs this criminal procedural tradition by recourse to a number of Mesopotamian myths that recount the way criminals, albeit not murderers, were convicted and punished. To him, this use of myth is attractive because myths can preserve remembrances of social conditions of greater antiquity than other sources.

[4]Jacobsen, "An Ancient Mesopotamian Trial for Homicide," 204–205.

However, in my opinion, reading this tradition of lynch justice into the record of the Nippur Murder Trial is a narrow way of reading, especially in light of the brevity of the other homicide records. These other records also omit elements indispensable to the adjudication of homicide. The absences are different in different documents. For example, the Nippur Murder Trial records the statements of the members of the Assembly of Nippur. They formally identify the accused and propose capital punishment as the remedy. A question about the culpability of the victim's wife arises from two members of the Assembly and is answered. There is no mention of a formal accusation or the presence of witnesses: The document only records the points of discussion of the Assembly of Nippur. However, in the first homicide case recorded in NSG 202, the widow makes the accusation. The accused produced witnesses to prove that he was innocent, but the details of their testimony are not recorded. Unlike the Nippur Murder Trial, the court's discussion is truncated. Does this mean that the court did not explain its ruling or question witnesses simply because it is not mentioned? The nature of these documents is such that only the contested matters are put down in writing. In the second case in NSG 202, the fact that Kali killed Guzani is mentioned. No indication of whether it was ascertained through the testimony of witnesses or the killer's confession is made. The document contains a quotation of Kali's protestation that he killed in self-defense and notes that he proved that an argument had occurred. The manner in which he offered proof is not included. An oath is considered sufficient to resolve the dispute in CT 29 42. The fact that these documents are not exact transcripts means that the reconstruction of the proceedings must be full of lacunae. The absence of a detailed establishment of the facts of the case through the testimony of witnesses, the killer's confession, the taking of oaths, or the like does not mean that they did not occur. The cuneiform law collections omit information on procedure and on distinguishing between intentional and unintentional homicide, as well as referring to odd cases. Genre, whether of legal record or law collection, shapes what is depicted as the adjudication of homicide.

This study focuses on a single type of offense, but its findings have ramifications for the analysis of other offenses. If biblical law on homicide is so different from cuneiform law except for a few cases, it would be worth investigating whether biblical and cuneiform law on other offenses exhibit the same relationship. The international documents demonstrate that while there is a general assumption that homicide is wrong, not much else regarding the remedy of homicide is shared in the ancient Near East. If there is so little shared with regard to a heinous offense like homicide, it would be doubtful that assumptions about other offenses would be possible. The exception to this would probably be in the realm of contract and economic law, where international trade would require a common basis to operate.

APPENDIX

Cuneiform Sources on Homicide

1. **The Reform of UruKAgina**

   PUBLICATION: Ukg. 4 xii 13–22 (= Ukg. 5 xi 20–29) = H. Steible and H. Behrens, *Die Altsumerischen Bau- und Weihinschriften* (Stuttgart: Franz Steiner, 1991).

   TRANSLITERATION AND TRANSLATION: Piotr Steinkeller, "The Reform of UruKAgina and an Early Sumerian Term for 'Prison,'" *AuOr* 9 (1991), 227–233.

   TRANSLATION: Jerrold S. Cooper, *Sumerian and Akkadian Royal Inscriptions: Pre-Sargonic Inscriptions* (AOS Translation Series I; Winona Lake, Indiana: Eisenbrauns, 1986), 73.

   DATE: circa 2350 B.C.E.[1]

2. **NSG 41**

   PUBLICATION: ITT 2789 = Henri de Genouillac, *Inventaire des Tablettes de Tello*, volume II/1 (Paris: Ernest Leroux, 1910), number 2789.

General note: Text 8 in O. R. Gurney, "Texts from Dur-Kurigalzu," *Iraq* 11 (1949), 138, apparently describes a slaying, but the text is too fragmentary for any conclusions to be drawn from it. ARM XIII 109 (G. Dossin et al., *Textes divers* [ARM XIII; Paris: Paul Geuthner, 1964], 116) might describe a parricide, but the text is difficult.

[1] Cf. Amélie Kuhrt, *The Ancient Near East, c. 3000–330 B.C.* (London: Routledge, 1995), 27.

TRANSLITERATION AND TRANSLATION: NSG 41 = Adam Falkenstein, *Die neusumerischen Gerichtsurkunden* (Bayerische Akademie der Wissenschaften, philosophisch-historisch Klasse 40; Munich: Bayerische Akademie der Wissenschaften, 1956), 2.67–69; Bernard J. Siegel, "Slavery During the Third Dynasty of Ur," *American Anthropologist* 40, issue 1, part 2 (1947), 24–25.

DATE: Neo-Sumerian period (twenty-first century B.C.E.)

3. **NSG 202**

PUBLICATION: TEO 6168 = Henri de Genouillac, *Textes économiques d'Oumma de l'époque d'Our* (TCL 5; Paris: Librairie Orientaliste/Paul Geuthner, 1922), number 6168.

TRANSLITERATION AND TRANSLATION: NSG 202 = Falkenstein, *Die neusumerischen Gerichtsurkunden,* number 202, 2.331–333.

DATE: Neo-Sumerian period (twenty-first century B.C.E.)

NSG 202 is a *Sammeltafel* from Umma, recording a number of cases, one of which involves homicide.

4. **NSG 121**

PUBLICATION: TEO 6165 = de Genouillac, *Textes économiques d'Oumma de l'époque d'Our,* number 6165.

TRANSLITERATION AND TRANSLATION: NSG 121 = Falkenstein, *Die neusumerischen Gerichtsurkunden*, number 121, 2.206–208.

DATE: Neo-Sumerian period (twenty-first century B.C.E.)

5. **The Nippur Murder Trial**

PUBLICATION: 2 N-T.54; duplicates: PBS VIII 173, 3N-T.340 + 3N-T.403 + 3N-T.273, 3N-T.426 = Edward Chiera, *Legal and Administrative Documents from Nippur* (Publications from the Babylonian Section VIII; Philadelphia: University Museum, 1914), number 173.

TRANSLITERATION AND TRANSLATION: Thorkild Jacobsen, "An Ancient Mesopotamian Trial for Homicide," in *Toward the Image of Tammuz and Other Essays on Mesopotamian History and Culture* (ed. William L. Moran; HSS 21; Cambridge, Massachusetts: Harvard University Press, 1970; originally published in *Analecta Biblica* 12 [1959]), 198–201.

TRANSLATION: Samuel Noah Kramer, *From the Tablets of Sumer* (3d edition; Philadelphia: University of Pennsylvania Press, 1981 [1st edition, 1956]), 57–58; Martha T. Roth, "Gender and Law: A Case Study from Ancient Mesopotamia," in *Gender and Law in the Hebrew Bible and the Ancient Near East* (ed. Victor H. Matthews, Bernard M. Levinson, and Tikva Frymer-Kensky; JSOTSup 262; Sheffield: Sheffield Academic Press, 1998), 173–184.

DATE:[2] reign of Ur-Ninurta of Isin (1923–1896 B.C.E.)
The so-called Nippur Murder Trial is recorded in Sumerian on a number of tablets. The homicide itself took place in the very late 1900s B.C.E. Two copies date from the reign of Rim-Sin of Larsa (1822–1763 B.C.E.). Four copies date from the reign of Samsiliuna and later (no earlier than 1749 B.C.E.). On these later copies, a number of trials are recorded.

6. **CT 29 42**

PUBLICATION: BM 78184 = *Cuneiform Texts from Babylonian Tablets in the British Museum* 29 (London: Trustees of the British Museum, 1971 [1910]), plates 42, 43, 41.

TRANSLITERATION AND TRANSLATION: P. Dhorme, "Mélanges," *RA* 8 (1914), 102–105; Arthur Ungnad, *Babylonische Briefe aus der Zeit der Ḫammurapi-Dynastie* (Leipzig: J. C. Hinrichs, 1914), 180–184.

DATE: Old Babylonian period, reign of Samsiliuna (1749–1712 B.C.E.)

7. **Riftin 46**

PUBLICATION, TRANSLITERATION, AND TRANSLATION: A. P. Riftin, "Iz vavilonskogo prava," in *Sergeju Fedoroviču Oldenburgu k pjatidesjatiletiju naučno-obščestvennoj dejatelnosti 1882–1932* [To Sergei Fedorovich Oldenburg on the Fiftieth Anniversary of his Scholarly Endeavors 1882–1932] (Leningrad: Izdatelstvo Akademii Nauk, 1934), 437–442.

TRANSLITERATION AND TRANSLATION: A. P. Riftin, *Staro-Vavilonskie iuridicheskie i administrativnye dokumenty y sobraniiakh SSSR* [Old Babylonian Judicial and Administrative Documents] (Moscow: Izdatelstvo Akademii Nauk, 1937), 91–94; B. Landsberger, "Gerichtsprotokoll über einen Mordprozess," *ZA* 43 (1936): 315–316; John David Fortner, "Adjudicating Entities and Levels of Judicial Authority in Lawsuit Records of the Old Babylonian Period" (Ph.D. dissertation, Hebrew Union College, 1996), 749–751.

DATE: 1792 B.C.E. (year 30 of Rim-Sin, 1822–1763)

8. **CCT 4 30a**

PUBLICATION: Sidney Smith, *Cuneiform Texts from Cappadocian Tablets in the British Museum IV* (London: British Museum, 1927), number 30a.

[2]The tablets themselves date to the late nineteenth century B.C.E. based on the stratigraphy of the site and the particular layer in which 2N-T.54 was excavated. The writing on PBS VIII 173 indicates that it is of approximately the same age as 2N-T.54. The duplicates appear to be at least from the reign of Samsiliuna (1749–1712 B.C.E.) or later. See Jacobsen, "An Ancient Mesopotamian Trial for Homicide," 196.

TRANSLITERATION AND TRANSLATION: Louis Lawrence Orlin, *Assyrian Colonies in Cappadocia* (The Hague: Mouton, 1970), 123–125.

DATE: Old Assyrian period

9. ARM III 18

PUBLICATION: ARM III 18 = J. R. Kupper, *Lettres* (TCL 24; ARM III; Paris: Paul Geuthner, 1948), plate 20, number 18.

TRANSLITERATION AND TRANSLATION: J. R. Kupper, *Correspondance de Kibri-Dagan* (ARMT III; Paris: Imprimerie Nationale, 1950), 34–37.

DATE: Old Babylonian period

10. ARM VIII 1

PUBLICATION: ARM VIII 1 = Georges Boyer, *Textes juridiques et administratifs* (TCL 29; ARM VIII; Paris: Paul Geuthner, 1957), number 1.

TRANSLITERATION AND TRANSLATION: Georges Boyer, *Textes juridiques* (ARMT VIII; Paris: Imprimerie Nationale, 1958), 2–7.

TRANSLATION: J. J. Finkelstein, in *ANET*[3], 545.

BIBLIOGRAPHY: Boyer, *Textes juridiques,* 167–168, 178–182; Reuven Yaron, "Varia on Adoption," *Journal of Juristic Papyrology* 15 (1965): 171–183, esp. 173–175.

DATE: Old Babylonian period

11. ARM XIII 145

TRANSLITERATION AND TRANSLATION: G. Dossin, J. Bottéro, M. Birot, et al., *Textes divers* (ARM XIII; Paris: Imprimerie Nationale, 1964), 151–152, number 145.

DATE: Old Babylonian period

12. ARM VI 43

PUBLICATION: ARM VI 43 = J. R. Kupper, *Lettres* (TCL 27; ARM VI; Paris: Paul Geuthner, 1953), 43.

TRANSLITERATION AND TRANSLATION: J. R. Kupper, *Correspondance de Baḫdi-Lim* (ARMT VI; Paris: Imprimerie Nationale, 1954), 66–69.

TRANSLATION: A. Leo Oppenheim, *Letters from Mesopotamia* (Chicago: University of Chicago Press, 1967), 103–104.

DATE: Old Babylonian period

13. ARM VI 37

PUBLICATION: ARM VI 37 = Kupper, *Lettres* (TCL 27; ARM VI; Paris: Paul Geuthner, 1953), 37.

TRANSLITERATION AND TRANSLATION: Kupper, *Correspondance de Baḫdi-Lim* (ARMT VI; Paris: Imprimerie Nationale, 1954), 58–61.

DATE: Old Babylonian period

14. ARM II 123

PUBLICATION: ARM II 123 = Charles-F. Jean, *Lettres* (TCL 23; ARM II; Paris: Paul Geuthner, 1941), 123.

TRANSLITERATION AND TRANSLATION: J. R. Kupper, *Correspondance de Baḫdi-Lim* (ARMT II; Paris: Imprimerie Nationale, 1950), 204–207.

DATE: Old Babylonian period

15. ARM V 35

PUBLICATION: G. Dossin, *Lettres* (ARM V; Paris: Paul Geuthner, 1951), number 35.

TRANSLITERATION AND TRANSLATION: G. Dossin, *Correspondance de Iasmaḫ-addu* (ARMT V; Paris: Imprimerie Nationale, 1952), 56–59.

DATE: Old Babylonian period

16. Wiseman Alalakh 17

PUBLICATION, TRANSCRIPTION, AND TRANSLATION: D. J. Wiseman, *The Alalakh Tablets* (London: British Institute of Archaeology at Ankara, 1953), number 17.

DATE: mid–fifteenth century B.C.E.

17. BBSt 9

PUBLICATION: BBSt 9 = L. W. King, *Babylonian Boundary-Stones and Memorial Tablets in the British Museum* (London: British Museum, 1912), plate 79.

TRANSLITERATION AND TRANSLATION: King, *Babylonian Boundary-Stones,* 51–69.

DATE: The *kudurru* was inscribed during the reign of Nabu-mukin-apli (978–943 B.C.E.). The homicide recounted in the *kudurru* occurred in the second year of Ninurta-kudurri-uṣur (986/985 B.C.E.).

18. TCL 12 117

PUBLICATION: TCL 12 117 = G. Contenau, *Contrats néo-babyloniens I* (TCL 12; Paris: Paul Geuthner, 1927), plate LVI.

TRANSLITERATION AND TRANSLATION: Ellen Whitney Moore, *Neo-Babylonian Business and Administrative Documents* (Ann Arbor: University of Michigan Press, 1935), 112–113.

DATE: Neo-Babylonian period

19. ABL 753

PUBLICATION: ABL 753 = Robert Francis Harper, *Assyrian and Babylonian Letters Belonging to the Kouyunyik Collections of the British Museum* (Chicago: University of Chicago Press, 1902), 7.808.

TEXT, TRANSLITERATION, AND TRANSLATION: T. G. Pinches, *An Outline of Assyrian Grammar* (London: H. J. Glaisher, 1910), 44.

TRANSLITERATION AND TRANSLATION: Manfried Dietrich, *Die Aramäer Südbabyloniens in der Sargonidenzeit* (AOAT 7; Kevelaer: Butzon & Bercker, 1970), 184–185.

DATE: Neo-Assyrian period

20. ADD 618

PUBLICATION: ADD 618 = C. H. W. Johns, *Assyrian Deeds and Documents: Volume 1* (2d edition; Cambridge: Deighton, Bell, and Co., 1924), number 618, pp. 470–471.

TRANSLITERATION AND TRANSLATION: J. Kohler and A. Ungnad, *Assyrische Rechtsurkunden* (Leipzig: Eduard Pfeiffer, 1913), number 660, pp. 388–389; Martha T. Roth, "Homicide in the Neo-Assyrian Period," in *Language, Literature, and History: Philological and Historical Studies Presented to Erica Reiner* (ed. by Francesca Rochberg-Halton; AOS 67; New Haven, Connecticut: American Oriental Society, 1987), 352–354; Theodore Kwasman, *Neo-Assyrian Legal Documents in the Kouyunjik Collection of the British Museum* (Studia Pohl, Series Maior 14; Rome: Pontificio Istituto Biblico, 1988), number 334, pp. 386–387; Remko Jas, *Neo-Assyrian Judicial Procedures* (SAA 5; Helsinki: The Neo-Assyrian Text Corpus Project, 1996), number 41, pp. 63–65.

TRANSLITERATION: J. N. Postgate, *Fifty Neo-Assyrian Legal Documents* (Warminster, England: Aris & Phillips, 1976), number 50, pp. 170–171.

TRANSLATION: Theophile J. Meek, "Mesopotamian Legal Documents," in *Ancient Near Eastern Texts Relating to the Old Testament,* 221.

DATE: eighth month, third day, 657 B.C.E.

21. ADD 321

PUBLICATION: ADD 321 = Johns, *Assyrian Deeds and Documents: Volume 1,* number 321, pp. 238–239.

TRANSLITERATION AND TRANSLATION: Kohler and Ungnad, *Assyrische Rechtsurkunden,* number 659, p. 388; Roth, "Homicide in the Neo-Assyrian Period," 357; Kwasman, *Neo-Assyrian Legal Documents,* number 341, p. 393; Jas, *Neo-Assyrian Judicial Procedures,* 65–66.

COLLATION: Simo Parpola, "Collations to Neo-Assyrian Legal Texts from Nineveh," *Assur* 2/5 (1979), 49.

DATE: reign of Assurbanipal (668–627 B.C.E.)

22. ADD 164

PUBLICATION: ADD 164 = Johns, *Assyrian Deeds and Documents: Volume 1,* number 164, pp. 97–98.

TRANSLITERATION AND TRANSLATION: Kohler and Ungnad, *Assyrische Rechtsurkunden,* number 658, p. 387; Kwasman, *Neo-Assyrian Legal Documents,* number 108, pp. 128–129; Theodore Kwasman and Simo Parpola, *Legal Transactions of the Royal Court of Nineveh, Part 1* (SAA 6; Helsinki: Helsinki University Press, 1991), number 264, p. 212; Jas, *Neo-Assyrian Judicial Procedures,* number 1, pp. 8–11.

TRANSLITERATION: Postgate, *Fifty Neo-Assyrian Legal Documents,* number 44, pp. 159–160.

DATE: eleventh[3] month, twenty-seventh day, 680 B.C.E.

23. ADD 806

PUBLICATION: ADD 806 = Johns, *Assyrian Deeds and Documents: Volume 2,* number 806, pp. 59–60.

TRANSLITERATION AND TRANSLATION: F. M. Fales and J. N. Postgate, *Imperial Administrative Records, Part II* (SAA 11; Helsinki: Helsinki University Press, 1995), number 222, pp. 149–150; Roth, "Homicide in the Neo-Assyrian Period," 357 (for ll. 1′–3′).

DATE: after the reign of Shalmaneser V (after 722 B.C.E.)[4]

24. Postgate Palace Archive 95

PUBLICATION, TRANSLITERATION, AND TRANSLATION: ND 219 = BM 131990 (British Museum) = J. N. Postgate, *The Governor's Palace Archive* (CTN II; London: British School of Archaeology in Iraq, 1973), pp. 123–124 and plate 44.

TRANSLITERATION AND TRANSLATION: Roth, "Homicide in the Neo-Assyrian Period," 358–359; Jas, *Neo-Assyrian Judicial Procedures,* number 43, pp. 66–67.

DATE: tenth month, twenty-seventh day, 740 B.C.E.

[3]Kwasman reads it as twelfth month, *Neo-Assyrian Legal Documents,* 128.

[4]This tablet must date from after the reign of Shalmaneser V because he is the later of the two kings mentioned in this tablet (the other king is Tiglath-Pileser III).

25. CTH 172

PUBLICATION: Emmanuel Laroche, *Catalogue des textes hittites* (Etudes et commentaires 75; Paris: Klincksieck, 1971), number 172 = KBo 1.10 + KUB 4, p. 96b.

TRANSLITERATION AND TRANSLATION: Horst Klengel, "Mord und Bussleistung im Spätbronzezeitlichen Syrien," in *Death in Mesopotamia* (ed. Bendt Alster; Mesopotamia, Copenhagen Studies in Assyriology 8; Copenhagen: Akademisk Forlag, 1980), 190; Albertine Hagenbuchner, *Die Korrespondenz der Hethiter* (Texte der Hethiter 16; Heidelberg: Carl Winter, 1989), 2.285, 291–292.

TRANSLATION: A. L. Oppenheim, *Letters from Mesopotamia* (Chicago: University of Chicago Press, 1967), 144; Gary Beckman, *Hittite Diplomatic Texts* (ed. Harry A. Hoffner, Jr.; SBL Writings from the Ancient World 7; Atlanta: Scholars Press, 1996), 136.

DATE: circa 1260 B.C.E.

26. El-Amarna 8

PUBLICATION: VAT 152 152 = H. Winckler and L. Abel, *Der Thontafelfund von El Amarna* (Mitteilungen aus den Orientalischen Sammlungen, Königliche Museen zu Berlin 1–3; Berlin: W. Spemann, 1889–1890), number 8; O. Schroeder, *Vorderasiatische Schriftdenkmäler der Königlichen Museen zu Berlin: Heft 11* (Berlin: J. C. Hinrichs, 1915), number 5.

TRANSLITERATION AND TRANSLATION: J. A. Knudtzon, *Die El-Amarna-Tafeln I* (Aalen: Otto Zeller, 1964 [1915]), 84–89.

TRANSLATION: William L. Moran, *The Amarna Letters* (Baltimore: The Johns Hopkins University Press, 1992), 16–17.

DATE: 1349–1334 B.C.E. (the overlap between the reigns of Amenophis IV/Akhenaten and Burnaburiyash II)[5]

27. RS 17.146

PUBLICATION: DO 4607 = Jean Nougayrol, *Le Palais Royal d'Ugarit IV/II: Textes Accadiens des Archives Sud (Archives Internationales)* (MRS 9/II; Paris: Imprimerie Nationale, 1956), plate XX.

TRANSLITERATION AND TRANSLATION: Jean Nougayrol, *Le Palais Royal d'Ugarit IV/I: Textes Accadiens des Archives Sud (Archives Internationales)* (MRS 9/I; Paris: Imprimerie Nationale, 1956), 154–157.

DATE: mid–thirteenth century B.C.E.

[5] For dates of the kings, see Moran, *The Amarna Letters*, xxxix.

28. RS 17.230

PUBLICATION: DO 4623 = Nougayrol, *Le Palais Royal d'Ugarit IV/II*, plate XXVIII; *Ugaritica* 3 (1956), p. 23, figure 29.

TRANSLITERATION AND TRANSLATION: Nougayrol, *Le Palais Royal d'Ugarit IV/I*, 153–154.

DATE: mid–thirteenth century B.C.E.

29. RS 18.115

PUBLICATION: DO 4833 = Nougayrol, *Le Palais Royal d'Ugarit IV/II*, plate LXXXIII.

TRANSLITERATION AND TRANSLATION: Nougayrol, *Le Palais Royal d'Ugarit IV/I*, 158–160.

DATE: mid–thirteenth century B.C.E.

30. RS 17.234

PUBLICATION: DO 4626 = Nougayrol, *Le Palais Royal d'Ugarit IV/II*, plate XXIX.

TRANSLITERATION AND TRANSLATION: Nougayrol, *Le Palais Royal d'Ugarit IV/I*, 173–174.

DATE: mid–thirteenth century B.C.E.

31. RS 17.299

PUBLICATION: DO 4653 = Nougayrol, *Le Palais Royal d'Ugarit IV/II*, plate XXXVI.

TRANSLITERATION AND TRANSLATION: Nougayrol, *Le Palais Royal d'Ugarit IV/I*, 182.

DATE: mid–thirteenth century B.C.E.

32. RS 17.369B + RS 17.69

PUBLICATION: DO 4709 + 4551 = Nougayrol, *Le Palais Royal d'Ugarit IV/II*, plate LXI.

TRANSLITERATION AND TRANSLATION: Nougayrol, *Le Palais Royal d'Ugarit IV/I*, 239–240.

DATE: mid–thirteenth century B.C.E.

33. RS 17.229

PUBLICATION: DO 4622 = Nougayrol, *Le Palais Royal d'Ugarit IV/II*, plate XXVII; *Ugaritica* 3 (1956), p. 16, figure 21.

TRANSLITERATION AND TRANSLATION: Nougayrol, *Le Palais Royal d'Ugarit IV/I*, 106.

DATE: mid–thirteenth century B.C.E.

34. RS 17.158

PUBLICATION: DO 4618 = Nougayrol, *Le Palais Royal d'Ugarit IV/II,* plate IV.

TRANSLITERATION AND TRANSLATION: Nougayrol, *Le Palais Royal d'Ugarit IV/I,* pp. 169–171; *ANET*³, 547.

DATE: mid–thirteenth century B.C.E.[6]

35. RS 17.42

PUBLICATION: DO 4538 = Nougayrol, *Le Palais Royal d'Ugarit IV/II,* plate IV; *Ugaritica* 5 (1968), pp. 658–660, figure 25–25A.

TRANSLITERATION AND TRANSLATION: Nougayrol, *Le Palais Royal d'Ugarit IV/I,* 171–172.

DATE: mid–thirteenth century B.C.E.

36. RS 17.145

PUBLICATION: DO 4606 = Nougayrol, *Le Palais Royal d'Ugarit IV/II,* plate XIX.

TRANSLITERATION AND TRANSLATION: Nougayrol, *Le Palais Royal d'Ugarit IV/I,* 172–173.

DATE: mid–thirteenth century B.C.E.

37. RS 20.22

PUBLICATION: Jean Nougayrol, *Ugaritica* 5 (MRS XVI; Paris: Imprimerie Nationale, 1968), 713ff, plates 36 and 36A.

TRANSCRIPTION AND TRANSLATION: Nougayrol, *Ugaritica* 5, 94–97.

BIBLIOGRAPHY: P. R. Berger, "Zu den 'akkadischen' Briefen," *Ugarit-Forschungen* 2 (1970), 286–287.

DATE: mid–thirteenth century B.C.E.

38. RS 17.251

PUBLICATION: DO 4641 = Nougayrol, *Le Palais Royal d'Ugarit IV/II,* plate XXXIII; *Ugaritica* 3 (1956), p. 41, figure 55.

TRANSLITERATION AND TRANSLATION: Nougayrol, *Le Palais Royal d'Ugarit IV/I,* 236–237.

DATE: mid–thirteenth century B.C.E.

39. RS 17.337

PUBLICATION: DO 4678 = Nougayrol, *Le Palais Royal d'Ugarit IV/II,* plate XLVI.

[6] H. Klengel, "Ini-Tešub," RLA 4.104–105. Ini-Teshub's Hittite contemporary is Tudhaliya IV.

TRANSLITERATION AND TRANSLATION: Nougayrol, *Le Palais Royal d'Ugarit IV/I,* 168–169.

DATE: mid–thirteenth century B.C.E.

40. Laws of Ur-Nammu (LU)[7]

PUBLICATION, TRANSLITERATION, AND TRANSLATION: Si. 277 = Fatma Yildiz, "A Tablet of Codex Ur-Nammu from Sippar," *Or* (1981): 87–97.

TRANSLITERATION AND TRANSLATION: Martha T. Roth, *Law Collections from Mesopotamia and Asia Minor* (SBL Writings from the Ancient World Series; Atlanta: Scholars Press, 1995), 13–22.

TRANSLATION: J. J. Finkelstein in *ANET*[3], 523–525; Willem H. Ph. Römer, "Aus den Gesetzen des Königs Urnammu von Ur," in *Rechts- und Worschaftsurkunden Historisch-chronologische Texte* (TUAT, Band 1/1; Gütersloh: Gütersloher Verlagshaus Gerd Mohn, 1982), 17–23.

DATE: Ur-Nammu's reign, 2112–circa 2095 B.C.E. (Shulgi's reign, 2094–2047 B.C.E.)

41. Laws of Lipit-Ishtar (LL)[8]

PUBLICATION, TRANSLITERATION, AND TRANSLATION: Miguel Civil, "New Sumerian Law Fragments," in *Studies in Honor of Benno Landsberger* (Assyriological Studies 16; Chicago: University of Chicago, 1965), 1–12.

TRANSLITERATION AND TRANSLATION: Roth, *Law Collections from Mesopotamia and Asia Minor*, 23–35.

TRANSLATION: S. N. Kramer in *ANET*[3], 159–160; Heiner Lutzmann, "Aus den Gesetzen des Königs Lipit Eschtar von Isin," in *Rechts- und Worschaftsurkunden Historisch-chronologische Texte,* 23–31.

DATE: Lipit-Ishtar's reign, 1934–1924 B.C.E.

[7]The putative authorship of Ur-Nammu as the lawgiver of this code has been debated because its first-person prologue is unique among the cuneiform law codes and some of the events of its historical narrative cannot be dated to Ur-Nammu's reign. Cf. S. N. Kramer, "The Ur-Nammu Law Code: Who Was Its Author?" *Or* 52 (1983), 453–456. However, some of the events must be dated to his reign, and not his successor and son, Šulgi. Piotr Michalowski and C. B. F. Walker, "A New Sumerian 'Law Code,'" in *DUMU-E$_2$-DUB-BA-A: Studies in Honor of Åke Sjöberg* (ed. Hermann Behrens, Darlene Loding, and Martha T. Roth; Occasional Publications of the Samuel Noah Kramer Fund 11; Philadelphia: The University Museum, 1989), 385, points out that it is unlikely that a war with the independent city of Anšan took place during the reign of Šulgi because it would be difficult to believe that Ur-Nammu would have allowed this city to remain independent during his reign. In the same way, one of the kings mentioned, Namaḫani, was the last independent ruler of Lagash. It was unlikely that he remained independent throughout the reign of Ur-Nammu.

[8]There is a possibility that the fragment on which these statutes are found does not actually belong to the Laws of Lipit-Ishtar.

42. Sumerian Laws Exercise Tablet (SLEx)

PUBLICATION, TRANSLITERATION, AND TRANSLATION: YBC 2177 = A. T. Clay, "A Sumerian Prototype of the Hammurabi Code," *Orientalische Literaturzeitung* 17 (1914), 1–3; Clay, "Sumerian Prototype of the Hammurabi Code," in *Miscellaneous Inscriptions in the Babylonian Collection* (Yale Oriental Series, Babylonian Texts 1; New Haven, Connecticut: Yale University Press, 1915), 18–27.

TRANSLITERATION AND TRANSLATION: Roth, *Law Collections from Mesopotamia and Asia Minor,* 42–45.

TRANSLATION: Finkelstein in *ANET*[3], 525–526.

43. Laws of Eshnunna (LE)

PUBLICATION, TRANSLITERATION, AND TRANSLATION: Albrecht Goetze, *The Laws of Eshnunna* (AASOR 31; New Haven, Connecticut: The American Schools of Oriental Research, 1956); Farouk N. H. Al-Rawi, "Assault and Battery," *Sumer* 38 (1982), 117–20.

TRANSLITERATION AND TRANSLATION: Roth, *Law Collections from Mesopotamia and Asia Minor,* 57–70; Émile Szlechter, *Les lois d'Ešnunna* (Publications de l'Institut de Droit Romain de l'Université de Paris 12; Paris: Centre National de la Recherche Scientifique, 1954); Reuven Yaron, *The Laws of Eshnunna* (2d edition; Jerusalem: The Magnes Press, 1988).

TRANSLATION: Rykle Borger, "Der Codex Eschnunna," in *Rechts- und Worschaftsurkunden Historisch-chronologische Texte,* 32–38; Goetze in *ANET*[3], 161–163.

DATE: early eighteenth century B.C.E.

44. Laws of Hammurapi (LH)

PUBLICATION, TRANSLITERATION, AND TRANSLATION: V. Scheil, *Textes élamites-sémitiques, deuxieme série* (Mémoires de la Délégation Perse 4; Paris: Ernest Leroux, 1902); E. Bergmann, Codex *Ḫammurabi: Textus Primigenius* (Editio tertia; Scripta Pontificii Instituti Biblici 51; Rome: Pontificium Institutum, 1953).

TRANSLITERATION AND TRANSLATION: G. R. Driver and John C. Miles, *The Babylonian Laws* (Ancient Codes and Laws of the Near East; Oxford: Clarendon, 1955); Robert Francis Harper, *The Code of Hammurabi* (Chicago: University of Chicago Press, 1904); J. Kohler and F. E. Peiser, *Hammurabi's Gesetz* (Leipzig: Eduard Pfeiffer, 1904); Roth, *Law Collections from Mesopotamia and Asia Minor,* 71–142; M. E. J. Richardson, *Hammurabi's Laws: Text, Translation and Glossary* (The Biblical Seminar 73; Semitic Texts and Studies 2; Sheffield: Sheffield Academic Press, 2000).

TRANSLATION: Rykle Borger, "Der Codex Hammurapi," in *Rechts- und Worschaftsurkunden Historisch-chronologische Texte,* 39–79; André Finet, *Le Code de Hammurapi* (Littératures anciennes du Proche-Orient 6; Paris: CERF, 1973); Meek in *ANET*^{3}, 163–180.

DATE: Hammurapi's reign, 1792–1750 B.C.E.

45. Middle Assyrian Laws (MAL)

TRANSLITERATION AND TRANSLATION: G. R. Driver and John C. Miles, *The Assyrian Laws* (Ancient Codes and Laws of the Near East; Oxford: Clarendon, 1935); Roth, *Law Collections from Mesopotamia and Asia Minor,* 153–194.

TRANSLATION: Rykle Borger, "Die mittelassyrischen Gesetze," in *Rechts- und Worschaftsurkunden Historisch-chronologische Texte,* 80–92; Guillaume Cardascia, *Les Lois assyriennes,* (Litteratures anciennes du Proche-Orient; Paris: Les Éditions de CERF, 1969); Meek in *ANET*^{3}, 180–188.

DATE: fourteenth century B.C.E.

46. The Hittite Laws (HL)

PUBLICATION, TRANSLITERATION, AND TRANSLATION: Edgar H. Sturtevant and George Bechtel, *A Hittite Chrestomathy* (William Dwight Whitney Linguistic Series; Philadelphia: Linguistic Society of America, 1935).

TRANSLITERATION AND TRANSLATION: Harry Angier Hoffner, *The Laws of the Hittites: A Critical Edition* (DMOA XXIII; Leiden: Brill, 1997); E. Neufeld, *The Hittite Laws* (London: Luzac & Co. Ltd.)

DATE: Old Hittite recension, circa 1650 B.C.E.; New Hittite recension, circa 1350–1200 B.C.E.

47. The Edict of Telepinus

PUBLICATION: CTH 19 = KBo III 1 + KBo XII 5 + KBo III 68 + KBo XII 7 (= BoTU 23 A) = KUB XI 1 (= BoTU 23 B) + KBo XIX 96 = KBo III 67 (= BoTU 23 C) + KUB XXXI 2 (= BoTU 23 G) + KUB XXXI 17

TRANSLITERATION AND TRANSLATION: Inge Hoffmann, *Der Erlass Telipinus* (Heidelberg: Carl Winter/Universitätsverlag, 1984), 52–53; Sturtevant and Bechtel, *A Hittite Chrestomathy,* 175–200.

TRANSLATION: Hoffner, "Hittite Laws," in Roth, *Law Collections from Mesopotamia and Asia Minor,* 237; Th. P. J. van den Hout, "The Proclamation of Telepinus," in *The Context of Scripture: Volume I, Canonical Compositions from the Biblical World* (ed. William W. Hallo; Leiden: Brill, 1997), 196–199; Hans-Martin Kümmel, in *Rechts- und Worschaftsurkunden Historisch-chronologische Texte,* 464–470.

DATE: mid–seventeenth century B.C.E.

Bibliography

Aaron, David. *Biblical Ambiguities: Metaphor, Sanctity, and Divine Imagery*. The Brill Reference Library of Ancient Judaism. Leiden: Brill, 2001.

Albertz, Rainer. *A History of Israelite Religion in the Old Testament Period*. Translated by John Bowden. Louisville Kentucky: Westminster/John Knox, 1994.

Albright, W. F. "The Judicial Reform of Jehoshaphat." In *Alexander Marx Jubilee Volume*, 61–82. New York: The Jewish Theological Seminary, 1950.

______. "The List of Levitic Cities." In *Louis Ginzberg Jubilee Volume*. New York: American Academy for Jewish Research, 1945.

Alt, Albrecht. "The Origins of Israelite Law." 1934. Translated by R. A. Wilson. In *Essays on Old Testament History and Religion*, 101–171. Reprint, Garden City, New York: Anchor Books, 1968.

______. "Zur Talionsformel." In *Kleine Schriften zur Geschichte des Volkes Israel*. 1934. Volume 1, 341–344. Reprint, Munich: C. H. Beck, 1953.

Anderson, Gary A. *Sacrifices and Offerings in Ancient Israel: Studies in Their Social and Political Importance*. HSM. Atlanta: Scholars Press, 1987.

Attenborough, F. L., ed. and trans. *The Laws of the Earliest English Kings*. Cambridge: Cambridge University Press, 1922.

Auld, A. Graeme. "Cities of Refuge in Israelite Tradition." *JSOT* 10 (1978): 135–146.

Bäntsch, Bruno. *Das Bundesbuch, Ex. XX 22–XXIII 33*. Halle: Max Niemeyer, 1892.

Barmash, Pamela. "The Narrative Quandary: Cases of Law in Literature." *Vetus Testamentum* 54 (2004): 1–16.

Barré, M. L. "Rabiṣu." In *Dictionary of Deities and Demons in the Bible*, 2d ed., edited by Karel Van der Toorn, Bob Becking, and Pieter W. van der Horst, 1287–1290. Leiden: Brill, 1995.

Bauer, Theodore. *Das Inscriftenwerk Assurbanipals*. Leipzig: J. C. Hinrichs, 1933.

Bellefontaine, Elizabeth. "Customary Law and Chieftainship: Judicial Aspects of 2 Samuel 14.4–21." *JSOT* 38 (1987): 47–72.

Bendor, S. *The Social Structure of Ancient Israel*. Jerusalem Biblical Studies. Jerusalem: Simor, 1996.

Berger, P.-R. "Zu den 'akkadischen' Briefen Ugaritica V." *Ugarit Forschungen* 2 (1970): 285–293.

Black-Michaud, Jacob. *Cohesive Force: Feud in the Mediterranean and the Middle East*. With a foreword by E. L. Peters. Oxford: Basil Blackwell, 1975.

Bloch, Marc. *Feudal Society*. Translated by L. A. Manyon. 1961. Reprint, Chicago: University of Chicago Press, 1974.

Bloch-Smith, Elizabeth. *Judahite Burial Practices and Beliefs About the Dead*. JSOTSup. Sheffield: JSOT Press, 1992.

Boecker, Hans Jochen. *Law and the Administration of Justice in the Old Testament and Ancient East*. Translated by Jeremy Moiser. 1976. Reprint, Minneapolis: Augsburg, 1980.

Bottero, Jean. *Mesopotamia: Writing, Reasoning, and the Gods*. Translated by Zainab Bahrani and Marc Van de Mieroop. Chicago: University of Chicago Press, 1992.

Bright, John. "The Apodictic Prohibition: Some Observations." *JBL* 92 (1973): 185–204.

Buss, Martin J. "The Distinction Between Civil and Criminal Law in Ancient Israel." In *Proceedings of the Sixth World Congress of Jewish Studies 1973*, volume 1, *51–*62. Jerusalem: World Union of Jewish Studies, 1977.

Campbell, J. K. *Honour, Family and Patronage: A Study of Institutions and Moral Values in a Greek Mountain Community*. Oxford: Clarendon Press, 1964.

Cassuto, U. *The Book of Genesis: Part I: From Adam to Noah; Part II: From Noah to Abraham* [Hebrew]. 1944. Publications of the Perry Foundation for Biblical Research in the Hebrew University of Jerusalem. Reprint, Jerusalem: Magnes Press, 1986.

Caudill, Bernice Calmes. *Pioneers of Eastern Kentucky: Their Feuds and Settlements*. Cincinnati, Ohio: Privately printed, 1969.

Cazelles, Henri. "L'auteur du code de l'alliance." *RB* 52 (1945): 173–191.

Chapman, Rupert. "Weapons." In OEANE, 5.334–339. New York: Oxford University Press, 1997.

Childe, V. Gordon. "The Urban Revolution." *The Town Planning Review* 21 (1950): 3–17.

Childs, Brevard S. *The Book of Exodus*. OTL. Philadelphia: Westminster, 1974.

Closen, G. E. "Der 'Dämon Sünde'." *Bib* 16 (1935): 431–442.

Crüsemann, Frank. *The Torah: Theology and Social History of Old Testament Law.* Translated by Allan W. Mahnke. Edinburgh: T & T Clark, 1996.

Daube, David. "Direct and Indirect Causation in Biblical Law." *VT* 11 (1961): 246–269.

______. *Studies in Biblical Law.* Cambridge: Cambridge University Press, 1969.

Delekat, L. *Asylie und Schutzorakel am Zionheiligtum: Eine Untersuchtung zu den privaten Feindpsalmen.* Leiden: Brill, 1967.

Deller, K. "Assyrisches Sprachgut bei Tukulti-Ninurta II (888–884)." *Or* 26 (1957): 268–272.

______. "Neuassyrisches aus Sultantepe." *Or* 34 (1965): 457–477.

______. "Progressive Vokalassimilation im Neuassyrischen." *Or* 36 (1967): 457–477.

______. "Die Rolle der Richters im neuassyrischen Prozessrecht." In *Studi in onore di Edoardo Volterra VIII,* 639–653. Milan: A. Giuffrè, 1971.

______. "Studien zur neuassyrischen Orthographie." *Or* 31 (1962): 186–196.

______. "Zur sprachlichen Einordnung des Inschriften Aššurnaṣirpals II. (883–859)." *Or* 26 (1957): 144–156.

______. "Zweisilbige Lautwerte des Typs KVKV im Neuassyrischen." *Or* 31 (1962): 7–26.

Dennis, Andrew, Peter Foote, and Richard Perkins, trans. *Laws of Early Iceland: Grágás, Volume 1.* University of Manitoba Icelandic Series III. Winnipeg: University of Manitoba Press, 1980.

Diakonoff, I. M. "Extended Families in Old Babylonian Ur." *ZA* 75 (1985): 47–65.

Diamond, A. S. *The Comparative Study of Primitive Law.* L.T. Hobhouse Memorial Trust Lecture. London: The Athlone Press, 1965.

______. "An Eye for an Eye." *Iraq* 19 (1957): 151–155.

______. *Primitive Law Past and Present.* London: Methuen & Co., Ltd., 1971.

Dinur, B. "The Cultic Character of the Cities of Refuge and the Ceremony of Asylum [Hebrew]." *EI* 3 (1954): 135–146.

Dressler, Joshua. *Understanding Criminal Law.* 2d edition. Legal Text Series. N.p.: Richard D. Irwin, 1995.

Driver, G. R. "Review of The Laws of Eshnunna." *Journal of the Royal Asiatic Society* (1972): 57–58.

Driver, S. R. *Deuteronomy.* 3d edition. ICC. Edinburgh: T & T Clark, 1901.

Duhm, Hans. *Die bösen Geisten im Alten Testament.* Tübingen/Leipzig: J. C. B. Mohr, 1904.

Edzard, Dietz Otto, and F. A. M. Wiggermann. "Maškim, Kommissar, Anwalt, Sachwalter." In RLA, 7.449–455. Berlin: Walter de Gruyter, 1987–1990.

Eichler, Barry L. "Literary Structure in the Laws of Eshnunna." In *Language, Literature, and History: Philological and Historical Studies Presented to Erica Reiner,* edited by Francesca Rochberg-Halton. AOS 67, 71–84. New Haven, Connecticut: American Oriental Society, 1987.

______. "Murder [Hebrew]." In *Encyclopaedia Miqra'it.* Volume 7, 426–431. Jerusalem: Mossad Bialiq, 1968.

Ellis, Maria deJ. "Taxation in Ancient Mesopotamia: The History of the Term *Miksu*." *JCS* 26 (1974): 211–215.

Eph'al, I. "The Western Minorities in Babylonia in the 6th–5th Centuries B.C." *Or* 47 (1978): 74–90.

Evans-Pritchard, E. E. *The Nuer: A Description of Their Modes of Livelihood and Political Institutions of a Nilotic People*. Oxford: Clarendon, 1940.

Faust, Avraham. "The Rural Community in Ancient Israel During Iron Age II." *BASOR* 317 (2000): 17–39.

Finkelstein, J. J. "Ammiṣaduqa's Edict and the Babylonian 'Law' Codes." *JCS* 15 (1961): 91–104.

———. "The Goring Ox: Some Historical Perspectives on Deodands, Forfeitures, Wrongful Death and the Western Notion of Sovereignty." *Temple Law Quarterly* 46 (1973): 169–290.

———. "The Hammurapu Law Tablet BE XXXI 22." *RA* 63 (1969): 11–27.

———. "A Late Old Babylonian Copy of the Laws of Hammurapi." *JCS* 21 (1967): 39–48.

———. "Law, the Law of the Ancient Near East [Hebrew]." In *Encyclopaedia Miqra'it*. Volume 5, 588–614. Jerusalem: Mossad Bialiq, 1968.

———. "The Laws of Ur-Nammu." *JCS* 22 (1969): 66–82.

———. "An Old Babylonian Herding Contract and Genesis 31:38f." *JAOS* 88 (1968): 30–36.

———. "On Some Recent Studies in Cuneiform Law." *JAOS* 90 (1970): 131–143.

———. *The Ox That Gored*. Prepared by Maria deJ. Ellis. Transactions of the American Philosophical Society 71/2. Philadelphia: The American Philosophical Society, 1981.

———. "Sex Offenses in Sumerian Law." *JAOS* 86 (1966): 355–372.

Fishbane, Michael. *Biblical Interpretation in Ancient Israel*. Oxford: Oxford University Press, 1985.

Flanagan, James W. "Chiefs in Israel." *JSOT* 20 (1981): 47–73.

Fox, Richard G. *Urban Anthropology: Cities in Their Cultural Settings*. Englewood Cliffs, New Jersey: Prentice-Hall, 1977.

Frank, Karl. *Lamashtu, Pazuzu und Andere Dämonen*. Leipzig: Harrassowitz, 1941.

Frazer, James G. *The Golden Bough*. Abridged edition. New York: MacMillan, 1951.

Freydank, Helmut. "Fernhandel und Warenpreise nach einer mittelassyrischen Urkunde des 12 Jahrhunderts v.u.Z." In *Societies and Languages of the Ancient Near East: Studies in Honor of I. M. Diakonoff*, 64–75. Warminster, England: Aris & Phillips Ltd., 1982.

Frymer-Kensky, Tikva. "Pollution, Purification, and Purgation in Biblical Israel." In *The Word of the Lord Shall Go Forth: Essays in Honor of David Noel Freedman in Celebration of His Sixtieth Birthday*, edited by Carol L. Meyers and M. O'Connor, 399–414. Winona Lake, Indiana: Eisenbrauns, 1983.

———. "Tit for Tat: The Principle of Equal Retribution in Near Eastern and Biblical Law." *BA* 49 (1980): 230–234.

Fuchs, Andreas, and Simo Parpola. *The Correspondence of Sargon II, Part III: Letters from Babylonia and the Eastern Provinces*. SAA 15. Helsinki: University of Helsinki Press, 2001.

Gagarin, Michael. *Drakon and Early Athenian Homicide Law*. New Haven, Connecticut: Yale University Press, 1981.

Gelston, A. "A Note on II Samuel 7, 10." *ZAW* 84 (1972): 92–94.

Ginat, Joseph. *Blood Disputes Among Bedouin and Rural Arabs in Israel: Revenge, Mediation, Outcasting and Family Honor*. Pittsburgh: University of Pittsburgh Press, 1987.

Gitin, Seymour, and Trude Dothan. "A Royal Dedicatory Inscription from Ekron." *IEJ* 47 (1997): 1–16.

Gluckman, Max. *Custom and Conflict in Africa*. Oxford: Basil Blackwell, 1965.

______. *The Judicial Process Among the Barotse of Northern Rhodesia*. Manchester: Manchester University Press, 1955.

______. "The Peace in the Feud." *Past and Present* 8 (1955): 1–14.

______. *Politics, Law and Ritual in Tribal Society*. Oxford: Basil Blackwell, 1977.

Gordon, Cyrus H. *Ugaritic Textbook*. An Or 38. Rome: Pontifical Biblical Institute, 1965.

Gottwald, Norman K. *The Tribes of Yahweh: A Sociology of the Religion of Liberated Israel, 1250–1050 B.C.E.* Maryknoll, New York: Orbis, 1979.

Graf, Karl Heinrich. "Die Sogenannte Grundschrift Des Pentateuchs." *Archiv für wissenschaftliche Erforschung des Alten Testaments* 1 (1869): 466–477.

Grayson, A. K. *Assyrian Rulers of the Third and Second Millennium B.C.* RIMA 1. Toronto: University of Toronto Press, 1986.

Greenberg, Moshe. "Avenger of Blood." In IDB, 1.321. Nashville, Tennessee: Abingdon, 1962.

______. "The Biblical Conception of Asylum." In *Studies in the Bible and Jewish Thought*. JPS Scholar of Distinction Series, 43–50. 1959. Reprint, Philadelphia: The Jewish Publication Society, 1995.

______. "Crimes and Punishments." In IDB, 1.733–744. Nashville, Tennessee: Abingdon, 1962.

______. "The Design and Themes of Ezekiel's Program of Restoration." *Int* 38 (1984): 181–208.

______. "More Reflections on Biblical Criminal Law." In *Studies in Bible*, edited by Sara Japhet. ScrHier 31, 1–18. Jerusalem: Magnes Press, 1986.

______. "Some Postulates of Biblical Criminal Law." In *Sefer Ha-Yovel Li-Yehezqel Koyfman*, edited by Menahem Haran, 5–28. Jerusalem: Magnes Press, 1960. Reprinted in *The Jewish Expression*, edited by Judah Goldin, 18–37. New York: Bantam, 1968.

Greengus, Samuel. "Legal and Social Institutions of Ancient Mesopotamia." In CANE, 469–84. New York: Scribners, 1995.

Gruber, Mayer. "The Tragedy of Cain and Abel: A Case of Depression." In *The Motherhood of God and Other Studies*. South Florida Studies in the History of Judaism 57, 121–131. Atlanta: Scholars Press, 1992.

Gunn, David M. *The Story of King David.* JSOTSup 6. Sheffield: JSOT Press, 1978.

Gurney, O. R. *The Middle Babylonian Legal and Economic Texts from Ur.* N.p.: British School of Archaeology in Iraq, 1983.

______. "The Sultantepe Tablets VII: The Myth of Nergal and Ereshkigal." *AnSt* 10 (1960): 105–131.

______. "Texts from Dur-Kurigalzu." *Iraq* 11 (1949): 131–141.

Gurney, O. R., and S. N. Kramer. "Two Fragments of Sumerian Law." In *Studies in Honor of Benno Landsberger.* Assyriological Studies 16, 13–19. Chicago: University of Chicago Press, 1965.

Haase, Richard. "Die Behandlung von Tierschäden in den Keilschriftrechten." *RIDA* 14 (1967): 11–65.

______. *Einführung in das Studium keilschriftlicher Rechtsquellen.* Wiesbaden: Otto Harrassowitz, 1965.

Halbe, Jörn. *Das Privilegrecht Jahwes Ex 34, 10–26.* Göttingen: Vandenhoeck & Ruprecht, 1975.

Hallo, William W. "Biblical History in Its Near Eastern Setting: The Contextual Approach." In *Scripture in Context: Essays on the Comparative Method,* edited by Carl D. Evans, William W. Hallo, and John B. White, 1–26. Pittsburgh: The Pickwick Press, 1980.

Halpern, Baruch. "Jerusalem and the Lineages in the Seventh Century BCE: Kinship and the Rise of Individual Moral Responsibility." In *Law and Ideology in Monarchic Israel,* edited by Baruch Halpern and Deborah W. Hobson. JSOTSup 124, 11–107. Sheffield: Sheffield Academic Press, JSOT Press, 1991.

Haran, Menahem. "Studies in the Accounts of the Levitical Cities." *JBL* 80 (1961): 45–54, 156–165.

______. *Temples and Temple-Service in Ancient Israel.* Winona Lake, Indiana: Eisenbrauns, 1995.

Hawkins, J. D. "'Great Kings' and 'Country-Lords' at Malatya and Karkamiš." In *Studio Historiae Ardens: Ancient Near Eastern Studies Presented to Philo H.J. ten Cate on the Occasion of his 65th Birthday,* edited by Theo van den Hout and Johan de Roos. Uitgaven Van Het Nederlands Historisch-Archaeologisch Instituut Te Istanbul 74, 73–85. Leiden: Nederlands Historisch-Archaeologisch Instituut te Istanbul, 1995.

______. "Karkamiš." In RLA, 5.426–446. Berlin: Walter de Gruyter, 1976–1980.

______. "Kuzi-Tešub and the 'Great Kings' of Karkamiš." *AnSt* 38 (1988): 99–108.

Hegel, G. W. F. *Philosophy of Right.* Translated by T. M. Knox. 1821. Reprint, Oxford: Oxford University Press, 1952.

Heltzer, Michael. *The Rural Community in Ancient Ugarit.* Wiesbaden: Dr. Ludwig Reichert Verlag, 1976.

Herzog, Zeev. *Archaeology of the City: Urban Planning in Ancient Israel and Its Social Implications.* Tel Aviv: Tel Aviv University, 1997.

Hess, Richard S. "One Hundred Fifty Years of Comparative Studies of Genesis 1–11." In *"I Studied Inscriptions from Before the Flood": Ancient Near Eastern, Literary, and Linguistic Approaches to Genesis 1–11,* edited by Richard S. Hess and David Toshio Tsumura. Sources for Biblical and Theological Study 4, 3–26. Winona Lake, Indiana: Eisenbrauns, 1994.

Hoebel, E. Adamson. *The Law of Primitive Man: A Study in Comparative Legal Dynamics*. Cambridge, Massachusetts: Harvard University Press, 1954.

Hoffmann, David Z. *Das Buch Leviticus*. Berlin: M. Poppelauer, 1905–1906.

Hoffmann, Inge. *Der Erlass Telipinus*. Heidelberg: Carl Winter/Universitätsverlag, 1984.

Hoffner, Harry A., Jr. "Incest, Sodomy and Bestiality in the Ancient Near East." In *Orient and Occident: Essays Presented to Cyrus H. Gordon on the Occasion of His Sixty-Fifth Birthday*, edited by Harry A. Hoffner, Jr. AOAT, 81–90. Kevelaer: Butzon & Bercker, 1973.

———. "Legal and Social Institutions of Hittite Anatolia." In CANE, 555–569. New York: Scribners, 1995.

———. "On Homicide in Hittite Law." In *Crossing Boundaries and Linking Horizons: Studies in Honor of Michael C. Astour on His 80th Birthday*, edited by Gordon D. Young, Mark W. Chavalas, and Richard E. Averbeck, 293–314. Bethesda, Maryland: CDL Press, 1997.

Hout, Th. P. J. "The Proclamation of Telepinus." In *The Context of Scripture*, ed. William W. Hallo, 196–199. Leiden: Brill, 1997.

Hurvitz, Avi. "Dating the Priestly Source in Light of the Historical Study of Biblical Hebrew a Century After Wellhausen." *ZAW* 100 (1988): 88–99.

———. "The Language of the Priestly Source and Its Historical Setting – the Case for an Early Date." In *Proceedings of the Eighth World Congress of Jewish Studies, 1981*, 83–94. Jerusalem: World Union of Jewish Studies, 1983.

———. *A Linguistic Study of the Relationship Between the Priestly Source and the Book of Ezekiel*. CahRB. Paris: J. Gabalda, 1982.

Jackson, Bernard S. *Essays in Jewish and Comparative Legal History*. Studies in Judaism in Late Antiquity. Leiden: E. J. Brill, 1975.

Jacobsen, Thorkild. *Treasures of Darkness: A History of Mesopotamian Religion*. New Haven, Connecticut: Yale University Press, 1976.

Jamieson-Drake, David W. *Scribes and Schools in Monarchic Israel: A Socio-Archaeological Approach*. Sheffield: Almond Press, 1991.

Japhet, Sara. *I & II Chronicles*. OTL. Louisville, Kentucky: Westminster/John Knox, 1993.

Jhering, Rudolf von. *Geist des römischen Rechts auf den verschiedenen Stufen seiner Entwicklung*. 1898. Reprint, Aalen: Scientia Verlag, 1968.

Jirku, Anton. *Das weltliche Recht im Alten Testament*. Gütersloh: T. Bertelsmann, 1927.

Johns, C. H. W. *Assyrian Deeds and Documents: Volume I*. 2d edition. Cambridge: Deighton, Bell, and Co., 1924.

———. *Assyrian Deeds and Documents: Volume II*. Cambridge: Deighton, Bell, and Co., 1901.

Johnson, Allan Chester, Paul Robinson Coleman-Norton, and Frank Card Bourne, eds. *Ancient Roman Statutes*. The Corpus of Roman Law II. Austin: University of Texas Press, 1946.

Johnson, Wallace. *The T'ang Code: Volume II, Specific Articles*. Princeton Library of Asian Translations. Princeton: Princeton University Press, 1997.

Kaufman, Ivan T. "The Samaria Ostraca: An Early Witness to Hebrew Writing." *BA* 45 (1982): 229–239.

Kiefer, Thomas M. *The Tausug: Violence and Law in a Philippine Moslem Society*. Case Studies in Cultural Anthropology. New York: Holt, Rinehart and Winston, Inc., 1972.

Kiernan, Steven C. "Extradition of a Convicted Killer: The Ira Einhorn Case." *Suffolk Transnational Law Review* 24 (2001): 353–385.

King, L. W. *Babylonian Boundary-Stones and Memorial Tablets in the British Museum*. London: British Museum, 1912.

Kirk, G. S. *Myth: Its Meaning and Functions*. Cambridge: Cambridge University Press, 1970.

Klawans, Jonathan. *Impurity and Sin in Ancient Judaism*. Oxford: Oxford University Press, 2000.

———. "The Impurity of Immorality in Ancient Judaism." *JJS* 48 (1997): 1–16.

Klengel, H. "Ini-Tešub." In RLA, 5.104–105. Berlin: Walter de Gruyter, 1976–1980.

———. *Syria, 3000–300 B.C.: A Handbook of Political History*. Berlin: Akademie-Verlag, 1992.

Knohl, Israel. *The Sanctuary of Silence: The Priestly Torah and the Holiness School*. Minneapolis: Fortress, 1995.

Koch, Klaus, ed. "Der Spruch 'Sein Blut bleibe auf seinem Haupt' und die israelitische Auffassung vom vergossenen Blut." *VT* (1962): 396–416.

———. *Um das Prinzip der Vergeltung in Religion und Recht des alten Testament*. Wege der Forschung. Darmstadt: Wissenschaftliche Buchgesellschaft, 1972.

Korošec, Victor. *Hethitische Staatsverträge*. Leipziger Rechtswissenschaftliche Studien. Leipzig: Theodor Weicher, 1931.

———. "Les Lois Hittites et leur évolution." *RA* 57 (1963): 121–144.

Koschaker, Paul. "Forschungen und Ergebnisse in den keilschriftlichen Rechtsquellen." *ZSS* 49 (1929): 188–201.

———. "Keilschriftrecht." *Zeitschrift der Morgenländischen Gesellschaft* 89 (1935): 1–39.

Kramer, S. N. "Ur-Nammu Law Code." *Or* 23 (1954): 40–51.

Kraus, F. R. *Ein Edikt de Konigs Ammi-Saduqa von Babylon*. Studia et documenta ad iura orientis antiqua 5. Leiden: Brill, 1958.

———. "Ein zentrales Problem des altmesopotamischen Rechtes: Was ist der Kodex Hammurabi?" *Genava* n.s. 8 (1960): 283–296.

Krecher, J. "Glossen." In RLA, 3.431–440. Berlin: Walter de Gruyter, 1957–1971.

Kuhl, Curt. "Die 'Wiederaufnahme' – ein literarkritischen Prinzip?" *ZAW* 10 (1952): 1–11.

Kuhrt, Amélie. *The Ancient Near East.* Routledge History of the Ancient World. London: Routledge, 1995.

Kümmel, Hans-Martin. "Der Thronfolgeerlass des Telepinu." In *Rechts- und Worschaftsurkunden Historisch-chronologische Texte*, Rykle Borger. TUAT. Band 1, 464–470. Gütersloh: Gütersloher Verlagshaus Gerd Mohn, 1982.

Lambert, W. G. "The Gula Hymn of Bullutsi-Rabi." *Or* 36 (1967): 105–132.

______. "The Laws of Hammurabi in the First Millenium." In *Reflets des deux fleuves, Volume de Mélanges offerts à André Finet,* edited by M. LeBeau and P. Talon. Akkadica Supplementum 6, 95–98. Leuven: Peeters, 1989.

Landsberger, Benno. *The Conceptual Autonomy of the Babylonian World.* Translated by T. Jacobsen, B. Foster, and H. von Siebenthal, with an introduction by T. Jacobsen. 1926. MANE. Volume 1, Fascicle 4. Reprint, Malibu, California: Undena Publications, 1976.

______. "Lexikalisches archive." *ZA* 41 (1933): 218–233.

______. *Three Essays on the Sumerians.* Introduction and translation by Maria deJ. Ellis. MANE 1/2. Los Angeles: Undena, 1974.

Lautner, J. G. *Die richterliche Entscheidung und die Streetbeendigung im altbabylonischen Prozessrechte.* Leipziger Rechtswissenschaftliche Studien 3. Leipzig: Theodor Weicher, 1922.

Leemans, W. F. "King Hammurapi as Judge." In *Symbolae iuridicae et historicae Martino David dedicatae II,* edited by J. A. Ankum, R. Feenstra, and W. F. Leemans, 105–128. Leiden: Brill, 1968.

Lerner, Renee Lettow. "The Intersection of Two Systems: An American on Trial for an American Murder in the French Cour d'Assizes." *University of Illinois Law Review* (2001), 791–856.

Levine, Baruch. "Late Language in the Priestly Source: Some Literary and Historical Considerations." In *Proceedings of the Eighth World Congress of Jewish Studies, 1981,* 69–82. Jerusalem: World Union of Jewish Studies, 1983.

______. *Leviticus.* The JPS Torah Commentary. Philadelphia: The Jewish Publication Society, 1989.

______. *Numbers 1–20.* AB. New York: Doubleday, 1993.

Levinson, Bernard M. *Deuteronomy and the Hermeneutics of Legal Innovation.* New York: Oxford University Press, 1997.

Liedke, Gerhard. *Gestalt und Bezeichnung alttestamenlicher Rechtssätze: Eine formgeschichtlich-terminologische Studie.* WMANT. Neukirchener-Vluyn: Neukirchener Verlag, 1971.

Lindgren, James. "Measuring the Value of Slaves and Free Persons in Ancient Law." *Chicago-Kent Law Review* 71/1 (1995): 149–217.

Liverani, Mario. *Prestige and Interest: International Relations in the Near East ca. 1600–1100 B.C.* History of the Ancient Near East/Studies I. Padua: Sargon, 1990.

Llewellyn, K. N., and E. Adamson Hoebel. *The Cheyenne Way: Conflict and Case Law in Primitive Jurisprudence.* Norman: University of Oklahoma Press, 1941.

Löhr, Max. *Das Asylwesen im Alten Testament.* Halle: Max Niemeyer, 1930.

Luckenbill, D. *The Annals of Sennacherib*. Oriental Institute Publications. Chicago: University of Chicago Press, 1924.

MacDowell, Douglas M. *Athenian Homicide Law in the Age of the Orators*. Manchester: Manchester University Press, 1963.

Machinist, Peter B. "Outsiders or Insiders: The Biblical View of Emergent Israel and Its Contexts." In *The Other in Jewish Thought and History: Constructions of Jewish Culture and Identity,* edited by Lawrence J. Silberstein and Robert L. Cohn, 35–60. New York: New York University Press, 1994.

———. "The Question of Distinctiveness in Ancient Israel." In *Ah, Assyria...: Studies in Assyrian History and Ancient Near Eastern Historiography,* edited by Mordechai Cogan and Israel Eph'al. ScrHier 33, 196–212. Jerusalem: Magnes Press, 1991.

Malamat, Abraham. "King Lists of the Old Babylonian Period and Biblical Genealogies." *JAOS* 88 (1968): 163–173.

———. "Mari and the Bible: Some Aspects of Tribal Organzation and Institutions." *JAOS* 82 (1962): 143–140.

Malul, Meir. *The Comparative Method in Ancient Near Eastern and Biblical Legal Studies*. AOAT 227. Neukirchen-Vluyn: Neukirchener Verlag, 1990.

Master, Daniel M. "State Formation Theory and the Kingdom of Ancient Israel." *JNES* 60 (2001): 117–131.

Mayes, A. D. H. *Deuteronomy*. New Century Bible Commentary. Grand Rapids, Michigan: Eerdmans, 1979.

Mazar, Benjamin. "The Cities of the Priests and Levites." Edited by Shmuel Ahituv and Baruch A. Levine. In *The Early Biblical Period: Historical Studies*, 132–145. 1960. Reprint, Jerusalem: Israeli Exploration Society, 1986.

McCarter, P. Kyle. *II Samuel*. AB. Garden City, New York: Doubleday, 1984.

McKeating, Henry. "The Development of the Law on Homicide in Ancient Israel." *VT* 25 (1975): 46–68.

McKenzie, Donald A. "The Judge of Israel." *VT* 174 (1967): 118–121.

McKillop, Bron. "Anatomy of a French Murder Case." *American Journal of Comparative Law* 45 (1997): 527–583.

Merz, Erwin. *Die Blutrache bei den Israeliten*. BWAT 20. Leipzig: J. C. Hinrichs'sche Buchhandlung, 1916.

Milgrom, Jacob. "The Alleged 'Demytholigization and Secularization' in Deuteronomy." *VT* 21 (1973): 156–161.

———. *Leviticus 1–16*. AB. New York: Doubleday, 1991.

———. *Numbers*. The JPS Torah Commentary. Philadelphia: The Jewish Publication Society, 1989.

———. "Sancta Contagion and Altar/city Asylum." In *Congress Volume: Vienna 1980*. SVT 32, 278–310. Leiden: Brill, 1981.

———. *Studies in Levitical Terminology, I: The Encroacher and the Levite; the Term 'Aboda*. Berkeley: University of California Press, 1970.

Miller, William Ian. *Bloodtaking and Peacemaking: Feud, Law, and Society in Saga Iceland*. Chicago: University of Chicago Press, 1990.

Mishaly, Ayala. "The Bēl Dāmē's [*sic*] Role in the Neo-Assyrian Legal Process." *Zeitschrift für Altorientalische und Biblische Rechtsgeschichte* 6 (2000): 35–53.

Moran, William L. "The Creation of Man in Atrahasis I 192–248." *BASOR* 200 (1970): 48–56.

Muhly, J. D. "Metals." In OEANE, 4.1–5. New York: Oxford University Press, 1997.

Nader, Laura. "The Anthropological Study of Law." In *Law and Anthropology*, edited by Peter Sack and Jonathan Aleck. The International Library of Essays in Law and Legal Theory, 1–32. New York: New York University Press, 1992.

Naveh, Joseph. "A Hebrew Letter from the Seventh Century B.C." *Israel Exploration Quarterly* 10 (1960): 129–139.

Nicolsky, N. M. "Das Asylrecht in Israel." *ZAW* 48 (1930): 146–175.

Nörr, Dieter. "Zum Schuldgedanken im altbabylonian Strassrecht." *ZSS* 75 (1958): 1–31.

Nougayrol, Jean. *Le palais royal d'Ugarit IV: Planches, textes accadiens des archives sud*. MRS 9. Paris: Imprimerie Nationale, 1956.

Oppenheim, A. Leo. *Ancient Mesopotamia*. Rev. edition. Completed by Erica Reiner. Chicago: University of Chicago Press, 1977.

______. "'The Eyes of the Lord.'" *JAOS* 88 (1968): 173–180.

Osumi, Yoichi. *Die Kompositionsgeschichte des Bundesbuchs Exodus 20,22b–23,33*. OBO 105. Freiburg, Switzerland; Gottingen: Universitätsverlag Freiburg/ Vanderhoeck & Ruprecht, 1991.

Otten, H. "Zum hethitischen Gewichtssystem." *AfO* 17 (1954–1956): 128–131.

Otto, Eckart. *Wandel der Rechtsbegründungen in der Gesellschaftgeschichte des Antiken Israel: Eine Rechtsgeschichte des "Bundesbuches" Ex XX 22–XXIII 13*. Studia Biblica III. Leiden: Brill, 1988.

Parker, Robert. *Miasma: Pollution and Purification in Early Greek Religion*. Oxford: Clarendon, 1983.

Parpola, Simo. *Neo-Assyrian Toponyms*. AOAT. Kevelaer: Butzon & Bercker, 1970.

Parpola, Simo., and Kazuko Watanabe. *Neo-Assyrian Treaties and Loyalty Oaths*. Edited by Simo Parpola. SAA 2. Helsinki: Helsinki University Press, 1988.

Paul, Shalom M. "Exod. 21:10, a Threefold Maintenance Clause." *JNES* 28 (1969): 48–53.

______. *Studies in the Book of the Covenant in the Light of Cuneiform and Biblical Law*. SVT 18. Leiden: Brill, 1970.

Petschow, Herbert. "Neufunde zu keilschriftlichen Rechtssammlungen." *ZSS* 85 (1968): 1–29.

Pfeiffer, Robert H. "The Influence of Hammurabi's Code Outside of Babylonia." In *Akten des XXIV Internationalen Orientalisten-Kongresses*, 148–149. Wiesbaden: Deutsche Morgenländische Gesellschaft, 1957.

Phillips, Anthony. *Ancient Israel's Criminal Law*. Oxford: Basil Blackwell, 1970.

______. "The Interpretation of 2 Samuel xii 5–6." *VT* 16 (1966): 243–245.

Posner, Richard A. *The Economics of Justice*. Cambridge, Massachusetts: Harvard University Press, 1981.

Pospíšil, Leopold J. *Anthropology of Law: A Comparative Theory*. New Haven, Connecticut: HRAF Press, 1974.

Postgate, Nicholas. *Early Mesopotamia: Society and Economy at the Dawn of History*. London: Routledge, 1992.

———. "More Assyrian Deeds and Documents." *Iraq* 32 (1970): 129–164.

———. "'Princeps Iudex' in Assyria." *RA* 74 (1980): 180–182.

Rad, Gerhard von. *Genesis*. Rev. edition. OTL. Philadelphia: Westminster, 1972.

Regev, Eyal. "Priestly Dynamic Holiness and Deuteronomic Static Holiness." *VT* 51 (2001): 243–261.

Reiner, Erica. *Šurpu: A Collection of Sumerian and Akkadian Incantations*. Archiv für Orientforschung. Graz: N.p., 1958.

———. "A Manner of Speaking." In *Zikir Šumim: Assyriological Studies Presented to F. Kraus*, 282–289. Leiden: Nederlands Instituut voor het Nabije Oosten, 1982.

Renger, Johannes M. "Institutional, Communal, and Individual Ownership or Possession of Arable Land in Ancient Mesopotamia from the End of the Fourth to the End of the First Millennium B.C." *Chicago-Kent Law Review* 71/1 (1995): 269–320.

Reventlow, H. Graf. "Sein Blut komme über sein Haupt." *VT* 10 (1960): 311–327.

Reviv, Hanokh. *The Institution of Elders in Ancient Israel* [Hebrew]. Texts and Studies. Jerusalem: Magnes Press, 1983.

Riccobono, S., ed. *Fontes iuris romani ante-iustiniani*. 2d edition. Florence: Barbera, 1941.

Rin, Svi. "The מות of Grandeur." *VT* 9 (1959): 324–325.

Roberts, Simon. "The Study of Disputes: Anthropological Perspectives." In *Disputes and Settlements: Law and Human Relations in the West*, edited by John Bossy, 1–24. Cambridge: Cambridge University Press, 1983.

Rofé, Alexander. "The History of the Cities of Refuge in Biblical Law." In *Studies in Bible*, edited by Sara Japhet. ScrHier 31, 205–239. Jerusalem: Magnes Press, 1986.

———. "Joshua 20: Historico-Literary Criticism Illustrated." In *Empirical Models for Biblical Criticism*, edited by Jeffrey H. Tigay, 132–147. Philadelphia: University of Pennsylvania Press, 1985.

Röllig, W. "Gurata." In RLA, 3.703. Berlin: Walter de Gruyter, 1957–1971.

Ross, J. P. "The 'Cities of the Levites' in Joshua XXI and I Chronicles VI." Ph.D. diss., University of Edinburgh, 1973.

Rost, Leonhard. *The Succession to the Throne of David*. Translated by Michael D. Rutter and David M. Gunn, with an introduction by Edward Ball. 1926. Historic Texts and Interpreters in Biblical Scholarship 1. Reprint, Sheffield: Almond, 1982.

Roth, Martha T. "Homicide in the Neo-Assyrian Period." In *Language, Literature, and History: Philological and Historical Studies Presented to Erica Reiner*, edited by Francesca Rochberg-Halton. AOS 67, 351–365. New Haven, Connecticut: American Oriental Society, 1987.

———. "Mesopotamian Legal Traditions and the Laws of Hammurabi." *Chicago-Kent Law Review* 71/1 (1995): 13–40.

———. "The Neo-Babylonian Widow." *JCS* 43–45 (1991–1993): 1–26.

———. "On LE 46–47A." *NABU* 3 (1990): 71.

———. "The Scholastic Exercise 'Laws About Rented Oxen.'" *JCS* 32 (1980): 127–146.

Rouland, Norbert. *Legal Anthropology*. Translated by Philippe G. Planel. Stanford, California: Stanford University Press, 1994.

Roux, Georges. *Ancient Iraq*. 3d edition. London: Penguin, 1992.

Saggs, H. W. F. *The Greatness That Was Babylon*. New York: Hawthorn, 1962.

———. "The Nimrud Letters IV: The Urartian Frontier." *Iraq* 20 (1958): 182–212.

San Nicolò, M., and A. Ungnad. *Neubabylonische Rechts- und Verwaltungsurkunden*. Leipzig: J. C. Hinrichs'sche Buchhandlung, 1935.

Scheil, V. *Textes Élamites-Anzanites*. Quatriéme série. Memoires de la Délégation en Perse 11. Paris: Librairie Ernest LeRoux, 1911.

Schloen, J. David. *The House of the Father as Fact and Symbol: Patrimonialism in Ugarit and the Ancient Near East*. Studies in the Archaeology and History of the Levant. Winona Lake, Indiana: Eisenbrauns, 2001.

Schroeder, O. "Zur Amarnatafel VAT 1704." *Orientalistische Literaturzeitung* 18 (1915): 174–176.

Schulz, Hermann. *Das Todesrecht im Alten Testament: Studien zur Rechtsform der Mot-Jumat-Sätze*. BZAW. Berlin: Verlag Alfred Töpelmann, 1969.

Schwartz, Baruch J. "The Bearing of Sin in the Priestly Literature." In *Pomegranates and Golden Bells: Studies in Biblical, Jewish, and Ancient Near Eastern Ritual, Law, and Literature in Honor of Jacob Milgrom*, edited by David P. Wright, David Noel Freedman, and Avi Hurvitz, 3–21. Winona Lake, Indiana: Eisenbrauns, 1995.

———. *The Holiness Legislation* [Hebrew]. Jerusalem: Magnes Press, 1999.

———. "'Term' or Metaphor – Biblical נשא עון/פשע/חטא [Hebrew]." *Tarbiz* 63 (1994): 149–171.

Schwienhorst-Schönberger, Ledger. *Das Bundesbuch (Ex 20,22–23,33): Studie zu seiner Entstehung und Theologie*. BZAW 188. Berlin/New York: Walter de Gruyter, 1990.

Scott, S. P., trans. and ed. *Corpus Iuris Civilis*. Volume 3. Cincinnati: Central Trust Co., 1932.

Shiloh, Yigal. "The Four-Room House: Its Situation and Function in the Israelite City." *IEJ* 20 (1970): 180–190.

Sick, Ulrich. *Die Tötung eines Menschen und ihre Ahndung in den keilschriftlichen rechtssammlungen unter Berücksichtigung rechtsvergleichender Aspekte*. Ph.D. diss., Eberhard-Karls-Universität, 1984.

Sigrist, M. "On the Bite of a Dog." In *Love and Death in the Ancient Near East: Essays in Honor of Marvin H. Pope*, edited by John H. Marks and Robert M. Good, 85–88. Guilford, Connecticut: Four Quarters Press, 1987.

Sjöberg, Åke. "Was There a Sumerian Version of the Laws of Hammurabi?" *AuOr* 9 (1991): 219–225.

______. "Zu einigen Verwandtschaftsbezeichnungen im Sumerischen." In *Heidelberger Studien zum Alten Orient,* edited by D. O. Edzard, 219–225. Wiesbaden: Otto Harassowitz, 1967.

Soden, Wolfram, von. "Kleine Beiträge zum Verständnis der Gesetze Ḫammurabis und Bilalamas." *ArOr* 17 (1949): 359–373.

______. "*Muškēnum* und die Mawālī des frühen Islam." *ZA* 56 (1964): 133–141.

Speiser, E. A. *Genesis.* 1962. AB. Garden City: Doubleday, 1985.

______. "'People' and 'Nation' of Israel." *JBL* 59 (1960): 157–163.

Spencer, John R. "The Levitical Cities: A Study of the Role and Function of the Levites in the History of Israel." Ph.D. diss., University of Chicago, 1980.

Sperling, David. "Blood." In ABD, 1.761–763. New York: Doubleday, 1992.

______. "Bloodguilt in the Bible and in Ancient Near Eastern Sources." In *Jewish Law in Our Time,* edited by Ruth Link-Salinger (Hyman), 19–25. N.p.: Bloch, 1982.

Spronk, K. "Synchronic and Diachronic Approaches to the Book of Nahum." In *Synchronic or Diachronic? A Debate on Method in Old Testament Exegesis,* edited by Johannes C. de Moor, 159–186. Leiden: Brill, 1995.

Stade, Bernhard. "Das Kainszeichen." In *Ausgewahlte Akademische Reden und Abhandlungen,* 229–273. Giessen: J. Ricker'sche Verlagsbuchhandlung, 1899.

Stager, Lawrence. "The Archaeology of the Family in Ancient Israel." *BASOR* 260 (1985): 1–35.

Starke, J. G. *Introduction to International Law.* 10th edition. London: Butterworths, 1989.

Starr, June, and Jane F. Collier. "Historical Studies of Legal Change." In *Law and Anthropology,* edited by Peter Sack and Jonathan Aleck. The International Library of Essays in Law and Legal Theory, 1–32. New York: New York University Press, 1992. Originally published in *Current Anthropology* 28 (1987): 367–372.

Steuernagel, C. *Der Rahmen des Deuteronomium.* 2d edition. 1894. Reprint, Halle: Max Niemeyer, 1923.

Stol, M. "Muškēnu." In RLA, 8.492–493. Berlin: Walter de Gruyter, 1993–1997.

Stone, Elizabeth. "Texts, Architecture and Ethnographic Analogy: Patterns of Residence in Old Babylonian Nippur." *Iraq* 43 (1981): 19–33.

Sulzberger, Mayer. *The Ancient Hebrew Law of Homicide.* Philadelphia: Julius H. Greenstone, 1915.

Tadmor, Hayyim. "Traditional Institutions and the Monarchy: Social and Political in the Time of David and Solomon." In *Studies in the Period of David and Solomon and Other Essays,* 239–257. Winona Lake, Indiana: Eisenbrauns, 1982.

Talmon, Shemaryahu. "The 'Comparative Method' in Biblical Interpretation – Principles and Problems." In *Congress Volume: Göttingen.* SVT 320–356. Leiden: Brill, 1978.

______. "The Presentation of Synchroneity and Simultaneity in Biblical Narrative." In *Literary Studies in the Hebrew Bible: Form and Content, Collected Studies,* edited by Shemaryahu Talmon, 112–133. Jerusalem: Magnes Press, 1993.

Talmon, Shemaryahu, and Michael Fishbane. "Issues in the Ordering of Selected Chapters of Ezekiel [Hebrew]." *Tarbiz* 42 (1972–1973): 35–38. (A translation of this article is "The Structuring of Biblical Books: Studies in the Book of Ezekiel," *Annual of the Swedish Theological Institute in Jerusalem* 10 [1976], 143–146.)

Thomas, D. Winton. "A Consideration of Some Unusual Ways of Expressing the Superlative in Hebrew." *VT* 3 (1953): 209–224.

Thompson, R. Campbell. *The Devils and Evil Spirits of Babylonia*. London: Luzac and Co., 1903.

Thureau-Dangin, F. *Une relation de la huitième campagne de Sargon*. TCL 3. Paris: Paul Geuthner, 1912.

Tigay, Jeffrey M. *Deuteronomy*. The JPS Torah Commentary. Philadelphia: Jewish Publication Society, 1996.

Todd, S. C. *The Shape of Athenian Law*. Oxford: Clarendon, 1993.

Toorn, Karel, van der. *Sin and Sanction in Israel and Mesopotamia*. Studia Semitica Neerlandica. Assen/Maastricht, the Netherlands: Van Gorcum, 1985.

Tsumura, David Toshio. "Genesis and Ancient Near Eastern Stories of Creation and Flood: An Introduction." In *"I Studied Inscriptions from Before the Flood": Ancient Near Eastern, Literary, and Linguistic Approaches to Genesis 1–11*, edited by Richard S. Hess and David Toshio Tsumura. Sources for Biblical and Theological Study 4, 27–57. Winona Lake, Indiana: Eisenbrauns, 1994.

Tur-Sinai, N. H. "At the Door Sin Couches [Hebrew]." *Tarbiz* 16 (1944): 8–10.

Van de Mieroop, Marc. *The Ancient Mesopotamian City*. Oxford: Clarendon, 1997.

Vanderhooft, David. "Dwelling Beneath the Sacred Place: A Proposal for Reading 2 Samuel 7:10." *JBL* 118 (1999): 625–633.

Van Selms, A. "The Goring Ox in Babylonian and Biblical Law." *ArOr* 18/4 (1950): 321–330.

Van Seters, John. *Prologue to History: The Yahwist as Historian in Genesis*. Louisville, Kentucky: Westminster/John Knox Press, 1992.

Vaux, Roland, de. *Ancient Israel*. New York: McGraw-Hill, 1961.

Veenhof, Klaas R. "'In Accordance with the Words of the Stele': Evidence for Old Assyrian Legislation." *Chicago-Kent Law Review* 4 (1995): 1717–1744.

Viberg, Åke. *Symbols of Law: A Contextual Analyis of Legal Symbolic Acts in the Old Testament*. Coniectanea Biblical Old Testament Series 34. Stockholm: Almqvist & Wiksell, 1992.

Vila, Bryan, and Cynthia Morris, eds. *Capital Punishment in the United States: A Documentary History*. Primary Documents in American History and Contemporary Issues. Westport, Connecticut: Greenwood Press, 1997.

Wagner, Volker. *Rechtssätze in gebundener Sprache und Rechtssatzreihen im israelitischen Recht: Ein Beitrag zur Gattungsforschung*. BZAW. Berlin: Walter de Gruyter, 1972.

Waldron, Jeremy. "Lex Talionis." *Arizona Law Review* 34 (1992): 25–51.

Wallace-Hadrill, J. M. "The Bloodfeud of the Franks." In *The Long-Haired Kings*. Medieval Academy Reprints for Teaching 11, 121–147. 1962. Reprint, Toronto: University of Toronto Press, 1982.

Walzer, Michael. "The Legal Codes of Ancient Israel." *Yale Journal of Law and the Humanities* 4 (1992): 335–349.

Watson, Alan. *Legal Transplants: An Approach to Comparative Law*. Charlottesville: University of Virginia Press, 1974.

———. *Rome of the XII Tables: Persons and Property*. Princeton: Princeton University Press, 1975.

Weber, Max. *Economy and Society: An Outline of Interpretive Sociology*. Edited by Guenther Roth and Claus Wittich, translated by Ephraim Fischoff. 1922. Reprint, Berkeley: University of California Press, 1978.

Weidner, Ernst F. "Das Alter der mittelassyrischen Gesetzestexte." *AfO* 12 (1937–1939): 46–54.

———. "Die Bibliothek Tiglatpilesers I." *AfO* 16 (1952): 197–215.

———. "Drei neue Fragmente des Kodex Hammurapi aus neuassyrischer Zeit." *AfO* 16 (1952): 323–324.

Weinfeld, Moshe. *Deuteronomy and the Deuteronomic School*. 1972. Reprint, Winona Lake, Indiana: Eisenbrauns, 1992.

———. *Deuteronomy 1–16*. AB. New York: Doubleday, 1991.

———. "On 'Demytholigization and Secularization' in Deuteronomy." *VT* 21 (1973): 230–233.

Weisman, Ze'ev. "The Place of the People in the Making of Law and Judgment." In *Pomegranates and Golden Bells: Studies in Biblical, Jewish, and Near Eastern Ritual, Law, and Literature in Honor of Jacob Milgrom,* edited by David P. Wright, David Noel Freedman, and Avi Hurvitz, 407–420. Winona Lake, Indiana: Eisenbrauns, 1995.

Wellhausen, Julius. *Prolegomena to the History of Israel*. With a preface by W. Robertson Smith, with a foreword by Douglas A. Knight. 1885. Reprint, Scholars Press Reprints and Translations Series. Atlanta: Scholars Press, 1994.

Wenham, Gordon J. *The Book of Leviticus*. New International Commentary on the Old Testament. Grand Rapids, Michigan: Eerdmans, 1979.

Westbrook, Raymond. "Biblical and Cuneiform Law Codes." *RB* 92 (1985): 247–264.

———. *Studies in Biblical and Cuneiform Law*. CahRB. Paris: J. Gabalda, 1988.

Westermann, Claus. *Genesis 1–11, a Commentary*. Translated by John J. Scullion. CC. Minneapolis: Augsburg Publishing House, 1984.

Wette, W. M. L., de. *Dissertatio critica exegetica qua Deuteronomium a prioribus Pentateuchi libris diversum, alius cujusdam recentioris actoris opus esse monstratur*. Halle, 1805.

Whitman, James Q. "At the Origins of Law and the State: Supervision of Violence, Mutilation of Bodies, or Setting of Prices?" *Chicago-Kent Law Review* 71/1 (1995): 41–84.

Wilson, E. Jan. *"Holiness" and "Purity" in Mesopotamia*. AOAT. Kevelaer: Butzon & Bercker, 1994.

Wilson, Robert R. "Enforcing the Covenant: The Mechanisms of Judicial Authority in Early Israel." In *The Quest for the Kingdom of God: Studies in Honor of George E. Mendenhall,* edited by H. B. Huffmon, F. A. Spina, and A. R. W. Green, 59–75. Winona Lake, Indiana: Eisenbrauns, 1983.

———. "Israel's Judicial System in the Preexilic Period." *Jewish Quarterly Review* 74 (1983): 229–248.

Wormald, Jenny. "The Blood Feud in Early Modern Scotland." In *Disputes and Settlements: Law and Human Relations in the West,* edited by John Bossy, 101–144. Cambridge : Cambridge University Press, 1983.

Wright, C. J. H. "Family." In ABD, 2.761–769. New York: Doubleday, 1992.

Wright, David P. "Deuteronomy 21:1–9 as a Rite of Elimination." *CBQ* 49 (1987): 387–403.

———. *The Disposal of Impurity*. SBLDS 101. Atlanta: Scholars Press, 1987.

Yaron, Reuven. "Enquire Now About Hammurabi, Ruler of Babylon." *Tijdschrift voor Rechtsgeschiedenis* 59 (1991): 223–238.

Yoffee, Norman. "Aspects of Mesopotamian Land Sales." *American Anthropologist* 90 (1988): 119–130.

———. "Too Many Chiefs (or, Safe Texts for the 90s)." In *Archaeological Theory: Who Sets the Agenda?* edited by Norman Yoffee and Andrew Sherratt, 60–78. Cambridge: Cambridge University Press, 1993.

Zevit, Ziony. "The *Eglâ* Ritual of Deuteronomy 21:1–9." *JBL* 95 (1976): 377–390.

General Index

Index of Citations

BIBLICAL TEXTS

Genesis

Exodus

Leviticus

Numbers

Deuteronomy

Joshua

Ezekiel

Joel

Micah

Zephaniah

Psalms

Job

Proverbs

Ruth

Song of Songs

Lamentations

Ezra

Nehemiah

1 Chronicles

2 Chronicles

EXTRA-BIBLICAL TEXTS

Cuneiform

Israelite

Phoenician

Post-biblical Jewish texts

Ugaritic

HEBREW TERMS ANALYZED

גֹּאֵל 98
גֹּאֵל חַדָּם 98, 110
דָּמוֹ בְרֹאשׁוֹ 98
דָּמוֹ עַל רֹאשׁוֹ 98
דָּמָיו בוֹ 98
דָּמִים 97–98
מָקוֹם 76, 78, 80
מִקְלָט 101
נָשָׂא 13
עֵדָה 88
רוֹצֵחַ 121